THE COMPLETE WORKS OF
FRANCIS A. SCHAEFFER
A CHRISTIAN WORLDVIEW

VOLUME FOUR
A Christian View of the Church

Second Edition

CROSSWAY BOOKS

A PUBLISHING MINISTRY OF
GOOD NEWS PUBLISHERS
WHEATON, ILLINOIS

The Complete Works of Francis A. Schaeffer: A Christian Worldview, Volume Four,
A Christian View of the Church copyright © 1982 by Francis A. Schaeffer.

Published by Crossway Books
      a publishing ministry of Good News Publishers
      1300 Crescent Street
      Wheaton, Illinois 60187

The Church at the End of the Twentieth Century: copyright © 1970 by Francis A. Schaeffer
The Church Before the Watching World: copyright © 1971 by Francis A. Schaeffer
The Mark of the Christian: copyright © 1970 by Francis A. Schaeffer
Death in the City: copyright © 1969 by L'Abri Fellowship
The Great Evangelical Disaster: copyright © 1984 by Francis A. Schaeffer

Published in this edition by arrangement with the original U.S. publishers.

All rights reserved. No part of this publication may be reproduced, stored in a retrieval system or transmitted in any form by any means, electronic, mechanical, photocopy, recording or otherwise, without the prior written permission of the publisher, except as provided in USA copyright law.

First printing: hardback, first edition, 1982
Fifth printing: paperback, second edition, 1985

Library of Congress Catalog Card Number: 84-72685

ISBN 13: 978-0-89107-335-2
ISBN 10: 0-89107-335-3

Printed in the United States of America

The Complete Works of Francis A. Schaeffer.
Complete Set: 0-89107-331-0
      Volume 1   0-89107-332-9
      Volume 2   0-89107-333-7
      Volume 3   0-89107-334-5
      Volume 4   0-89107-335-3
      Volume 5   0-89107-336-1

VP		16	15	14	13	12	11	10	09	08	07	06
30	29	28	27	26	25	24	23	22	21	20	19	18

THE COMPLETE WORKS OF
FRANCIS A. SCHAEFFER
A CHRISTIAN WORLDVIEW

VOLUME ONE: A CHRISTIAN VIEW OF PHILOSOPHY AND CULTURE

Book One: The God Who Is There
Book Two: Escape From Reason
Book Three: He Is There and He Is Not Silent
Book Four: Back to Freedom and Dignity

VOLUME TWO: A CHRISTIAN VIEW OF THE BIBLE AS TRUTH

Book One: Genesis in Space and Time
Book Two: No Final Conflict
Book Three: Joshua and the Flow of Biblical History
Book Four: Basic Bible Studies
Book Five: Art and the Bible

VOLUME THREE: A CHRISTIAN VIEW OF SPIRITUALITY

Book One: No Little People
Book Two: True Spirituality
Book Three: The New Super-Spirituality
Book Four: Two Contents, Two Realities

VOLUME FOUR: A CHRISTIAN VIEW OF THE CHURCH

Book One: The Church at the End of the Twentieth Century
Book Two: The Church Before the Watching World
Book Three: The Mark of the Christian
Book Four: Death in the City
Book Five: The Great Evangelical Disaster

VOLUME FIVE: A CHRISTIAN VIEW OF THE WEST

Book One: Pollution and the Death of Man
Book Two: How Should We Then Live?
Book Three: Whatever Happened to the Human Race?
Book Four: A Christian Manifesto

Preface to Volumes I–V

We are reediting and republishing the twenty-one books written by me between 1968 and 1981. Various people asked for this, so that they would be available in permanent form. I agreed to the work involved in it because we have found that all the books are contemporary for the 1980s. We think they are more contemporary now than when they were first published.

These books are now published as five hardback volumes. Thus, all my printed work which is in book form will be available in five companion volumes.

Much reediting has gone into this. They are the same books, yet brought up to date and clarified where time has shown they need clarification.

A section of *The God Who Is There* which seems to have been rather widely discussed and, it seems to me, at times misunderstood and misstated has been what is sometimes called "Schaeffer's apologetics." This section is enlarged as an added appendix on pages 175-187 of Volume I of this series.

All the books are to be read and understood together (along with my wife Edith's books). They together are a unit.

They were written to be read and useful to both Christians and non-Christians. Time has proved this to be the case far beyond our hopes.

They were not written to be only used on the academic scene, though they have been used there, but also for the less academic—though, of course, we realize that they do take care and study and are not popular reading to be pursued while dozing in an armchair. Some have thought the terminology difficult, but I have letters from many parts of the world saying that it was the use of this terminology that for them showed that Christianity has something to say to twentieth-century people, and that it was this terminology which was the bridge which caused them to study the books and to be helped by them. We have tried to make the terminology easier where possible.

The Bible translations have been maintained as they were in the original editions: that is, the *King James* in the earlier books, and the *New International Version* in *Whatever Happened to the Human Race?* and *A Christian Manifesto.*

Another choice to be made was whether to leave the word *man,* as designating men and women, or go to the recent usage of indicating in each case that *she* or *he* is meant. When the earlier books were written, this was not a problem. In my later books the newer way of speaking and writing has been used. However, bringing the earlier books in line in this regard would have been a horrendous task. Please therefore forgive me, anyone who would be disturbed, and please read the usage in the older accepted way. I would be overwhelmingly sorry if anyone would be "put off." Please read it as "man" equaling a human being and all human beings—whoever you are—women and men, children and adults.

The basic trilogy has been: *The God Who Is There, Escape from Reason,* and *He Is There and He is Not Silent.* All the others fit into these as spokes of the wheel fit into the hub.

The early books broke ground in calling for the Lordship of Christ in the arts—art, literature, cinema, philosophy and so on. *How Should We Then Live?, Whatever Happened to the Human Race?* and *A Christian Manifesto* bring this body of thought forward into the area of a Christian's duty, under the Lordship of Christ, in the whole of life as a citizen, especially in the area of law, government, and standing for a high view of human life.

We have been overwhelmed at the way these books have been used over such a wide spectrum of kinds of people and geographically. I can truly say it has brought us to awe and worship. These new five volumes are now published in the hope that they too will be so used.

To make these present volumes more useful for some, at the end of each volume there is a list of translations in the various countries and the publishers for the books in that volume.

This venture would not have been possible without the hard work and wisdom of Dr. Jeremy Jackson and Ranald Macaulay who gave me their suggestions. I thank them profoundly.

Francis A. Schaeffer, 1982

Contents

BOOK ONE: THE CHURCH AT THE END OF THE TWENTIETH CENTURY

Preface	3
Chapter 1. The Roots of the Student Revolution	5
Chapter 2. The International Student Revolution	23
Chapter 3. The Church in a Post-Christian Culture	37
Chapter 4. Form and Freedom in the Church	51
Chapter 5. The Practice of Community and Freedom	61
Chapter 6. The Threat of Silence	69
Chapter 7. Modern Man the Manipulator	79
Chapter 8. Revolutionary Christianity	87
Appendixes	
A. Learning From the Past to Do Better in the Future	97
B. What Difference Does Inerrancy Make?	103

BOOK TWO: THE CHURCH BEFORE THE WATCHING WORLD

Introduction	115
Chapter 1. A Historical Critique of Theological Liberalism	117
Chapter 2. Adultery and Apostasy—The Bride and Bridegroom Theme	133
Chapter 3. Practicing Purity in the Visible Church	151
Appendix: Some Absolute Limits	165

BOOK THREE: THE MARK
OF THE CHRISTIAN 181

BOOK FOUR: DEATH IN THE CITY

Chapter 1. Death in the City   209
Chapter 2. The Loneliness of Man   219
Chapter 3. The Message of Judgment   225
Chapter 4. An Echo of the World   235
Chapter 5. The Persistence of Compassion   247
Chapter 6. The Significance of Man   257
Chapter 7. The Man Without the Bible   265
Chapter 8. The Justice of God   277
Chapter 9. The Universe and Two Chairs   287

BOOK FIVE: THE GREAT EVANGELICAL DISASTER

Preface   303

Part I: Introduction

Chapter 1. What Really Matters?   307

Part II: The Watershed of the Evangelical World

Chapter 2. Marking the Watershed   327
Chapter 3. The Practice of Truth   345

Part III: Names and Issues

Chapter 4. Connotations and Compromise   367
Chapter 5. Forms of the World Spirit   379
Chapter 6. The Great Evangelical Disaster   401

Part IV: Conclusion

Chapter 7. Radicals for Truth   409

Notes to Volume Four   413

List of Translated Editions and Publishers of the
    Books in Volume Four   425

Acknowledgments   429

Index: An Index for All Five Volumes Appears at the End
    of Volume Five

The Church at the End of the Twentieth Century

Preface

In this book I have attempted to describe the sociological milieu in which the church of Jesus Christ now finds itself. Those who have read my previous books, especially *The God Who Is There* and *Escape From Reason,* will find some repetition in Chapter One of this present book. However, three things should be kept in mind: (1) For those who have not read the other books, this base—"how we got to be where we are"—must be laid, or the rest of the book floats in space. (2) New material is added which will be helpful in viewing the total context in its specific sociological perspective. (3) Even for those who have read the other books, listened to my taped lectures, or heard me lecture in person, a review will still not be amiss, for the material in Chapter One should be consciously before all of us as we consider "where we are" in regard to the church in the midst of the present and future sociological situation.

Furthermore, this analysis emphasizes and reemphasizes the fact that modern problems in many fields are really not many, but one basic problem with a number of results in what at first may seem to be unrelated fields or disciplines. Thus, the modern cultural problem, the sociological problem, the problem of governing our

3

countries today, the problems of ecology and epistemology are all related, for the basic problem of modern man gives the specific form in which each of these confronts us. And if our comprehension of this relatedness is not clear at its base, we cannot give basic solutions to effect a cure.

On the other hand, I would urge those who have not read the other books, and who may easily feel Chapter One moves too quickly, to read the book-length treatments in *The God Who Is There* and *Escape From Reason*.

Francis A. Schaeffer
Switzerland

CHAPTER ONE

The Roots of the Student Revolution

People are asking if the church has a future as we come to the close of the twentieth century. To consider this, we must first think through where we are and what we can expect as we approach the end of this century. Let us first consider the international student revolution in the 1960s and its relationship to society as a whole, and let us begin this by tracing quickly how in our society we got to be where we were at that time.

The international student revolution was a watershed in our culture and society. It did not spontaneously appear from nowhere. Its true and deepest roots are seen in the stream of intellectual history which flows from the European Renaissance and before. It was a revolution that was not merely cultural or psychological. Its source was not to be found in a simplistic analysis of the generation gap. The roots strike deep into the history of man and his attempt to understand who he is and where he came from.

It is just such intellectual history that we must grasp if we are to comprehend the ferment on our campuses in the 1960s and the results in a change in our society which is shaping the 1980s.

The Rise of Science
The birth of modern science is a good place to begin. Modern

science arose out of a Christian mentality. Alfred North White-head, for example, emphasizes the fact that modern science was born because it was surrounded by a Christian frame of reference. Galileo, Copernicus, Francis Bacon, Kepler, and scientists up to and including Newton believed that the world was created by a reasonable God, and therefore we could find out the order of the universe by reason.

Oppenheimer stressed the same thing: modern science could not have been born at all without a Christian milieu, a Christian consensus. As Francis Bacon (1561-1626) said in *Novum Organum Scientiarum:* "Man by the Fall fell at the same time from his state of innocence and from his dominion over nature. Both of these losses, however, can even in this life be in some part repaired; the former by religion and faith, the latter by the arts and the sciences." A few years ago I read something from Galileo which was very moving to me. Galileo stressed the fact that when he looked at the universe in all its richness and its beauty (he did not mean merely aesthetic beauty, but its unity in the midst of its complexity), he was called to only one end—to worship the beauty of the Creator.

This was the birth of our modern thinking in the area of science, and it produced various results. It led, for example, to the certainty of the uniformity of natural causes. There was a uniformity of natural causes, not in a closed system, but in one that was open to reordering.

Early modern scientists believed that God and man could operate into the machine and reorder the flow of cause and effect.

This had a number of results. First, it meant that nature was important. Second, it implied a clear distinction between nature as the object and myself as the observer. There was an objective basis for knowledge—something out there—and there was, therefore, a clear distinction between reality and fantasy. The people who gave birth to modern science knew that God had created the universe, that it was there, not as Eastern thinking has it, as an extension of the essence of God, but as something other than God and as something other than what is spun out of the mind of man. Today this objective basis for knowledge has been undermined, and the distinction between reality and fantasy has become difficult—sometimes impossible—to maintain.[1]

Furthermore, as is obvious from the quotation above, Bacon believed that man was wonderful, even though he was fallen. He believed in the fall of man in the biblical sense—that man is a sinner shut away from God on the basis of his moral guilt. Nevertheless, man is wonderful.

This is the very opposite of modern man. Modern man has been told that reason has led to the conclusion that man is a zero. This is a part of the tension of our present generation. It did not exist when modern science began. In those days, in other words, the machine was no threat—neither the machine of the cosmos, nor the machines that man made.

The Particular and the Universal

The Greeks long before understood that there was a dilemma between the particulars and the universals. It was not only Plato who wrestled with this, but he especially understood exactly what Jean-Paul Sartre has said in our generation: a finite point has no meaning unless it has an infinite reference point. He is right. Unless the particulars have a universal over them, the particulars have no meaning. Whether a particular is an atom, or a chair, or you, there must be a relationship to something which gives it meaning, or these things all become a zero.

The Greeks sought answers to the dilemma in two different realms. First of all, in the area of the *polis*. The Greek concept of *polis* involves far more than just a city, though that is the literal definition of the word. It implies a whole society. And the Greeks found that society as society could not give ample meaning to the particulars.

Second, they tried to place the particulars in relation to their gods. But the difficulty with the Greek gods is that they never were big enough to be an infinite reference point. Greek literature shows this in the way the Fates are treated. Sometimes the Fates are in control, and sometimes the gods control the Fates. Thus, neither society nor their gods gave the Greeks a sufficient universal.

Moving very rapidly to another crucial point in history, the high Renaissance, one encounters Leonardo da Vinci, the first modern mathematician. Leonardo tried to find an infinite reference point from the standpoint of rationalism or humanism. What rationalism or humanism is must be made clear here, because it is so easily confused with the word *rational*. Rationalism means that man begins from himself alone and tries to build all the answers on this base, receiving nothing from any other source and specifically refusing any revelation from God. Such rejection of revelation has led in our era to the position of the early Wittgenstein and the movie *The Silence* by the film maker, Ingmar Bergman. There is no one there to speak. Leonardo felt this silence in regard to a rationalistic universal back in his day.

Leonardo first tried to find an infinite reference point by means of mathematics. But he realized as a mathematician that if you begin with mathematics, you only get to particulars and to mechanics. You do not discover or produce a universal.[2]

Recognizing that mathematics could not give him the proper base, Leonardo then tried to see if the artist could paint the soul. By *soul,* he did not mean the same thing as a theologian does. Rather he meant the universal. He failed.

The fact is that man, beginning with only particulars, can never derive the universal. And that is as true in metaphysics as in morals.

Rousseau and Autonomous Freedom
Next, in order to understand not only the student revolution but our present society, one must properly understand Jean-Jacques Rousseau. The Durants in their history of mankind begin their study of modern man quite properly with Rousseau. They rightly say that you cannot understand modern man without understanding him. Back in the time of the high Renaissance, the intellectuals wrestled with the problem of nature and grace, a subject dealt with especially in *Escape From Reason.* Jean-Jacques Rousseau was concerned with nature and freedom. This is the background of the autonomous freedom which modern man seeks. Rousseau saw that by his time rationalistic man had reduced the created world (nature) to an autonomous machine. By the time of Rousseau men were already feeling threatened by the machine, and so to offset this they set up autonomous freedom as against the machine. Reasonably you cannot have both an autonomous machine, a machine that encompasses everything including man, and autonomous freedom at the same time. Nevertheless, Rousseau put forth the concept.

The lines of opposition are clear. On the one hand is a determinism—an autonomous machine; on the other hand is a man who desires autonomous freedom to stand against the restriction of the machine and all restrictions. What began to develop was a Bohemian life. In this situation, the artist living the Bohemian life became the hero. In the autonomous life, not only were the constraints of Scripture being cast away, but all restraints. Civilization began, therefore, to be seen as the threatening force, the demonic force which limited the individual's freedom.

The Bohemian life never worked out well in practice. Rousseau himself wrote on how to raise children. But his theories failed to work even for himself. Most people do not realize that he had children whom he put in an institution and never or rarely visited. Here is the problem of the autonomous freedoms: it leads to the selfish and the ugly.

Gauguin the artist did exactly the same thing. He went off to Tahiti to find his ideal away from culture and away from society; but all the time he was away, his family back in Paris was writing to him, asking for money for the food they lacked. But the logic of autonomous freedom nullified the desire to care. He left an illegitimate son in Tahiti—about the only contribution he made there. This child in Tahiti had to snatch small amounts of money from the tourists through the years by painting very poor pictures and signing them "Gauguin." Not very pretty—the result of the concept of autonomous freedom, the Bohemian life.

At the end of his life Gauguin himself recognized that this autonomous freedom was not going to work, and he shows this in his great painting, *What? Whence? Whither?* which hangs now in the Boston Museum of Art. It took him two years to do this painting, and the French inscription painted on the canvas itself tells us what he was doing. He asks, "Where are we going?" In his letters he called attention to the last three figures, a very beautiful Tahitian girl, an old woman, and an ugly bird, of which there is no counterpart in nature. He makes plain in his letters what he is saying in this painting: Notice the last three figures. Notice the old woman—she is dying, and who is watching her? Nobody but a bird that doesn't exist. There is the dilemma. Autonomous freedom did not work out even in Gauguin's own lifetime.

Modern Science and Modern, Modern Science
Later we come to the difference between modern science and what I call modern, modern science. Modern science was born, as I have indicated, from the Christian concept that man on the basis of reason could understand the universe because a God of reason had created it. Modern, modern science, however, extended the idea of the uniformity of natural causes by adding a new phrase—

in a closed system. This little phrase changed all of life because it put everything within the machine.

At first science dealt with physics, chemistry and astronomy. You could add a few more subjects perhaps, but there it ended. But later as psychology was added and then social sciences, man himself was in the machine.

If everything is put into the machine, of course there is no place for God. But also there is no place for man, no place for the significance of man, no place for beauty, for morals or for love. When you come to this place, you have a sea without a shore. Everything is dead. But the presupposition of the uniformity of natural causes in a closed system does not explain the two basic things that are before us: (1) the universe that exists and its form, and (2) the mannishness of man.

As Sartre says, the basic philosophic question is that something is there rather than nothing being there. You have to explain the something that is there. Einstein adds a note: when we examine the universe, we find that it is like a well-formulated word puzzle; namely, that you can suggest any word, but finally only one will fit. In other words, you not only have a universe that is there that has to be explained, but it is a very special kind of a universe, a universe exceedingly complex and yet with a definite form.

Modern man in his philosophy, his music and his art usually depicts a chaotic situation in the universe. But when you make a Boeing 707, it is beautiful. Why? Because it fits into the universe. The universe is not really the chaos that they picture.

There is also the problem of the uniqueness of man. Over 60,000 years ago—if you accept modern dating—man buried his dead in flower petals. If we look at Chinese bronzes, though they are far separated from us in time and culture, we find they conform to ourselves. They were made by somebody else, but they are also a part of me. There is the mannishness of man. The cave paintings at 20,000—30,000 B.C. are even more illustrative. From these one can show that man has always felt himself to be different from non-man.

Modern man says, "No, we are just machines—chemically determined or psychologically determined." But nobody consistently lives this way in his life. I would insist that here is a presupposition which intellectually, in the laboratory, would be cast out simply because it does not explain what is.

On the other hand, the biblical position, which begins with a personal rather than an impersonal beginning, gives us a different answer. The real issue is to decide, with intellectual integrity, which set of presuppositions conforms to what is.

But many of us catch our presuppositions like measles. Why do people fit into the post-Christian world? I would urge that it is not because of facts, but because our present almost monolithic culture has forced upon us the other answer—namely, the uniformity of natural causes, not in an open system beginning with a personal God, the way the early scientists believed, but in a closed system. It is not that the facts are against the Christian presuppositions, but simply that the Christian view is presented as unthinkable. The better the university, the better the brainwashing tends to be.

The results of following the implications of modern man were clearly developed in the nineteenth century. Nobody has expressed it better than the Marquis de Sade, who was one of the early modern chemical determinists. De Sade's position (and he lived by it) was that if you have determinism, then whatever *is* is right. You can say that things are nonsocial. Or you can think of the liberal theologian, Paul Tillich's concept of the demonic as being a force for disintegration rather than for integration, but that is all you can say. You cannot say that anything is right or wrong. Morality is dead. Man is dead.

Nietzsche is a key to this. He was the first man who cried, in the modern sense, "God is dead," but he was brilliant enough to understand the results. If God is dead, then everything is gone. I believe that it was not just his venereal disease in Switzerland which caused him to become insane. I believe that Nietzsche made a philosophic statement in his insanity. He understood that if God is dead, there are no answers to anything and insanity is the end. This is not too far philosophically from the modern Michael Foucault, for example, who says that the only freedom is in insanity.

We must never forget what one is left with in such a situation. If we do not begin with a personal Creator, eventually we are left (no matter how we string it out semantically) with the impersonal plus time plus chance. We must explain everything in the uniqueness of man, and we must understand all of the complexity of the universe on the basis of time plus chance.

The difficulty of explaining man and the universe on such a basis was recognized by Darwin himself. In his autobiography and in letters published by his son he wrote: "With my mind I cannot believe that these things come by chance." He said this as an old man many times over. Twice he added a strange note to this effect: "I know in my mind this can't be true, but my mind is only a monkey's mind, and who can trust a mind like that?" On this basis, how could one accept any conclusions of the human mind, including Darwin's theory?

More recently, Murray Eden at MIT used high-speed computers to ask a question: Beginning with chaos at any acceptable amount of time up to eight billion years ago, could the present complexity come by chance? The answer is absolutely *No*.

Cosmic Alienation
But modern man does in fact assume—wittingly or unwittingly—that the universe and man can be explained by the impersonal plus time plus chance. And in this case man and his aspirations stand in total alienation from what is. And that is precisely where many people today live—in a generation of alienation: alienation in the ghettos, alienation in the university, alienation from parents, alienation on every side. Sometimes this takes the form of "dropping out," sometimes it takes the form of "joining the system" to get along as easily as possible and to get as much from the system as possible. Those who are only playing with these ideas and have not gotten down into the real guts of it forget that the basic alienation with which they are faced is a cosmic alienation. It is simply this: there is nobody there to respond to you. There is nobody home in the universe. There is no one and nothing to conform to who you are or what you hope. That is the dilemma.

Let me use an illustration I have used previously. Suppose, for example, that the room in which you are seated is the only universe there is. God could have made a universe just this big if he wished. Suppose in making the only universe there were a room made up of solid walls, but filled up to the ceiling with liquids: just liquids and solids and no free gases. Suppose then that fish were swimming in the universe. The fish would not be alienated from the universe because they can conform to the universe by their nature. But suppose if by chance, as the evolutionists see chance, the fish suddenly developed lungs. Would they be higher or lower? Obviously, they would be lower, because they would drown. They would have a cosmic alienation from the universe that surrounded them.

But man has aspirations; he has what I call his mannishness. He desires that love be more than being in bed with a woman, that moral motions be more than merely sociological something-or-others, that his significance lie in being more than one more cog in a vast machine. He wants a relationship to society other than that of a small machine being manipulated by a big machine. On the basis of modern thought, however, all of these would simply be an illusion. And since there are aspirations which separate man from his impersonal universe, man then faces his being caught in a terrible, cosmic, final alienation. He drowns in cosmic alienation, for there is nothing in the universe to fulfill him. That is the position of modern man. There is nothing there to fulfill him in all that there is.

Remember the cry of the modern artist, often the prophet of today, as he cries out about cosmic alienation. Just before his death Alberto Giacometti said: *I've never been able to picture the situation of man. If I could, no one could look at it because it would be too horrible.* If you go into a good museum where his work is displayed properly, there are always huge areas around the individual figures. In Giacometti there is a concept of total loneliness.

Charlie Chaplin also expressed it. In the modern age Chaplin was not the clown, he was the thinker. For modern man, there is no god, there are no angels, no other conscious life in the universe. All the concepts of conscious life in other parts of the universe are merely statistical elongation and projection. So when Charlie Chaplin heard that there were no conscious beings on Mars, he said, "I feel lonely." He is the modern philosopher speaking with force. If God is not there, who is there?

It would not make any difference for the Christian if there is conscious life somewhere else in the universe, but so far there is no proof that such exists. We know there are angels, but for modern man's knowledge, all conscious life is shut up on this planet. Thus, without God being there, man has good reason to be lonely.

Or take Mortimer Adler's book, *The Difference of Man and the Difference It Makes.* Adler writes that if we do not soon find a difference with man, we will treat him like a machine. Thousands of our generation have decided that that is now no longer a prophecy, but a fact. And let me add that we can expect men to be treated like machines if we believe that people are machines.

The situation students face in the universities today can be instructive. Most of their professors have been teaching that man is a machine. The result: students are being treated like machines. Their reaction is right; student revolt or apathy and the desire to get as much out of the system as possible for a hedonistic life is understandable.

Modern Man as Mystic

Let us understand further that modern man could not tolerate being shut up finally into the mere stuff of machinery. And so modern man has become a mystic.

Rousseau and Kant both lead in this direction, but I will start a bit later in history. Kierkegaard is the key. Some may feel that I have attributed to Kierkegaard the attributes peculiar to his followers and not to him, and surely that is a point that could be argued. It may be correct, But whether Kierkegaard or Kierkegaardianism gave birth to it, we now have a divided universe, something man has not faced in past history. Before this, philosophers and thinkers were always striving for a unified field concept, a concept that would include all of life and all of knowledge.

Modern man, however, has accepted a total dichotomy. Beginning with rationalism, rationally you come only to pessimism. Man equals the machine. Man is dead. So those who followed Kierkegaard put forth the concept of an optimism in the area of nonrationality. Faith and optimism, they said, are always a leap. Neither has anything to do with reason.

This new way of looking at knowledge is, I feel, at the heart of the generation gap one heard so much about a few years ago. In this now accepted dichotomy there is no exchange at all between reason which leads to pessimism and anything which leads to optimism. Any optimism concerning God or beauty, any concept of the significance of man or of moral motions, always has to be in the area of nonreason. This is the situation, therefore, at the heart of the generation gap: modern man has come to the place where he has given up his rationality in order to hold on to his rationalism.

So modern man holds on to his rationalism (that man should understand the world by starting totally from himself), even though it has led him to give up hope for a unified field of knowledge and to give up confidence in rationality—which all men in the past rightly fought for, because God has made man in His own image and a part of this image is reason.

Therefore, modern man is a mystic, but his mysticism is quite different from that of, say, the Roman Catholic mystic of the past. Modern man is a mystic in the sense of his leaping "upstairs"—as I have used this language in *Escape from Reason* and *The God Who Is There*.[3] He seeks optimism on the basis of nonreason. He does not know why he must leap; yet he feels forced to make the leap against his reason.

Christians know why the non-Christian must leap. He must leap because he has been made in the image of God. No matter how far he is separated from God by false intellectual systems and by his guilt and his sin, he has not become non-man. He is still made in the image of God, even though he is a rebel and separated from God.

Modern man finds he must leap into the irrational, even though he does not know why he must leap. Holding to the uniformity of natural causes in a closed system, he is left with only the impersonal plus time plus chance. This does not explain man's aspirations; and so, feeling really damned, caught in his own kind of hell, he leaps upstairs.

The Common Man as Mystic

This leap began in philosophy, moved into the arts with the post-Impressionists, into music after Debussy, into other cultural areas (in the English-speaking world) with T. S. Eliot, and finally into theology with Karl Barth. It is the total irrational leap. It spread in various ways: first through the intellectuals, to the educated people; then it swept around the middle class; and it has also influenced the masses through the common media. Open *Time* or *Newsweek,* the British newspapers, *L'Express* or *Der Spiegel* on the Continent, and one sees the message carried down to the common man.

What is taught is that there is no final truth, no meaning, no absolutes, that it is not only that we have not found truth and meaning, but that they do not exist.

The student and the common man may not be able to analyze it, but day after day, day after day, they are being battered by this concept. We have now had several generations exposed to this, and we must not be blind to the fact that it is being accepted increasingly.

In contrast, this way of thinking has not had as much influence on the middle class. Many of these keep thinking in the old way as a memory of the time before the Christian base was lost in this post-Christian world. However, the majority in the middle class have no real basis for their values, since so many have given up the Christian viewpoint. They just function on the "memory." This is why so many young people have felt that the middle class is ugly. They feel middle-class people are plastic—ugly and plastic— because they try to tell others what to do on the basis of their own values, but with no ground for those values. They have no base, and they have no clear categories for their choices of right and wrong. Their choices tend to turn on what is for their material benefit.

Take, for example, the faculty members who cheered when the student revolt struck against the administration and who immediately began to howl when the students started to burn up faculty manuscripts. They have no categories to say this is right and that is wrong. Many such people still hang on to their old values by memory, but they have no base for them at all.

A few years ago John Gardner, head of the Urban Coalition, spoke in Washington to a group of student leaders. His topic was on restoring values in our culture. When he finished, there was a dead silence. Then finally one man from Harvard stood up and in a moment of brilliance asked, "Sir, upon what base do you build your values?" I have never felt more sorry for anybody in my life. He simply looked down and said, "I do not know." I had spoken that same day about what I am writing in the first part of this book. It was almost too good an illustration of my lecture. Here was a man appealing to the young people for a return to values, but he is offering nothing to build on; a man who was trying to tell his hearers not to drop out, and yet giving no reason why they should not. Functioning only on a dim memory, these are the parents who have turned off their children when their children ask why and how. When their children cry out, "Yours is a plastic culture," they are silent. We had the response so beautifully stated in the 1960s in the Beatles' *Sergeant Pepper*: "She is leaving home— we gave her everything money could buy." This is the only answer many parents can give.

They are bothered about what they read in the newspapers concerning the way the country and the culture are going. When they read of the pornographic plays, see pornographic films on T.V., they are distressed. They have a vague unhappiness about it, feel threatened by all of it, and yet have no base upon which to found their judgments.

And tragically, such people are everywhere. They constitute the largest body in our culture—northern Europe, Britain, and also in America and other countries as well. They are a majority—what was called for a time the "silent majority"—but they are weak as water. They are people who like the old ways because they are pleasant memories, because they give what to them is a comfortable way to live. But they have no basis for their values.

Education, for example, is accepted and pressed upon their children as the only thinkable thing to pursue. Success is starting the child at the earliest possible age and then, within the least possible years, his obtaining a Master's or a Ph.D. degree. Yet if the child asks why?, the only answers are, first, because it gives social status, and then because statistics show that if you have a university or college education you will make more money. There is no base for real values or even the why of a real education.

Huxley and the Drug Culture

It would likewise be possible to study the irrational leap toward nonrational values in existentialism, looking at the three French, German and Swiss philosophers—Jean-Paul Sartre, Martin Heidegger and Karl Jaspers. The early Wittgenstein, too, is central. But here I will limit myself to just one more aspect before discussing the student rebellion of the 1960s in more detail.

That aspect is best seen in Aldous Huxley. You cannot understand the student revolution without understanding him. Huxley was the father of the cult of drug taking. Huxley did not suggest drugs as an escape. Rather, he said, because reason is not going to take us anywhere, one should give healthy people drugs and help them have some kind of experience which hopefully would be optimistic.

Huxley never gave up on this. In the last chapter of *The Humanist Frame,* which was edited by his brother Julian, it is clear that Aldous held this position to the end. He also made his wife promise that when he was dying she would give him LSD, so he would die in the midst of a trip. This was the drug world of the 1960s. I spoke with hundreds of people on drugs at that time, but I never met a really serious drug taker (of course, this was not every little girl who began to smoke marijuana simply because everybody around was smoking it) who did not understand that he was following Huxley's concept of the upper-story leap, the upper-story hope.

Modern Theology and God Words
Modern theology has not helped us. From Karl Barth on, it is an upper-story phenomenon. Faith is a totally upstairs leap. The difficulty with modern theology is that it is really no different from taking drugs. You may try drugs, you may try modern liberal theology. It makes no difference—both are trips, separated from reason.

What we are left with is god words. Students coming out of all kinds of backgrounds say, "I'm sick of god words." And I must respond, "So am I." These theologians have cut themselves off from any concept of propositional, verbalized revelation in the Bible. They are left upstairs with only connotation words and no content. For them any concept of a personal God is dead, and any content about God is dead. They are cut off from any categories of absolute right and wrong, and thus they are left with situational ethics. That is all. As you listen to him, the modern theologian is only saying what the surrounding consensus is saying, but in theological terms. There is no help here.[4]

John Cage and Hissing Oneself
The irony of such a situation is played up by an event that happened to John Cage, the modern composer who writes music from a theory of chance, random selection. Leonard Bernstein once offered him the New York Philharmonic Orchestra. After Cage directed some of his own chance music, he started to take his bows and he thought he heard steam escaping from the steam pipes. Then he realized that the musicians were hissing. As John Cage explains it, it must have been a traumatic experience. But I have often thought about what I would like to have said to the musicians there that night. I am sure that if one had had an hour with those musicians, one would have found that most of them really believed philosophically exactly what John Cage believes—that the universe begins with the impersonal plus time plus chance. Why were they hissing, then? They were hissing because they did not like the results of their own position when they heard it in the medium to which they were sensitive. They were hissing themselves.

A great number of parents and professors are also hissing themselves. They do not like what students do. They do not like what that whole generation is doing. But what they do not face is what the musicians did not face—that basically they believe the same things and they are dishonest, or at least not consistent, in not doing what their children do. Their sons and daughters have simply taken what they have taught and carried it to its logical conclusion.

Malcolm Muggeridge has written much that is worthwhile, but to me the most striking thing he ever wrote was the article in the *New Statesman* (March 11, 1966) that showed he had changed his direction from the New Guardian Leftism to the new Malcolm Muggeridge. He called it "The Great Liberal Death-Wish." He simply admitted that he had realized that the goal toward which he had been optimistically moving was not going to be realized. The liberalism in which he had his hopes had cut away all the groundwork and left no categories with which to make moral judgments. Muggeridge still feels this strongly. Liberalism has committed suicide because it has cut away its foundation. So the faculty screamed with glee when students stormed the administrative offices, but squealed once they turned against the faculty. They had cut away their own foundations, and they had no categories with which to say what is right and what is wrong; they had no way to stop the flood they had loosed.

Law Is King
This is a complete contrast to the original base upon which government was built in the United States. We had freedom and form, form and freedom. Almost all human discussion can turn upon the question of form and freedom—in the arts, in government, in society. Of course, we have had in the United States in the past a far from perfect situation and much for which we must say we are sorry. Yet the northern European Reformation culture has had a form and a freedom that no culture in the world has ever had before—unless it was a few small Greek city-states for a few years, and there is a doubt in my mind concerning that. But the northern European countries built upon the Reformation had form and freedom. There was a specific Anglo-Saxon form of this—Samuel Rutherford, for example, the great leader of the second Reformation in Scotland, and his book, *Lex Rex* (law is king).

How could law—rather than arbitrary judgments of individuals or an elite—be king? Simply because God had spoken, there was a base upon which to build law. Law is to be seen not as floating on a sociological set of statistics, but on a solid foundation. This notion came into the United States Constitution largely through Locke. Locke secularized this base, though even he cheated sometimes and quoted from the Gospels. The American Constitution rested on *Lex Rex* toned down through Locke, through such men as Jefferson, and directly through the great Witherspoon.

There is a huge painting by Paul Robert, a Swiss artist from a great family of artists, who painted in the Supreme Court Building in Switzerland just before 1900. Through Hugh Alexander of Geneva he had become a Christian, and then he began to express his Christianity in his art. When he was asked to paint the mural on the stairway leading up to the old Supreme Court offices, he expressed in painting what Samuel Rutherford had expressed in words. The title of the painting is *Justice Instructing the Judges.* In the foreground are different forms of litigation—the wife against the husband, the architect against the builder, etc. Above them stand the Swiss judges with their little white dickeys. How are these people with their little white dickeys going to judge the litigation? A whole sociological theory is involved here. Robert's answer is this: justice (no longer blindfolded with her sword vertical, as is common) is unblindfolded with her sword pointing downward to a book on which is written "The Word of God." Here is *Lex Rex,* because justice is not merely statistical averages. Here is something to build on.

Compare this with Wittgenstein's and Bergman's understanding of the problem of silence. In Paul Robert's world-view we are no longer like the fish in the room; no longer do we face cosmic alienation; no longer is there a lack of categories to explain why some things are right and some things are wrong. There is revelation from outside man—propositional, verbalized revelation. It is not the Christians who have to leap. It is humanistic man who must leap into a mysticism with nothing there.

It is a matter of presuppositions. Many people catch their presuppositions like some children catch childhood diseases. They have no idea where they come from. But that is not the way the thinker chooses his presuppositions. His presuppositions are selected on the basis of which presuppositions fit what is; that is, what presuppositions give solid answers concerning what is. It is only the Christian presuppositions which explain what is—in regard to the universe and in regard to man.

Jesus' Answer to Camus
Consider further Camus in *The Plague.* Nothing is better for considering modern man's dilemma. Modern man asks, "Where does

justice come from? How can I move?" Camus says, "You can't.
You're really damned." The more you feel the tension of injustices, the more your damnation as modern man and the modern
rationalist increases. In *The Plague,* which is Camus' center piece,
as the rats bring the disease into Oran, Jean Tarrou is faced with a
dilemma. Either he may join with the doctor and fight the plague,
in which case he will be humanitarian, but (in Camus' construc-
tion) he will be fighting God. Or, he can join with the priest and
refuse to fight the plague, in which case he will be nonhumanitar-
ian. And poor Camus died with this dilemma upon him. He never
solved it.

By contrast, of course, there is the magnificent account in the
Bible of Jesus Christ in front of the tomb of Lazarus. Jesus who is
God, and claims to be God in the full Trinitarian sense, stands in
front of the tomb, and He is angry. The Greek makes that plain.
As Jesus stands there in His anger, we should notice something.
The Christ who claims to be God can be angry at the result of the
Fall and the abnormal event which He now faces *without being
angry at Himself.*

It is titanic. Suddenly I can fight injustice knowing I am not
fighting what is good. It is not true that what is is right. I can fight
injustice knowing there is a reason to fight injustice. Because God
does not love everything, because He has a character, I can fight
injustice without fighting God.

The Context of the Student Revolt
Here, then, is the context in which the student revolt of the 1960s
and our present society can be understood. This is how we came
to be where we were in the 1960s, and society of the 1980s is an
extension of that, but with apathy rather than explosion—that is,
apathy except when material affluence is threatened. Society has
reaped the rewards of its escape from reason. From modern science to modern, modern science, from man made in the image of
God to man the machine, from freedom within form to determinism and autonomous freedom, from harmony with God to cosmic
alienation, from reason to drugs and the new mysticism, from a
biblically based theology to god words—this is the flow of the
stream of rationalistic history. Out of this stream came the student
revolution and that which has followed.

CHAPTER TWO

The International Student Revolution

Now that we have seen *how* we got to be where we are, we will look further at *where* we are. By what steps did the student revolt boil up?

It began at Berkeley in the fall of 1964, and there the various student protests tended to take two different but related forms. First, there was the free speech movement that began as an attempt to give students a chance to engage in politically relevant activity—political recruitment, speeches, etc.—on the university campus itself. Within this movement there were students of all shades of political persuasion.

At the same time another element emerged. The hippie movement cried out for absolute, autonomous freedom. They stood, whether consciously or not, in the stream of Rousseau, Thoreau, the Bohemian life and hedonism. Any authority was met with the cry of "fascist" or "Cossack." In their definition a fascist or Cossack included anybody who suggested any restraint on freedom of the individual. Basically, with these students the rebellion was apolitical. The hippies simply dropped out of society, literally doing nothing much one way or another for or against society. They just opted out.

There was a short-lived third stream as well—the filthy speech movement, which had its major fling some months after the free speech movement began. This rebellion took the form of grabbing the microphone and shouting four-letter words into the ears of all within reach of the amplifying system. A rather crazy idea of freedom if you stop to think about it! This stream was important in that it has influenced the vocabulary of much of the radical rhetoric and was a factor in opening the way for the acceptance of the permissive language of films, the stage, and T.V. today.

But whether it was the free speech people or the hippies (who often were involved with drugs), their first sentence was: "We live in a plastic culture."

This sentence was not wrong; it was right. The evangelical, orthodox church should have been saying it for twenty years before that. If we had, the young people might not have been in the dilemma they were. But orthodox Christians no longer constituted the status quo, and yet had hardly noticed that was the fact. Most Christian leaders try to plead with the young people to "maintain the conservative position" without realizing that the conservative position means the majority position or the generally accepted position, and Christians no longer hold the majority position. We who hold to historic Christianity are now a minority.

The only way to reach our young people is no longer to call on them to maintain the status quo. Instead we must teach them to be revolutionary, as Jesus was revolutionary against both Sadducees and Pharisees. In this biblical sense we must be revolutionary. If we are going to say anything meaningful to our generation, whether for individual conversion or for a cultural transformation in which Christ is Lord of all, we must build upon the understanding that the generation in which we live is plastic. *Plastic* is a good word here, for plastic is synthetic and it also has no natural grain or form. The church has failed to speak in anything like the way God would have had it speak. It largely acted as though the Christian base could be removed, and it would make no practical difference to society, culture or its own young people.

The New Industrial State
But if on one side there was the hippie and the free speech movement, there was yet another direction. Appearing at the same time was John Kenneth Galbraith. *The New Industrial State* was the book in which Galbraith clearly stated this direction, though he

had outlined it earlier in the Reith Lectures. Galbraith did not use the same words, but he agreed with the hippies that we live in a plastic culture. Culture has lost its way, and we should now have somebody new to direct it. Who should direct it? Galbraith's answer was: the academic and especially the scientific elite, plus the state. To those who know Plato, it all sounds very familiar. The philosopher-kings were to be reinstated.

Trouble in Utopia
Of course, problems arose in both views. Within the hippie and the free speech movement, one problem was pointed up very early by Allen Ginsberg. He made the shrewdest comment that I think has been offered when he, Alan Watts, Gary Snyder, and Timothy Leary met together at a symposium in San Francisco during the apex of hippieism. Leary and others were speaking warmly of the virtues of drugs and of the great future coming under the new absolute freedom. On the basis of hedonism we come to a golden tomorrow. Every man will be personally free, having no restraints. Man, especially under the influence of drugs, would come to his utopia. Ginsberg pricked that balloon with a single sentence. He simply said, "But, Tim, somebody must make the posters." The simple fact is, freedom without form produces nothing.

The Galbraith side, however, had its own problems. If we have an academic, scientific, state elite without any controls upon it, without any outside universal to guide it, it will undoubtedly lead in the direction of an establishment totalitarianism. Please repeat the term *establishment elite* in your mind until the term is permanently stuck there.

The problem is that you cannot trust the scientist just because he wears a white coat. It is as simple as that. Inside the coat he is still a fallen man. Even those who are not Christians should understand enough about people to know you cannot trust them merely because of the color of hat or coat they wear. The best illustration of this was Edmund R. Leach, the anthropologist at Cambridge. But I will reserve for the last chapter a fuller discussion of what he exemplified—scientific manipulation of facts.

The Response of the Anarchists
Out of the free speech, hippie side there came two other answers. There were two other branches. In the first, total freedom led to a new anarchy. This group of students believed that things have

become so bad that they could not possibly be worse. Therefore, they would destroy everything, and without reason hope that out of the ashes of destruction would spring forth something better, simply because it could not be worse. They were the bombers in the cities in the United States. Theirs was a vain, romantic dream. These were the forerunners of the terrorists in the 1970s and the 1980s. Even though he thinks he is tough, eventually the anarchist is a romantic. He hopes something better will come, though he has no reason so to hope.

The Response of the New Left
Second, out of the free speech and the hippie movements the New Left came. It derives from what, as I said, Ginsberg pointed out: someone needs to make the posters. Herbert Marcuse pointed the way. Marcuse was the philosopher of the New Left, the one who bound the student movement together over almost the whole world. As Galbraith put forth the concept of an establishment totalitarianism, Marcuse put forth the concept of a left-wing totalitarianism. It explained the change in the campus revolutions from Wisconsin and Columbia onwards. It explained what happened at the University of Wisconsin, at Columbia University, at the Sorbonne and in West Berlin. One of the leaders of the Sorbonne revolution spoke over the French radio. Another student called up on the phone and said, "Give me a chance to speak." But the answer was "No, just shut up—I'll never give you a chance to speak." The same thing happened wherever the New Left took over. Here is the complete opposite to the original free speech movement—a few hundred tell thousands they must be still.

Many students lived in a halfway house, as it were. They did not believe what their parents believed, they would not defend their parents' values; but neither did they have a base for their own beliefs, nor would they hold them for long if challenged. They had no real system of values and hence, even in the university, they allowed an elite to tell them to be still.

Some quit the New Left because it dawned on them that they were building a new fascist regime, a new fascism in the sense that an elite without any controls upon it, with no universals to impose upon it, was telling everyone else to shut up and listen to them alone.

We must not delude ourselves. These university movements,

whether in West Germany or Italy or Tokyo or the United States, were only the pilot plan. They were meant to be the pattern for society. What we have going on is a war, and those who are being attacked are often oblivious. What happened then on our campuses was not meant for the universities alone—it was meant for the total society.

This then was, and is, the situation. Whether it is a left-wing (or liberal) elite or an establishment elite, the result is exactly the same. There are no real absolutes controlling either. In both cases, one is left with only arbitrary absolutes set by an authoritarian society or state, or some elite, with all the modern means of manipulation under its control.

Three Alternatives to Christianity
Before explaining what I take to be the proper Christian response, I wish to summarize the three basic alternatives to that Christian response. If one abandons the Christian solution—the return to the absolutes and universals possible because of God's speaking clearly to man—there are three (and only three) possible alternatives.

The first is hedonism—namely, that every individual does exactly what he wants to do. Hedonism can function as long as you have one man. But as soon as you have more than one person in society, chaos immediately follows. Imagine two hedonists meeting each other over a swift stream on a single log. Here you have the dilemma. But hedonism really still holds many, even though they stay in the system. They are there for their own hedonistic advantage.

The second possibility, if you do not have an absolute, is the dictatorship of 51 percent, with no controls and nothing with which to challenge the majority. This is sociological law—the law of averages, the law of majority opinion. In the United States, Oliver Wendell Holmes and the Yale University Law School were the first to act upon such open sociological law. The concept of *Lex Rex,* that there is a real base to build on, is gone, and even the Constitution is viewed as a less than firm form of restraint. The courts are making sociological law.

But one must understand where this leads. It means that if Hitler was able to get a 51 percent vote of the Germans, he had a right to kill the Jews.

Our Christian forefathers who built the Reformation concept of government with its checks and balances did not believe in the dictatorship of 51 percent. In Scandinavia, Switzerland, Holland, Canada, the United States, there were checks and balances in government. The English had the Crown, the House of Lords, the House of Commons and the Prime Minister, and the courts balanced against each other. The Swiss were so insistent on the matter of checks and balances that the Supreme Court building was not even allowed to be in the same city as the rest of the government. Today the Supreme Court is still in Lausanne and the rest of the government in Berne. But in current political thinking—in the absolute power of 51 percent, law only by consensus—all this is laid aside. No longer can the little man with the open Bible say to the 51 percent, you are wrong. No longer is there an absolute anywhere with which to measure and judge. A shifting and arbitrary consensus rules.

The third possibility is an elite or a dictator—that is, some form of authoritarianism wherein a minority, the elite, or one man tells the society what to do. Again in this case arbitrary absolutes are set up, free from the control of any universal. In the 1970s the Supreme Court assumed this position in the United States, imposing their views of what was good for society. The abortion ruling was a clear example. This important shift in regard to human life was imposed with the people given no chance to vote upon it.

I would say it again: if you do not have an absolute that resides somewhere, to which you can appeal, these are the only three sociological possibilities. The professors in the universities and others did not seem to realize when they cut away the Christian position that it was going to lead to one of these three positions. They destroyed the base and short-sightedly did not know what would follow.

The largest block of people are those who in the 1970s were called the "silent majority." They are the majority in the United States, England and many other countries. They can elect whomever they will under our present democratic voting procedures.

These, however, must be clearly understood to consist of two unequal parts: (1) the Christians, standing in the stream of historic Christianity, living under the propositional revelation of God as He has spoken in the Bible, and therefore having absolutes; and (2) the majority of what was called the silent majority, who are living on the memory of the practical advantages that Christian culture gave, but without a base for these advantages. Their values are affluence (they are practical materialists) and personal peace at any price. Having no base, no absolutes, most of them will compromise liberty if they are finally forced to choose between their affluence and personal peace on the one hand and giving up a piece of liberty on the other. They are no closer to the true Christian than was the hippie community and the New Left. In fact, they are probably further away, for they have no values that deserve the name *values*. Affluence and personal peace at any price as the controlling factors of life are as ugly as anything could be.

The students of the 1960s who reached the place of disillusionment then tended to drift into the majority of the silent majority. Many continued to smoke marijuana, etc., but they no longer had any reason to do anything that disturbed their form of peaceful life; they had, and have, no ideals to cause them to do anything but protect their own life-style. Many of the original Berkeley free speech people, or people like them, will never again risk anything to speak for free speech if it is costly.

The problem is that though the pendulum may swing from the *liberal* to the *conservative* side, if economic well-being is not forthcoming (for example, the control of inflation), having no base for real values, there could easily be another swing to some form of an elite which gave the promise of affluence and personal peace.

The danger is that the evangelical, being so committed to middle-class norms and often even elevating these norms to an equal place with God's absolutes, will slide without thought into accepting some form of an establishment elite.

The Christian Response

If this is the situation, what then is the Christian response? Some Christians have supposed that the choice is between a revolutionary stance and some kind of reconciliation. The Christian, it is assumed, is to choose reconciliation. But we cannot have reconciliation in a world like ours unless something happens first. We are headed for the disaster I have described above, and no nice soft talk of reconciliation and the contentless word *love* is going to have any meaning in such a setting. We must have something stronger.

We must have a Christian revolution. Love, yes. But let us understand that if we are to have it, we need to know what it is. We need what the Reformation of the sixteenth century built on, that which derives from Scripture itself—that God is not only a

God of love, but a God of holiness. He is a God with character. Everything is not equally right before God, and because of this we have our absolutes and categories. We are not left with silence as the early Wittgenstein saw it; God has spoken in propositions to man.

Because God has spoken in a propositional, verbalized way in the Bible, we can have categories, in relationship to knowing (we do not have to be lost between fantasy and reality), to morals, to law, and to social action. In this setting, man is no longer dead. He has been separated from God by his true moral guilt, but he is not dead. Man is wonderful, made in the image of the personal God. Here is the answer both to Rousseau and to the mechanical world, whether in chemical determinism or psychological determinism. And in the substitutionary death of Christ who died upon the cross in space and time and history, there is a way for our true moral guilt to be removed and for man to return to fellowship with God.

Here, then, is the basis for a revolution built on truth. We can, by God's grace, build again. To young people who want a revolution, let me say this: You cannot be a revolutionary simply by some minor thing like letting your hair grow and cultivating a beard. To be a real revolutionary, you must become involved in a real revolution—a revolution in which you are pitted against everybody who has turned away from God and His propositional revelation to men—even against the user of god words. This is a revolution in which we may again hope to see good results, not only in individuals going to Heaven, but in Christ who is Lord becoming Lord in fact in this culture of ours to give us even in this fallen world something of both truth and beauty.

Cobelligerents, Not Allies

Let me suggest three implications of what a true revolution will mean in the light of where we are. First, Christians must realize that there is a difference between being a cobelligerent and an ally. At times we will seem to be saying exactly the same thing as those without a Christian base are saying. If there is social injustice, say there is social injustice. If we need order, say we need order. In these cases, and at these specific points, we would be cobelligerents. But we must not align ourselves as though we are in any camp built on a non-Christian base. We are an ally of no such camp. The church of the Lord Jesus Christ is different—totally different; it rests on the absolutes given to us in Scripture.

My observation of many young pastors and others is this: suddenly they are confronted by some two camps and they are told, "Choose, choose, choose." By God's grace they must say, "I will not choose between these two. I stand alone with God, the God who has spoken in the Scripture, the God who is the infinite-personal God, and neither of your two sides is standing there. So if I seem to be saying the same thing at some one point, understand that I am a cobelligerent at this particular place, but I am not an ally."

The danger is that the older evangelical with his middle-class orientation will forget this distinction and become an ally of an establishment elite, and at the same time his son or daughter will forget the distinction and become an ally of some "leftish" elite. We must say what the Bible says when it causes us *to seem to be saying* what others are saying, such as "Justice!" or "Stop the meaningless bombings!" But we must never forget that this is only a passing cobelligerency and not an alliance.

The Preaching and the Practice of Truth

Second, we and our churches must take truth seriously. The great tragedy is that in all our countries, evangelicalism under the name of evangelicalism is destroying evangelicalism. Orthodoxy under the name of orthodoxy is destroying orthodoxy. Take the Free University of Amsterdam, that great school which under Abraham Kuyper really spoke for God, not only in theology but in its understanding of culture. Today the Theology Department in the Free University discredits the Scripture. In America it is the same. We have theological seminaries that call themselves evangelical and no longer hold to the Scriptures, especially the first half of Genesis, as fully inspired in their historic content. In England it is the same. T. H. Huxley spoke as a prophet in 1890 when he said that there would come a day when faith would be separated from all fact (especially all pre-Abrahamic history), and faith would go on triumphant forever. That is where not only the liberal theologians are, but also the evangelical, orthodox theologians who begin to tone down on the truth, the propositional truth of Scripture which God has given us.

The key here is antithesis. If a statement is true, its opposite is not true. We must take this very seriously. Many of us in the name of evangelicalism are letting it slip through our fingers. Unless we accept the modern twentieth-century concept that religious truth is only psychological truth, then if there is that which is true, the opposite is not true. Two religions that teach exactly opposite things may both be wrong, but they cannot both be right. We must act upon, witness, and preach this fact: what is contrary to God's revealed propositional truth is not true, whether it is couched in Hindu terms or traditional Christian terms with new meanings.

All the areas of our personal and corporate life, especially our corporate religious life, must be affected. The early church allowed itself to be condemned, both by the secular and religious authorities. They said, "We must preach, we must witness publicly; we must obey God rather than man." In Acts 4:19, 20 they said: In obedience to God, we must say what we have seen, and we must say what we have heard regardless of any authority that would tell us to be quiet. They practiced antithesis.

Students from London School of Economics, Harvard, the Sorbonne, from Africa and Asia and from the ends of the earth, have come to L'Abri with their packs on their backs. But if you think they would listen to us if we were not willing to say that what Christianity teaches (what God has spoken) stands as an antithesis to its opposite, you do not understand your own children or your own age. Our credibility is already minus 5 if we do not say what is false and wrong in contrast to what is true and right. It is minus 405 if we are not willing to stand practically in the arena of antithesis. Some Christians think they will be listened to more if they give in a bit at some points concerning the Scripture, but they are mistaken—they have given away the answers which are needed.

But if first we must speak Christianity with a clear content and an emphasis on truth as over against what is not true, equally we must *practice* truth. This was the stress in my speech to the Berlin Congress on Evangelism, "The Practice of Truth," and it has been what I have stressed at many places, and at many times, since.

We must practice the truth even when it is costly. We must practice it when it involves church affiliation or evangelistic cooperation. There is a difference between having a public discussion with a liberal theologian and inviting him to pray in our program. There is a difference between personal fellowship with a Christian and publicly acting in such a way that others would conclude it makes no difference when central points have been compromised.

This is a time to show to a generation which thinks that the concept of truth is unthinkable that we do take truth seriously. This means we must carefully consider the principle of the purity of the visible church and what discipline in regard to both life and doctrine means. We may differ at certain points in application, but the concepts must be discussed and put into practice under the leadership of the Holy Spirit. Two biblical principles have to be considered in their interrelationship: (1) the principle of the purity of the visible church; and (2) the principle that the world has a right to judge whether we are Christians and whether the Father sent the Son, on the basis of observable love shown among all true Christians.[1]

If we practice latitudinarianism either individually or corporately in an age like our own, we have removed our credibility before the non-Christian, post-Christian, relativistic, skeptical, lost world.

If you think that those who have rejected the plastic culture and are sick of hypocrisy are going to be impressed when you talk about truth and at the same time practice untruth, you are wrong. They will never listen. You have cut the ground from under yourself. We live in a generation that does not believe that such a thing as truth is possible, and if you practice untruth while talking about truth, the real thinkers will just say, "Garbage!"

True Christian Community
Third, our churches must be real communities. With an orthodoxy of doctrine there must equally be an orthodoxy of community. Our Christian organizations must be communities in which others see what God has revealed in the teaching of His Word. They should see that what has happened in Christ's death and reconciliation on the cross back there in space and time and history is relevant, that it is possible to have something beautiful and unusual in this world in our communication and in communities at this point of history. We may preach truth. We may preach orthodoxy. We may even stand against the practice of untruth strongly. But if others cannot see something beautiful in our human relationships, if they do not see that upon the basis of what Christ has done our Christian communities can stop their infighting, then we are not living properly.

The Christian community and the practice of that community should cut across all lines. Our churches have largely been preaching points and activity generators. Community has had little place. In the New Testament church this practice of community was not just a banner, but cut all the way down into the hard stuff of the material needs of the members of the community. This was the reason for the appointing of the first deacons. It was also practiced at long distance; the Gentiles of Macedonia, for example, gave to the needy Jewish Christians in Jerusalem. Such gifts were not considered less spiritual than those gifts sent to Paul to help him in his missionary preaching. Such gifts were not forced; they were made on the basis of free loving community. They were viewed as something normal among the Christians. This was a practiced orthodoxy of community.

This went across *all* lines. I shall never forget the prayer of a young person at the close of my last lecture at Buck Hill Falls a number of years ago. She prayed, "Forgive me for hating adults." May God forgive us, the orthodox of all kinds and ages, for the lack of integration in the Christian groups, across *all kinds* of lines.

I want to see us treating each other like human beings, something that the humanistic student rebels desired but were unable to produce. Every Christian church, every Christian school, every mission should be a community which the world may look upon as a pilot plant.

When a big company is going to put several million dollars into building a plant, it first builds a pilot plant to show it can be done. Every Christian community everywhere ought to be a pilot plant to show that we can have horizontal relationships with men and that this can result in a community that cares not only for Man with a capital "M," but for the individual—not only for upper-case Human Rights, but for the whole man in all his needs.

Unless people see in our churches not only the preaching of the truth but the practice of the truth, the practice of love, and the practice of beauty; unless they see that the thing that the humanists rightly want but cannot achieve on a humanist base (human communication and human relationship), is able to be practiced in our communities, then let me say it clearly: they will not listen and they should not listen.

True Revolution
But if Christians can take these factors into account—(1) the difference between being a cobelligerent and an ally, (2) the preaching and the practice of truth even at great cost in our Christian groups, and (3) the observation of community within those churches and Christian groups that stand under the Scripture—then we will have the possibility of a stirring of a fresh revolution.

It will be a real revolution—a real reformation and revival in the orthodox evangelical church. And then by God's grace, a Christian consensus may become active again.

We do not need 51 percent of the people to begin to have an influence. If 20 percent of the American population were really regenerate Christians, clear about their doctrines, beliefs and values, taking truth seriously, taking a consistent position, we could begin, not to have an overwhelming consensus, but at least to have a vital voice again in the midst of our community. But if this reformation and revival, this positive revolution, does not occur, if we do not begin to put a base back under our culture, the base that was there in the first place and now is completely gone, then I believe with all my heart that we will have a revolution from either the left or the establishment in order to give at least an illusion of what the people want concerning material well-being.

And if this revolution comes from either side, our culture will be changed still further. The last remnants of Christian memory in the culture will be eliminated, and freedoms will be gone. If the revolution comes from the establishment, it will be much more gradual, much less painful for the Christian—for a while. But eventually it will be as total. We must not opt for one as against the other just because it seems to give a little peace for a little time. That is an enormous mistake, because both are equally non-Christian and eventually both will be equal in smashing out the freedoms which we have had.

CHAPTER THREE

The Church in a Post-Christian Culture

Is there a future for the church in the midst of the twentieth century? That question is foremost in the minds of many Christians.

In the previous chapter I set forth three things that are necessary if the church of the Lord Jesus Christ is to be a revolutionary force in the midst of twentieth-century upheaval and revolution: (1) the church must distinguish between being a cobelligerent and an ally; (2) it must be careful to stand clearly for truth, both in doctrine and in practice even when it is costly; and (3) it must be more than merely a preaching point and an activity generator; it must show a sense of community.

The Truth of Christianity
Now I want to look more closely at the third point—the individual Christian and the Christian community. But even this very practical consideration is built firmly on the basis of the second point mentioned above—the stress on truth in doctrine and practice.

There will be little meaning to Christian community until we understand what *Christian* means, and understand who make up a Christian community.

The liberal theologians in their stress on community speak and act as though we *become* Christians when we enter the horizontal relationship of community. But this is a totally wrong starting-point. If this were so, Christianity would have no more final value than the humanistic community. And that is the trouble with modern man—he can find no sufficient value for humanistic community, for he can find no sufficient value for the people who make it up. If the individual person is a zero, then community is only adding zeros.

We must hold to the great Reformation concepts and Reformation creeds, and prior to these the orthodox creeds, back to the one that we often recite together—the Apostles' Creed, and then the Nicene Creed, and the Chalcedonian Christology. All these we must hold to, but this is not the final concept of truth the Bible puts forth. The final great concept of truth is that Christianity is true to what is there.

I often think that one of the reasons there is such an air of unreality in much of the church, and for many people, is that they do not really understand what is meant when we say Christianity is true. It is not that it is merely true to a creed, though we should be true to our creeds. It is not even that it is true to the Bible, though certainly our Christianity should be true to the full inspiration of Scripture. But it is rather that Christianity is true to what is really there. It explains why the universe is here and why it has its complexity and its form. It gives us the truth about who man is and the great requirement, the truth that God is there. It tells us that our final environment is not impersonal, but personal. We have an intellectual knowledge which in the middle of the twentieth century we can hold with integrity.

But this knowledge must be practical. Our knowledge concerning the existence of God should flow on into an adoration of this God with our whole selves, including the intellect. Christianity is not only a scholasticism; rather, I would insist strongly, it is the highest and the only true mysticism—because it is the only mysticism that allows a person to come into contact with God as a whole person, without leaving the intellect hanging outside. And it will not do merely to understand this; it must flow on in practice individually and then corporately.

God Exists
Both the individual's and the community's life turns upon the existence of a personal relationship with God. Everything hangs

on this point. There will be no reality either in our individual or corporate Christian living and spiritual life except on the basis of a personal relationship with the God who is there. And any concept of a really personal relationship with the God who is there turns upon the fact that God exists and is personal and that I, a man, am made in His image and therefore am personal. God is infinite. I am finite. But if He is personal and I am personal, made in His image, it is not unnatural that I should be in a personal relationship with the God who is there.

Let us understand that the beginning of Christianity is not salvation: it is the existence of the Trinity. Before there was anything else, God existed as personal God in the high order of Trinity. So there was communication and love between the persons of the Trinity before all else. This is the beginning.

The naturalness of my individual relationship with God does not turn upon the fact of salvation; it turns upon who God is and who I am. Now to enter into this relationship, we must have salvation. But the relationship of an individual man, though finite, to the infinite God who is there should never take us by surprise. This is the kind of God we have, and this is the kind of man He has made in His image, distinct from the trees, the plants and the machineline portion of the universe.

The first commandment is to love God with all our heart, soul and mind. This commandment was not merely spoken by Jesus, but written in the Old Testament, and surely represents the purpose of man's existence—to love God. But it is a meaningless command unless we understand the kind of God who is there and the kind of man that I am.

The theologian who talks about loving God and has no real certainty of any correlation between his use of the word *God* and God's being there is talking nonsense. It is ridiculous to speak of loving a God who is not there. Take, for example, the liberal theologian who says there is no reality in prayer. Bishop Robinson in *Honest to God* showed this clearly in his notion that there is no real vertical relationship with God. It is impossible to have such a relation with God simply because God, for Robinson, was not the kind of God who would make a vertical relationship have any meaning. But God is a personal God, and therefore the call to love Him is not nonsense.

Or, on the other hand, take the humanist who thinks man is a machine. If I am a machine, whether chemically or psychologically determined, then my loving God has no meaning. Furthermore, if God is the great philosophic other, or the impersonal everything—pantheism in some sense—then the call to love God is either an illusion or a cruel hoax.

Everything that Christianity has ever had turns on the existence and character of God and the existence and nature of man—the existence and nature of "me." Therefore, the adequate base for individual and corporate Christian living is a personal relationship with the God who is there and who is personal.

Furthermore, how we function must witness to the fact that we know God is there. All too often we say God exists and then go on in just a scholastic orthodoxy. Often, as far as the world can see, our whole organizational program is set up as though God isn't there and we have to do everything ourselves on a Madison Avenue basis.

Suppose we awoke tomorrow morning and we opened our Bibles and found two things had been taken out, not as the liberals would take them out, but *really* out. Suppose God had taken them out. The first item missing was the real empowering of the Holy Spirit, and the second item the reality of prayer. Consequently, following the dictates of Scripture, we would begin to live on the basis of this new Bible in which there was nothing about the power of the Holy Spirit and nothing about the power of prayer. Let me ask you something: what difference would there be from the way we acted yesterday? Do we really believe God is there? If we do, we live differently.

The Guilt of Man

Of course we know, as we look across mankind and as we look in our own hearts, that man is not what he was originally made to be. I must acknowledge that individually I have deliberately sinned, deliberately done what I know to be wrong. And if I am to be in the place for which I was made—that is, in a personal relationship with this God who exists—something is needed in order to remove this true moral guilt which I have.

The Bible speaks to the man without the Bible—the man who is totally untrained in its content—and it speaks to the man with the Bible—the man who has had intimate exposure to its message. In both cases, it speaks of the fact that all men have sinned individually and as such are under moral guilt before God. This is a tremendous contrast to twentieth-century thinking in which man has guilt-feelings but no true moral guilt, because there are no absolutes before which a man is, or can be, morally guilty. Guilt-feelings are all that are possible. But biblically all men stand truly morally guilty before God because each has deliberately sinned.

In the first four chapters of Romans, Paul speaks to the Greek and the Roman world, which was very much like our own world both in intellectual intensity and in decadence. There he lays out why a man needs to be a Christian and how he may become one. From the fifth chapter on, Paul speaks to Christians as Christians. The intriguing thing is that it is in the fifth chapter where he is speaking to Christians that he introduces Adam and Adam's revolt against God in order to explain to the Christian the origin of sin in the world. When he talks to the non-Christians in the first chapters and tells them why they should understand that they have true moral guilt, he points out that they have individually and deliberately done those things that they knew were wrong.

Thus in Romans 1:32—2:3 Paul speaks to the man without the Bible:

> Who, knowing the judgment of God, that they who commit such things are worthy of death, not only do the same, but have pleasure in [consent with] them that do them. Therefore, thou art inexcusable, O man, whosoever thou art that judgest; for wherein thou judgest another, thou condemnest thyself; for thou that judgest doest the same things. But we are sure that the judgment of God is according to truth against them who commit such things. And thinkest thou this, O man, that judgest them who do such things, and doest the same, that thou shalt escape the judgment of God?

Let me use an illustration again that I have used in other places. If every little baby that was ever born anywhere in the world had a tape recorder hung about its neck, and if this tape recorder only recorded the moral judgments with which this child as he grew bound other men, the moral precepts might be much lower than the biblical law, but they would still be moral judgments. Eventually each person comes to that great moment when he stands before God as Judge. Suppose, then, that God simply touched the tape recorder button and each man heard played out in his own words all those statements by which he had bound other men in moral judgment. He could hear it going on for years—thousands and thousands of moral judgments made against other men, not aesthetic judgments, but moral judgments. Then God would simply say to the man, though he had never heard the Bible, now where do you stand in the light of your own moral judgments?

The Bible points out in the passage quoted above that every voice would be stilled. All men would have to acknowledge that they have deliberately done those things which they knew to be wrong. Nobody could deny it.

We sin two kinds of sin. We sin one kind as though we trip off the curb, and it overtakes us by surprise. We sin a second kind of sin when we deliberately set ourselves up to fall. And no one can say he does not sin in the latter sense. Paul's comment is not just theoretical and abstract, but addressed to the individual—"O man"—any man without the Bible, as well as the man with the Bible.

In Romans 2:17 he speaks to the man with the Bible and says the same thing. God is completely just. A man is judged and found wanting on the same basis on which he has tried to bind others.

The Necessity of Judgment

But let me stress this warning—it is more than just; it is necessary. It is the only message that is able to speak into the twentieth-century mentality because it is the only message which really gives an answer to the two great problems of all men—modern man and man throughout the ages. First, man needs absolutes, universals, something by which to judge.

If one has no basis on which to judge, then reality falls apart, fantasy is indistinguishable from reality; there is no value for the human individual, and right and wrong have no meaning.

There are two ways to get away from God's judgment of men. One is to say that there is no absolute. But one must be aware that if God does not judge on a 100 percent basis, he is indeed like an old man in the sky. And worse—not only is man left in relativism, but God Himself is bound by relativism. God must be the Judge whose own character is the law of the universe, or we have no absolute. We do not need to be embarrassed as we speak of the individual coming to God to be judged in the full historic sense of judgment. It is quite the other way. If this is not true, then we no longer have an absolute, and we no longer have an answer for twentieth-century man.

The other way to get away from God's judgment of the individual is to take away the significance of man, to say that he is a machine, or that he is chemically or psychologically determined, that his actions in this world are not his own. In such a case, of course, he is not responsible and cannot be justly judged. But a true significance is the second need of man; and if man is not really significant, then in the name of Christianity we have plunged man back again into the caldron of twentieth-century thought where man becomes zero.

My point is simply this: the individual is not separated from God by creation. It is natural that he should be in personal relationship with God; he is separated from God because of his rebellion against God, and therefore we must stress the solution which the Scripture gives.

Christianity's Way Out

What then is this solution? Paul says it is the same for both the man without the Bible and the man with the Bible. Here is an amazing solution for the problem of man. It only fails to be amazing if we have heard it so long that we simply do not listen. But if you could imagine yourself suddenly coming face to face with this answer for the first time, so that you were not turned off by evangelical phraseology, but really were caught by the full force of God's solution to the dilemma, man's true guilt, you would understand that the word *amazing* is not too strong.

"For I am not ashamed of the gospel of Christ; for it is the power of God [the Greek word is *dunamis,* the dynamite of God, the explosive power of God] unto salvation to everyone that believeth; to the Jew first, and also to the Greek" (Romans 1:16). Paul enlarges in Romans 3:23-26: "For all have sinned, and come short of the glory of God." Remember to whom Paul is speaking—the intellectual and sophisticated Greek and Roman world. "For all have sinned, and come short of the glory of God." It is stronger in the Greek—for all have sinned (in the past) and they are falling short (in the present) of the glory of God. But they are "justified freely [*gratis*]" (v. 24).

There is no humanistic note added to salvation here. Man keeps trying to add a humanism to salvation. Whether it is the Judaizers at the time of Paul, or the classical Roman Catholic Church with the addition of works, or the modern theologian—it does not matter. Man always tries to sneak a humanistic element into salvation. But in the area of individual salvation Scripture rejects all humanism. Man is justified freely "through the redemption that is in Christ Jesus, whom God hath set forth to be a propitiation through faith in his blood, to declare his righteousness for the remission of sins that are past, through the forbearance of God; to declare, I say,

at this time his righteousness, that he might be just, and the justifier of him who believeth in Jesus."

Talk about the atom bomb! This is totally explosive—into the
midst of the humanism of any age and expressly into the humanism of the twentieth century. All too often we pass by this 26th
verse too lightly: "To declare, I say, at this time his righteousness,
that he [himself] might be just, and [yet] the justifier of him who
believeth in Jesus." God keeps His absolute standard, and yet there
is a way for the individual to be reconciled to Him, to be in a
personal relationship to Him, which gives meaning to life. It is at
this point that the individual is understood to be the complete
contrary of a zero.

Somebody Knows My Name
Christ's death does not leave us with an impersonal relationship to
God. Salvation is not merely a magnificent theological or intellectual formula; it is this, but it is much more. The Good Shepherd
knows the sheep by name.

Many Christians have heard this for fifty or sixty years, and
when they read it again they are half asleep. But there are also
those who are inhabitants from the midst of the twentieth century,
who live in a world of silence, a world in which no one speaks, the
world of the early Wittgenstein and Bergman, a world in which
there is a desperate longing for communication and love, a world
in which no one is there. To these people I would say, "The Good
Shepherd knows the sheep by name. One who becomes a Christian is not merely an IBM card."

Those students who are caught in the universities and feel the
impersonality of the great machine of society and the university
manipulating the little machine, can they not understand that here
is an entirely different thing? Somebody knows your name in that
great crowd. Somebody knows your name as you protest against
the computer-controlled university and society. Because He is
infinite, He can know each one personally as though no one else
were there. Because the Good Shepherd is truly a man, but more
than a man (the second person of the Trinity and has been forever), He, being infinite, can know each one personally as though
no one else were there.

When by God's grace I accept Christ as my Savior, my Messiah,
my real moral guilt before God is gone, and I am returned to the
place for which I was created—a person-to-person relationship
with a personal God. This is vertical, personal relationship. Now I

can say, "Abba, Father." "Abba" is simply a transliteration from the Aramaic, *Father,* a translation from the Greek. In Greek, *father* can signify either a gentle or an austere father. But *Abba* is a word that will not allow this. *Abba* is *papa, daddy*. If it is done with reverence, the personal God, the Creator of the universe, may now be spoken of as Papa, as Daddy, whatever your favorite word is for father. You may call him that as long as you come in His way, the nonhumanist way, through the finished substitutionary work of Christ as He died in space and time on the cross, and as you do it with awe and reverence.

What we have here is a tremendous personal relationship with the Father—a tremendous father-to-son, or father-to-daughter relationship. Now when I say, "Our Father who art in heaven," it is not a figure of speech. (The liberals tell me it is, but it is not.) It's reality. He is my Father. I may call him Daddy. I may call him Papa.

The universe is no longer silent and impersonal now. There is someone there who loves me, and I may speak and He hears. Together we may speak, and He as the personal God hears, and He, not being a part of the machine, can work in space and time, back into history, on the basis of our prayer.

Suddenly the great syndrome of the twentieth century is smashed. I live now in a different universe, a different world.

Notice, then, that the three problems of modern man fall into place upon this analysis and this solution. First, God is really holy: absolutes do exist. Second, all men do not need to be lost. Third, man is significant. He is not a stick or a stone, not merely a programmed computer. Here you have suddenly brought together the three explosive answers which modern man really needs.

But it is not only an answer to the needs of the twentieth-century man; it is God's solution to the basic problem of all time. Man has been separated from God not by creation, but by rebellion. And God has given a solution that should get us all really excited. This is finally the only thing sufficient to turn us on. I am tired of the evangelical orthodoxy that has ceased to be excited with our answer.

Communication and the Individual
The first step in understanding Christian community, then, is understanding the individuals who make up the community, for the individual is important to God. And the individual is impor-

tant as the individual. Christ is not interested simply in a faceless mass.

Because God is personally interested in individual men, He has given them knowledge, knowledge which the individual man desperately needs and may have. God has given it in propositional, verbalized communication in the Bible. And that should not be surprising. It is only astonishing if you fail to remember who man is: man has been made in the image of God. God has made him to communicate horizontally with other men on the basis of verbalization, and so it is not surprising that the personal God would communicate to him in verbalized form.

Even the strongest atheist agrees that this is not surprising if you begin with the Christian beginning. If there is a personal God on the high order of the Trinity, so that communication has existed for all eternity, and if He has made man in His own image to be the verbalizer (and, by the way, all modern anthropology so marks man—this is the clear distinction between man and non-man), then it is not surprising that He would give us true information on the basis of verbalization.

God has given us two kinds of propositional revelation in the Bible: first, didactic statements and commands; second, a record of how He Himself has worked in space-time history. With these two together we really have a very adequate knowledge, both as knowledge and as a basis for action.

God has not given us exhaustive knowledge, but He has given us true knowledge—about Himself and about the space-time cosmos. Let me repeat: it is not exhaustive knowledge, but it is true knowledge.

Furthermore, Jesus came as prophet, priest and king. He is the giver of knowledge; He is the revealer of the Godhead bodily. But we must beware lest we begin to make a distinction between the knowledge which Jesus gives and the knowledge which the Bible gives. Jesus Himself will not allow any dichotomy here. Jesus says He is the giver of knowledge, but He always quotes the Scripture as though it were also a statement of knowledge to the individual. The Bible and the testimony of Christ stand side by side. What we have here, then, is a Person-to-person imparting of knowledge.

Christian Community

Now we are ready to start talking about the community. I would stress again, however, that a person does not come into relationship with God when he enters the Christian community, whether it is a local church or any other form of community. As I have said, the liberals have gone on to promote other concepts of community. They teach that the only way you can be in relationship to God is when you are in a group. The modern concept is that you enter into community; in this community there is horizontal relationship; in these small I-thou relationships you can hope that there is a big I-Thou relationship.

This is not the Christian teaching. There is no such thing as a Christian community unless it is made up of individuals who are already Christians through the work of Christ. One can talk about Christian community until one is green, but there will be no Christian community except on the basis of a personal relationship with the personal God through Christ. The Christian community is made up of those whom the Good Shepherd knows by name as His sheep, those who are in relationship with God, who stand in a living way as a branch to the vine, the bride to the Bridegroom, those who have come to the living God through the work of Jesus Christ as He died upon the cross.

This is the difference between the sacraments of baptism and the Lord's Supper. Baptism is once for all. It represents a man's acceptance of Christ as Savior and then being baptized at that moment with the Holy Spirit. It is a once-for-all situation. The Lord's Supper is taken constantly because it represents Christians' feeding upon Christ, which should be constant, moment by moment—to use the modern word, existential. These are the ones who should be making up the Christian community.

We have looked carefully at the individual as he stands in relationship to God. The community stands in the same place. I think we have failed here. We have had a fixed, static concept of the church, that somehow or other the church is not a breathing reality. But even though Christianity is individual, it is not individualistic. One must come to God as an individual, but after we have come one at a time, God did not make us to be alone horizontally.

The first thing God did after He made man was to create someone who would be his counterpart, Eve, different from himself and yet his counterpart—so that there would be a proper, horizontal, finite, personal relationship as well as the vertical personal relationship with the infinite-personal Creator. That is what God wants. God has called us in the New Testament—the Old as well, but in a slightly different form—to come into an understanding that there is to be community, a relationship between those who are already Christians.

Note this: you can have individual Christians and no Christian community, but you cannot have a Christian community without having individual Christians. On the other hand, as evangelical, orthodox men and women, we can understand and fight for the need of the individual coming to God and then we can stand individualistically, in a poor sense, rather than in a practicing community. But we must not stand in sheer individualism; once we are Christians, there should be community. As I have used the term before, there is to be an orthodoxy of community as well as an orthodoxy of doctrine.

There are, of course, many forms of Christian communities— local churches, theological schools, Christian colleges, missions, etc. All of these are, or should be, Christian communities, though differing slightly in form. However, they are not entirely equal because, except for the local church, all the others have come into existence to meet the changing needs of the years. In the New Testament, however, the church form has been commanded by God Himself for the era in which we live—that is, until Christ's return.

Existential Living
But regardless of its outward form, the Christian community as a community should understand that its first relationship is not horizontal, but vertical. The Christian community is made up of those who are in a personal relationship with God, and then the community *as a unit* is to strive to be first of all in a relationship with God. Its first job is not toward the lost, though it has a task there. The first thing the Christian community should do is to stand *as a community* in a living, existential, moment-by-moment relationship to God. The congregation, the Christian college student body, the family, whatever the community is, this fellowship of believers should stand in awe and worship waiting before God.

Do we really do this? All too frequently as soon as we get together, we function like the Board of Trade. Not too long ago I was talking to a man whose family owns great cotton mills in England. He said, "You're right. You're right. I go to two kinds of meetings—Christian meetings among Christian brothers, and business meetings at the cotton mill. Sometimes I suddenly sit up in the middle of the meeting and ask myself, 'Which meeting am I in?' "

Community relationship to God does not come mechanically. Even when a group stands for the purity of the visible church and for the historic Christian faith, it does not mean that we, *as a group*, mechanically and automatically practice a relationship upward to God. It is something that must be consciously and continuously sought after. The individual, and then the group, must consciously look to Christ for help and consciously look to the leadership of the Holy Spirit not only theoretically but in reality, consciously understanding that every relationship must first be toward God before it has meaning out toward men. And only after the vertical relationship—first individually and then as the group—is established are we ready to have horizontal relationships and a proper Christian community. It is a long way to come. But there is no other way to achieve authenticity.

But as we come now as a community consciously realizing our calling, we can know who we are in our horizontal relationships. First of all, to these around me in my Christian community, I am a man among men. I am one flesh, one blood with them. They are made in the image of God, and I am made in the image of God. We have one Creator—one origin. Second, I am a brother in Christ with them because they and I, by God's grace, have come under the finished work of Jesus Christ.

Therefore, as we meet in our groups, we know who we are. We are not like those who march in our streets and do not know who they are—who call for community, but have no basis for community beyond biological continuity. Now we are ready to begin real personal living, to practice the orthodoxy of community corporately. Real personal Christian living individually and corporately as a community that rests upon the individual's and the community's personal relationship with a personal God gives us the possibility of Christian community before the eye of an observing world. But there is no use taking all this time, this whole chapter, to understand what Christian community is if we do not practice it! We will continue through the remainder of this book to think about what that practice means in the midst of our post-Christian culture.

CHAPTER FOUR

Form and Freedom in the Church

We now come to the fourth consideration needed if the church is going to be what it should be, ready for what lies ahead in the years at the end of the twentieth century. Those already given are: first is the difference between being a cobelligerent and an ally; the second, the preaching and practice of truth, even if at great cost; the third, the practice of the orthodoxy of community within true Christian groups and between true Christian groups. Now the fourth is the consideration of what form and what freedom the Bible gives in regard to the church as the church—or we could speak of it as the boundary conditions set forth in the New Testament on the polity of the church.

Note here that we are not just speaking of Christian work in general, but the church as the church—what is often spoken of today as the institutional or organized church. Does it have a future?

The church of Jesus Christ is, of course, first of all the church invisible. It is the body of believers united by faith in Christ in the full biblical sense, whether or not they are members of an external organization. It includes the church today at war in the present world and the church of the past whose members are already at peace. It is the church universal. When Jesus said, "I will build my church" (Matthew 16:18), this was what He meant. And the writer of Hebrews, in 12:22, 23, had the same thing in mind—the unity of the entire body of believers of all times and all places.

The Visible Church

But one of Jesus' remarks also points to the visibility of the church. In Matthew 18:17 Jesus says, "And if he shall neglect to hear them, tell it unto the church; but if he neglect to hear the church, let him be unto thee as an heathen man and a publican." So here we have already indicated the fact that the church is not only to be invisible, but visible as well. It would be meaningless to command to bring before the invisible church a brother in Christ with whom we have had a difference. There is an indication here that there is a structure to which we may bring our brother when we have had a falling out—a structure which makes a distinction between those in that structure and those out of it.

As we turn to the book of Acts, we find this concept is recognized and applied by the early church. Acts 13:1, 2 concerns the group of Christians at Antioch. Antioch is important, because it is the place where most church historians and exegetes feel that for the first time full Gentiles (not just "God-fearers," Gentiles like Cornelius who believed but had not taken on the full Jewish rites) were reached by the Christian Jews.

The text begins: "Now there were in the church that was at Antioch . . ." Thus, there was a functioning local congregation called "the church." From here on the New Testament clearly indicates that churches were formed wherever some became Christians.

Salvation, as I have emphasized already, is individual, but not individualistic. People cannot become Christians except one at a time, and yet our salvation is not solitary. God's people are called together in community. Hence at Antioch individual Christians are not now acting individualistically; they are acting as a unit.

Not only the officers among the believing Jews, but apparently the members at Antioch as well couldn't refrain from telling the good news to their Gentile neighbors. Manaen especially is singled out and called "the foster brother of Herod." Here, then, is a member of the aristocracy who was a member of the church at Antioch.

This church covered the whole spectrum of society. It was as wide as the culture which it faced. Undoubtedly it had simple people in it, but it could also have Herod's foster brother. It had Jews, and it had Gentiles. It was, in fact, from the very beginning the ideal local church. It encompassed the whole spectrum of the surrounding society, including, furthermore, those who, like Herod's foster brother and a slave, could not come together in any other setting.

Similarly, you will notice that though they were not all "professional ministers" or "missionaries," yet they were all tellers. Christians felt a burden for being tellers into their own culture, and this is how the Gentiles became Christians at Antioch. But also they felt a burden for sending Paul and Barnabas abroad.

In a sense we have a complete picture of what the local church ought to be: individuals were becoming Christians, but not individualistic ones; the congregation covered the full spectrum of the society; the members were all tellers, not only at home but abroad. And when the Holy Spirit said that Barnabas and Saul should be sent on the first missionary journey, the members did not function only as individual Christians, but as a unit, as a church.

I am often asked, "Is the institutional church finished as we face the end of the twentieth century?" My answer is very much No, for the church is clearly given as a New Testament ordinance until Christ returns. However, that is a very different thing from forgetting that the New Testament gives freedoms as well as forms as to what the institutional church may be like.

Let us consider what limits the New Testament places upon the institutional church—that is, what form the New Testament imposes. We have already dealt with the command for orthodoxy of doctrine and life and orthodoxy of community. Now we are thinking of the New Testament statements concerning the polity of the church as a church. *The first of these is that local congregations are to exist and that they are made up of Christians.*

The Formation of Local Churches

If we look ahead to Acts 16:4, 5, we hear about the missionary journey upon which Paul and Barnabas had been sent from the church at Antioch. "And as they went through the cities, they delivered them the decrees to keep, that were ordained of the apostles and elders who were at Jerusalem. And so were the churches established in the faith, and increased in number daily."

As the missionary journey progressed, once more individuals were brought to salvation, but they soon joined together in a specific, observable structure, an organization with form. Throughout Paul's missionary journey we see a stress on the formation of churches.

In Romans 16:16 Paul writes, "Salute one another with an holy kiss. The churches of Christ salute you." The reference is to churches, not just the church. In 2 Corinthians 11:28, Paul refers to "the care of all the churches." Romans 16:3, 4 contains some very instructive statements about the early churches that were formed. "Greet Priscilla and Aquila." (In Greek the word is *Prisca,* a term of fondness for Priscilla.) "Greet Prisca and Aquila, my helpers in Christ Jesus, who have for my life laid down their own necks; unto whom not only I give thanks, but also all the churches of the Gentiles." It is not *church,* but *churches;* individual churches were formed.

Paul continues, "Likewise greet the church that is in their house." Aquila and Priscilla were then in Rome. But when they were in Asia, as we learn in 1 Corinthians 16:19, they also had a church in their home. Apparently wherever Priscilla and Aquila went, people were saved and a church was then started.

It is interesting, however, that the church was in their home. Lightfoot says that there were no church buildings as such before the third century. Since Lightfoot made that statement, however, archaeologists have found a most interesting place in Rome. Roman houses—unless they were the great mansions—were relatively small. What archaeologists found was a place with the facade of two houses still untouched, but with the internal walls torn out to make a larger room. And from everything that was found there, the archaeologists believe that this was a church building. This structure is dated at the end of the second century. But whether one accepts Lightfoot's starting point in the third century, or whether one dates it at the end of the second century, it really makes no difference. There is no biblical norm as to where, and where not, the church should meet. *The central fact is that the early concept of the church had no connection with a church building.* The church was something else: a group of Christians drawn together by the Holy Spirit in a place where they worked together in a certain form, a form which we will examine as we go now through various verses in the New Testament.

First Corinthians 4:17 and 7:17 also give the most clear statements one could have that churches were considered as churches and not just as an abstract or invisible concept. Individual churches were formed as people became Christians, and these were definite, specific entities.

In 1 Corinthians 11:18, we have a note which is unhappy, and yet which is surely encouraging for us. "First of all, when ye come together in the church, I hear that there are divisions among you; and I partly believe it." It is unfortunate and yet it is encouraging to us that already at this early time we find troubles and problems in the church. The church is not a church building, mind you, but a congregation of believers. And this congregation of believers was not perfect because there is nothing perfect in a fallen world. And Christians are not perfect until Jesus comes. Since there is discipline in the church, this does not mean that something is held aloft as an ideal totally beyond our imagination and our experience. This is not a picture of a perfect congregation, but it is a congregation made up of Christians.

Right up to the year 100 (if you take the book of Revelation as having been written then) John, writing under the inspiration of the Holy Spirit, directs the book of Revelation to individual churches. Hence, up to the end of the New Testament, individual churches existed and were important enough for letters to be addressed to them. The picture is clear. As Paul moves over the Roman Empire, as Aquila and Priscilla move over the Roman Empire, as other Christians move over the Roman Empire, individuals are saved and local congregations are organized. And this, I believe, is a pattern that holds for the church until Jesus comes.

The first biblical norm, then, is that there should be churches made up of Christians. Not to have such churches would be contrary to this norm.

Second, it seems clear that these congregations met together in a special way on the first day of the week. Though there are not many references, they do seem definite. Consider 1 Corinthians 16:2 and Acts 20:7. Each first day of the week they met as a statement that "He is risen, He is risen indeed!"

But let us notice that no specific time of the day is given as a norm. The day is set; the time of the day is left totally open.

Local Church Polity
The letters of Paul and the book of Acts indicate something of the specific form these congregations took. We know, for example,

that the churches had officers. Acts 14:23 reads, "And when they had ordained (or appointed) elders in every church, and had prayed with fasting, they commended them to the Lord, on whom they believed." Scholars have discussed how these elders were chosen; I personally think that there is no clear indication. But there is no doubt of the fact that there were elders. The church did not sit there as a group of believers with no form. *The third norm, therefore, is that there are to be church officers (elders) who have responsibility for the local churches.* Missionaries on missionary journeys produced not only individual Christians, but also churches with officers.

Elders and Deacons

As one reads the New Testament, a rather detailed picture begins to emerge; the church begins to take on dimension and life. There is, for example, the remarkable passage (Acts 20:17-37) which describes Paul saying good-bye to the church at Ephesus, a church he dearly loved and where he had spent so much time. He did not want to go to the city itself, where he knew he would be forced to stay longer, so he went to the seaport of Miletus, about thirty or forty miles from Ephesus, and asked the elders to meet him there.

Paul then addressed this statement to them in the 28th verse: "Take heed, therefore, unto yourselves, and to all the flock, over which the Holy Ghost hath made you overseers, to feed the church of God, which he hath purchased with his own blood." Notice how the elders are given a double charge. They are to watch out for those who will bring in false doctrine. They are called upon to exert discipline, but they are not merely to be like a court, as if this is their only or their chief function. They are also to feed the flock. They have a responsibility to see that the church is not anemic. The elders are not to forget either side; both are necessary. They must see that the Word of God is brought to the church so that, on the one hand, false doctrine and false life are kept out (or if they arise, that discipline is applied), but, on the other hand, that the church does not dry up like an old pea in a pod. They are to feed the church by the Word of God. This surely has the concept of teaching, but the use of the word "feed" carries more with it; it implies that the church is to live. The officers have a responsibility for maintaining real life in the church.

Paul implies in 1 Timothy 5:17 that there were two kinds of elders: "Let the elders that rule well be counted worthy of double honor, especially they who labor in the word and doctrine." Here, then, is an indication that in the early church some elders gave special attention to preaching and teaching. That is, there were elders who were especially committed to preaching and teaching the people, or as it is expressed here, "labor in the word and in doctrine."

In addition to elders, there are also deacons. Acts 6:1-6 says that they were the men who were to care for the distribution of gifts to meet a material need. *The fourth norm, then, is that there should be deacons responsible for the community of the church in the area of material things.* If the practice of community in the church were being taken as seriously as it should be, this would be no small task! Deacons would indeed need to be men of the Spirit, as the first deacons were. Consider, for example, what this would mean when poorer blacks from the ghetto joined a more wealthy "middle-class" or "upper-class" congregation.

Discipline

The fifth norm is that the church is to take discipline seriously. First Corinthians 5:1-5 is one example among many which calls for careful discipline based on the principle of the purity of the visible church in doctrine and in life. The New Testament stresses such purity, for the church is not to be like an amoeba so that no one can tell the difference between the church and the world. There is to be a sharp edge. There is to be a distinction between one side and the other—between the world and the church, and between those who are in the church and those who are not.

Paul writes, "It is reported commonly that there is fornication among you, and such fornication as is not so much as named among the Gentiles, that one should have his father's wife. And ye are puffed up, and have not rather mourned, that he that hath done this deed might be taken away from among you. For I verily, as absent in body but present in spirit, have judged already, as though I were present, concerning him that hath done this deed, in the name of our Lord Jesus Christ, when ye are gathered together, and my spirit, with the power of our Lord Jesus Christ, to deliver such an one unto Satan. . . ." The fact is that discipline in the church is important. For a church not to have discipline in life and doctrine means that it is not a New Testament church on the basis of the New Testament norms.

Qualifications for Office
The sixth norm is that there are specific qualifications for elders and deacons. Not only does the Bible set forth the offices of the church, but it also describes the kind of men who should hold these offices. The qualifications for elders and deacons are given in two places—1 Timothy 3:1-13 and Titus 1:5-9. These describe what the elders and deacons should be like. The church has no right to diminish these standards for the officers of the church, nor does it have any right to elevate any other standards as though they are then equal to these which are commanded by God Himself. These and only these stand as absolute.

In Titus 1:5 Paul writes, "For this cause left I thee in Crete, that thou shouldest set in order the things that are wanting (left undone), and ordain elders in every city, as I had appointed thee." So although churches had been formed, the situation was still incomplete. The form was not yet full because elders with the proper qualifications had not yet been appointed or ordained. So Titus is to take care of what has been left undone; he is to bring this church up to the level of the form that the New Testament church should have.

The First Church Council
Form did not end with the local church. Acts 15 shows that these churches were not entirely separated one from the other. Representatives from individual churches at a time of real crisis met together in Jerusalem in what has often been called the Jerusalem Council. The issue was crucial: how any person is to be saved (Acts 15:1). It was a major doctrinal question bearing on the problem of the Judaizers who were saying that a man must be saved not only by faith in Christ, but also by the addition of the Jewish ceremonial law: "Certain men who came down from Judaea taught the brethren, and said, Except ye be circumcised after the manner of Moses, ye cannot be saved." So they met together as office-bearer (verse 6) in a formal way.

First of all, there was discussion (verses 7-12). The King James Version calls it "disputing," but this implies the wrong tone. There was much questioning, much discussion, but not what we would call disputing. Verse 7 reads, "And when there had been much questioning, Peter rose up, and said unto them, Men and brethren, ye know how that a good while ago God made choice among us. . . ." What follows is Peter's testimony in the situation. Afterwards, "all the multitude kept silence, and gave audience to Barnabas and Paul, declaring what miracles and wonders God had wrought among the Gentiles by them" (verse 12).

Hence, on the question of salvation there was discussion and testimony first by Peter and then by Barnabas and Paul. It would seem from the 13th verse that a kind of moderator was also present here: "And after they had held their peace, James answered, saying, Men and brethren, hearken unto me." There is very little detail as to the exact form here, but the general picture is clear. Somebody—James, the half-brother of Christ—drew the discussion together and related it to Scripture (verses 15-17), the basis of the church's authority. Their solution was not merely something they generated out of themselves. It was rooted in Old Testament Scripture—in this case, Amos. James quoted, "After this I will return, and will build again the tabernacle of David, which is fallen down; and I will build again its ruins, and I will set it up; that the residue of men might seek after the Lord, and all the Gentiles, upon whom my name is called, saith the Lord, who doeth all these things (or who maketh these things of old)." So here we find a meeting, a moderator, an appeal to Scripture, and a conclusion. It does seem to me therefore that *the seventh norm is that there is a place for form on a wider basis than the local church.*

I would add as *the eighth biblical norm that the two sacraments of baptism and the Lord's Supper are to be practiced.*

Form and Freedom
Now it is important to realize two things. First, these are the New Testament forms commanded by God. These norms are not arbitrary—they are God's form for the institutional, organized church and they are to be present in the twentieth century as well as any century. Second, there are vast areas which are left free. There is *form,* and there is *freedom.*

Someone may feel that something else is clearly commanded beyond the eight norms I have given. Others may question whether one of these is really a norm. But do not let us get bogged down at that point. My primary point as we prepare for the end of the twentieth century is, on the one hand, that there is a place for the institutional church and that it should maintain the form commanded by God, but, on the other hand, that this also leaves vast areas of freedom for change. It is my thesis that as we cannot bind men morally except where the Scripture clearly commands (beyond that we can only give advice), similarly *anything the New Testament does not command concerning church form is a freedom to be exercised under the leadership of the Holy Spirit for that particular time and place.*[1] In other words, the New Testament sets boundary conditions, but within these boundary conditions there is much freedom to meet the changes that arise both in different places and different times.

I am not saying that it is wrong to add other things as the Holy Spirit so leads, but I am saying that we should not fix these things forever—changing times may change the leading of the Holy Spirit in regard to these. And certainly the historic accidents of the past (which led to certain things being done) have no binding effect at all. It is parallel to the evangelical church being bound by middle-class mores and making them equal with God's absolutes. To do this is sin. Not being able, as times change, to change under the Holy Spirit is ugly. The same applies to church polity and practice. In a rapidly changing age like ours, an age of total upheaval like ours, to make nonabsolutes absolutes guarantees both isolation and the death of the institutional, organized church.

CHAPTER FIVE

The Practice of Community and Freedom

Let us return for a moment to the concept of the orthodoxy of community in relationship to the task of the deacons who are responsible for the community of the church in the area of material things.

The Bible tells us the attitudes that should exist specifically in the churches of the Lord Jesus Christ and, I think we can say, in other Christian groups as well. Notice 1 Corinthians 16:1, 2: "Now concerning the collection for the saints, as I have given order to the churches of Galatia, even so do ye. Upon the first day of the week let every one of you lay by him in store, as God hath prospered him, that there be no gatherings when I come." Here the tithe is not mentioned, but proportional giving is. They were meeting together on the first day of the week, as we meet on the first day of the week. And there was a call in the midst of the church to supply the needs of the saints.

Here is where I feel we, as evangelicals, have rather lost our way. We have made a complete distinction between our giving for missionary purposes and for the material needs of Christians. We have lost our way and ignored the tough stuff—the care of each other's material needs.

This is not by any means to minimize giving for missions. Although Paul sometimes made tents, he also sometimes received gifts so that he did not need to make tents. True. But what I am pointing out is that there is no hard and sharp line in this giving. There is a strong emphasis on the fact that the local congregations within the proper polity had a huge sense of community—a sense of community which reached into all of life and all of life's needs, including the material needs.

How They Love One Another

The testimony has come down to us from the early churches—not in the Scripture, but by an apparently accurate tradition—that in the Greek and Roman world the cry went out, "Behold, how they love one another." And I would suggest that this is precisely what we must be striving for. It is exactly parallel to marriage. According to the Scripture, there is a form for sexual relationship. This form is not man-made, and it must not be set aside. This form is found in marriage.

But the difficulty within evangelical circles is that we often forget that within the proper form of marriage there is to be an interplay of personality which is beautiful. There is both form and a freedom for reality of personal interplay within the form. The form is necessary. But we must understand that form is not all there is, or sexuality becomes frigid and dead. So if we have a totally faithful marriage that is also ugly, it is certainly not what it ought to be; it does not portray what God means marriage to be. We can speak a great deal against sexual laxity in the whole area of sexual morality, but merely speaking of this is not enough. We must show to a world that is looking for beauty in the midst of twentieth-century ugliness that in the proper form (marriage), there can be a freedom of personal interplay which is beautiful.

The Practice of Community

It is the same for the church. Let us hold, until the time when Jesus comes, the polity which the Bible gives us. And let us have community within the church which includes all of life and all of life's needs—including the material needs. Recall the first positive characteristic required of an elder in Titus 1:8—that he is to be a man of hospitality. An elder is not only to measure up in some poor way to the negative stipulations. There is a positive: the elder's home is to be open to people. There are to be the kinds of human relationships that are necessary to show community within our groups, to give what humanism longs for and cannot produce.

Humanism talks much of Man with a capital M, but hardly anything of the individual man. It has produced a humanism out of the Enlightenment that has ended in ugliness. We must exhibit community that is real and not just an inscription on a banner we carry on Saturday afternoon between four and five.

People are looking at us to see if when we say we have truth, it is then possible for this truth not only to take men's souls to Heaven, but to give all of life meaning in the present time, moment by moment. They are looking to us to produce something that will bring the world to a standstill—human beings treating human beings like human beings. The church should be able to do this because we know who we are and we know who they are— first, men made in the image of God, then brothers within the church and Christian community on the basis of the shed blood of the Lord Jesus Christ. The church will not stand in our generation, the church will not be a striking force in our generation unless it keeps a proper balance between form and freedom in regard to the polity of the church, unless it keeps the strength of the Christian dogmas and at the same time produces communities with beauty as well as truth.

All too often when people listen to the church, especially to the liberal church, they only hear god words. And all too often when they listen to the evangelical and orthodox church, they come to conclude that they also are hearing only god words. And that should lead to our sorrow and our tears and our asking for forgiveness. When the Scripture talks about community and hospitality, it is not talking in vague generalities; it is talking about the stuff that counts and is open to observation. James writes, "If ye fulfill the royal law according to the scripture"—and here he goes back to Christ as giving the royal law—"Thou shalt love thy neighbor as thyself, ye do well" (James 2:8). And in verses 15, 16 James, under the leadership of the Holy Spirit, puts teeth into the command: "If a brother or sister be naked, and destitute of daily food, and one of you say unto them, Depart in peace, be ye warmed and filled; notwithstanding ye give them not those things which are needful to the body, what doth it profit?"

There is no use saying you have community or love for each other if it does not get down into the tough stuff of life. It must, or we are producing ugliness in the name of truth. I am convinced that in the twentieth century people all over the world will not listen if we have the right doctrine, the right polity, but are not exhibiting community.

This is not the world's call. It is God's call. Under the shed blood of the Lamb of God there is to be a substantial healing of everything that the Fall brought forth. It will not be perfect, but it must be substantial. And one of those things is the divisions between people. We must show by God's grace that in a substantial way these can be healed.

The book of Acts puts even more teeth in this: "Then the disciples, every man according to his ability, determined to send relief unto the brethren who dwelt in Judaea" (Acts 11:29). Here is something striking: the Greeks are sending money to the Jews. As the church at Antioch cut across the whole social spectrum, from Herod's foster brother down to the slave, the church and its community also cut across the difference between Jew and Gentile—not only in theory but in practice. When those in Antioch heard that the Jews had a material need in a different geographical location in Judea, they gathered together their funds and sent Barnabas and Paul on a long journey in order to meet the material needs of their brothers.

Let me say it very strongly again: there is no use talking about love if it does not relate to the stuff of life in the area of material possessions and needs. If it does not mean a sharing of our material things for our brothers in Christ close at home and abroad, it means little or nothing.

At the very beginning of the New Testament church, there were the deaths of two people who lied to God at this particular point. "Neither was there any among them that lacked; for as many as were possessors of lands or houses sold them, and brought the prices of the things that were sold" (Acts 4:34). The communists say this is communism. It is not. Communism includes force. There is no force here. In Acts 5:4 Peter addresses Ananias: "While it remained, was it not thine own? And after it was sold, was it not in thine own power? Why hast thou conceived this thing in thine heart? Thou hast not lied unto men, but unto God." The church brought no force. The state was not involved. But there was a force stronger than that of any state in regard to the Christians' caring for each other's material needs, a force of love, a force of brotherhood, and a force of community which covered all the facets of life.

Freedom and Form

Does the church have a future in our generation? Only if it shows not only the form of Scripture at the point of proper polity, but also the form of the Scripture at the point of proper community. If it does not show both together, we have missed the whole lot. One stands along with the other.

We call ourselves Bible-believing Christians. Some of us have stood together shoulder to shoulder since the early thirties in the battle for Bible-believing Christianity. That is beautiful. We must still stand regardless of the cost until Jesus comes. But let us understand that when we call ourselves Bible-believing Christians, this cuts in two directions: it means that we speak when the Bible speaks, and we are silent when the Bible is silent.

Our forefathers understood this in the Westminster Assembly when they said that the church's authority was administrative and declarative. They meant that in the area of doctrine and the area of conduct, the church has a right to bind other people's conscience only where it can show that the principle was derived from a definite exegesis of the Scripture.

We must speak where the Scripture has spoken. But let us notice that we must also respect the silences. Within every form, there is freedom. Whether one is painting a picture, or dealing with a sociological problem, or raising a child, it is the same. The formation of a school, for example, and the order in a school rests on the balance of form and freedom. I suggest that where the Bible is silent, it indicates a freedom within the scriptural form.

God could have added one more chapter to the book of Acts and given us much more detail. He did not. We surely cannot say the Bible is mistaken. We must believe not only that what is said is—by God's will and inspiration—final, but also that where there is silence we are granted freedom under the leadership of the Holy Spirit.

If the church will allow freedom for changing situations, churches will be here until Jesus comes back. But let us not mistake historical accidents and what is sociologically comfortable out of our past for God's absolutes either in rules of personal dress or in the forms that individual churches take in individual situations.

Can we not believe that the Holy Spirit will lead us in the area of silences? Is it not true that we Bible-believing Christians often cease being Bible-believing when we begin to teach that what is sociologically comfortable is equal to God's absolutes? I suggest that many of us do it all the time.

Here is the feeling of death that people complain of so often. Here is the source of much of the confusion in our Christian schools and churches. The difference between God's absolutes and those things that are only a product of historic accident is not understood or is minimized.

I have an advantage because I work over many countries, and I see that godly people have been led by historic accidents into very different forms of the church. Different periods of time show this as well. There have been times, in the early days, for example, when the church met only in homes. Those of you today who meet in beautiful church buildings should thank God that He has given you a building bigger than a house in the midst of your needs. But do not confuse the building with an absolute. Do not confuse the church with a church building. It may burn to the ground. But destroying the building does not destroy the church.

There was a time when Priscilla and Aquila had a church in their home. Was that less a church? Of course not. What, then, does it indicate? It indicates that the Holy Spirit can lead at different times with freedom. Did He lead your group to build a building? I can well believe He did. Does it mean then that Aquila and Priscilla were wrong? No. Does it mean that Aquila and Priscilla were led of the Holy Spirit to have a church in their home? Yes. Does that mean you are wrong? No. So we have form and freedom.

The community we are called upon to make observable to the watching world is just as much an absolute form as the norms given concerning church polity. Community and polity stand together. But within this double form there are freedoms in which the Holy Spirit may lead different people at different times, different congregations thereby meeting different needs.

Ossified Conservatism

The church has a place, but not if it ossifies. I think too often we are killing ourselves. We fail to distinguish the things that are open to change from those that are not. We must make ourselves available to the existential leading of the Holy Spirit. Often that is not the way we think, especially those of us who are conservative. Sometimes people say we are conservative in our theology because we are conservative in everything. That is a jibe, but sometimes it is right.

Let me give two illustrations. The first is a group of German missionaries in South America. They have their own form. Their services must be in German because they have always been in German. And so they go to the Indians in South America and make them learn German so they can hear the gospel.

If that sounds too incredible—surely your group is not so foolish—don't be too hasty. I know a church in the United States in which some of the people have a real burden for the blacks. It is a church that loves the Lord in its doctrine, and these people in it have achieved what I think is one of the outstanding breakthroughs in working with the blacks. One of the men in the church has felt this work is his special calling and has given much of his life to it. He gets up early every Sunday morning, wakes up the little black children in the neighborhood, and gets them out of bed. Because they have been up late at night, they must be awakened. He helps dress them and brings them to Sunday school. Here they are given graham crackers and milk, so the youngsters have something to eat.

But notice: these little children are not ready to get up for the morning church service at an early hour because in the ghetto they have been up half the night. So he suggested in this church—he was one of the elders—that they change the service to a later hour. And the roof fell in. A change was unthinkable. We may laugh or cry at the German missionaries, but this is surely as bad.

Many evangelicals and conservatives tend to be low-church people. That is, very often they speak out against those who have any formalized form of liturgy. But in reality the low-church evangelical has his own form of liturgy which often is absolutely unchangeable. It is inconceivable to move the service from 10:00 to 10:45 or from morning to afternoon, or to change the order of the service, or to consider having the pastor stand in a privileged position only once on Sunday, rather than twice—to preach on Sunday morning, but answer questions Sunday night.

We have all sorts of possibilities. There should be different kinds of services at different places and different times. Many would be preferable to what most churches now have. May our churches be open to these possibilities.

An Old-Fashioned Spiritual Problem
Refusal to consider change under the direction of the Holy Spirit is a spiritual problem, not an intellectual problem. There is a bad concept of old-fashionedness and there is a good concept. The good concept is that some things never change because they are

eternal truths. These we must hold to tenaciously and give up nothing of this kind of old-fashionedness. But there is a bad sense. I often ask young pastors and professors who are wrestling with these things a simple question: can you really believe that the Holy Spirit is ever old-fashioned in the bad sense? The obvious answer is No. So if we as evangelicals become old-fashioned—not in the good sense, but the bad—we must understand the problem is not basically intellectual, but spiritual. It shows we have lost our way. We have lost contact with the leading of the Holy Spirit who is never old-fashioned in the bad sense.

There is a place for the church until Jesus comes. But there must be the balance of form and freedom in regard to the polity and the practice of community within that church. And there must be a freedom under the leadership of the Holy Spirit to change what needs to be changed, to meet the changing needs in that place and in the moment of that situation. Otherwise, I do not believe there is a place for the church as a living church. We will be ossified, and we will shut Christ out of the church. His Lordship and the leadership of the Holy Spirit will become only words.

Let us be thankful there is a given form. Then let us be careful to make sure that we are not bound by unbiblical forms, by forms which we have become used to and which have no absolute place in the church of the Lord Jesus Christ. In regard to the polity and practice of the church, except for the clearly given biblical norms, every other detail is open to negotiation among God's people under the leadership of the Holy Spirit.

CHAPTER SIX

The Threat of Silence

I believe the church today is in real danger. It is in for a rough day. We are facing present pressures and present and future manipulations which will be so overwhelming in the days to come that they will make the battles of the last forty years look like kindergarten child's play.

The evangelical church seems to specialize in being behind. We began to talk about the pressures of the black-white crisis and the urban problems only after most of society had been talking about them for a long time. And, of course, these are real and a part of the whole, but the major problem we are going to face—as I see it, and I could be wrong and I hope I am—in the next twenty years or so is revolution with repression. Society is going to change. I believe that when my great-grandchildren grow to maturity, they will face a culture that has little similarity to ours. And the church today should be getting ready and talking about issues of tomorrow and not about issues of thirty and forty years ago, because the church is going to be squeezed in a wringer. If we have found it difficult in these last years, what are we going to do when we are faced with the real changes that are ahead?

We already are, of course, losing many of our young people,

losing them on every side. It would be impossible to say how many have come to L'Abri from Christian backgrounds. And these young people have said, "You are our last hope." Why? Because they are smart enough to know that they have been given no answers. They have simply been told to believe. Doctrines have been given them without relating them to the hard, hard problems which these young people are facing. Those who come to us and say something of the nature that we are their last hope usually then speak of two things which discouraged them. First, they have not been given reasonable answers to reasonable questions. Second, they have not seen beauty in the Christian group they were in. This matter of "beauty" is related to the orthodoxy of community we spoke about in a previous chapter. These things should make us ask questions. Where are we going? And what is our problem?

What Lies Ahead
Whether we live in the United States, Britain, Canada, Holland or other "Reformation countries," it really does not matter. The historic Christian faith is in the minority. Most Christians, especially those of us who remember what the United States was like forty-five or fifty years ago, go on as if we were in the majority, as though the status quo belongs to us. It does not.

One of the greatest injustices we do to our young people is to ask them to be conservative. Christianity today is not conservative, but revolutionary. To be conservative today is to miss the whole point, for conservatism means standing in the flow of the status quo, and the status quo no longer belongs to us. Today we are a minority. If we want to be fair, we must teach the young to be revolutionaries, revolutionaries against the status quo.

Do you wonder why the young people leave home? Youngsters come to L'Abri from the richest families in the world, from the greatest luxury. Why? Because they are sick of their parents making gods of affluence and thinking that one adds enough meaning to life merely by adding one more automobile to an already crowded garage. These young people are not wrong in this. They may have the wrong solution, but they are right in their diagnosis. Many of their parents, in the majority of what in the 1970s was called the silent majority, may sound like Christians, but they have no base. They may say what we have heard in the past, and they may say what Christians might say, but it is not the same.

Often they are merely repeating from memory what is comfortable for the moment.

Here we are, then, the historic, Bible-believing Christian minority. If what was called the silent majority in the 1970s are not given the material affluence they consider their right, there will be much pressure to some form of establishment elite.

What about the church in this situation? Certainly, at least at first, an establishment elite will be less harsh on the church than a left-wing elite if that should come into power. But that is a danger. The church will tend to make peace with the establishment and identify itself with it. It will seem better at first, but not in the end. If the church is identified with the establishment in the minds of young people, in the minds of those who will be coming forth to be men and women in the next twenty years, I believe the church will be greatly hindered.

In the United States many churches display the American flag. The Christian flag is usually put on one side and the American flag on the other. Does having the two flags in your church mean that Christianity and the American establishment are equal? If it does, you are really in trouble. These are not two equal loyalties. The state is also under the norm of the Word of God. So if by having the American flag in your church you are indicating to your young people that there are two equal loyalties or two intertwined loyalties, you had better find some way out of it. The establishment may easily become the church's enemy. Before the pressure comes, our young people (from kindergarten on), our older people, and our officers must understand this well: there are not two equal loyalties; Caesar is second to God. This must be preached and taught in sermons, Sunday school classes, and young people's groups.

It must be taught that patriotic loyalty must *not* be identified with Christianity. As Christians we are responsible, under the Lordship of Christ in all of life, to carry the Christian principles into our relationship to the state. But we must not make our country and Christianity to be synonymous.

This has always been important, but should certainly be so today. If a pastor stands in the pulpit and preaches this way, and the people come in and hear him making plain that he is not confusing the two loyalties, then even if they differ on certain specific questions, at least the pastor has maintained credibility with them. But the really important thing is not our credibility with other men, but our rightness with God. Equating any other loyalty with our loyalty to God is sin. And we had better get our priorities straight now before the pressures in our society overwhelm both us and society as we have known it. If the pressures are great now, there is every reason to be sure they will get greater.

Pressures on Society

In looking ahead into the next years at the end of this century, let us consider the special pressures on our society at this time, the pressures which open the way for a slide into accepting various forms of loss of liberty.

The first of these is the increasing loss of the Reformation memory as the years pass. This present generation has been raised by the first full post-Christian generation, and thus the memory is all but gone. In government and in morals, the base is gone and the hedonistic, subjective whims of a 51 percent majority, or an elite, are all that is left. Only sociological averages and arbitrary judgments remain.

Because of the sweep of intellectual history—the philosophy and world-views which cast away the revelational base, the modern, modern science that reduced man to a machine, the escape from reason that has led to the modern upstairs mysticism—the notion of a government and a law based on God's character and His revelation in Scripture is now no longer operative in political theory or in application. Even the very memory of it is all but gone.

Hence, society in the "Reformation countries" faces a major pressure—a pressure that strikes at its very roots. That which was its base is gone, and the perspective with which everything else is viewed has shifted.

The Loss of Truth

A second, very closely related pressure is the fact that modern men no longer believe in truth. They no longer believe in antithesis. Modern man believes only in dialectical synthesis. There is a thesis; it has an antithesis. Neither is true or false. "Truth" for today lies only in a synthesis. And even that synthesis is not true forever, for tomorrow there will arise another thesis different from today's and out of the combination of these will come "truth" for tomorrow. But in no case will any of these "truths" be absolute. *Truth* in the classical sense, that which accurately represents what is real for all time and all places, does not exist—not even as an ideal.

This is just as true on our side of the Iron Curtain as it is on the other. If you could snap your fingers today—and I am not minimizing the danger of communism—if you could snap your fingers at this moment and there would be no communists left in the Western world, you would not solve the problem. The real problem is that modern man, whether or not he is a communist, no longer believes in truth but only in synthesis. Modern man thinks truth is unfindable. The generations that have preceded us may not have found truth, but they thought finding it was possible. They held it at least as an aspiration. Modern man no longer holds it as an aspiration.

Modern man no longer expects that truth exists even in the scientific world. All we are left with is statistical averages. Once I was speaking of science to a British university audience. Suddenly a young man in the scientific world stood up. "Sir," he said, "you don't realize how much the scientific enterprise is only the upper-middle class doing science as a form of gamesmanship." I am sure he is right. Often science is not engaged in the lofty objective of defining truth, but in filling up the time with small details so that no great conclusions will have to be faced.

Furthermore, there are no, or few, philosophies in the traditional sense of philosophy. There are antiphilosophies. Existentialism is an antiphilosophy because while it tries to deal with the really big questions, it does so apart from reason. Linguistic analysis does not even try to deal with the big questions. By definition its proponents have shut themselves up and limited their work to the definition of language. They do not ask the big questions. Language leads to language.

This is the end of the Renaissance. The Enlightenment with all its humanistic pride has come to the place of despair.

Drugs, of course, add to the sense of a loss of truth as truth. And the destruction of normal syntax and normal language in the Theatre of the Absurd, etc., is meant to hack away still further at any hope of truth. Much of modern art, music and movies tends in the same direction. And most of all, the general acceptance of the absolute dichotomy of the upper and lower stories (of which I speak in *The God Who Is There* and *Escape From Reason*) destroys truth as a unified concept and leaves modern man under the pressure of the relative.

The Demise of Leadership

A third pressure upon our society is that there is no natural leadership which can give direction to our culture. That is, there is no natural leadership—no group in the United States or even Britain—who are respected and accepted as natural leaders, especially by the young. Of course, the situations in Britain and the United States are not exactly alike. The House of Lords, which used to give balance to the House of Commons, could be removed now and it would make little difference. The royal family likewise does little to maintain the government and cultural values. Again, this is felt especially among the young. British aristocracy has become a kind of Wodehouse character to many people in England.

The simple fact is, however, that the same thing could be said about "the upper class" in the United States. No longer are there any leaders who naturally command the respect and admiration of large bodies of American citizens, especially those under thirty-five.

A Sociological Breakdown

A fourth pressure upon our society is the practical sociological breakdown. It is not only the dropouts. Those who have a 9 A.M. to 5 P.M. mentality are everywhere today. Talk to any businessman, and he will tell you he can find few to take responsibility. Talk to the policeman on the beat, and he will tell you few will help him when somebody is in trouble.

Some years ago *Newsweek* carried a story of a policeman who was moonlighting by driving a taxicab. Some people tried to hold him up. He had his revolver with him, so he got out and held the thieves in the car. For over half an hour he pleaded with people to help him. Windows went up and then were slammed down. He stood there until he thought he could no longer hold out. Finally, a policeman on duty came along and he was helped, but he had been caught in the midst of a total sociological breakdown.

The worst case, perhaps, was the horrible thing that happened in New York some years ago. A girl was gradually raped and stabbed to death while some thirty people who knew what was going on never even picked up a phone to call the police. They did not want to be involved.

The upshot is this: society treats men like machines because modern man has come to conclude that man is a machine. Those who think that our universities and our intellectuals are teaching that man is an animal are far, far behind. To modern man, man is only to be equated with clanking machinery. And because man sees man as a machine, he tends to treat men on the level of the subhuman.

Related to this is the effect of modern technology. The machine is given dominance over man. The machine is King. This would be serious and bring pressure under any circumstances, but when man does not know who he is and when he views other men as machinery, the pressure on society is overwhelming.

The Population Explosion and the Ecological Problem

A fifth great pressure that previous societies have not known is the increased number of people and with it ecological destruction. These two could be discussed separately, but they are closely related.

One would think that in the Alps where I live there would be peace, but everywhere you turn the mountains are being ripped up to make roads across them, so that it is getting harder and harder to find a quiet place. We know the problem in the United States. So we make national parks, and pretty soon the national parks are destroyed because so many people come into them that the trails are covered with asphalt to keep them from being worn away, and they are no better than Broadway.

Along with this goes ecological destruction. Read the papers carefully and you will see that, openly or not so openly, the idea is put forward that the only way to deal with the increased numbers of people and the ecological problem is by a curtailing of liberty.

The Atomic Bomb

Sixth, of course, is the pressure of the A-bomb or the H-bomb. For a certain kind of person this builds up a titanic pressure. Why? Because modern man has nobody in the universe but man. There is no God, there are no angels. And scientifically so far there is no proof that there is any other conscious life anywhere in the universe except on the earth. The only value that is left to a man like Bertrand Russell is the biological continuity of the human race. As Charlie Chaplin put it, "I feel lonely."

Modern man is lonely in a cosmic sense because as far as he is concerned, he is the only conscious observer. He has been thrown up by chance, and he is the only observer there is. If the hydrogen bombs drop in their total force and wipe out the human race, all that is left will be the universe, hard and cold, with nobody to look at it, nobody to observe it, nobody to see its beauty, nobody to see its order. There will be no one to see the blowing of a tree, hear the song of a bird, see the formation of a cloud or the rising of the sun. This is where modern man is living. And it is terrifying. What is the use? If the hydrogen bombs fall, the world is silent.

Think for a moment, if you will, what this would mean. Suppose you wrote the greatest sonnet that was ever written, and you put it on tape and hooked it up to a machine that has the highest amplification that any machine has ever been able to give. Suppose you hooked this up to solar batteries so that it would play for 1,000 years. Suddenly, then, suppose the hydrogen bomb dropped. There is no God, there are no angels, there is no conscious intelligent life anywhere else in the universe and in all the galaxies that would be able to be conscious of the playing of the sonnet. What difference would it make if the sonnet played on in the unhearing, unheeding coldness of the galaxies even for 5,000 years? This is modern man's pressure.

None of us want the bomb to fall, but do note that for modern man, what we have said above gives him a special terror.

The Biological Bomb

There is a seventh pressure which is the greatest yet. It is often called the biological bomb, a "bomb" much greater than the hydrogen bomb. I am not being spectacular: the genetic engineers have made most of the basic breakthroughs on this. It is the misuse of genetic knowledge.

Aldous Huxley's *Brave New World* was not a joke. As he described it, babies were grown in test tubes. They were bred in intellect and physical ability for the level of labor the state wished them to perform. So if a man was needed for a certain manual job, he would be bred for that level, another man to another level, and on up through the whole line. That was Huxley's vision forty years ago. It is much closer today.

Modern man has no moral imperative for what he *should* do, and consequently he is left only with what he *can* do. And he is doing what he can do even though he stands in terror. And the biggest terror of all is: who is going to shape the human race?

It will not be just a matter of male and female, not merely a matter of preventing deformed babies. That is not where it ends. It is rather like Aldous Huxley and drugs. It is not that you give the drugs to the sick, but to the healthy. Here it is the same. Not just that you deal with a baby who may be born deformed. Now we are going to fool with the babies who are not deformed.

And with the development of the biological bomb, even today men are on the verge of being able to make new deadly viruses as super-weapons, viruses for which there are no cures. Unlike the H-bomb, these will be easily made by any small nation.

Where We Stand

These, then, are some of the pressures on twentieth-century society and the church. The collapse of the Reformation concept of government, the loss of truth, the demise of any generally accepted leadership group, the breakdown in personal responsibility, the growth of population and the ecological problem, the hydrogen bomb, and the biological bomb—tremendous pressures these are! And these pressures open the way for the manipulators.

CHAPTER SEVEN

Modern Man the Manipulator

It is obvious: the future is open to manipulation. Who will do the manipulating? Will it be the new elite on the side of an establishment authoritarianism or another elite? Whoever achieves political or cultural power in the future will have at his disposal techniques of manipulation that no totalitarian ruler in the past has ever had. None of these are only future; they all exist today waiting to be used by the manipulators.

Scientific Manipulation

First of all, consider what Galbraith puts forward. He proposes that we turn everything over to the new philosopher-kings of the academic and especially the scientific state elite. But wait: can we really trust the government of a scientist merely because he is a scientist? Can we actually believe that such people will not manipulate just because they are scientists? One could give illustration after illustration where so-called scientific men are not objective.

Recall that, as Alfred North Whitehead said, Christianity produced modern science because it gave a context in which the early scientists such as Galileo, Copernicus and Francis Bacon believed that the universe could be understood by reason—the universe had been created by a reasonable God. Therefore, they were not surprised that man by his reason could find out the order of the universe. Modern man no longer has this assumption.

I am convinced that science as we have known it with a commitment to objectivity will have difficulty in continuing now that this philosophy is gone. I work with many men in the scientific world, and many of them agree that objectivity is growing weaker. A clear illustration is Edmund Leach, a man who gave Reith Lectures in England, a brilliant man, a leading anthropologist at Cambridge University. Leach said in *The New York Review of Books* (February 3, 1966) that in the past there were two theories of evolution. The dominant theory was that the evolutionary process began in one place, and therefore all races have come from a common base. The second theory of evolution, which once was as strong as this (although in the intervening years it has become much weaker and today is only a minor voice), was that evolution began at different points, widely separated not only in geographic location but in time. With this there was the concept that a race is higher if it has evolved longer.

Leach said in this article that the last time this second theory, this theory of multiple evolution, was put forward, the man who stood against it was the president of Princeton University, a Christian. The reason he rejected it was theological.

Leach says that he does not stand against this other form of evolution for this reason, but because if one holds this view it promotes an attitude of racism, that one race is greater than another. Therefore, he chooses the other form of evolution.

Note well: this is a nonobjective sociological science. Conclusions are determined by the way a scientist *wants* the results to turn out sociologically. It is a science which will manipulate society by the manipulation of scientific "fact." I do not believe that man without absolutes, without the certainty that gave birth to modern science in the first place, will continue to maintain a high sense of objectivity. On one side, I think science will increasingly become only technology. On the other side, it will become sociological science and be a tool of manipulation in the hands of the manipulators.

Beware, therefore, of the movement to give the scientific community the right to rule. They are not neutral in the old concept of scientific objectivity. Objectivity is a myth that will not hold simply because these men have no basis for it. Keep in mind that to these men morals are only a set of averages. Here, then, is a present form of manipulation which we can expect to get greater as one of the elites takes more power.

Manipulation of Law
In a previous chapter we have already looked at the shift from the Reformation concept of law (which has a base to begin from in God's having spoken) to modern sociological law (in which the courts make law on the basis of what they conceive to be the immediate sociological or economic good). In this view, even the Constitution and the previous body of law are viewed loosely as far as any constraint is concerned. Just as sociological science is a source of manipulation open to the manipulators, so sociological law gives an endless range of manipulation.

Manipulation of History
Another form of manipulation is the manipulation of history. In *Newsweek,* March 10, 1969, there was a little squib by Arnold Toynbee. He said that the races have always interbred in America and gave as proof of it that George Washington was out having sexual intercourse with a Negro slave in the slave quarters and he caught a cold, which was the cause of his death. Even *Newsweek* felt it necessary to put a little note at the bottom of the page, saying that there is no authority for such a statement.

Is it a joke? No. People will be manipulated if they think you are talking history instead of mere subjective fantasy. There are dozens of such cases within the last few years.

History as history has always presented problems, but as the concept of the possibility of true truth has been lost, the erosion of the line between history and the fantasy the writer wishes to use as history for his own purposes is more and more successful as a tool of manipulation.

Perhaps the clearest illustration was *Luther,* written by the English dramatist, John Osborne. This play made a great reputation for him, but it was a twisting of history, especially in the last lines. At the end of the play Martin Luther is challenged by Staupitz, the old man who supposedly had headed the monastery which Luther had left. Staupitz asks, "When you were before the Diet in Worms . . . why did you ask for that extra day to think over your reply?" Luther reflects and says, "I wasn't sure." Staupitz leaves, Luther takes his young son from his wife's arms and stands alone, softly talking with the child. "We must go to bed, mustn't we? A little while, and you *shall* see me. Christ said that, my son. I hope that'll be the way of it again. I hope so. Let's just hope so, eh? Let's just hope so." The lights go out, and the play ends.

The *London Times* drama critic said, "Isn't it interesting that Osborne had to add that sentence in order to make it a modern play?" Luther never would have said that. Luther's certainty based on the Bible is manipulated out of existence with one clever but false line that thousands take as history. Here is a distortion of fact, a destruction of Christian ideals and the Protestant base via contorted history.

Michener's *Hawaii* was another perfect example. Here under the writing of what sounds like history a whole adverse view of Christianity is manipulated in the reader's mind. The same thing was true of Rolf Hochhuth's *Soldiers,* in which Churchill is totally plowed. There is not an iota of evidence that Churchill had a Polish general killed. And yet Hochhuth by turning upon Churchill was able with tremendous force to discredit any concept of authority. The people who went to see this drama came away certain that Churchill was a knave and that you cannot trust anybody in authority.

Manipulation in Religion
Manipulation is on every side, and nowhere more so than in liberal theology and religion. Modern theology with its religious connotation words takes the words *Christ* or *God* or the other great Christian words and makes them a banner which has high motivation value but no content. The man who wishes to do the manipulation can simply grab the flag, march in the direction he wishes, and we are supposed to follow.

Perhaps the clearest illustration here is situational ethics. The Cambridge morality which followed the Cambridge theology said it is Christlike to sleep with a girl if she needs you. To call something Christlike causes people to move in this direction without ever realizing that in so doing, the sexual ethic of Jesus Himself is being violated.

I think, however, that the new theologians, both the Roman Catholic progressives and the Protestant theologians, are going to win in the use of contentless religious words. I suggest that for two great reasons they stand in a stronger position than, say, those who would manipulate with the use of contentless religious words in the direction of the Eastern religions. First, they have the continuity of religious organization. They control the machinery of most of the major denominations. Second, they use the same words that the ears of people are used to, and they do not bring in strange and exotic words such as the followers of Eastern religions do.

I would not be surprised if in the future even communism will be manipulating its people on the basis of religious terms rather than atheism. Certainly, however, here in the West we are open to complete manipulation on the basis of contentless religious words. This is not theoretical. Remember that Julian Huxley, the atheist, has been suggesting this use of religion for years.

The ecological pressure opens the door to manipulation by religious terms in a different way. Many are saying that we must accept a concept of pantheism if the problem of ecology is to be met. Thus here pantheism is being suggested not as truth but as a form of manipulation of society.[1] It should be noted that this is not at odds with most liberal theology today, for most of it already has pantheistic tones.

Manipulation in the Theater and Art

In the Theatre of the Absurd, in Marcel Duchamp's "environments" and "happenings," in much of television, in the cinema, in psychedelic sound, and in art, we are being removed from the control of our reason.

In art museums throughout the world, the viewers are at the mercy of the artists. People, even children, who go through the art galleries are being manipulated whether they know it or not. No matter how long they contemplate, say, Duchamp's *The Bride Undressed by Her Bachelors Yet* or *Le passage de la vierge a la mariee* (The passage of the virgin to the married state), they may not understand the content of the painting. But the artist plays with the viewer as if he were putty. The young couple holding hands, looking at Duchamp's work, will have a harder time saying no to their urges that evening. Reason is bypassed. Man is manipulated.

It should be noted most carefully that the giving up of the control of reason that is so universal today in the acceptance of the upper and lower stories makes all these forms of manipulation that much more possible and complete.

Manipulation in Television

Television is perhaps an even worse offender. Malcolm Muggeridge has commented on this. He points out that people think they see reality when they see those television pictures, but what they do not realize is that they are looking at pure fantasy. They are looking at an edited situation that does not present what is, but what the man at the console wants you to think is. You feel you know everything because you have actually seen the picture with your own eyes, but in every situation you have been given an edited version.

I learned this lesson a number of years ago when I was lecturing in St. Louis. I was speaking at a conference there, and some people were kind and provided me with a room where I could get some rest. So my son Franky and I went up to the room, and he turned on the television set. As I sat there waiting for the next time I was going to lecture, I began to read in a paper about the war in Vietnam. On the television there was a war picture. Quite unconscious of what was happening, I read about the war in Vietnam and out of the corner of my eye watched the war picture. And all of a sudden it dawned on me that what I was looking at on the television screen, which I knew with my mind was fantasy, was more real in its impact than the war I was reading about in the paper where real people were dying. When what is shown on television is carefully edited, this force of the seen is then an absolute form of manipulation.

I have also been on the other end of this manipulation by editing when I have been on TV talk shows trying to make a point. Somebody at the controls knows that you are going to say something he does not like, and so he switches the camera and the mike and you're dead. You sound like a fool no matter how right your answer is going to be. The television viewer says to himself, "Schaeffer is a fool"—and he may be, but this does not prove it. A simple fact: people think they are seeing reality when they sit in front of that crazy box, but they are being manipulated in subtle but strenuous ways.

Related to this is the subliminal use of television and the cinema. You can flash something on any television or movie screen so fast that you never know you saw it, and yet it affects you and you tend to do what you were told. This again is not theoretical; it has been perfectly proven. Once it was tested by flashing "Drink Coca-Cola, Drink Coca-Cola, Drink Coca-Cola" on a cinema screen. Nobody knew they had seen it, and yet Coca-Cola was cleared out for blocks around after the cinema.

With Coca-Cola it may seem not to be serious, but with political manipulation it would be. By law no Western country may use this. But do we think that there are other countries under dictatorial rule that would not use it? Are we so naive? If a country really came down into the groove where I think our society is going, if one of the elites really took over power and in desperation it was this or nothing, are we so naive to think the elite would fail to use it if it had the power to do so? Let's not fool ourselves. No totalitarian government, including Hitler's and Stalin's, has ever had these forms of manipulation.

Chemical and Electrical Manipulation

Arthur Koestler adds a further note. In *The Ghost in the Machine* he said that evolution is not yet complete. Not believing in the fall of man, he explained man's dilemma this way: man has evolved with a lower and an upper brain that are not in harmony. What we must ask our scientists to do is to develop a super-drug that will bring the two halves into proper relationship. Such a drug would make man passive and prevent his constant quarreling. How does Koestler propose that the drug be given to the population? He has suggested that the way we may administer it is in the water supply.

Koestler is not alone in these suggestions of chemical or mechanical manipulation. *Newsweek* (December 1, 1969) said that by the 1990s drugs to blunt curiosity and initiative will be available for use. The *St. Louis Globe Democrat* (October 27, 1969) reported that Dr. Kermit Krantz, head of the Gynecology and Obstetrics Department of Kansas City University's medical school, urged putting "the pill" in all the world's water supplies if it would solve the problem of overpopulation. Whether "the pill" is ever so used or not, this form of manipulation is an acceptable concept in modern men's minds.

Furthermore, the computer itself can be dangerous. The computer has entered into a new age: it can watch you. The great eye can be upon you—recording every single thing you do from your birth to your death. This too is not tomorrow; it is ready today. One computer expert on the West Coast, a man who has as many basic computer patents as anybody in the world, has become so disturbed by the big, all-recording banks of computers that he is spending the end of his life trying to make little inexpensive computers so that men can fight the big computers. The existence of the computer and the control it puts into the hands of those in power steps up the power of each of the forms of modern manipulation in the hands of the manipulators.

Becoming Aware
I hate being an alarmist, and I do not think I am. Anything I have said that is alarmism, I hope you will simply forget. But these things are something that the church must be aware of. Many young scientists come to L'Abri, and I half facetiously say to some of them, "Maybe the biggest contribution you can ever make to Christianity is to make something you can put on the spigot or the faucet that will strain out everything except water!"

The church is confronted with people who really believe that democracy is dead, who really believe that such an age is gone. I agree, unless we can return to a Reformation base with real reformation and real revival. These are the things the evangelical church should be getting prepared for.

CHAPTER EIGHT

Revolutionary Christianity

We are surrounded on every side with the loss of truth, with the possibility of manipulation that would have made Hitler chuckle, that would have caused the rulers of Assyria to laugh with glee. And we not only have the possibilities for these manipulations, but people are trained on the basis of the loss of truth and the loss of the control of reason to accept them.

Where are we? Exactly where Romans 1:21, 22 says we are. Man has rebelled against God, and God is letting man go on to the natural conclusion, and man believes a lie. This is the end—the big lie. Our generation is more ready to believe the big lie than any in the history of Western man.

This is not a day for a sleepy church—a church that is merely operating on the basis of memory and is afraid to be free where it needs to be free within the form of Scripture.

What then must we as Christians do? What do we need? The task of this final chapter is to answer those questions. Initially, I will direct attention to two general requirements. But our Christianity is nothing if not a practical, moment-by-moment affair. So I will end by giving some specific, practical suggestions.

Hot Christianity

First, for ourselves and for our spiritual children, we need a Christianity that is strong, one that is not just a memory. The games of yesterday are past. We are in a struggle that the church has never been in before.

Basically, let me paraphrase Marshall McLuhan and reverse him. He said in a day of cool communication—that is, in a day when you are manipulating people—if anybody wants to sell his product, he must not use hot communication. In other words, when people have been trained to respond like a salivating dog to the ringing of a bell, you must not try to feed things through reason. It will not work.

I would reverse this. In a day of increasing cool communication, biblical Christianity must make very plain that it will deal only with hot communication. Biblical Christianity rests upon content, factual content. It does not cause people to react merely emotionally in a first-order experience.

Let me repeat from Chapter One, some evangelicals have their own form of cool communication. Patting people on the head, they say, "Don't ask questions, dear; just believe."

It is even stronger than this. Much of our gospel, as we preach it, has little or no content. We sometimes fall into the trap of saying the same thing the liberal says, only in our own evangelical jargon instead of his. What tends to come across is gobbledygook—a contentless statement without meaning.

We can see it in the theological area because many evangelicals today feel that it is safe now to praise Karl Barth, seemingly not understanding that Karl Barth was the one who really opened the door to the new theology and all that flowed from it. Many evangelicals are drifting in this direction by treating the early chapters of Genesis the way the new theology treats the whole Bible—namely, separating the Bible's statements about space-time history from "religious truth." If we are really going to preach meaningfully into the twentieth century, we must have the courage to understand this must not be done.

I would also remind you—as I have done in another book—of what J. S. Bezzant, an old-fashioned liberal, says in *Objections to Christian Beliefs*. Speaking of the neo-orthodox position, he writes, "When I am told that it is precisely its immunity from proof which secures the Christian proclamation from the charge of being mythological, I reply that immunity from proof can 'secure' nothing whatever except immunity from proof, and call nonsense by its name." A brilliant sentence. But we may do this in the name of evangelicalism if we do not make clear that we speak of truth, and if we let people in various areas and disciplines squeeze out from under the control of Scripture.

Every single preaching of the gospel must be related to strong content. We must not fall into the cheap solution of beginning to use these cool means of communication and cause people to seem to make professions of faith. If we fall into this kind of manipulation, we have cut Christianity down to the ground because we are only adding to the loss of the appropriate control which reason should have. We are throwing ourselves wide open to future problems. Christianity must fight for its life to insist that it deals with content—content which stands in contrast to that which is not true.

The New Testament itself says that we must strain through the grid of reason everything that comes into our mind.

Consider what John says in 1 John. If a spirit, a prophet, knocks on your door tonight, what do you say to him? John says that you should ask him an intellectual question—whether Christ has come in the flesh. This is a question of the reason and not of the emotions. It is one of the sharpest intellectual questions one could frame, because when you ask a prophet or spirit whether Christ has come in the flesh, you are asking him two things: whether Christ has had an existence before the incarnation and whether the incarnation has taken place.

In other words, the Bible insists on the church of Jesus Christ dealing, in the words of McLuhan, in the area of hot communication.

This is no time for Christianity to allow itself to be infiltrated by relativistic thinking from either the secular or the theological side. It is a time for the church to insist, as a true revolutionary force, that there is a truth. It is possible to know that truth, not exhaustively but truly.

Compassionate Christianity

Second, our Christianity must become truly universal, relevant to all segments of society and all societies of the world.

Why are we in trouble with the blacks? Simple. When white evangelical Christians held the consensus, they did not have enough care and compassion for the blacks to care for them in practical ways. Not that the white evangelical church should have made the blacks white or converted them to a mode of living dominated by "white" historical accidents. But the white Christians should have so loved them that they shared with them Christianity and all that flows from it, and this should have included social justice, but also making sure that the black pastors had as good a theological training as the white pastors.

What, then, would have resulted would not have been a violation or an elimination of a black man's blackness, but the black community today would have been far different if white Christians had had proper compassion. And, furthermore, the white community today would be far different. It is our lack of compassion that has brought us to the place we are now.

Unfortunately, it is not just the blacks. It involves, for example, Jews as well. The rationalistic Jews of eastern Europe came into New York City by the thousands. What churches went out to reach them for Christ? Practically none.

We let them live first of all in Harlem—the early Harlem. There they were. We did not care. We took their labor. We left them alone. And now the *rationalistic* Jews and their children, with all the brilliance of the Jewish mind, are shaping our culture through the theater, through works of art, through writing in the newspapers and news magazines and elsewhere. That is where we are. We have an enormous guilt behind us for a lack of compassion, not just for the blacks but for all people we have ignored.

Think of black Harlem. You know what Harlem was called in days past? The poor man's Paris. Why? Because everybody thought he could go to Paris and could sleep with anybody he wanted to sleep with, do any creepy thing he wanted to do, if he paid enough money for it. In days gone by many whites made Harlem that. The white man made black Harlem his Paris for every kinky thing he wanted to do.

We have had an enormous lack of compassion. We have said that we believe that men are lost, but what evidence for this have we shown the world when it comes to the blacks and the Jews and others as well?

Beginning in the 1960s we began doing exactly the same thing with the new outsider—the radical young. What did we do to assimilate this new radical element? Very little. We drove them away from us in school, in our churches, and very often even in our families. If any of these young were different from us in the most unimportant and unessential detail, we simply did not have love and compassion for them. I am talking about community. We failed to show any community at all if their life-styles differed from our own mentality.

The early Christian church cut across all lines which divided men—Jew and Greek, Greek and barbarian, male and female; from Herod's foster brother to the slave; from the naturally proud Gentiles in Macedonia who sent material help to the naturally proud Jews who called all Gentiles dogs, and yet who could not keep the good news to themselves, but took it to the Gentiles in Antioch. The observable and practical love in our days certainly should also without reservation cut across all such lines as language, nationalities, national frontiers, younger or older, color of skin, education and economic levels, accent, line of birth, the class system of our particular locality, dress, short and long hair among whites and African and non-African hairdos among blacks, the wearing of shoes and the nonwearing of shoes, cultural differentiations, and more traditional and less traditional forms of worship.

I want to tell you it can work. In L'Abri—let me keep saying, it's far from perfect—what do we find? Many young people from evangelical circles come every year. They arrive and say we are from such and such a school, from an evangelical background, and you are our last hope. We have heard that there may be some answers, some beauty here. What do they do? They try us out. They come to church in their blue jeans or their different clothes. They see if they are going to be accepted. When we pass the test we can begin to talk, but we have to pass the test. This is a community. This is compassion. This is the area where we must function.

When in the 1960s it was "the thing" to go about with bare feet, was there any absolute reason to wear shoes? I can't find it in the norms of the New Testament. Many a time our little chapel is jammed, and these students come and there they sit. Those who preach don't preach for twenty minutes; they preach for an hour and a quarter on Sunday morning. And these students come and sit. In the 1960s they sat with their bare feet; they still sit in their blue jeans, and they sit in their weird clothes, and they learn that it doesn't matter to us.

In reality, therefore, I don't think we have to worry only about youth. What we have to worry about is the church. If the church is what it should be, young people will be there. But they will not just "be there"; they will be there with the blowing of horns and the clashing of high-sounding cymbals, and they will come rejoicing.

In the midst of its imperfections and the circle of its weaknesses, what is happening at L'Abri proves this to be the case. Even when the church is a little bit of what it should be, the young people will come. They will come in their own way; they will come from the ends of the earth when the church is in some poor fashion what God meant it to be.

So much for general requirements. What about the specific tasks, the specific things we can do, by the power of the Holy Spirit, to make the church come alive for today—and tomorrow?

Open Your Home for Community
Don't start a big program. Don't suddenly think you can add to your church budget and begin. Start personally and start in your homes. I dare you. I dare you in the name of Jesus Christ. Do what I am going to suggest. Begin by opening your home for community.

I have seen white evangelicals sit and clap their heads off when black evangelicals get up to talk at conference times. How they clap! That's nice, because twenty years ago the evangelicals would not have been clapping. But I want to ask you something if you are white. In the past year, how many blacks have you fed at your dinner table? How many blacks have felt at home in your home? And if you haven't had any blacks in your home, shut up about the blacks. On the basis of Scripture, open your home to the blacks and if they invite you, go with joy into their homes. Have them feel at home in your home. Then you will be able to begin to talk with them, but not before, and your church can jump across this division as it should. And if you are a black Christian, it all cuts equally the other way: how many whites have you invited to your home in the last year? How many have eaten at your table?

L'Abri is costly. If you think what God has done here is easy, you don't understand. It's a costly business to have a sense of community. L'Abri cannot be explained merely by the clear doctrine that is preached; it cannot be explained by the fact that it has been giving intellectual answers to intellectual questions. I think those two things are important, but L'Abri cannot be explained if you remove the third. And that is there has been *some* community here. And it has been costly.

In about the first three years of L'Abri, almost all our wedding presents were wiped out. Our sheets were torn. Holes were burned in our rugs. Indeed once a whole curtain almost burned up from somebody smoking in our living room. Blacks came to our table. Orientals came to our table. Everybody came to our table. What happened at L'Abri could not have happened any other way.

You see, you don't need a big program. You don't have to convince your session or board. All you have to do is open your home and begin. And there is no place in God's world where there are no people who will come and share a home as long as it is a real home.

The Unantiseptic Risk

How many times have you risked an unantiseptic situation by having a girl who might easily have a sexual disease sleep between your sheets? We have girls come to our homes who have had several abortions by the time they are seventeen. Is it possible they have venereal disease? Of course. But they sleep between our sheets. How many times have you let this happen in your home? Don't you see this is where we must begin? This is what the love of God means. This is the admonition to the elder—that he must be given to hospitality. Are you an elder? Are you given to hospitality? If not, keep quiet. There is no use talking. But you can begin.

If you have never done these things or things of this nature, if you have been married for years and years and had a home (or even a room) and none of this has ever occurred, if you have been quiet, especially as our culture is crumbling about us, if this is so—do you really believe that people are going to Hell? And if you really believe that, how can you stand and say, "I have never paid the price to open my living place and do the things that I can do on my own level"?

I have a question in my mind about us as evangelicals. We fight the liberals when they say there is no Hell. But do we really believe people are going to Hell?

Let me add a note to put this in balance: I have known families who have been moved with compassion and have opened their homes for those who were too much for them as a family unit. With the father out to work, it proved too much for the wife to handle and for the family unity. And in their compassion and feeling of responsibility, they kept the individual beyond the time they could help.

It *is* easier in a community like L'Abri, but that is not the point. Every Christian, every family unit, should see that a compassionate open home is a part of their Christian responsibility, and should practice it *up to the level of their capacity*. This will not be static; sometimes a family can do more, and sometimes less.

However, this should not be an excuse for doing nothing or little. And then beyond that, the church should share responsibility. And a group of Christians should exist and be available where the more difficult ones can be shown a practical love and community.

It's not only in a place like L'Abri in the Alps where all this has meaning. When I was a pastor in the United States, I knew what it meant to go down to the nightclubs at night and fish the drunks out at 3 or 4 o'clock in the morning and take them to their homes. Do you?

Back in the forties in St. Louis when my wife, Edith, had a black cleaning woman come in, she ate lunch with her every day. When they ate together, Edith put a candle in the middle of the table so the table setting would have beauty. Have you ever done that? This is the way community begins. There is no other way. Everything else is false if it is further away than this.

Structure Your Church for Community

I'll tell you another thing you can do. You can consider restructuring your regular church meetings. There is nothing in the Scripture that says you have to have a worship service at 10 o'clock Sunday morning. You could have it at any time—3 P.M., 10 P.M. or even 2 A.M. And think of the folly of some churches that dare not omit an "invitation" in the evening because that service must be "evangelistic." It is always evangelistic whether or not an unsaved person ever comes into that church. Try to stop it, and pretty soon people say you are not evangelistic because you are not going through a certain form. But you must try.

There is also nothing in the New Testament that says you have to have a prayer meeting on Wednesday night. Why, then, do you have such a prayer meeting? Because you have always had one on Wednesday night? But suppose nobody came on Wednesday night. Who says you can't have the prayer meeting on Sunday night? If you have young people or others who would come one time but not another, why not change your services?

We must have the courage to change all kinds of things in our services. Stay within the limits of the form of the New Testament, but count everything else free under the leadership of the Holy Spirit. Begin to talk to your boards, begin to talk to your session, have prayer meetings about what you can change in your service to make our churches living things in the generation which we are facing.

Furthermore, you can quit having so many meaningless meetings in your church. You can eliminate those that meant something yesterday but not today, and then officers and people can spend more time opening their homes to other people. Not just so everyone can sit with their feet up and watch the little black box for three more hours. But so that you can have some family life and can talk to your children about the things they need to know in such a day as ours; read to your children. Then you can open your home to a wider community. There are dozens of meetings in almost every church that could just as well be scrapped—meetings that have nothing to do with the norms of Scripture and therefore are not sacred as such.

It isn't too hard to begin. Of course as soon as you start, it will be difficult because often you will have to buck the evangelical establishment. But Christian kids who come to L'Abri speaking of the unreality they see among the evangelicals are not talking about this kind of home. If they saw their parents opening their home at expense to their furniture and rugs, if they were told to pray not merely for the lost out there somewhere, but for specific people whom they knew sitting at the table in their own home, the unreality would be gone.

Do you ever open your home to the crazy friends of your own children? When your kids come home and they have brought some crazy kook? The kids that your own children bring—are they welcome? Ask them and you will get some honest answers.

If our children see us paying prices this way in our homes, and then see it moving over and beginning in our churches, we can be sure that this sense of unreality that is such a blight, such a cancer in the evangelical church, will begin to dissipate.

The Bible says we are to give out cups of cold water. How many have we ever given out to one of those who are different from ourselves? Don't try to get your church to begin if you haven't begun it for yourself.

Do you talk against the affluent society? That's another thing that we evangelicals are good at now. We are against the affluent society. How many times have you risked your share in that society, getting nicked and scratched in the name of Jesus Christ? How many times have you risked breaking the springs in your car crowding kids into it to take them somewhere? Don't talk about being against the affluent society unless you put that share of the affluent society which is your hoard on the line. And don't dare respond that these things I'm saying are not a part of the teaching of the Word of God concerning rich and real community.

But Christian pastors come to me and say, "Don't you understand? If I begin this, I'm going to get kicked out of my church. If I bring blacks and the long-haired kids into my home, if I really get close to them and they begin to love me and trust me and then come to church, I may get kicked out." We send martyrs off to the end of the earth and say, go ahead and die for Jesus Christ. Why not here at home?

A revolution is coming and is here. If we don't have the courage in Jesus Christ to take a chance of getting kicked out of our churches and being ostracized today, what are we going to do when the revolution comes in force? If we don't have the courage to open our homes and begin to admit these things into the churches, slowly begin to make the changes that can be brought within the forms of the polity of the New Testament, then don't be concerned about having courage when the pressure comes—we won't have it!

Pray that the Lord will send you the people of His choice. But don't pray that way unless, no matter who these people are across the whole board of twentieth-century man, you are willing to take them into your home, have them at your table, and introduce them to your family.

It is not a day for small games. We need to teach a Christianity of content and purity of doctrine. And we need to practice that truth in our ecclesiastical affairs and in our religious cooperation if people, young and old, are to take our claim of truth seriously. We need to understand the difference between being a cobelligerent and an ally and not get confused about which is which. We must have and practice an orthodoxy of community. And we must be free to change those things in our church polity and practice which need changing. We would have thought the Christians of North Korea, for example, not only foolish, but resisting the wisdom of the Holy Spirit if, instead of going underground, they had maintained their old habits of time and place of meetings which would have made them vulnerable to those who desired to destroy them in the takeover of North Korea. Are we doing any better in the light of the overwhelming changes which have already come in our culture and society?

Learning From the Past to Do Better in the Future

A half century ago, liberals were taking over the power centers of almost every major old-line denomination in the United States. At that time, Bible-believing Christians divided into two groups: one was composed of those who left those denominations; the second, of those who stayed in their denominations and tried to build *a greater evangelical establishment*. Looking back over the years, there have been problems on both sides.

Looking back to the thirties, I can now say that an early mistake was made after we left the Presbyterian Church in the United States of America (Northern—now part of the United Presbyterian Church in the U.S.A.). It was a mistake that marked the "separatist movement" for years to come. There were many who, before the division, said they would not tolerate a liberal takeover; but when the time came, many of these remained in. Without judging their motives, it is true to say that the few who came out felt deserted and betrayed. Some of those who stayed in urged that the Constitutional Convention Union—the vehicle for all of their working together previously—should not be dissolved so as to enable those who stayed in and those who came out to continue to work together. But in exasperation and, perhaps, some anger, those who left dissolved it at once. All the lines of a practical example of observable love among the brethren were destroyed.

The periodicals of those who left tended to devote more space to attacking people who differed with them on the issue of leaving than to dealing with the liberals. Things were said that are difficult to forget even now. Those who came out refused at times to pray with those who had not come out. Many who left broke off all forms of fellowship with true brothers in Christ who had not left. Christ's command to love one another was destroyed. What was left was frequently a turning inward, a self-righteousness, a hardness. The impression often was left that coming out had made those who did so so right that anything could then be excused. Having learned such bad habits, they later treated each other badly when the resulting new groups had minor differences among themselves.

To be really Bible-believing Christians we need to practice, *simultaneously*, at each step of the way, two biblical principles. One principle is that of the purity of the visible church: Scripture commands that we must do more than just talk about the purity of the visible church, we must actually practice it, even when it is costly. The second principle is that of an observable love among all true Christians. In the flesh we can stress purity without love, or we can stress love without purity; we cannot stress both simultaneously. To do so we must look moment by moment to the work of Christ and of the Holy Spirit. Without that, a stress on purity becomes hard, proud, and legalistic; likewise, without it a stress on love becomes sheer compromise. Spirituality begins to have real meaning in our lives as we begin to exhibit simultaneously the holiness of God and the love of God. Without this simultaneous exhibition our marvelous God and Lord is not set forth. It is rather a caricature of him that is shown, and he is dishonored.

Happily, the hardness generally has greatly diminished over the years among the groups that withdrew—but we paid a terrible price for what was there in the earlier days.

One of the joys of my life occurred at the 1974 Lausanne Congress on World Evangelization. Some men from the newly formed Presbyterian Church in America asked me to attend a meeting there, made up of men who had just left the Presbyterian Church in the U.S. (Southern) to form the PCA, and some men who had not left. Spokesmen representing both sides said that meeting was possible because of my voice and especially my book, *The Church Before the Watching World*. I could have wept, and perhaps I did. We can do better than we would naturally do—but not without foreseeing the fleshly dangers and looking to our living Lord for His strength and grace.

I see the second problem of those who left the UPCUSA as a confusion over where to place the basic chasm that marks off our identity. Is the chasm placed between Bible-believing churches and those that are not, or is it between those who are Presbyterian and Reformed and those who are not? When we go into a town to start a church, do we go there primarily motivated to build a church that is loyal to Presbyterianism and the Reformed Faith? Or do we go to build a church that will preach the gospel that historic, Bible-believing churches of all denominations hold, and then, on this side of that chasm, teach what we believe is true to the Bible with respect to our own denominational distinctives? The answers to these questions make a great deal of difference. There is a difference of motivation, of breadth and outreach. One view is catholic and biblical and gives promise of success—on two levels: first, in church growth and healthy outlook among those we reach; second, in providing leadership to the whole church of Christ. The other view is inverted and self-limiting—and sectarian.

Those who did not leave the liberally controlled denominations 50 years ago also developed two attitudes. The first was the birth of a general latitudinarianism. If those who came out were inclined to become hard, some of those who stayed in tended to become soft. Some said: This is not the moment to come out, but we will do so if such-and-such occurs. Some developed their own kind of hardness—a decision to stay in no matter what happened.

If one accepts an ecclesiastical latitudinarianism, it is easy to step into a cooperative latitudinarianism that easily encompasses doctrine, including one's view of Scripture. This is what happened historically. Out of the ecclesiastical latitudinarianism of the thirties and the forties has come the letdown with regard to Scripture in certain areas of evangelicalism in the eighties. Large sections of evangelicalism act as though it makes no real difference whether we hold the historic view of Scripture, or the existential methodology that says the Bible is authoritative when it teaches religious things but not when it touches on what is historic or scientific, or on such things as the male/female relationship.

Not all who stayed in the liberal-dominated denominations

have done this, by any means. I do not believe, however, that those who made the choice to stay in no matter what happens can escape a latitudinarian mentality. They will struggle to paper over the difference regarding Scripture so as to keep an external veneer of evangelical unity—when indeed there is no unity at that crucial point of Scripture. When doctrinal latitudinarianism sets in, we can be sure both from church history and from personal observation that in one or two generations those who are taught by the churches and schools that hold this attitude will lose still more, and the line between evangelical and liberal will be lost.

Unless we reject the existential methodology as a whole, we will be confused in our thinking, and succumb to the general relativism of our day and compromise our ecclesiastical duties.

The second problem for those who did not leave the liberally controlled denominations is their natural tendency constantly to move back the line at which the final stand must be taken. For example, could such well-known evangelical Presbyterians as Clarence Macartney, Donald Grey Barnhouse, and T. Roland Phillips have stayed in a denomination in which the crucial issues are the ordination of women and the refusal to ordain a young pastor whose only "fault" is that while he says he will not preach against the ordination of women, he will not change his own view that it is unbiblical? Can you imagine that these men would have considered it a victory to have stalled the ordination of practicing homosexuals and lesbians? What do you think Macartney, Barnhouse, and Phillips would have said? Such a situation in their denomination would have been inconceivable to them.

Evangelicals must beware of false victories. The liberal denominational power structure knows how to keep Bible-believing Christians off balance. There are many possible false victories they can throw to evangelicals to prevent them from making a clear pullout. There are still those who say, "Don't break up our ranks. Wait a while longer. Wait for this, wait for that." Always wait, never act. But fifty years is a long time to wait while things are getting worse. Because of my failing health, I am in a good position to say that we do not have forever to take that courageous and costly stand for Christ we sometimes talk about.

Let us now shift our focus. What does the future hold? What can we expect for ourselves, our congregations, our physical and spiritual children in the days ahead? America is moving at great speed toward a totally humanistic society and state. Do we suppose this trend will leave our own little projects, lives, and churches untouched? When a San Francisco Orthodox Presbyterian congregation can be dragged into court for breaking the law against discrimination because it dismissed an avowed, practicing homosexual as an organist, can we be so deaf as not to hear all the warning bells?

Unfortunately, the liberal denominations support humanistic trends, publicly and financially as well as formally. Is this what evangelicals should support, by denominational affiliation, with their names and their finances? If so, they support not only what is wrong, but what will destroy us in the rapidly worsening scene.

In what presbytery in the UPCUSA can you bring an ordained man under biblical discipline for holding false views of doctrine and expect him to be disciplined? We should first of all, of course, do all we can on a personal, loving level to help the liberal; but if he persists in his liberalism he should be brought under the discipline, because the visible church should remain the faithful bride of Christ. The church is not the world. When a denomination comes to a place where such discipline cannot operate, then before the Lord her members must consider a second step: that step, with regard to the practice of the principle of the purity of the visible church, is with tears to step out. Not with flags flying, not with shouts of hurrah or thoughts that in this fallen world we can build a perfect church, but that step is taken with tears.

Evangelicals who come to this point must still keep on loving the liberals, and must do so because it is right. If we do not know how to take a firm stand against organized liberalism and still love the liberals, we have failed in half of the call to exhibit simultaneously the love and the holiness of God—before a watching world, before a watching church, before our children, before the watching angels, and before the face of the Lord Himself.

This is not a day of retreat and despair. Christians can still make a difference if they put the Lord before ease in their congregations. But they need to have pastoral examples as well as teaching. Pastors cannot give either clear teaching or clear example if they exhibit a relativistic, latitudinarian stance toward liberalism, instead of a loving, clear, and courageous one. Pastors cannot give the example and leadership an often latitudinarian evangelical establishment needs today if they do not pay the price necessary. They must not just talk about the truth; they must practice truth where it is costly.

Evangelicals must work on the basis of a proper hierarchy of things. The real chasm must be between true Bible-believing Christians and others, not at a lesser point. The chasm is not between Lutherans and everybody else, or Baptists and everybody else, or Presbyterians and everybody else. If evangelicals do not exhibit this truth in the way they teach in their seminaries and in the churches they build, they cannot give the leadership the whole church of Christ needs. Further, not to do this is to fail to show love and unity among all true Christians as commanded by Christ. His command is for observable love and observable unity among all true Christians, not just among those of one denomination. The real chasm is between those who have bowed to the living God and His Son Jesus Christ—and thus also to the verbal, propositional communication of God's Word, the Scripture—and those who have not.

Let us be careful to keep things in their proper order. Let us find ways to show the church and the world that while we indeed maintain our denominational distinctives and do not minimize them, because we believe they are biblical, evangelicals are brothers in Christ in the severe battles of our day.

Learning from the mistakes both sides have made in the past, pastors who leave liberal-dominated denominations, with their congregations, can raise a testimony that may still turn both the churches and society around—for the salvation of souls, the building up of God's people, and at least the slowing down of the slide toward a totally humanistic society and an authoritarian suppressive state.

Having done all these necessary things, let us never forget that while our call is first to be the faithful bride of Christ, that is not our total call. We are also called to be the bride in love with the divine bridegroom. This is our call for the days ahead.*

March 1980

---

*An address delivered in Pittsburgh at the Consultation on Presbyterian Alternatives, March 1980.

What Difference Does Inerrancy Make?

As I think back to eight years ago, and how at that time there was real danger that a weakened view of Scripture would come into, infiltrate, and take over much of the evangelical camp, to see four thousand of you here today is a testimony to the grace of God which fills me with deep emotion. And I do not believe it's the end of something; I believe it's the beginning of something, not just for the Bible, but for the praise of the Creator of the heavens and the earth—the One who has spoken to us, and without error, in this marvelous book.

I would begin by reading a little thing which I wrote for the folder that went out giving the call for this conference.

> Unless the Bible is without error, not only when it speaks of salvation matters, but also when it speaks of history and the cosmos, we have no foundation for answering questions concerning the existence of the universe and its form and the uniqueness of man. Nor do we have any moral absolutes, or certainty of salvation, and the next generation of Christians will have nothing on which to stand.

The International Council on Biblical Inerrancy was begun by those who were deeply concerned for the Scripture as God's

Word, as "Thus saith the Lord." It was called into being because a significant section of what is called evangelicalism had allowed itself to be infiltrated by the general world-view, the viewpoint, of our day. This by which it had become infiltrated *was really a variant of what had dominated liberal theological circles under the name of neo-orthodoxy.*

Two weeks ago, I was on the Milt Rosenberg radio show in Chicago, and he had a young liberal pastor who graduated from a very well-known liberal theological seminary programmed with me for a three-way discussion. Rosenberg is a clever master of discussion, and with *A Christian Manifesto* and the question of abortion as the discussion points, he kept digging deeper and deeper into the difference between the young liberal pastor and myself. The young liberal pastor brought up Karl Barth, Niebuhr, and Tillich, and we discussed them. It became very clear in that three-way discussion that the young liberal pastor never could appeal to the Bible without qualifications. And then the young liberal pastor said, "But I appeal to Jesus." My reply on the radio was that on his view of the Bible he could not really be sure that Jesus lived. His answer was that he had an inner feeling, an inner response, that told him that Jesus had existed.

The intriguing thing to me was that one of the leading men of the weakened view of the Bible who is called an evangelical, and who certainly does love the Lord, in a long and strenuous but pleasant discussion in my home a few years ago, when pressed backwards as to how he was certain concerning the resurrection of Jesus Christ, had used almost the same words. He said he was sure of the resurrection of Jesus Christ because of the inward witness. They both answered finally in the same way.

My point is that this Council was called into being because a significant and influential section of what is called evangelicalism has become infiltrated by a point of view that had a specific relationship to the view that had dominated liberal theological circles under the name of neo-orthodoxy. To me, this was curious at the time when I saw it happening a certain number of years ago because where this ends had already been demonstrated by the Niebuhr, Tillich, God is dead syndrome. But equally significant is that both end with no other final plea than "an inner witness." There is no final, objective authority.

This points up that the infiltration is even more encompassing. Namely, that as the neo-orthodox roots are only the theological expression of the surrounding world-view of existentialism, so also what was put forth as this new view of Scripture in evangelicalism is also an infiltration of the general world-view of existentialism. That is, that though the Bible has errors in it, yet "a religious word" somehow breaks through from it—which finally ends in some expression such as "an inner feeling," "an inner response," or "an inner witness."

This reminds us of the secular existential philosopher Karl Jasper's term, "the final experience," and any number of terms which are some form of the concept of the final authority being an inner witness. In the neo-orthodox form, the secular existential form, and this new evangelical form, truth is left finally as only subjective.

All this stands in sharp contrast to the historic view presented by Christ Himself and the historic view of the Scripture in the Christian church, which is the Bible being objective, absolute truth. Of course, we all know that there are subjective elements involved in our personal reading of the Bible and in the Church's reading of the Bible. But nevertheless, the Bible *is* objective, absolute truth in all the areas it touches upon. And therefore, we know that Christ lived, and that Christ was raised from the dead, and all the rest, not because of some subjective inner experience, but because the Bible stands as an objective, absolute authority. That is the way we know. I do not downplay the experience that rests upon this objective reality, but this is the way we know—upon the basis that the Bible is objective, absolute truth.

Or to say it another way: the culture is to be constantly judged by the Bible, rather than the Bible being bent to conform to the surrounding culture. The early church did this in regard to the Roman-Greek culture of its day. The Reformation did this in its day in relation to the culture coming at the end of the Middle Ages. And we must never forget that all the great revivalists did this concerning the surrounding culture of their day. And the Christian church did this at every one of its great points of history.

The contrast to this other view of Scripture—in which the Church is being infiltrated and dominated by the view of the culture at that passing moment—is the Word of God as absolute, judging the passing, changing, *fallen* culture. This Council, as I said, was called into being to stand opposed and, in love, to try to rectify this infiltration—out of concern for the Scripture as God's

Word, as "Thus saith the Lord." And we can be glad the Lord has brought us to the day in which all of us are gathered here.

Notice though what the primary problem was, and is: infiltration by a form of the world-view which surrounds us rather than the Bible being the unmovable base for judging that ever-shifting fallen culture. The Council's position stands at the point of the call *not* to be infiltrated by this ever-shifting fallen culture which surrounds us, but rather judging that culture upon the basis of the Bible.

The topic of this talk is, "What Difference Does Inerrancy Make?" Overwhelmingly, the difference is that with the Bible being what it is, God's Word as absolute, as God's objective truth, we do not need to be, *and we should not be,* caught in the ever-changing fallen cultures which surround us. Those who do not hold the inerrancy of Scripture do not have this high privilege. To some extent, they are at the mercy of the fallen, changing culture. And Scripture is thus bent to conform to the changing world spirit of the day instead of their having a solid authority upon which to judge and to resist the views and values of that changing, shifting world spirit.

We, however, must be careful before the Lord. If we say we believe the Bible to be the inerrant, authoritative "Thus saith the Lord," we do not face the howling winds of change which surround us with confusion and terror. And yet, the other side of the coin is that if this *is* the "Thus saith the Lord," we must live under it. And without that we don't understand what we have said when we say we stand for an inerrant Scripture.

In my book *A Christian Manifesto,* I deal with the consequences of the view now so widely held in our culture that the final reality is some form of energy or mass, shaped into its present form by pure chance. Because of this view, it is increasingly perceived that there are no final values, mores, or a basis for law. Therefore, quite properly on this view that the final reality is only mass or energy shaped into its present form by pure chance, there are not and there *cannot be* any fixed values. All things are relative, and the final value is what makes the individual or society happy, feel good, at the moment. This is not just the hedonistic young person doing what feels good; it is society and even law as a whole.

This has many facets, but one is the breakdown of all stability in society. Nothing is fixed, there are no set standards, only what makes one happy is dominant. This is even true in regard to human life. The January 11, 1982, issue of *Newsweek* had a cover story of about five or six pages which showed conclusively that human life begins at conception. All students of biology should have known this all along. Then one turned the page, and the next article was entitled "But Is It A Person?" The conclusion of that page was, "The problem is not determining when actual human life begins, but when the value of that life begins to outweigh other considerations, such as the health or even the happiness of the mother." The terrifying phrase is "or even the happiness." Thus, even acknowledged human life can be and is taken for someone else's happiness.

With no set values, all that matters is my or society's happiness at the moment. I must say I cannot understand why even the liberal lawyers of the Civil Liberties Union are not terrified at that point.

And, of course, it is increasingly accepted that if a newborn baby is going to make the family or society unhappy, it too should be allowed to die. All you have to do is to look at your television programs and this comes across increasingly like a flood. And it's upon such a view that Stalin and Mao allowed (and I'm using a very gentle word when I say "allowed") millions to die for what they considered the happiness of society. This then is the terror that surrounds the church today. The individual's or society's happiness takes supreme preference even over human life.

One of the things which increasingly has troubled Christians, and others who are thoughtful people, concerning this concept of no fixed standards is the resulting instability of the family. The family is as much a casualty of the modern relativism as is human life.

Now let us realize that we are in as much danger at this point of being infiltrated by the surrounding thought forms as those whose infiltration by the existential theological thought forms led to the formation of this Council. We, because we find ourselves in a society with no fixed standards, are surrounded by a "no-fault" everything. Each thing is psychologically pushed away or explained away so that there is no right or wrong. And, as with the happiness of the mother taking precedence over human life, so anything which interferes with the happiness of the individual or society is dispensed with. This too can be called nothing less than hedonism.

And we can say the Bible is without mistake and still destroy it if we bend the Scripture by our lives to fit this culture instead of judging the culture by the Scripture. The no-fault divorce laws in many of our states are not really based upon humanitarianism, or kindness. They are based on the view that there is no right and wrong. And thus, all is relative, which means that society and the individual acts on what seems to them to give happiness for them at the moment.

Do we not have to agree that much of the church has bent Scripture at the point of divorce to conform to the culture rather than the Scripture judging the present viewpoints of the fallen culture?

Through the ages, the church has held three views concerning the attack upon the family which comes by the breakup of families. The first view that has been held through the centuries is that which has been held up to the recent past, for example, by the Church of England. That is, that there is no acceptable basis for divorce and remarriage. The second view which has been discussed and held through the ages is based on Jesus' words in Matthew 5:31, 32. That is, that there is only one basis for divorce and remarriage—sexual infidelity. Note that this would not say there is no fault by the "innocent" party, nor would it say that there *must* be a divorce. But it does say that adultery is a basis for divorce and remarriage. The third view that has been held through the centuries is based on I Cor. 7:15. It is that held by the Westminster Confession of Faith, and it happens to be that which after much consideration is my own view. That is, that there are two biblical bases: adultery, and permanent desertion that cannot be rectified by the church, or as the Westminster Confession of Faith puts it, by the magistrates—that is, by the civil authority.

Now, these three views can be discussed, and people can hold one or the other, feeling that they are basing their views on Scripture. But to go beyond this means that as the mother has the right to kill her baby for her happiness, I have the right to attack, not just the family in general, but contrary to Scripture, I attack the family by breaking up my own family. I find it hard to say, but here is an infiltration by the surrounding society that is as destructive to Scripture as is a theological attack upon Scripture. Both are a tragedy. Both bend the Scripture to conform to the surrounding culture.

When Dr. Koop, Franky, and I were in the midst of the seminars for *Whatever Happened to the Human Race?,* one of us received a letter from someone in the evangelical ranks. The writer holds a good view theologically concerning the Scripture, and I would also say I like him. In his letter, however, he said, "I see the emergence of a new sort of fundamentalist legalism." Later he explained what he meant like this: "That was the case in the thrust concerning false evangelicals in the inerrancy issue, and is also the case on the part of some who are now saying that the evangelical cause is betrayed by any who allow any exceptions of any sort in government funding in abortion." He links the two issues of Scripture and abortion together.

This needs clarification. I know of no Protestant who does not take into consideration the health of the mother if, with tears, the doctor cannot save *both* of his patients—the child and the mother. It is all the other qualifications which are tacked on to the statement, "I am against abortion . . . except for this, for that, for the other," that raises the question if it is understood that it is human life as such that is involved in contrast to some individual's or society's concept of happiness.

In the light of the question "What Difference Does Inerrancy Make?" I would like to consider the phrase "a new sort of fundamentalist legalism" in regard to all the points I've touched upon so far in this talk. I'll repeat the phrase: "fundamentalist legalism."

If what is involved is the heartless, loveless, fundamentalist legalism some of us have known so well in the past, of course we do not want it, and we reject it in the name of Christ. The love of God and the holiness of God must always be evident simultaneously. And if anyone has wandered off and returns, the attitude should not be one of pride that we have been right, but rather joy, and the playing of songs, happy music, joyous music, singing of joyous songs, and I would add, even dancing in the streets because, and if, there has been a true return.

Again, if the term "fundamentalist legalism" means the downplaying of the humanities, as unhappily has so often been the case, the failure to know that the intellect is important, that human creativity by Christians and non-Christians is worth study, if it means the downplaying of the scholarly, if it means the downplaying of the Lordship of Christ in all of life, then my work of some forty years and all my books and films speak of my total rejection of this.

Again, if the term "fundamentalist legalism" means a confusion of primary and secondary points of doctrine and life, that too should be rejected.

But, when all this is said, when we come to the central things of doctrine, including maintaining the Bible's emphasis that it is without mistake, and the central things of life, then something must be considered. *Truth carries with it confrontation.* Truth *demands* confrontation; loving confrontation, but confrontation nevertheless. If our reflex action is always accommodation regardless of the centrality of the truth involved, there's something wrong.

As what we may call holiness without love is not God's kind of holiness, so what we may call love without holiness, including when necessary confrontation, is not God's kind of love. God is holy, and God is love.

We must, with prayer, say no to the theological attack upon Scripture. We must say no to this, clearly and lovingly, with strength. And we must say no to the attack upon Scripture which comes from our being infiltrated in our lives by the current worldview of no fault in moral issues. We must say no to these things equally.

The world of our day has no fixed values and standards, and therefore what people conceive as their personal or society's happiness covers everything. We are not in that position. We have the inerrant Scripture. Looking to Christ for strength against tremendous pressure because our whole culture is against us at this point, we must reject the infiltration in theology and in life equally. We both must affirm the inerrancy of Scripture and then live under it in our personal lives and in society.

God's Word will never pass away, but looking back to the Old Testament and since the time of Christ, with tears we must say that because of lack of fortitude and faithfulness on the part of God's people, God's Word has many times been allowed to be bent, to conform to the surrounding, passing, changing culture of that moment, rather than to stand as the inerrant Word of God judging the form of the world spirit and the surrounding culture of that moment. In the name of the Lord Jesus Christ, may our children and grandchildren not say that that can be said about us.*

March 1982

---

*An address delivered in San Diego at a plenary session of the Congress on the Bible, March 1982.

The Church Before the Watching World

Introduction

This book is addressed to twentieth-century Christians as they face a very practical problem. As Christians we say we believe in truth and in the practice of truth, and yet we face much untruth in the visible church. The problem is not new; error was present in the early church when councils were held to combat it. It was present in the medieval church until the Reformation reaffirmed the biblical faith. And it is present today.

The biblical teaching is clear. As the bride of Christ, the church is to keep itself pure and faithful. And this involves two principles which seem at first to work against each other: (1) the principle of the practice of the purity of the visible church in regard to doctrine and life; and (2) the principle of the practice of an observable love and oneness among *all* true Christians regardless of who and where they are.[1] These two principles are, in turn, based on the character of God Himself, for God is holy and God is love. In *The Mark of the Christian* I have developed the implications of the second principle for the visible church. The present book will concentrate on the first principle. More specifically, it will focus on doctrinal purity. But both principles, because they are based upon the character of God, must be practiced simultaneously. So while we look closely here at the first principle, we must not forget to practice the second.

The issues involved in the principle of the purity of the visible church in our day in regard to doctrine and life break down logically into several questions. (1) How has the present impurity in the churches come about, and what is it? (2) Why should Christians and churches be concerned with doctrinal purity? (3) How can doctrinal purity in the church be maintained in practice? A chapter will be devoted to each of these questions. An appendix, "Some Absolute Limits," will discuss in a different and perhaps unique fashion for modern man the ways in which the trend toward a lack of doctrinal purity can be recognized before it advances beyond the germinal stage.

Although many of the details of this book are drawn from ecclesiastical history in the United States, churches almost everywhere face similar problems in slightly different historic settings. In countries as diverse as Korea, Holland and England, one finds almost exact parallels to the American scene. And it is well for Christians in other countries to have a comprehension of what has occurred in the United States ecclesiastically in the last forty-five years because in the shifting balances of world influence American money and American energy have carried these issues directly from America to Europe and most of the "missionary" countries of the world. Thus, both the principles and the illustrations given here will, I believe, be valuable to churches in every country.

CHAPTER ONE

A Historical Critique of Theological Liberalism

What is the character and form of modern doctrinal impurity, and how did it arise? In every age, of course, the church has faced the problem of doctrinal error. The history of Christendom in the last 300 years, however, has its own peculiar character. In the course of these 300 years, there have been a number of important historical changes in the nature of the challenge to the biblical perspective. It is especially important to understand the development of such theology as it moves from what we may term the *old liberalism* to the *new liberalism* (existential theology).

Before we take up the details, however, we must stress the fact that the reason we reject liberal theology, old and new, is not that we are opposed to scholarship. Constantly through the years great Bible-believing scholars have engaged in what is usually called *lower criticism*—the question of what the best biblical text really is. Take, for example, such men as Robert Wilson at Princeton Theological Seminary before the changes which came in that institution. It is natural that biblical Christians should find textual study important, because since Scripture is the propositional communication from God to men, obviously we are interested in the very best text possible. Consequently, Christian scholars have labored through the years in the area of lower criticism.

Higher criticism is quite a different matter. Picking up where lower criticism leaves off, it attempts to determine upon its own subjective basis what is to be accepted and what is to be rejected after the best text has been established. The "new hermeneutic" is a case in point, for here there is no real distinction between text and interpretation; both are run together.

The real difference between liberalism and biblical Christianity is not a matter of scholarship, but a matter of presuppositions. Both the old liberalism and new liberalism operate on a set of presuppositions common to both of them, but different from those of historic, orthodox Christianity.

The Birth of Liberalism

But how did theological liberalism come about? In order to understand this, we must go back about 250 years to Germany where theological liberalism was born. At that particular time, the German universities and German intellectuals were moving toward modern naturalism. That is, they were moving away from the concept held by the early scientists (such men as Copernicus, Francis Bacon, Galileo and Newton), who believed in the uniformity of natural causes in a limited system, open to reordering by both God and man. They were moving into the concept of the uniformity of natural causes in a closed system, a concept which makes everything that exists a cosmic machine.

That is, an ideological and philosophical shift was taking place. In the academic disciplines surrounding the faculties of theology, the view of the older science (a science whose concept of the uniformity of natural causes in an open system was completely consistent with biblical thought) was being replaced by what I call modern, modern science (a concept which, by the uniformity of natural causes in a closed system, eventually leaves no room for God or a significant man). In the academic world, then, a new view was gradually becoming dominant—a total consensus. The result was that the theological faculties became isolated from the other faculties, and, not being able or willing to stand alone, these faculties capitulated in their theology by accepting the naturalism of the other faculties.

I believe the reason they capitulated was that their theology was already less than it should have been. By the middle of the eighteenth century in the German universities, the theology of the Reformation, having "the burning heart," was coming to an end. What remained of orthodox theology had largely become only repetitive. Such a theology, of course, can never stand for long.

In church history a cycle seems to recur: living orthodoxy moves to dead orthodoxy and then to heterodoxy. It would seem that this was the case in the German universities at that particular time. The German theologians did not accept their own form of naturalism because they were forced to do so by the facts. They did so to conform, and liberal theology has been conforming ever since. For, from that day to this, liberal theology has been a theology of naturalism.

It is interesting, but not surprising, that from the time theology became naturalistic, it has tended simply to follow the curve of secular naturalism. It really says nothing different from the surrounding consensus; whatever the surrounding nontheological consensus is, theological liberalism has conformed to it. If we were to draw a graph giving the curve of the shifting secular naturalistic consensus in red ink and then the teaching of liberal theology in green ink, we would find almost identical curves, with the theological liberalism simply following a few years later and using religious terms instead of secular ones. Liberal theology uses different terminology, and yet says the same thing just a short time later. It has a naturalistic perspective that is totally opposite from the perspective of historic Christianity and the Bible.

The Biblical Perspective

Basically, the biblical perspective is this. First, there is an infinite-personal God who exists and who has created the external universe, not as an extension of His own essence, but out of nothing. Something of the nature of this created universe can be found out by reason because that is the way the infinite-personal God has created it.[1] The universe is neither chaotic nor random, but orderly. Cause and effect is real, but this cause and effect is not in a closed system, but rather in an open system—or, to say it in a different way, it is a cause-and-effect system in a limited time span. Though this universe has an objective existence apart from God, it does not operate solely on its own; it is not autonomous. God is not a slave to the cause-and-effect world He has created, but is able to act into the cause-and-effect flow of history.

Second, God has made man in His own image, and this means, among other things, that man too can act into the cause-and-effect flow of history. That is, man cannot be reduced to only a part of the machine; he is not an automaton.

Third, not only can God act into the world, but He is not silent;

He has spoken to men in the historic, space-time situation. The Bible and Christ in His office of prophet have given a propositional, verbalized communication to men that is true about God, true about history, and true about the cosmos. This should not take us by surprise, for if God has made man in His own image and has made us so that we can verbalize facts propositionally to each other on a horizontal level of communication, then it is natural that the infinite God who is personal would also communicate vertically to man in the same way. Of course, we must be careful to make a distinction here. Although God has not given us exhaustive knowledge (only He is infinite), He has given us true knowledge (what I have often called true truth)—true knowledge about Himself, about history, and about the cosmos.[2]

Fourth, the universe as it is now is not normal; that is, it is not now as it was when it was first created. Likewise, man is no longer as he was when first created. Therefore, from God's side there is the possibility of a qualitative solution for man as he is now and for man's cruelty, without man ceasing to be man.

We should notice at this point how opposed the biblical perspective is to naturalism (the uniformity of cause and effect in a closed system), for naturalism discounts by presupposition this possibility. It bases its understanding of human life and the form of the universe by presuppositionally shutting itself up to finite man totally starting from himself. Man gathers whatever particulars he can and then tries to make universals (and tries to find meaning only from himself), while ruling out the possibility of knowledge from all other sources. Naturalism leaves no room for propositional truth being given by God to man, no room for miracle, and eventually leaves no room for the significance of man.

While there are certainly many more details that could be included in the biblical perspective if one were to make the outline more complete, the present description will suffice for our critique of liberalism here.[3]

The Steps to Modern Naturalism

Historically, in the shift from theological orthodoxy to today's present existential theology, three major steps were taken. The first step I have already indicated: the movement from a belief in the uniformity of natural causes in a system open to reordering by God and man, to the concept of the uniformity of natural causes in a closed system. Let us consider this step more fully.

During the period between the Renaissance and Reformation, and the age of Rousseau, Kant and Hegel, the mood of the secular thinkers was optimistic. They believed that on the basis of rationalism, man could rationally find a unified answer to all of knowledge and life.

According to *rationalism,* as I am using the term here, man can understand the universe by beginning from himself without any recourse to outside knowledge, specifically outside knowledge or revelation from God. The term *rationality* sounds very similar, but the difference in meaning is profound. Rationality means that reason is valid. The first axiom in the classical concept of rational methodology is that A is A and A is not non-A. That is, if a proposition is true, then its opposite is not true. Or, in the area of morality, if a certain thing is right, then its opposite is wrong. One should not, therefore, confuse the terms *rationalism* and *rationality*.

The secular thinkers we are referring to in this period believed optimistically that they could begin only from themselves (this is rationalism), apply reason (rationality), and come to a unified concept of knowledge and of life. They thought that this would lead them to find true answers. They were optimists at this time on the basis of reason.

Where did liberal theology stand in that same period? As I mentioned, liberal theology simply echoed the surrounding rationalistic consensus. In this period the liberal theologians were also optimistic. They believed on the basis of rationalistic scholarship that they could find the historical Jesus while eliminating the supernatural from the biblical account. They believed that they could take reason, apply it to the Bible, and come up with the historical Jesus while getting rid of the supernatural element they found in the biblical account. By presupposition, they were naturalists, and the supernatural made them uncomfortable. But notice that they were simply following what the secular thinkers had already said. The liberal theology was operating in the more limited area of its own discipline, but within that area it was saying the same thing and it had the same mentality.

The Step to Despair

What, then, was the second step? This step came from the development from Rousseau, Kant and Hegel. The secular rationalistic philosophers concluded that on a rational basis they could not find a unified answer to knowledge and to life. Their quest ended in failure. In other words, accepting the validity of reason and arguing as reasonably as they could, basing their arguments only in rationalism, they finally concluded that they could not put all the pieces together. Their optimism was gone.

What, then, happened to liberal theology? Liberal theology simply followed suit. Liberal theologians had been optimistic about being able to separate the historical Jesus from the supernatural elements of the Gospel accounts, but with Albert Schweitzer's analysis of their failure in his book, *The Quest of the Historical Jesus,* they had to admit that they were not going to be able to do it. This was the end of an era. They discovered that the supernatural and the historical Jesus were so united that if all the supernatural was removed, no historical Jesus remained. And if one kept the historical Jesus, some supernatural had to stay. So their end was failure, and their optimism was gone.

The Step to Modern Mysticism

The third step for both the secular and the religious thinkers was a very interesting one and follows on from Hegel and even more Kierkegaard. For after the failure of rationalism, if rationality was maintained there were two possibilities. The first was to become nihilistic. That is, on the basis of reason, they could have concluded that all is blackness and then given up hope.[4] Their other rational alternative was to conclude that *rationalism* was wrong, that men—being finite—cannot gather enough particulars to make up the universals. That in fact, men need knowledge outside of themselves if they are ever to find a satisfactory answer to life. In other words, it would have been reasonable to accept the possibility of revelation or at least the necessity for revelation. But, of course, to do this they would have had to give up their presupposition of rationalism. The point is that they could have taken either of these alternatives and yet have remained men of reason.

It must have been a hard moment for them; they had to choose between these two alternatives if they were going to keep their rationality. Instead, they did something new. They did what previously would have been unthinkable to educated men: they split the field of knowledge. They held on to their rationalism by letting go of the concept of a unified field of knowledge. Non-Christian philosophers had formerly thought that they would be able to come up with a unity on the basis of reason, but they abandoned this hope.

Rather, they now accepted that on the basis of reason men will always come to pessimism—man is a machine and meaningless. Therefore, they developed a concept of nonreason, an attempt of man to achieve meaning and significance outside the framework of rationality. For them, everything which makes human life as human life worth living falls in the area of nonreason, what I call in my other books the upper story.

It is crucial that we understand the situation here. The areas of reason and nonreason are held to be completely apart. Picture the line between reason and nonreason as a solid concrete wall with barbed wire in the middle charged with 10,000 volts of electricity. Then you can begin to understand how there can be no interchange between the lower story with reason which leads to despair and the upper story of hope without reason. Everything that is worthwhile for human life—meaning, values, love, etc.—is in the area of nonreason. In what we may now call the new humanism, we have a semantic mysticism with no facts.

Existential Theology

How does liberal theology fit into this? Liberal theology makes the same shift as secular naturalism. Karl Barth and his disciples, and the theology that sprang up out of the Lutheran world at the University of Lund, Sweden, developed what has come to be called transcendental theology, neo-orthodoxy, or existential theology. Karl Barth, however, is basically the originator of the movement, and it will be sufficient to concentrate on his contribution.

First, one must realize that to the end of his life he continued to accept the higher critical theories. Thus for him there were many mistakes in the Bible. Some have said that Karl Barth's contribution was to sound a bell in the midst of this century's great need for authority. What he really did was give liberal theology a peg in midair. To put it simply, he tried the impossible feat of producing an authority while accepting the results and techniques of higher criticism. To him the Bible has mistakes in it, but a "religious word" breaks through from it. To Karl Barth and his followers, a statement in the Bible can be historically false and yet religiously true. It was a very simple step but entirely revolutionary. With it theology stepped from the solid earth of rationality into a land where anything can happen.

Karl Barth's basic position was this: Of course, the Bible has all kinds of mistakes in it, but it doesn't matter; believe it religiously.

In his first *Romerbrief* (1919) he indicated his relationship to Kierkegaard, and in his *Dogmatics*, II, it is plain that Karl Barth is an existentialist as far as epistemology is concerned.

At the end of his life Barth struggled to hold back the natural direction which he had opened to someone like Tillich and to the death-of-God theology which followed. He did not like what was produced; nevertheless, he was the one who opened the door.

The older liberalism was a heresy from a Christian viewpoint; but from a classical, philosophical viewpoint, it was respectable. The older liberalism was demonstrated most clearly perhaps by a man like Harry Emerson Fosdick in the United States. He and others like him gradually spun a rosy idealism which overlooked the world as it is. But they stayed within the circle of thought wherein one man says, "What I say is true," and another man, if he holds the opposite, says, "No, your view is false and mine is true." They changed the definition of words so that their terminology needed a whole new series of definitions; but at least when one understood their definitions, there was a certain stability in the matter.

But the newer liberals, the existential theologians, do not define their terms so clearly; and, furthermore, they want to say that two mutually contradictory statements may very well both be true. At one time they themselves made this obvious by saying that their position stressed both-and, rather than either-or. In a very real sense, this theology is the child of Hegel. Hegel's teaching led to the concept that a *thesis* naturally leads to an *antithesis,* and these together lead to a *synthesis.* (To come to this conclusion, one sets aside the methodology of antithesis.) But even this synthesis is only relative, for it too generates its own antithesis, then further synthesis, and so on *ad infinitum.*

The new liberals, therefore, often said *both-and* to two mutually exclusive propositions. One example is saying both that Christ rose physically from the dead and that He did not rise physically from the dead. This is not just a modern problem of semantics. For example, some of the most far-out Roman Catholic progressive theologians at the World Congress on the Future of the Church who met in Brussels in September 1970 insisted that they believed in the bodily resurrection of Jesus, yet also said that if one had been there that day, this event could not have been verified by the use of normal means of verification. This is understandable in the context of the both-and mentality. Or, to say it another way, the bodily resurrection is an upper-story matter.

I remember hearing a certain existential theologian speaking some years ago. After he had finished, I overheard one old Christian saying to another, "Wasn't it wonderful?" The other answered, "It was wonderful, but I couldn't understand it." True Christianity is quite different. When the Bible says, "In the beginning God created the heavens and the earth," a child and a philosopher can understand that it means God created the heavens and the earth in antithesis to the idea that God did not create the heavens and the earth. It does not mean that we can plumb to the exhaustive depths of all God knows about this, but it does mean that the basic facts have been clearly expressed in terms of antithesis. With the paradox-ridden new liberal theology, statements have a way of seeming to be profound while actually being only vague. To get the full impact of this, just read a chapter in the works of B. B. Warfield, J. Gresham Machen, Abraham Kuyper, Martin Luther or John Calvin, and then read a chapter by one of the existential theologians.

Let me take another illustration. One of the clearest expressions of the both-and type of thinking came to me when a pastor raised on this theology said to me, "The classical Roman Catholic priest is closer to you than I am." When I asked him what he meant, he said, "The priest holding the historic Roman Catholic position and you at least agree that one is right and one is wrong. But we say you are both right." In other words, as far as "religious truths" are concerned to this man, he would express "religious truths" in such a way that one person could say that Christ is the only mediator between God and man, and another person could say that Mary and the saints intercede for us and they both would be right.

While I was in Finland some years ago, a Bible-believing university professor there used the following illustration. A new liberal, he says, is like a shopkeeper who keeps many things under the counter. When the old-fashioned liberal comes in and asks for old-fashioned liberalism, the new liberal reaches under the counter and says, "That is *just* what we have here." When the Bible-believing Christian comes in, the new liberal reaches under the counter and says, "That is *just* what we have here." The new theology is able to do this because of its both-and mentality. Opposites can still be religiously true.

Take, for example, the concept of the Fall. The old liberal, in casting aside the fact of man's sinfulness as taught in the Bible, built for himself an idealistic world that didn't exist. The utopia built by man was to arrive tomorrow. The new liberal, a man like Reinhold Niebuhr, for example, said that man is very deeply flawed (he may even use the word *sinner* to describe this). Therefore, he seemed closer to the true world than the old-fashioned liberal. But how did man get to be a sinner, and what *is* sin? The Bible tells us that man fell in the Garden of Eden. The new liberal says that it does not matter if historically there ever was a Garden of Eden; he tries to lay hold of the realism that man is cruel while dispensing with the Bible's explanation of how he came to be this way. Thus he hangs his peg in midair, casting aside the historicity of the Scripture and yet trying to retain the results that the Bible teaches.

In the matter of individual doctrines, this leads the new liberal into many strange places. The upshot of this position is that there is no clear line between God the Father and God the Son, no clear line concerning the deity of Christ, no clear line between Christ and the sinfulness of man, or between what Christ did for us and what happens to us subjectively. We are told that the really important thing is what happens to us now.

Furthermore, there is no clear line between a lost man and a saved man. With the loss of antithesis there is an implicit or explicit universalism in the new liberalism. One existential theologian in Holland told me in a conversation that the division among men is not vertical but horizontal. When I asked him what he meant, he said it is not that some men are justified before God and some are not, but that all men are right and all men are wrong. Of course, no Christian is perfect, but by his terminology and in our talk it was clear that this was not what he meant.

Hence, the existential theologian speaks to the world as though the world were the church and to the church as though it were the world. There never is a clear line, because any real concept of antithesis is foreign to him.

It is interesting that way back in the summer of 1949, Dr. Hedeinus, an atheistic professor of philosophy at the University of Uppsala, Sweden, wrote a book in which he criticized the theological professors at Lund, accusing them of being "atheists, clothed as bishops and pastors." He further commented that if Christianity is something reasonable that an intelligent man can believe, it should be able to be put into words that can be understood. In short, he said, If the new liberalism is Christianity, I do not want it; its concepts cannot even be put into understandable words, and

it is in a worse position than I am. This, of course, is exactly what
J. S. Bezzant said much later in *Objections to Christian Belief* when
he called this type of theology nonsense.[5]

The Bible and the Word of God
I have emphasized that there are no clear doctrinal lines in the new
theology, but I must make one exception. The new liberals do
raise a definite chorus that the Bible is *not* the Word of God. Their
well-known words are, "The Bible is not the Word of God, but
contains the Word of God." Historically Protestantism has centered its authority in the Bible. But the new liberals, although they
have cut loose from this, still act as if they have an authority. It is
as though a man had torn down a bridge and then walked across
on thin air as if the bridge were still there.

In theory the new liberal said, especially some years ago, that
the Bible contains the Word of God and that God will make
certain portions of the Bible the Word of God to the individual as
he reads it. That is why neo-orthodoxy was sometimes called
"crisis theology." A man is reading along, and some portion of the
Bible suddenly becomes the Word of God to him; this is a *crisis,* as
though lightning had struck him from above. Such is the theory.
But in practice each individual reader must decide for himself
what is the Word of God in the Bible and what is not.

For example, consider the Oslo Youth Conference back in
1947, which took place at a time that was something of a high-
water mark for neo-orthodoxy in its most hopeful form, before its
problems began to show up to the neo-orthodox theologians
themselves. In a very real way this was parallel to the secular
existentialists' first hopefulness that was followed later on by difficulties. Think, for instance, of the early euphoria of the followers
of Karl Jaspers as they accepted the concept of the final experience.
As a matter of fact, there is a very specific parallel between Jaspers'
term and concept of the final experience and the terms and concepts of the crisis theology. In any case, the Oslo Youth Conference officially concluded thus: "The criterion of inspiration was
generally taken to be the testimony of any passage to, or its
accordance with, the spirit of Jesus Christ." In other words, the
young people were to decide what part of the Bible is the Word of
God and what isn't on their own subjective judgment as to what
part showed the spirit of Jesus Christ.

The authority which was being built in midair was and is a

product of one's own subjective judgment. In short, they were saying, "Such and such is true. Why? Because I say it is true." It is at this point that the English theologian Michael Green's statement that Bultmann is infallible for twenty minutes each Sunday morning is so very perceptive.

Even a cursory reading of Barth's writings and those of his followers will show that they dogmatically reject (as did the older form of liberalism) the historical view of Christianity that the original writings of the Bible were so inspired by God as to be kept free from error. Emil Brunner has said, "The Bible contains a lot of statements of fact, of ethics, and of doctrine, that are in contradiction to knowledge we have otherwise gained. There can be no harmony of the Gospels. That is bunk, dishonesty." Brunner writes furthermore, "This overemphasis upon the intellectual aspect of the Faith came out in two facts—both of them well-known, but, as it seems to me—never fully understood. The first of these facts was the equation of the 'Word' of the Bible with the 'Word of God'; this produced a doctrine of Verbal Inspiration, with all its disastrous results." It is interesting to note that Brunner admits that his view was not the view of Calvin, for he has written, "In the thought of Calvin a tendency to take a rigidly literal view of the Bible, which developed into the doctrine of Verbal Inspiration, comes out in the fact that Revelation and Scripture are regarded as identical." Or take the words of another representative of this position, H. T. Kerr, Jr., writing in *Theology Today*, again in the heyday of the hopeful era of neo-orthodoxy: "The crisis at the moment is evidenced by the transition from an older, traditional authority in terms of inerrancy and verbal infallibility to the current existential view that the Word of God is somehow written and yet apart from the words of the Bible."

It should also be pointed out that to the new liberal, the Word of God comes to us through other sources than the Bible. Other religious writings, and writings that are not religious at all, can become the source of the Word of God. In this regard, Reinhold Niebuhr wrote an article in which he spoke about the place of women in the offices of the church: "Some fundamentalist theologians will seek to disinherit her by quoting texts. Perhaps the church should overcome these sub-Christian standards [he is not referring here to quoting texts, but to the treatment of women by the church] more readily if it ceased arguing about them on Christian grounds and recognized more frankly that there are primitive depths as well as sublime heights in religion not known in secular idealism. That need not persuade us to become secularists, but it might make us willing to let secular idealism speak the Word of God on occasion." In other words, to Niebuhr there are times when secular idealism can speak the Word of God to us better than the Bible.

Incidentally this attitude about the Bible can more recently be seen in the new Roman Catholic theologians. While they say that they now give more emphasis to the Bible and less to tradition, yet their view of the Bible is now the same as Niebuhr's which has just been quoted. Therefore, they now can find parallel truths in non-Christian teachings as well.[6]

A Scandinavian Lutheran theologian has said that modern Lutheranism follows Luther in all points except his view of the Bible. Obviously, if a man does not have the Bible of Luther or Calvin, he does not have the same view of Christianity as Luther or Calvin. Calvin and Luther could speak with authority and clarity because their feet were fixed on the Bible as the Word of God. That gave them an objective and absolute standard. The new liberal cannot speak with clarity or true authority because the basis of his judgment is subjective.

I have devoted considerable space to elucidating the nature of the new theology both in its earlier developing form and now because this is, after all, the basic form in which present-day doctrinal impurity is expressed. When the visible church faces the principle of the purity of the visible church today, it finds that its primary difficulties are associated with this new theology. Hence, I feel it is important that we understand what is involved and see how definitely this is related to the secular existential philosophy of today. Once again naturalistic theology is only saying the same things as naturalistic secular thought.

The New Hope Becomes Despair
It is interesting, however, that this third step of modern upper-story mysticism with regard to the things that really matter has not produced the results that were intended. At first the new secular humanism seemed like a great hope; for even though reason leads to despair, these secular humanists thought meaning and hope could be found in the existential experience. But the existential experience, like all pegs hung in midair, has proved to be not a hope but a damnation.

Take, for example, the philosophy of Karl Jaspers who, as I mentioned previously, says that the meaning of life must be found in the "final experience." But, of course, the final experience is completely separated from all reason. Therefore, a person cannot talk about its content even to himself. All he can say is that he has had such an experience. It is, however, more than this. Because this type of thought has severed the meaning of life from any connection to reason, the secular or religious existentialist is left with no categories of truth, and no categories of right and wrong. Down in the lower story, reason tells him that he is only a machine, that he may be expressed in a mathematical formula. Upstairs in the upper story of nonreason, he has become something of a Greek shade unable to distinguish between fantasy and reality.

Wittgenstein in his *Tractatus* came to this same place, saying that in the area of all values, ethics, meaning and love there is nothing but silence. He then turned from his positivism and gave birth to linguistic analysis, where one eventually deals only with language that leads only to language.[7]

The euphoria of the new theological liberals is past, and they saw the difficulties with their position just as those saying the same thing in secular terms saw their difficulties. In other words, naturalistic theology follows naturalistic humanism not only in its attempt at answers, but also in the despair which follows from a failure of those answers. For example, the death-of-God theology says that in the area of reason there is no reason to say that God is there. And on the basis of naturalistic theology, that is correct. It is worth remembering here what Dr. Hedeinus said about the Lund theologians being atheists in bishop's garments.

On the basis of liberal theology's presuppositions, every liberal theologian should be a God-is-dead theologian. But most of them still try to escape by abandoning reason and leaping into the upper story, saying that here one can have an existential, a "religious," experience. But this existential experience is completely separated from reason.

Most liberals do not like this later (but now largely faded) God-is-dead theology, and they object loudly. They wish to continue to use the word *God,* but they are in the same situation as the God-is-dead theologians, because while they use the word *God,* all content about God is gone. They are left with "contentless-connotation" religious words, and thus the situation still parallels the trend of secular thought.

Words like *Jesus* are separated from all reason and have no real base. So what is the word *Jesus*? A contentless banner which men take and say, in effect, "Follow me on the basis of the motivational force of the word *Jesus*." This is really no different from rock groups who used the word *Jesus* in their songs. When we listened to the rock groups of the early 1970s, what did we hear? *Jesus, Jesus, Jesus*. We should not have misunderstood—most of these singers did not believe that a single word of this had anything to do with reason or with truth other than motivational "truth." Likewise in the new liberalism, seen one way Jesus is a trip, and seen another way he is a contentless banner that is useful in psychology and sociology.

After the counterrevolution of the 1960s there were some in California and elsewhere, coming out of the drug culture, who were continuing the same language and life forms and who happily were true Christians of a deep and beautiful kind. But unhappily, many of the cries of "Jesus, Jesus" heard from the "Jesus freaks" of the time only equalled, "Jesus is better than hash." What was the difference between these two groups? The real Christians turned totally from the upper-story concept of the trip and turned to the clear content of the Bible. They were in the stream of Bible-believing Christianity. The others still kept the upper-story trip or banner philosophy, or at best they returned to almost contentless emotionalism. As the years have passed, the two groups produced very different results. The first group went on as Christians in the historic stream of Christianity. The second group disappeared or drifted off to pantheism or other such paths.

This is also where the modern liberal theology still is—only contentless religious words in an upper-story experience. With the non-Christian "religious freaks," the word *Krishna* and the word *Christ* were interchangeable for the same reason that the modern existential theologians' ecumenism includes Hindus and Buddhists as well as any people who use the word *Christ*.

When the young people say to us, "I hate god words," if we are to be Christians we must say, "I hate god words too." For such god words are separated from all verification and falsification; they can be made to mean anything. The new theologians seem to be saying something more than secular thinkers are saying because they use such religious words. But they are really saying the same things with a different set of linguistic symbols. There is many a liberal theologian today who uses the word *God* to equal no god— to give optimism in what is to him a totally pessimistic predicament, using words only as psychological tools to give psychological help or to aid in sociological manipulation.

Liberalism as a System

Liberalism in theology is one unified system. In a most basic sense, it did not change with the birth of existential theology. The new existential theology is no closer to historic, biblical Christianity than is the old liberalism. It is really farther away. At least the old liberalism affirmed the concept of truth and spoke in antithesis.

Having come this far in our study of the new liberalism, it is obvious that it should be judged more completely than on some peripheral point which it produces in the area of morals or doctrine. It should not be judged, for example, because its universalism weakens evangelism, but because as a total unity it is wrong. Unless we see the new liberalism as a whole and reject it as a whole, we will, to the extent that we are tolerant of it, be confused in our thinking, involved in the general intellectual irrationalism of our day and compromising in our actions.

The new theology is simply modern thought using religious words. It is under the line of anthropology,[8] dwelling only in the world of men. It is faced with "a philosophic other" that is unknown and unknowable. The new theology is in the circle of the finite, and it has no meaning and no authority beyond the authority and the meaning which finite men can give it.

In other words, not having any propositional, verbalized communication from God to man, in all forms of liberal theology, old and new, man is on his own with only religious words rather than religious truth. Historic Christianity has nothing in common with either the old or the new secular rationalism, and it has nothing in common with either the old or the new liberal theology. Historic Christianity and either the old or the new liberal theology are two separate religions with nothing in common except certain terms which they use with totally different meanings.

CHAPTER TWO

Adultery and Apostasy— The Bride and Bridegroom Theme[1]

This study is one that I consider exceedingly important for our own generation: "Adultery and Apostasy—The Bride and Bridegroom Theme." Ephesians 5:25b-32 reads: "Christ also loved the church, and gave himself for it, that he might sanctify and cleanse it with the washing of water by the word; that he might present it to himself a glorious church, not having spot, or wrinkle, or any such thing; but that it should be holy and without blemish. So ought men to love their wives as their own bodies. He that loveth his wife loveth himself. For no man ever yet hated his own flesh, but nourisheth and cherisheth it, even as the Lord the church; for we are members of his body, of his flesh, and of his bones. For this cause shall a man leave his father and mother, and shall be joined unto his wife, and they two shall be one flesh. This is a great mystery, but I speak concerning Christ and the church."

You have here a very remarkable and very strong statement which Christ makes concerning the church as His bride. Notice, however, how God very carefully here intertwines this with the marriage relationship. The two ideas are so fused together that it is almost impossible in an exegetical study to divide them even, as it were, with an instrument as sharp as a surgeon's scalpel. Thus you have in Ephesians 5:21-25: "Submitting yourselves one to another in the fear of God. Wives, submit yourselves unto your own husbands, as unto the Lord. For the husband is the head of the wife, even as Christ is the head of the church; and he is the savior of the body. Therefore, as the church is subject unto Christ, so let the wives be to their own husbands in everything. Husbands, love your wives, even as Christ also loved the church, and gave himself for it." And verse 33: "Nevertheless, let every one of you in particular so love his wife even as himself; and the wife, see that she reverence her husband."

So there is here a very strong intertwining of teaching about the two relationships: the man-woman relationship and the Christ-Christian relationship with the Christ-church relationship.

When you examine the New Testament, you find that the brideship is thought of in two ways. In some places the emphasis is upon the fact that each Christian is, individually, the bride of Christ, and in other places it is the church as a unity that is the bride of Christ. But there is no contradiction in this; there is merely unity in the midst of diversity. The church is collectively the bride of Christ, and it is made up of individual Christians, each one of whom is the bride of Christ.

Paul says (verse 32) that he is speaking of a great mystery. What a tremendous mystery!—the fact that Christ, the eternal second person of the Trinity, has become the divine Bridegroom.

The Biblical Norm
Notice that this passage in Ephesians does not stand alone. In many places in the New Testament this same sort of illustration is used intertwiningly. In John 3:28, 29, we find John the Baptizer introducing Christ under these terms: "Ye yourselves bear me witness, that I said, I am not the Christ, but that I am sent before him. He (that is, the Christ) that hath the bride is the bridegroom." In John's introduction of Christ to the Jewish people, we find that he says: Here is the Lamb of God; and, next, here is the one who is going to be baptized by the Holy Spirit and who is going to baptize by the Holy Spirit; and also here is the Bridegroom of the bride.

Romans 7:4 contains a very striking, almost overwhelming use of this teaching: "Wherefore, my brethren, ye also are become dead to the law by the body of Christ" (and then comes a double "in order that") "*in order that* ye should be married to another, even to him who is raised from the dead." So we are dead to the law in order that we should be married to Christ. But that is not the end of it: ". . . *in order that* we should bring forth fruit unto God." The picture here is overwhelming. As the bride puts herself in the bridegroom's arms on the wedding day and then daily, and as therefore children are born, so the individual Christian is to put himself or herself in the Bridegroom's arms, not only once for all in justification, but existentially, moment by moment. Then the Christian will bear Christ's fruit out into the fallen, revolted, external world. In this relationship we are all female. This is the biblical picture, one that we would not dare use if God Himself did not use it.

The Old Testament, like the New, emphasizes the bride and the Bridegroom aspect. In the Old Testament it is God and His people; God is the husband of His people. See Jeremiah 3:14—"Turn, O backsliding children, saith the Lord; for I am married unto you." And, of course, there is no basic difference. The church continues. The church is new at Pentecost in one sense; yet in another sense it existed from the first man who was redeemed on the basis of Christ's coming work.

We have in 2 Corinthians 11:1, 2, "Would to God ye could bear with me a little in my folly; and, indeed, bear with me. For I am jealous over you with godly jealousy; for I have espoused (engaged) you to one husband that I may present you as a chaste virgin to Christ." And in the great culmination of Revelation 19:6-9 we have the picture of the church at the end of this present era—when Christ has returned. And what is the great event? It is nothing less than the marriage supper of the Lamb: "And I heard, as it were, the voice of a great multitude, and like the voice of many waters, and like the voice of mighty thunderings, saying, Alleluia! For the Lord God omnipotent reigneth. Let us be glad and rejoice, and give honor to him; for the marriage of the Lamb is come, and his wife hath made herself ready. And to her was granted that she should be arrayed in fine linen, clean and white; for the fine linen is the righteousness of saints. And he saith unto me, Write, Blessed are they who are called unto the marriage supper of the Lamb. And he saith unto me, These are the true sayings of God."

This theme, which is seen throughout the Old and New Testaments, culminates in this last great Lord's Supper where Christ Himself will serve His people. And there need be no hurry and there need be no rush, with millions and millions being served from the hands of the risen Lord. And they, being risen physically from the dead, will partake with their resurrected bodies. We look forward to this as we repeat the words of 1 Corinthians 11:26 each time in the Communion service: "For as often as ye eat this bread, and drink this cup, ye do show the Lord's death till he come."

Thus we find that the man-woman relationship of marriage is stressed throughout the Scriptures as a picture, an illustration, a type, of the wonder of the relationship of the individual and Christ and the church and Christ. What a contrast this is to the Eastern thinking. When, for example, Shiva came out of his ice-filled cave in the Himalayas and saw a mortal woman and loved her, he put his arms around her, she disappeared, and he became neuter. There is nothing like this in the Scriptures. When we accept Christ as our Savior, we do not lose our personality. For all eternity our personality stands in oneness with Christ.

Just as there is a real oneness between the human bride and bridegroom who really love each other, and yet the two personalities are not confused, so in our oneness with Christ, Christ remains Christ and the bride remains the bride. This great understanding of the way Scripture parallels the human man-woman relationship and our union with Christ guides our thinking in two directions. First, it makes us understand the greatness and the wonder and the beauty of marriage. And, second, it helps us to understand profoundly something of the relationship between God and His people and between Christ and His church. We understand in a real way something of this relationship as we understand in a real way something of the marriage relationship.

My personal opinion is that the marriage relationship is not just an illustration, but rather that in all things—including the marriage relationship—God's external creation speaks of Himself. We properly reject pantheism, but the orthodox man is in danger of forgetting that God has created the objective world—all the parts of His external creation—so that it speaks of Himself. The external, objective universe does speak of Him. While God is not the world, the world is created by God and speaks about God.

The Bible and Sexual Adultery

In our generation, people are asking why promiscuous sexual relationships are wrong. I would say that there are three reasons.

(There may well be more, but in this study I want to draw attention to these three.) The first one, of course, is simply because God says so. God is the Creator and the Judge of the universe; His character is the law of the universe, and when He tells us a thing is wrong, it *is* wrong—if we are going to have a God of the kind the Scripture portrays.

Second, however, we must never forget that God has made us in our relationships to really fulfill that which He made us to be, and therefore, too, a right sexual relationship is for our good as we are made. It is not to our real fulfillment to have promiscuous or homosexual relationships. This is not what God has made us for. Promiscuity tries to force something into a form which God never made it for, and in which it cannot be fulfilled.

The third is the reason we are dealing with most fully in this study: promiscuous sexual relationships are wrong because they destroy the picture of what God means marriage, the relationship of man and woman, to be. Marriage is set forth to be the illustration of the relationship of God and His people, and of Christ and His church. It rests upon God's character, and God is eternally faithful to His people. And we who are Christians should live every day of our lives in glad recognition of the faithfulness of God to His people, a faithfulness resting upon His character and upon His covenants, His promises. The relationship of God with His people rests upon His character and His promises, and sexual relationship outside of marriage breaks this parallel which the Bible draws between marriage and the relationship of God with His people.

Thus if we break God's illustration by such a relationship, it is a serious thing. Both in the Old and New Testaments the Bible speaks out strongly against all sexual promiscuity—all sexual practice outside of marriage. Scripture does not deal with it lightly. Along with all other forms of wrong sexual relationships, the Bible condemns adultery. (*Adultery* means the sexual unfaithfulness of a person who is married.) The Bible never allows us to tone down the seriousness of adultery.

In Matthew 5:32, for example, Jesus says, "But I say unto you that whosoever shall put away his wife, saving for the cause of fornication, causeth her to commit adultery; and whosoever shall marry her that is divorced committeth adultery." In the Jewish setting engagement was tantamount to marriage, and all forms of unfaithfulness are included here. What He is saying here is that unfaithfulness is so great a sin that the other person has a proper right to end the marriage and remarry upon the basis of adultery.

Then, of course, in the law in Exodus 20:14, one of the Ten Commandments says: "Thou shalt not commit adultery." The Old Testament was not only the religious book of the Jews, but also their book of basic civil law, and as such was related to the commands of God in the theocracy. In Leviticus 20:10 as well, God does not allow us to think that adultery is a small thing: "And the man who committeth adultery with another man's wife, even he who committeth adultery with his neighbor's wife, the adulterer and the adulteress shall surely be put to death." Furthermore, Deuteronomy 22:22 reads: "If a man be found lying with a woman married to an husband (later there are other directions for the punishment of sexual intercourse with an unmarried woman), then they shall both of them die, both the man that lay with the woman, and the woman. So shalt thou put away evil from Israel."

The book of Proverbs over and over again warns against adultery and its serious consequences. In the book of Jeremiah God continues to speak concerning this. Look at the first part of verses 10 and 11 of Jeremiah 23: "For the land is full of adulterers," and then, "For both prophet and priest are profane." The prophet and the priest are not free from adultery any more than the people are free from adultery. Jeremiah emphasizes the fact that indeed there is a great tragedy here; the people of God are given to adultery.

The book of Jeremiah came at a crucial time in Jewish history, a time, we learn from Jeremiah 5:7, 8, when they had an affluent economy. They were in a time of materialistic well-being, and at the same time they were under the judgment of God: "How shall I pardon thee for this? Thy children have forsaken me, and sworn by them that are no gods; when I had fed them to the full (here is the affluent society), they then committed adultery, and assembled themselves by troops in the harlots' houses. They were like fed horses in the morning; every one neighed after his neighbor's wife." So they are fed, they are filled with affluence, their stomachs are full of food, they have time on their hands. In this situation, what do they turn to? They are like the horse that, well fed, stands and neighs on one side of the stall. God uses overwhelmingly strong terms in discussing adultery.

The New Testament reveals exactly the same attitude. For example, in Galatians 5:19: "Now the works of the flesh are manifest, which are these: adultery, fornication, uncleanness, lasciviousness, idolatry, witchcraft (etc.).'' This is not to say that sexual sin is worse than any other sin. Such a concept of sin is completely warped and twisted. If you compare this list of sins with others in the New Testament, you will notice that sexual sin is not always, by any means, named first. The Holy Spirit very carefully breaks up the listing of the sins in the New Testament, thus indicating that, except for the great sin of turning from God, you must not put one sin above the other. Other sins are also sins, and so the lists sometimes mention them in one order, sometimes in another. But that is a different thing from forgetting that God very strongly condemns sexual sin. All sin is equally sin. Nevertheless, while this is true, God never allows us to tone down the condemnation of sexual sin. Sexual sin shatters the illustration of God and His people, of Christ and His church.

The Bride of Christ and Spiritual Adultery

But there is another level in our understanding of adultery. In 2 Corinthians 11:1, 2, which we have looked at before, we read: "Would to God ye could bear with me a little in my folly; and, indeed, bear with me. For I am jealous over you with godly jealousy; for I have espoused you to one husband, that I may present you as a chaste virgin to Christ." Here is the first step: men have become Christians and thus are the bride of Christ. Then Paul adds this in verse 3: "But I fear, lest by any means, as the serpent beguiled Eve through his subtility, so your minds should be corrupted from the simplicity that is in Christ." Here is the second step: the bride of Christ can be led away and can become less than the bride should be. As there can be physical adultery, so too there can be unfaithfulness to the divine Bridegroom—spiritual adultery.

No one is perfect. None of us is totally faithful to our divine Bridegroom. We are all weak. Many times we are unfaithful in a positive or a negative way in our thoughts or our actions. But the Scripture makes a clear distinction between the imperfection of all Christians and the spiritual adultery which results when those who claim to be God's people stop listening to what God has said and turn to other gods. As far as the Bible is concerned, the latter is apostasy.

The Bible takes the great and tremendous sin of adultery and shows us how important it is. And then it takes apostasy (turning away from God), calls it spiritual adultery (turning away from the divine Bridegroom), and says, This is even more important! But isn't that to be expected? If the Bible speaks out against breaking the illustration, shattering the symbol, how much more should we expect it to condemn the violation of the reality of which marriage is the symbol.

There is a stigma in the use of the term *adultery*, even in the world in the second half of the twentieth century. Even if there has been open and blatant adultery between a husband and wife, when they go to the law for a divorce, often the word is avoided and called something else, nice names; and in many states there is "no fault" divorce, so that adultery never can be named. The world still finds the term *adultery* to be something which it does not like, at which it winces. And it is the same with *apostasy*. Men like to tone down on these terms. They like to speak of these things in polite language. But God does not. The world still winces at the term *adultery*, even in the post-Christian second half of the twentieth century; but this is the term which God takes and applies as a strong phrase, like a knife, crying out to His people. We find He uses the term *adultery*, and parallel terms, over and over again, in regard to the people of God turning away from Himself.

In Exodus 34:12-15 he says: "Take heed to thyself, lest thou make a covenant with the inhabitants of the land where thou goest, lest it be for a snare in the midst of thee: But ye shall destroy their altars, break their images, and cut down their groves. For thou shalt worship no other god; for the LORD, whose name is Jealous, is a jealous God; lest thou make a covenant with the inhabitants of the land, and they go a whoring after their gods, and do sacrifice unto their gods, and one call thee, and thou eat of his sacrifice." When the people of God turned aside to these gods, the false gods round about, what does God call it? He says, Do you not understand what you are doing? You are going whoring, you are caught in the midst of a spiritual adultery.

Leviticus 20:5, 6 also uses the strongest terms: "Then I will set my face against that man, and against his family, and will cut him off, and all that go a whoring after him to commit whoredom with Molech (a false god I will be discussing later), from among their people." Notice here that God uses the same expression. For God's people to turn from God is spiritual adultery. Judges 2:17 says: "And yet they would not hearken unto their judges, but they went a whoring after other gods, and bowed themselves unto them." The term "bowed themselves unto them" is a sexual term used of a wife giving herself to her husband. And here God uses it with all this force when He says: Do you not see that you have acted like an adulterous woman bowing down in the sexual position before another man? In the book of Psalms (73:27) we read again: "For, lo, they that are far from thee shall perish; thou hast destroyed all them that go a whoring from thee."

Isaiah 1:21 says, "How is the faithful city become a harlot!" Who is this? This is Jerusalem, Jerusalem the golden. This is Jerusalem the city of God, Zion. What has she become? A prostitite. Why? Because she has turned from her rightful husband and become a streetwalker with false gods. And consider Jeremiah 3:1: "They say, If a man put away his wife, and she go from him, and become another man's, shall he return unto her again? Shall not that land be greatly polluted? But thou hast played the harlot with many lovers; yet return again to me, saith the Lord." God is saying, My faithfulness goes right on, though what you are doing is wounding Me. In regard to this passage, remember that the New Testament says the same thing; we can make the Holy Spirit sad (Eph. 4:30). He is a Person, and when we turn away from Him and teach and do those things which are contrary to the character of God as revealed in Scripture, we wound the Holy Spirit. He is sad. And the Old Testament says that when the people of God turn away from God, it is not nothing to God; it saddens the husband, who is God.

The sixth verse of the same chapter continues: "The Lord said also unto me in the days of Josiah, the king, Hast thou seen that which backsliding Israel hath done? She is gone up upon every high mountain and under every green tree, and there hath played the harlot." Here is a picture of the hills, of the trees, of the places where they worship. And Jeremiah says, These have become your lovers. The ninth verse says: "And it came to pass through the lightness of her whoredom, that she defiled the land, and committed adultery with stones and with stocks." He says, This is what you are worshiping instead of the living God. How does God describe it? He pictures it as a perverse adultery with these objects.

In Ezekiel 6:9 God is speaking, not Ezekiel. "I am broken with their whorish heart." God is saying about His people who have turned away into apostasy, "I am broken with their whorish heart, which hath departed from me, and with their eyes, which go a whoring after their idols." Notice how God is concerned about His people. This is not a neutral thing, a matter of indifference, to God. *God* is not just a theological term; he is not a "philosophical other." He is a personal God, and we should glory in the fact that He is a personal God. But we must understand that since He is a personal God, He can be grieved. When His people turn away from Him, there is sadness indeed on the part of the omnipotent God.

Ezekiel 16:30-32 pounds on: "How weak is thine heart, saith the Lord God, seeing thou doest all these things, the work of an imperious whorish woman, in that thou buildest thine eminent place in the head of every way (this reference is to a brothel; God is saying, your idols built on every street corner are like a brothel), and makest thine high place in every street; and hast not been as an harlot, in that thou scornest hire, but like a wife that committeth adultery, who taketh strangers instead of her husband!" This is pursued further in Ezekiel 23, where the whole chapter is given over to this concept. God says, There are two cities, Jerusalem in the south and Samaria in the north, and they have both committed spiritual adultery; he describes it there in the strongest terms.

Let us move on to Hosea 4:12: "My people ask counsel of their stocks, and their staff declareth unto them; for the spirit of whoredoms hath caused them to err, and they have gone a whoring from under their God." Notice the last expression again, where the sexual picture is used so vividly by God. He says, This is what you have done; you have moved out and you have taken this position under another god, a god that is no god—a god that is nonsense, nothing more than a stick, nothing more than your own staff. You commit spiritual adultery with these things; this is who you are and what you are and where you are.

Notice also Hosea 4:13: "They sacrifice upon the tops of the mountains, and burn incense upon the hills, under oaks and poplars and elms, because the shadow of them is good; therefore your daughters shall commit whoredom, and your spouses shall commit adultery." This points to another whole stream of biblical teaching that I will not discuss here except in connection with this one verse: the Old Testament says that if God's people turn away in spiritual adultery, it will not be long until the following generations are engaged in physical adultery, for the two things go hand in hand. And if any generation proves this, it's our generation. John Updike was right in his book *The Couples*. The whole novel is an illustration of the last pages in which the church is burned down. In reality, however, the church was "burned down" before the book began, and there was nothing left for Piet, the main character, except his promiscuous sexual life.

Our generation proves this with overflowing force. Let there be spiritual adultery, and it will not be long until physical adultery sprouts like toadstools in the land. In the 1930s liberalism took over many of the denominations in the United States, and in the 1980s our generation is sick with promiscuous sex and twisted sex. It is the same in Britain and other countries. These things are not unrelated. They are cause and effect.

Again in Hosea 9:1 we read: "Rejoice not, O Israel, for joy, like other peoples; for thou hast gone a whoring from thy God, thou hast loved a reward upon every cornfloor." Here again in Hosea 9, apostasy is spiritual adultery. Notice the form of speech God uses. A woman is out harvesting, and there is a freedom in the midst of the harvest. She takes a gift of money from some man to sleep with him on the cornfloor in the midst of the harvesting. This is what those who had been God's people had become; the wife of the living God is this in her apostasy.

You may say now, have we not read enough of these verses? We have not read the half of what you will find as you go through the Scriptures. God says, I do not want you to forget; I do not look upon spiritual adultery lightly.

I have deliberately chosen examples from all parts of the Old Testament—sections from the law, from different places in the historic books, from the books of poetry, and from the prophets. The whole of the Old Testament speaks in the same terms and carries the same force, the same thrust, as it proceeds.

You may say, Is this not just an Old Testament view? The answer is, No; it is the way the New Testament speaks as well. Revelation 17:1-5 reads:

> And there came one of the seven angels who had the seven vials, and talked with me, saying unto me, Come hither; I will show unto thee the judgment of the great whore that sitteth upon many waters; with whom the kings of the earth have committed fornication, and the inhabitants of the earth have been made drunk with the wine of her fornication. So he carried me away in the Spirit into the wilderness and I saw a woman sit upon a scarlet-colored beast, full of names of blasphemy, having seven heads and ten horns. And the woman was arrayed in purple and scarlet color, and decked with gold and precious stones and pearls, having a golden cup in her hand, full of abominations and filthiness of her fornication; and upon her forehead was a

name written, MYSTERY, BABYLON THE GREAT, THE
MOTHER OF HARLOTS AND ABOMINATIONS OF THE
EARTH.

This language is definitely not in the Old Testament alone. It is
brought to its highest pitch in the New Testament when the apostate church of the last days, and the culture it produces, is described in these terms.

Spiritual Adultery Today
Now let us notice where we have come. When those who claim to
be God's people turn aside from the Word of God and from the
Christ of history, this is far more heinous in the sight of God than
the worst case of infidelity in marriage, for it destroys the reality,
the great central Bridegroom-bride relationship. I have taken care
to emphasize that God does not minimize promiscuity in sexual
relationships, but apostasy—spiritual adultery—is worse. And the
modern liberal theologian is in that place. How do we look at it? I
would suggest we must be careful to look at it no less clearly than
God does. Consider the liberal theology of our day. It denies the
personal *God who is there*. It denies the divine, historic Christ. It
denies the Bible as God's verbalized Word. It denies God's way of
salvation. The liberals elevate their own humanistic theories to a
position above the Word of God, the revealed communication of
God to men. They make gods which are no gods, but are merely
the projection of their own minds.

As we describe their theories, we tend to dress them up in polite
terms, in fine clothes, carefully weaving these clothes so as not to
offend. We dress up our attitudes and statements in fine words in
regard to "the progressive theology" in the Roman Catholic
Church. But it is not progressive theology; it is regressive theology, a humanism being spoken in classical Roman Catholic terms.
In Protestantism, we call it *liberalism,* which is a strange word to
apply to it, for it is only humanism in classical Protestant terms.

Of course, we must treat men as human beings while having
discourse with them, and that very much includes the liberal
theologians. We must treat them as made in the image of God,
even if they are actively in rebellion against God, and we must let
them know that we love them as individuals. But this does not
mean that we should forget that apostasy must be named as apostasy. Apostasy must be called what it is—a spiritual adultery. We
must have politeness and struggle for human relationships with

the liberal theologians with whom we discuss. But as to the system they teach, there is to be no toning down concerning what it is. As I said, in our generation we tend to tone down the word *adultery* in divorce cases, for we do not much like the word. Far more in the religious realm we tone down the terms *spiritual adultery* and *apostasy*. But in doing this we are grievously wrong, because the Bible's perspective should be our own, and this is the way God speaks of it and looks upon it, and so this is the way God's people are called to look upon it.

This spiritual adultery is worse, much worse, than physical adultery. But it is also much worse, let me say, than the Jews following their idols. Oh, how God spoke out against the Jews following their idols! What strong figures of speech He used in love in order to bring them to their senses. But modern liberal theology is worse than this, for it turns against greater light, against greater blessing. Modern liberal theology is worse than following the Molech of old.

Do you know the facts concerning Molech? Molech, whose idol was in the valley of Hinnom, was a heathen god whom the Jews were constantly warned against following. What kind of a god was Molech? He was the god of the sacrifice of newborn babies. This was the central act of his worship; the firstborn of every woman's body had to be sacrificed to Molech. According to one tradition, there was an opening at the back of the brazen idol, and after a fire was made within it, each parent had to come and with his own hands place his firstborn child in the white-hot, outstretched hands of Molech. According to this tradition, the parent was not allowed to show emotion, and drums were beaten so that the baby's cries could not be heard as the baby died in the hands of Molech. And there, I would say, stand many in our day. Many of those who come to me, those with whom I work, are the children destroyed by a worse than Molech. Men—men who were supposedly the men of God—have stood by while their children were eaten up by modern theology. And then we are told that there is supposed to be no emotion shown.

Some of you who read this bear yourselves the marks of these things from the background from which you come. All of us are marked by this in some way, to some extent, because our Western, post-Christian world has been undercut by this liberal theology. Every scar this present generation has, every tear cried, every baby which some of you who read this have willfully aborted, every drug trip you have taken cannot be separated from the fact that the church has turned away and become unfaithful. This generation are the babies in the hands of Molech. And are we, as mere dilettantes, supposed to stand by and hear their cries and cover them up by beating loudly the drums of a profitless discussion? I tell you, No. We are to weep and to act.

What is the liberal theology like? It can only be paralleled with what God says in Proverbs 30:20 about the adulterous woman: "Such is the way of an adulterous woman; she eateth, and wipeth her mouth, and saith, I have done no wickedness." What a picture! Not everyone whose theology has been somewhat infiltrated by liberal theology should be likened to this, but the real liberal theologian (whether the old liberal-type theologian or the newer existential theologian) stands in this place. They say they have done no evil by their spiritual adultery, while not only the church but the whole post-Christian culture shows the results of their unfaithfulness.

There is no adulterous woman who has ever been so soiled as the liberal theology, which has had all the gifts of God and has turned away to a worship of something that is as destructive as Molech was to the babies whose parents were led astray from the living God to worship this idol. We must show love to the man with whom we discuss. Yes, and we fight for this at L'Abri. We must fight for the fact that he is not to be treated as less than a man. Nothing is more ugly than the orthodox man treating another man as less than a man and failing to show that he takes seriously Christ's teaching that all men are our neighbors. We do not discuss with the liberal only to win, but to help others, and to try to help him as well. But to treat lightly what liberal theology has done—not for a moment.

God's Word for Our Generation

What does God say to our generation? Exactly the same thing that He said to Israel 2,500 years ago when He said through Ezekiel: "I am broken with their whorish heart, which hath departed from me, and with their eyes, which go a whoring after their idols." I believe that this is how God looks at much of the modern church, and on our Western culture. I believe that this is how He looks on much of our cinema, much of our drama, much within our art museums. And above everything else, this is the way He looks into the churches in which a gospel that is no gospel is being preached. God is saddened. Should *we* not be moved?

He is the same God; He is the living God, He is the unchanging God. He is the God who is there. And will He not do in the midst of this situation what He did in the midst of the Jewish situation in the time of Isaiah in the Northern Kingdom, and in the time of Jeremiah and Ezekiel and Daniel in the Southern Kingdom? Will He not judge our culture? Will He not call it adulterous? I tell you in the name of God He will judge our culture unless there is a return to a Christian base for the culture—and that begins with true repentance and renewal in the church.

Now what should be our response? Listen to Jeremiah speak in 13:27—"Woe unto thee, O Jerusalem!" Indeed, as redeemed people we should know the joy of Christ, but as we look around us in much of the church and in our culture, can we fail to cry tears? Must we not also have this message? "Woe unto thee, O Jerusalem!" For like Jerusalem, much of the church has turned apostate. Within two or three generations in our northern European countries, we have turned aside. In Germany over a longer period, but in most of our countries so quickly have we turned aside: "Woe unto you, O Jerusalem! Woe to you, O liberal church! Woe to you, O apostate Christendom!" We must say these words while we cry for the individual and while we never fail to treat him as a human being. We must not speak more lightly than Jeremiah. We must not be any less moved. Our response must not be merely a theoretical discussion of an intellectual nature. It must be the cry, "Woe, O liberal church! Woe, O apostate Christendom!"

It is not just a question of abstract theology that is involved, not just an academic difference. It is not that I should get my Ph.D. and go off and sit in some faculty and merely make polite academic conversation. It is the difference between loyalty to the living God and spiritual adultery—spiritual adultery against the Creator and the Judge of the universe. Spiritual adultery, mind you, against the only adequate Bridegroom for man—individual man and mankind—the only adequate Bridegroom for all people in all the world. Spiritual adultery against the only One who can fulfill the longing of the human heart. To turn away from the divine Bridegroom is to turn to unfulfillment. This is not only sin; it is destruction.

We have seen how desperately wrong and sinful physical adultery is, but notice that Jesus gives a priority. In Matthew 21:31 Jesus says to the religious leaders of His day: "Verily I say unto you that the publicans and the harlots go into the kingdom of God before you." It is not that Jesus minimized the sexual sin, but here

He tells the religious leaders of His day, who have turned away from God, that the harlots and those who collect taxes for the Romans will go into the kingdom of God before them. As these men walk through the streets and see such a woman walking down the way, they will not speak to her. They will not even look at her. They turn away from her. They show their disgust publicly. But Jesus is saying, Look at her! Don't you understand? She will get into the kingdom of God before you ever will. Both are sinful. But God Himself in the words of Christ puts down a priority. Sexual sin is sinful, but spiritual adultery is worse. God Himself puts down a hierarchy in these things.

What is apostasy? It is spiritual adultery. No other words will do. This must be taken into account as we consider *the practice of truth*. Do not be only academic when you speak concerning the new Molech. You yourself have the burn marks of the new Molech. Everyone in our culture—especially the university generation and younger—has them. Nobody escapes, even if he was raised in a Christian home and has been a Christian from the time he was young. There is not one of us in our culture who does not have some burn marks from the new Molech upon his skin—not one.

God's Word for Us
But for ourselves, we who by God's grace belong to the people of God, we who are Christ's, we who are God's, we who have been redeemed on the basis of the blood of the Lamb—let us understand that we are now called, on the basis of this study, to take one more most crucial step. We are *to act* as that which we are. Who are we? We are not just those going to Heaven. We are even now the wife of God. We are at this moment the bride of Christ. And what does our divine Bridegroom want from us? He wants from us not only doctrinal faithfulness, but our love day by day. Such a study as this should not be ended by merely looking with clear perspective upon those who are unfaithful.

I must ask myself, "But what about you, Schaeffer?" And what about you, each one of you who knows the grace of God? What should be our attitude? Our attention must swing back now to ourselves. We have a crucial question to ask about ourselves.

We must ask, "Do I fight merely for doctrinal faithfulness?" This is like the wife who never sleeps with anybody else, but never shows love to her own husband. Is that a sufficient relationship in marriage? No, 10,000 times no. Yet if I am a Christian who speaks and acts for doctrinal faithfulness but do not show love to my divine Bridegroom, I am in the same place as such a wife. What God wants from us is not only doctrinal faithfulness, but our love day by day. Not in theory, mind you, but in practice.

For those of us who are the children of God, there can only be one end to this study concerning adultery and apostasy. We must realize the seriousness of modern apostasy; we must urge each other not to have any part in modern apostasy. But at the same time we must realize that we must love our Savior and Lord. We must be the loving, true bride of the divine Bridegroom in reality and in practice, day by day, in the midst of the unfaithfulness of our day. Our call is first to be the bride faithful, but that is not the total call. The call is not only to be the bride faithful, but to be the bride in love.

CHAPTER THREE

Practicing Purity in the Visible Church

Born-again Christians, whatever their background—Reformed, Lutheran, Baptist, Brethren, Congregational, Anglican or whatever their distinctives—have certain basic things in common. One of these is this task: to exhibit simultaneously the holiness of God and the love of God.

In *The Mark of the Christian* I expressed and developed this thought in a slightly different way. There I spoke of the need for the *simultaneous* practice of two biblical principles. The first is the principle of the practice of purity of the visible church (not the invisible church we join when by God's grace we cast ourselves upon Christ, but the visible church). The Scriptures teach that we must *practice,* not just *talk* about, the purity of the visible church. The second is the principle of an observable love and oneness among all *true* Christians. *The Mark of the Christian* stresses from John 13:34, 35 that according to Jesus Himself, the world has the right to decide whether we are true Christians, true disciples of Christ, on the basis of the love we show to all true Christians. John 17:21 provides something even more sobering in that Jesus gives the world the right to judge whether the Father has sent the Son on the basis of whether the world sees observable love among all true Christians.

In *The Church at the End of the 20th Century,* I emphasize another related parallelism: the call of God to practice simultaneously the orthodoxy of doctrine and the orthodoxy of community in the visible church. The latter of these we have too often all but forgotten. But one cannot explain the explosive dynamite, the *dunamis,* of the early church apart from the fact that they practiced two things simultaneously: orthodoxy of doctrine and orthodoxy of community in the midst of the visible church, a community which the world could see. By the grace of God, therefore, the church must be known simultaneously for its purity of doctrine and the reality of its community. Our churches have so often been only preaching points with very little emphasis on community. But exhibition of the love of God in practice is beautiful and must be there.

We have, then, two sets of parallel couplets: (1) the principle of the practice of the purity of the visible church, and yet the practice of observable love among all true Christians; and (2) the practice of orthodoxy of doctrine and observable orthodoxy of community in the visible church.

The heart of these sets of principles is to show forth the love of God and the holiness of God *simultaneously.* If we show either of these without the other, we exhibit not the character, but a caricature of God for the world to see. If we stress the love of God without the holiness of God, it turns out only to be compromise. But if we stress the holiness of God without the love of God, we practice something that is hard and lacks beauty. And it is important to show forth beauty before a lost world and a lost generation. All too often people have not been wrong in saying that the church is ugly. In the name of our Lord Jesus Christ, we are called upon to show to a watching world and to our own young people that the church is something beautiful.

Several years ago I wrestled with the question of what was wrong with much of the church that stood for purity. I came to the conclusion that in the flesh we can stress purity without love or we can stress the love of God without purity, but that in the flesh we cannot stress both simultaneously. In order to exhibit both simultaneously, we must look moment by moment to the work of Christ, to the work of the Holy Spirit. Spirituality begins to have real meaning in our moment-by-moment lives as we begin to exhibit simultaneously the holiness of God and the love of God.[1]

Let us consider, then, the exhibition of the holiness of God in relationship to the purity of the visible church. To do this, I want to go back into history. I will use the United States, first because it is my own country, and second because in the United States the whole course of events has occurred in a much shorter period than in most other countries and therefore can be seen and comprehended easily, though most countries have gone and are going through parallel situations. I come from the Presbyterian tradition. I will go back into the Presbyterian history of the 1930s and beg those of other backgrounds to learn from our mistakes.

In the 1930s, most large denominations in the United States came under the control of liberalism. The Presbyterian Church in the U.S.A. (now called the United Presbyterian Church) is one of the clearest cases of all because it was a very strong doctrinal church, and thus the shift can be clearly observed. I do not mean that everyone in the Presbyterian Church (or in these other denominations) became liberal; certainly not every pastor became liberal, but the denomination as a denomination definitely came under the control of those who held to liberal theology.

Let us go back first of all to 1924, one year after the Auburn Affirmation was signed. In the Presbyterian Church the Auburn Affirmation was the liberals' public declaration of war upon the historic Christian faith. It threw down the gauntlet. The conservatives of the church decided that the way to meet this challenge was to elect a moderator of the General Assembly who would clearly be Bible-believing. As a result, 1924 saw elected as the moderator of the Northern Presbyterian Church an orthodox, Bible-believing man, Dr. Clarence Edward McCartney. The conservatives were jubilant. The secular newspapers carried the story of the conservative victory, and the conservatives rejoiced. But while all the rejoicing was going on, the liberals consolidated their power in the church bureaucracy. And because they were allowed to do so, the election of the conservative moderator proved to mean nothing. By 1936 the liberals were so in control that they were able to defrock Dr. J. Gresham Machen, putting him out of the ministry.[2]

It seems to me that by the end of the 1930s almost all the major Protestant denominations in the United States came under the control of those holding liberal theological views, and that now in the 1970s and 1980s those denominations not dominated by liberal theology in the 1930s are in the same place of decision as the others were in the 1930s. It is to be noted that the Roman Catholic

Church now also has many in the hierarchy, many theologians and teachers, called the progressives, who are existential theologians who believe and teach the same things as the existential theologians in the Protestant churches do, but using traditional Roman Catholic, rather than Protestant, terms.

Two of the Protestant denominations in the United States now in the place of decision, interestingly enough, have recently tried to protect themselves, as did the Northern Presbyterian Church, by electing a conservative executive officer. But I would urge the true Christians today in these denominations to learn from the mistakes of the Presbyterian Church. Do not think that merely because a Bible-believing man is elected as an executive officer or is appointed to an important position, that this will give safety to a denomination. If the two power centers in modern denominations, the bureaucracy and the seminaries, remain in the control of the liberals, nothing will be permanently changed. There must be a loving but definite *practice* of the purity of the visible church in any denomination if it is really to dwell in safety. The holiness of God must be exhibited in ecclesiastical affairs. We must practice truth, not just speak about it.

It must be understood that the new humanism and the new theology have no concept of true truth. Relativism has triumphed in the church as well as in the university and in society. The true Christian, however, is called upon not only to teach truth but to practice truth in the midst of such relativism. And if we are ever to practice truth, it certainly must be in a day such as ours.

This means, among other things, that, after we have done all we can on a personal level, if they persist in their liberalism, the liberals in the church should come under discipline. For, as I pointed out in the preceding chapter, the church must remain the faithful bride of Christ. And, as I explained in detail in the first chapter, the liberals are not faithful to the God of the Bible, the God who is there. Historic Christianity, biblical Christianity, believes that Christianity is not just doctrinal truth, but flaming truth, true to what is there, true to the great final environment, the infinite-personal God. Liberalism, on the other hand, is unfaithfulness, spiritual adultery toward the divine Bridegroom. We are involved, therefore, in a matter of loyalty, loyalty not only to the creeds, but to the Scripture and beyond that to the divine Bridegroom—the infinite-personal divine Bridegroom who is there in an absolute antithesis to His not being there.

We not only believe in the existence of truth, but we believe we have the truth—a truth that has content and can be verbalized (and *then* can be lived)—a truth we can share with the twentieth-century world. Do you think our contemporaries will take us seriously if we do not practice truth? Do you think for a moment that the really serious-minded twentieth-century young people—our own youth as they go off to universities, who are taught in the fields of sociology, psychology, philosophy, etc., that all is relative—will take us seriously? In an age that does not believe that truth exists, do you really believe they will take seriously that their fathers are speaking truth and believe in truth? Will their fathers have credibility, if they do not practice antithesis in religious matters?

It is therefore necessary for the true Christians in the church to oppose McLuhanesque "cool" communication employed by the liberal theologians with the "hot" communication of theological and biblical content.[3] It is only thus that we can practice the exhibition of the holiness of God.

We believe in the hot communication of content, and as our age cools off more and more in its communication, as content is played down and reason is plowed under, I believe the historic Christian faith must more and more consciously emphasize content, content, and then more content. In this we are brought face to face in a complete antithesis with the existential theologian. If we are to talk truth at all, we must have content on the basis of antithesis, and to do this we must have discipline with regard to those who depart from the historic Christian faith. It is thus that we can practice the exhibition of the holiness of God.

At the same time, however, we must show forth the love of God to those with whom we differ. Forty-five years ago in the Presbyterian crisis in the United States, we forgot that. We did not speak with love about those with whom we differed, and we have been paying a high price for it ever since. We must love men, including the existential theologians, even if they have given up content entirely. We must deal with them as our neighbors, for Christ gave us the second commandment telling us that we are to love all men as our neighbors.

We must stand clearly for the principle of the purity of the visible church, and we must call for the appropriate discipline of those who take a position which is not according to Scripture. But at the same time we must visibly love them as people as we speak

and write about them. We must show it before both the church
and the world. We must say that the liberals are desperately wrong
and that they require discipline in and by the church, but we must
do so in terms that show it is not merely the flesh speaking. This is
beyond us, but not beyond the work of the Holy Spirit. I regret
that years ago we did not do this in the Presbyterian Church; we
did not talk of the need to show love as we stood against liberalism. And as the Presbyterian Church was lost, that lack has cost us
dearly.

But with prayer both love and concern for truth can be shown.
Several years ago at the Roosevelt University auditorium in Chicago, I had a dialogue with James Pike. I asked those in L'Abri to
pray for one thing—that I would be able to present a clear Christian position to him and to the audience, and at the same time end
with a good human relationship between the two of us. It was
something I could not do in my self, but God answered that
prayer. A clear statement was raised, with a clear statement of
differences, without destroying him as a human being. At the
close he said, "If you ever come to California, please visit me in
Santa Barbara." Later, when Edith and I were out in Santa Barbara, we went to his place and were able to carry on further a
discussion with him without one iota of compromise, and yet
again not destroying him but letting him know that we respected
him as a human being.

We also talked about the possibility that his belief that he was
talking to his son "on the other side" was really a matter of demonology. And James Pike did not get angry, though he was
close to crying. It is possible to make clear statements, even the
necessary negative ones, if simultaneously we treat men as men.

I will never forget the last time I saw him as Edith and I were
leaving the Center for the Study of Democratic Institutions. He
said one of the saddest things I have ever heard: "When I turned
from being agnostic, I went to Union Theological Seminary, eager for and expecting bread; but when I graduated, all that it left
me was a handful of pebbles."

Who is responsible for the tragedy of James Pike? His liberal
theological professors who robbed him of everything real and
human. We cannot take lightly the fact that liberal theological
professors in any theological school are leaving young men and
women with a handful of pebbles and nothing more.

Yet, even in the midst of this situation, by God's grace we must do two things simultaneously. We must do all that is necessary for the purity of the visible church to exhibit the holiness of God; and yet, no matter how bitter the liberals become or what nasty things they say or what they release to the press, we must show forth the love of God in the midst of the strongest speaking we can do. If we let down one side or the other, we will not bear our testimony to God who is holy and who is love.

Let us again go back to the Presbyterian struggles of the thirties when true Christians did not remember to keep this balance. On the one hand, they waited far too long to exert discipline, and so they lost the denomination, as did the Christians in almost every other denomination. On the other hand, some of them treated the liberals as less than human, and therefore they learned such bad habits that later, when those who formed new groups developed minor differences among themselves, they continued to treat each other badly. Beware of the habits we learn in controversy. Both must appear together: the holiness of God and the love of God exhibited simultaneously by the grace of God. It will not come automatically. It takes prayer. We must write about it in our denominational papers. We must talk about it to our congregations; we must preach sermons pointing out the necessity of standing for the holiness of God and the love of God *simultaneously,* and by our attitudes we must exhibit it to our congregations and to our own children.

It is important to notice the principle we are speaking about here and the language we use to express that principle. It is not the principle of *separation.* It is *the practice of the principle of the purity of the visible church.* Words are important at this point, because we make attitudes with the words we choose and use year after year. So I repeat: the principle is the practice of the purity of the visible church. That principle may have to be exhibited in various ways, but that is the principle. The church belongs to those who by the grace of God are faithful to the Scriptures. Almost every church has in its history a process for exercising discipline, and when needed this should be used in the practice of the positive principle.

Dr. Briggs was put out of the ministry of the Presbyterian Church in the late 1890s because he was the first man who brought liberalism into Union Theological Seminary. But by the 1930s the older type liberals were able to put out Dr. Machen because of his clear stand for the Scriptures and for the gospel.

Think: before 1900 Dr. Briggs could be disciplined; in the 1930s

Dr. Machen was disciplined and put out of the ministry. What had happened in the intervening years? Discipline had not been consistently applied by the faithful men of the church. The church was able, indeed, to discipline Dr. Briggs, but after that faithful men waited too long. Though they had achieved one outstanding victory, after that first burst of discipline they did nothing, until it was far too late. Discipline in the church, as in the family, is not something that can be done in one great burst of enthusiasm, one great conference, one great anything. Men must be treated in love as human beings, but it is a case of continual, moment-by-moment, existential care, for we are not dealing with a merely human organization but with the church of Christ. Hence, the practice of the purity of the visible church first means discipline of those who do not take a proper position in regard to the teaching of Scripture and to the creeds.

Why is it so unthinkable today to have discipline? Why is it that at least two denominations in the United States are now so much in the hands of the liberals that it is officially and formally no longer possible to have a discipline trial, ever—even in theory? It is because both the world and the liberal church are totally caught up in the grasp of synthesis and relativism. It was not unthinkable to our forefathers to conduct discipline hearings, because they believed that truth existed. But because the world and the liberal church no longer believe in truth as truth, any concept of discipline in regard to doctrine has become unthinkable.

I believe that all of the larger Protestant denominations which were not lost in the thirties are today in the midst of this battle of which we are speaking. To make the ecclesiastical sweep complete, we must note that since Vatican II in the Roman Catholic Church the progressive theologians have much power—existential theologians using Roman Catholic terms. Thus the view of existential theologians now controls or is influential in most of the ecclesiastical field.

When a church (like the Northern Presbyterian Church forty-five years ago) comes to the place where it can no longer exert discipline, then with tears before the Lord we must consider a second step. If the battle for doctrinal purity is lost, we must understand that there is a second step to take in regard to the practice of the principle of the purity of the visible church. It may be necessary for true Christians to leave the visible organization with which they have been associated. But note well: if we must leave our church, it should always be with tears, not with drums playing and flags flying. This is no place for naturally bombastic men to bombast.

We are not practicing a cold separation. Separation is a negative concept and builds a poor mentality. The Bible's final emphasis is never on negation but on affirmation. The Bible's principle of the practice of the purity of the visible church is a positive concept.

Still, we must decide what price we are willing to pay for maintaining this principle. If we do not, then we are not free under Christ. Before we ever come to a place where this horrible decision in regard to a church must be made, a prior issue must be already settled. The church as an organization is not first; Christ is first. Therefore, once Christ is no longer King and Lord in a church, then that church cannot have our loyalty. If we ever have to come to this second stage of the practice of the principle of the purity of the visible church, I pray that Christ will be put first in our decision.

If, unhappily, the Christians of a church come to this place, then I would suggest that there is another lesson to be learned from what I have observed as I have worked with various churches over many countries. We must face the fact that if we come to that unhappy moment, it will not be a simple situation where all the faithful Christians will come out at the same time. And this sets up an emotional tension among *true* Christians. I watched it in the Presbyterian Church in the 1930s as a young man. I have watched it in other countries—for example, in Holland and England. Those who have stood side by side for years suddenly feel a tension between them.

This results in two different tendencies. First, those who come out tend to become hard; they tend to become absolutists even in the lesser points of doctrine. One must realize that there is a great difference between believing in absolutes and having an absolutist mentality about everything. They tend to lose their Christian love for those *true* Christians who do not come out. Men who have been friends for years suddenly become estranged.

Second, those who stay in have an opposite tendency toward a growing latitudinarianism; this has tended to happen in evangelical circles in the United States. The tendency is to go from ecclesiastical latitudinarianism to cooperative comprehensiveness. Thus Christians may still talk about truth, but tend less and less to practice truth. The next step comes very quickly, say, in two or

three generations. If one stays in a denomination that is completely dominated by liberals and he gives in to the ecclesiastical latitudinarianism which becomes a cooperative comprehensiveness,
there is a tendency to drift into doctrinal comprehensiveness and
especially to let down on a clear view of Scripture.[4]

There is, therefore, a danger for both those who come out and
those who stay in. And in the name of the Lord Jesus Christ, we
must face these dangers in order to help each other. If a division
comes in a liberal church or denomination, true Christians must
not polarize. In the Presbyterian Church in 1936 we made this
mistake, and we have never fully recovered from it. Most of those
who left totally broke off fellowship with true brothers in Christ
who stayed in.

In 1936, when Dr. Machen was going to be put out of the
church, the General Assembly was meeting in Syracuse, New
York. The leading conservative Presbyterian pastor in Syracuse,
the Rev. Walter Watson of the First Ward Presbyterian Church,
did something which showed great ecclesiastical courage. The
Sunday before the General Assembly acted, he opened his pulpit
to Dr. Machen. Dr. Machen preached with everyone knowing
that before the next Sunday he was going to be defrocked by a
liberally controlled General Assembly.

The following week *The Philadelphia Bulletin* (June 11, 1936)
carried an article with a heading, "New Church Gets Under Way:
Presbyterian Constitutional Covenant Union Dissolves." Just a
headline, but what did it mean? *The Philadelphia Bulletin* reported
that the Rev. Walter Watson who had shown such courage the
week before had said to those who were leaving the church, You
must start a new church, but I plead with you in the name of the
Lord Jesus Christ not to dissolve the Constitutional Covenant
Union. This Constitutional Covenant Union was the organization
to which the Bible-believing Christians within the Presbyterian
Church belonged. The newspaper article read as follows:

> The Rev. Watson asked for less haste in dissolving the Union. He
> pointed out that there were thousands in the established church "who
> had not seen the light yet and the only way we can reach them is
> through an organization similar to the Covenant Union." "I foresee,"
> he said, "that for a while at least this new denomination will only be a
> little one with only a dozen churches, but in five or ten years we can
> expect several hundred thousand members."

Instead of following his advice, those who came out dissolved the Union and largely ceased to have any fellowship with the true brothers in Christ who had stood with them in the battle up to that moment. For forty-five years we have suffered painfully for this decision. This price is still being paid because in the 1980s as a number of local churches are leaving the Northern Presbyterian Church (as its liberal leadership has led it to greater and greater extremes), some of these withdrawing local churches show little enthusiasm for joining the denominations begun by those who left in the 1930s.

Here is what happened back in the 1930s. Since they largely broke off fellowship with the true Christians in the liberal denominations and had little or nothing to do with them, the Reformed churches in this country—both in the North and the South—have become more and more liberal. The true Christians who remained in those churches became discouraged by the attitude of those who had already left, and this was a factor for some of them remaining in the established churches. Man after man has talked to me in the last few years saying, "Back there I was hurt, I was injured. And because of that I have just stayed where I am, and I have been discouraged." Surely both they and those who came out, but who forgot the mark of the Christian, must bear the responsibility for this. And let us realize that the situation is not uniquely American. I have seen the same unhappy thing in European countries during the thirty-three years that I have lived and worked here.

Thus, it is clear—we discourage our brothers in Christ unless consciously and prayerfully ahead of time we are prepared for the situation—ready with a simultaneous, clear doctrinal stand and an exhibition of real, *observable* love among true Christians. This must be consciously thought about and prayed about and written about, for it does not come automatically. In the moment itself, tensions run high and there is little time for working on our attitudes then.

I plead with you, therefore: if, or when, that moment comes for you when loyalty to Christ brings you to the place of leaving your local church or denomination because of a theology false to Christ and the Scriptures, find some way to show an observable love among *true* Christians before the world. Don't divide into ugly parties. If you do, the world will see an ugliness which will turn it off. Your children will see the ugliness, and you will lose some of your sons and daughters. They will hear such harsh things from your lips against men who they know have been your friends that they will turn away from you. Don't throw your children away; don't throw other people away by forgetting to observe, by God's grace, the two principles simultaneously—to show love and to practice the purity of the visible church.

Finally, we must not forget that the world is on fire. We are not only losing the church, but our entire culture as well. We live in the post-Christian world which is under the judgment of God. I believe today that we must speak as Jeremiah. Some people think that just because the United States of America is the United States of America, because Britain is Britain, they will not come under the judgment of God. This is not so. I believe that we of Northern Europe since the Reformation have had such light as few others have ever possessed. We have stamped upon that light in our culture. Our cinemas, our novels, our art museums scream out as they stamp upon that light. And worst of all, modern theology screams out as it stamps upon that light. Do you think God will not judge our countries simply because they are our countries? Do you think that the holy God will not judge?

And if this is so in our moment of history, we need each other. Let us keep our doctrinal distinctives. Let us talk to each other about our distinctives as we keep our distinctives.

But in a day like ours, let us recognize the proper hierarchy of things. The real chasm is not between the Presbyterians and everybody else, or the Lutherans and everybody else, or the Anglicans and everybody else, or the Baptists and everybody else, etc. The real chasm is between those who have bowed to the living God and thus also to the verbal, propositional communication of God's Word, the Scriptures, and those who have not.

As a Bible-believing Presbyterian I feel very close to true Christians from other traditions and true Christians with other distinctives. I feel no separation in Christ. I come and I shake their hands, and I speak as though I have known them forever. If we get down to certain points of doctrine, we differ; but the things that I have spoken of are not rooted in Presbyterianism or in other distinctives—they are rooted in historic Christianity and in the scriptural faith. While I feel close to Bible-believing Christians who are not Presbyterians, I am not close to non-Bible-believing Presbyterians. This is where the division lies.

So in a day like ours, when the world is on fire, let us be careful to keep things in proper order. Let us find ways to show the world that while we maintain and do not minimize our distinctives, yet we who have bowed before God's verbalized, propositional communication, the Bible, and before the Christ of that Bible are brothers in Christ. This we must do in the face of liberal theology. We must practice an observable and real oneness—before God, before the elect angels, before the demonic hosts, before the watching liberals, and before the watching world.

Some Absolute Limits

Though genuine Christians may, and in fact do, disagree over certain points of Christian thinking, there are absolute limits beyond which a Christian cannot go and still stand in the historic stream of Christianity. My purpose here is to discuss some of these absolute limits.

Circles and Cliffs

There are some Christian groups who see doctrine as being just statements of certain dogmas worded precisely according to their own terminology. If a person varies at all from this particular formulation, he is ruled out. These groups insist that there is no room for variation at all. Doctrines, even nondoctrinal intellectual positions, must be held and formulated in the exact way they dictate, and every Christian must use the exact verbal forms they employ.

Often if a person is raised in this kind of thinking, what occurs is that as soon as he feels in any way that he cannot subscribe to the wording as it is given, then he is severely tempted to let the pendulum swing completely away from that position. This is especially true in the case of young people and students. Not knowing that there is legitimate freedom within the proper form, they throw Christianity away entirely. Out of such groups there is a constant stream of people who are going overboard and turning completely away from the Christian position.

To me, this is not the proper mentality. Rather, we should picture a circle within which there is freedom to move. Visualize, for example, what must have occurred on the floor of the Westminster Assembly when the Westminster Confession of Faith was being worked out. Men with varying views in regard to doctrinal detail (for example, eschatology) met together for a long time (1643-1647). What they did was to make certain statements that encompassed all the views that they agreed were faithful to the Scripture. In other words, when the Westminster Confession of Faith was framed, men with slightly different views in detail agreed that they could subscribe to this Confession. It laid down a circle in which (with their differences of doctrinal detail) they could move with freedom. The statements of the Confession were not meant to be of a merely repetitive nature, but were meant to be a limit inside of which were those propositions which were accepted as faithful to Scripture and outside of which were those which were unacceptable in the light of Scripture. Thus there was a definite form, but within this form there was freedom for some variation.

In short, the Christian doctrinal and intellectual position lays down a circle rather than a point. Or, to say it another way, doctrines are not merely lines to be repeated. This gives freedom to express the doctrines in various ways; one is not required to repeat over and over again the same formulations in exactly the same words.

Our study here should lead us to a circle of such a nature that it will warn us when we come to a place of danger. We should see the edge of the circle as an absolute limit past which we "fall off the edge of the cliff" and are no longer Christians at this particular point in our thinking. Nothing, it seems to me, could be more valuable than to recognize some of the places where the ultimate borderline rests.

Let us take, for example, a young man raised in an orthodox group who goes off to a university. He is fighting for his life, often without having the lines of demarcation, the absolute limits, carefully laid out. He only feels vaguely, "I have to stand for this; I have to stand for that." But he does not see the real reasons for the limits; he has been given a repetitive orthodoxy, and sometimes what he has been taught to stand for is only a projection of the position and not the position itself. Not knowing that he has freedom to move within the circle, if he moves at all everything tends to slip through his fingers.

Hence, it is tremendously important that we lay down some of these areas where, in our generation, we come to the edge of the cliff.

Let me first expand my analogy. With regard to the true Christian position, it seems to me that there are always two sides to the cliff, or rather, two cliffs, one on either side of the area of freedom. It is easy to fall or throw oneself over the cliff in one direction just because one is trying to escape falling off the cliff on the other side. Therefore, I want first to lay down what seem to me to be some of the absolute limits beyond which we fall off a cliff or step outside the circle. I say *some* of the absolute limits; others could be considered. And then I want to show, on the other hand, that there are contrary errors into which we can slide, and that these throw us down the other cliff and put us equally out of the circle. If we consciously visualize these cliffs between which proper Christian doctrine is to be found, then I think we can see the freedom we have to formulate, phrase, and rephrase our creeds and doctrinal statements. We will see that we need not be limited to sheer memorization. Yet at the same time, we will be warned before we fall off the cliff. Another way to put it is to imagine that these absolute limits are like the lens of an electric eye. When you approach one, the gong rings, you know you are in danger, and you back up.

There are at least two ways to get at these limits. One way is to study the swings of the pendulum in church history. Often the church has come to a point of danger only to let the pendulum swing completely over the opposite point of danger. The second way to get at the absolute limits is by analysis of the concepts involved, and that will be my method here.[1]

The doctrinal areas that concern us fall into two major divisions: (1) those that comprise the intrinsic aspects of the Christian system, by which I mean the things as true before the Fall as after the Fall; and (2) those concepts that are true only after the Fall.

God and Significance
We will take the intrinsic concepts first. Of these, the primary concept is that God exists and that He is free.

Christianity does not have a deterministic system. We must

always keep away from any sense of a deterministic system—regardless of the phrases used to state such a system. The reason Christianity is nondeterministic is that in Christianity we have a nondetermined God. This cannot be stressed too strongly. God did not create because He had to. He is "there" and He is "free," and His freedom includes the important point that He did not have to create. Nothing can be more basic than this. Any time you begin to get toward the point that "God is not free," a little bell ought to ring.

People may very well say to you, "Well, God needs the creation as much as the creation needs Him, because God needs to love something." Or they may say, "God needs to be face to face with something." But the reason this is not so is the Trinity. Because God is a personal God on the high order of Trinity, God Himself was everything He needed in the area of communication and love. The persons of the Trinity loved each other and communicated with each other before the creation of all things. Therefore we must never cross this line: God exists, and He did not need to create. He willed to create. See Revelation 4:11.

There is, however, the other cliff. There is the danger of saying that man has no significance. But this opposite danger is met by this statement: according to the Bible, once man has been created he can glorify God.

The first point of the Westminster Catechism is this: "The chief end of man is to glorify God, and to enjoy Him forever." It would be scripturally false to leave out the second phrase—"and to enjoy Him forever." The men who formulated the catechism showed great wisdom and insight in saying, "and to enjoy Him forever." Nevertheless, the first phrase is the first phrase: "The chief end of man is to glorify God." And in Christianity we have a nondetermined God who did not need to create because there was love and communication within the Trinity; and yet having been created, we as men can glorify God. That is tremendous.

But we must feel the force of both sides of the issue. If we fail to emphasize that we can glorify God, we raise the whole question of whether men are significant at all. We begin to lose our humanity as soon as we begin to lose the emphasis that what we do makes a difference. We can glorify God, and both the Old and New Testament say that we can even make God sad.

To summarize, then, the first basic absolute limit: God is free and did not need to create; yet, having been created, men, though finite, can glorify God. What you and I do makes a difference to God.

Chance and History
The second absolute limit is related to the first: God created out of nothing, and the infinity of the Judeo-Christian, personal God is of such a nature that when He created He did not need to put chance back of Himself. There is no chance back of God. This is one boundary line beyond which we fall off the cliff.

But likewise we fall off the cliff on the other side if we do not affirm that history has meaning. In Christianity, cause and effect in space-time history has real meaning. The rational moral creatures whom God created (of which we know two classes—angels and men) influence history by choice. In twentieth-century terms, man is not programmed. It is especially and overwhelmingly important to understand that Adam was not programmed.

Even nonpersonal elements of God's creation have a significance in history on their own level. The wind is the cause that blows down the tree. In other words, mechanical cause and effect is significant in history, and, on another level, moral and rational creatures are significant in history by choice. But in one way, neither is more stupendous than the other. As far as significance is concerned, the fact that the material universe that God has made has a reality of cause and effect is just as stupendous as the fact that moral, rational creatures affect history by choice. The marvel is that God created a universe with significance, that the things He created have significance.

One can say this in another way: the things God has made have a real objective existence. They are not just in the mind of God. Michelangelo's painting on the ceiling of the Sistine Chapel gives us a perfect illustration. In his painting of the creation of man, God points His finger out toward man whom He has just created. His other arm is thrown back and underneath are several figures. All but one are clearly angels (*putti*), but one figure stands out as different, and it is clear from her breasts that she is a girl. Tradition tells us that this is Eve. Question: Is this a Christian or non-Christian painting? There is no way to tell what was in Michelangelo's mind when he painted the picture. But there are two possibilities. The first is that God knew what Eve would look like, and *therefore* even though she was not as yet created when Adam was created, she was at that time just as much in existence as she ever would be. If this is what is being pictured, it fits into Eastern thinking, but not Christian thinking. The other possibility is that the painting simply indicates that God knew that He was going to create Eve and knew what she would look like before He created her. In this case, the concept is Christian.

The distinction is important. It made a great deal of difference to Adam whether Eve was only in the mind of God or whether an actualized, flesh and blood, beautiful Eve was before Adam as he woke from his sleep. The Bible teaches that God created things with a real, objective existence. The first corollary, then, is the objective existence of the things which God has made.

Another corollary is this: God, having created history, acts into history. It is not that history has no meaning to God; it is not as though He is suspended above it. For example, it was not the same to God before and after Jesus died on the cross (see John 7:39). And, furthermore, God does not deal with me today as if I were a seventeen-year old boy, nor does He deal today with Abraham in Ur of the Chaldees. God has not put chance back of Himself, and, on the other side, having created history, He truly acts into history at every given moment in such a way that He respects its being there; that is, He acts into it truly.

These two corollaries are just as true before the Fall as after the Fall. But there is a third corollary, relating to the second absolute limit, and it is true after the Fall but not before. That corollary is this: since the Fall, there is a work of the Holy Spirit with each man who becomes a Christian, and yet for each man there is a true conscious side to justification.

All too often the situation regarding man's salvation is discussed as an independent concept, and it is forgotten that it has a place under the second basic principle—that is, that there is no chance back of God. But there is a real marvel, a real wonder that should make us worship when we realize that these things are not just intellectual or doctrinal propositions, but that they are true to what is. It is really personally significant that though God did create things with true significance, yet He put no chance back of Himself.

What this means since the Fall is that when man accepts Christ as Savior, there is a work of the Holy Spirit, yet man is not simply a zero; there is a conscious side to justification.

If we fail to see that there is a conscious side to justification, we soon come to the place where we must say that either the gospel is not universally offered or that man is a zero. But neither is the case. The Bible makes very plain that the gospel is universally offered and that man is significant. So if on one hand you get to the place where you begin to have scruples about the universal offer of the gospel, or if on the other hand you make man a zero, you have fallen off a cliff.

Hence, it seems to me that we can equally fall off either side of the cliff. We can fall off on the side of putting chance back of God, or we can fall off the cliff on the other side by denying the conscious side of justification and making man a zero.[2]

Unity and Diversity

The third absolute limit is this proposition: the persons of the Trinity must be kept distinct. There is true unity and diversity, not behind God but in God. This is true not just since creation but eternally; it is ontologically true of the Trinity before the creation of anything else. There is the unity of one God and yet three Persons who are of such a nature that they are distinct even to the extent that there is true communication and true love between the persons of the Trinity forever. As Jesus said, "thou lovedst me before the foundation of the world" (John 17:24). Recall as well God's words in Genesis: "Let *us* make man in *our* own image" (Gen. 1:26). This is love and communication. It may sound simple, but it is overwhelming. Everything in the Christian system stands or falls at this particular place. We must never cross this line. This is an absolute cliff, for the whole concept of personality is involved.

Furthermore, there is a total distinction between the Creator and anything created, and this distinction is absolute. In the early creeds, the church rightly understood that this distinction is to be kept even to the level of the two natures of Christ—the divine and human. This is made clear in both the Nicene and the Chalcedonian formulations—that in the Person of Jesus Christ the two natures are without any confusion.

Yet if one goes too far, he falls off the cliff on the other side. For there is a unity in the Person of Jesus Christ. There are two natures, but one Person. It is not that one nature acts and then another nature acts, but that the Person of Jesus Christ acts. This is what historic Christianity has insisted upon since the early councils, and the New Testament clearly indicates that this is so.

Yet there is another area in which one finds distinctness and yet unity. It is of *a totally different order,* but it still forms a boundary line to a circle, an edge to a cliff. On the one hand, there is an absolute distinction between the creature and the Creator, and yet there is a mystical union of the believer with Jesus Christ. I cannot say too strongly that this is of a totally *different* order than God as Trinity, but it is a line which must not be crossed, for it too forms the edge of a cliff. I would add too that there is not only a mystical union of individual believers with Christ, but there is also a mystical union of the church with Christ. And this carries with it a further corollary: while the Bible emphasizes the value of each individual, and while we must reject the overwhelming loss of this concept in modern society, the alternative is not bare individualism; there is a unity of the church as the body of Christ. In the church, the individual persons who are Christians are unified as the body of Christ.

To summarize this absolute limit, one can simply say that on one side there is the cliff of confusion and on the other side the cliff of a loss of unity. In other words, on the one hand the Persons of the Trinity must be kept distinct up to the high level of love and communication between the Persons of the Trinity before the creation of the world; also, the Creator and creation must be kept absolutely distinct even to the point of a lack of confusion between the two natures of Christ. And on the other hand, there is the total unity of the Trinity and the total unity of the Person of Jesus Christ; and there is the reality of the mystical union of the believers with Christ and the reality of unity in the body of Christ. In each of these (on very different levels), the one cliff is confusion, the other cliff is the loss of unity.

Holiness and Love
We come now to a fourth limit: the absolute cliff concerning the holiness of God. God has a character, and His holiness is part of His character. We do not believe, as some modern theologians would have it, that God's holiness only means His being God. Rather, it means that there are some things that conform to His nature and some things that do not. God's holiness, in other words, involves moral content.

Modern theologians are apt to take holiness to mean simply God's metaphysical otherness. But this is not what the Bible teaches. The biblical God is not Tillich's god, "god behind God"; and He is not a god who is everything and therefore nothing. To repeat: there are those moral actions which conform to God's character and those that do not.

Of course, this has tremendous ramifications, for the fact that God is holy means something to the individual and it means something to the group. It demands holiness in our personal life and holiness in the church in both life and doctrine. All these stand not as isolated factors, but together upon the reality that God is holy.

And yet we must immediately respond that we fall off the opposite cliff if we forget that God is love. There is a great emphasis on love today. It is often viewed as having almost no direction, as being an unmotivated love—love that is to be equal in all directions. But God's love is not contentless or directionless for the simple reason that God does not "lack content." He has a character. The great statements of truth in the Bible, the great doctrines and the law of God—these lay down the tracks for love. We can, therefore, fall into heresy in two ways. We can forget either God's holiness or His love, and we cannot say which of these is worse.

We must realize that love alone is not the end of the matter. It rests upon the character of God, and God is the God who is holy and the God who is love. We must not choose between love and holiness, for to forget either is equally vicious. But we do have to realize that the talk of love which so surrounds us today is often a love without tracks. Therefore, when we begin to deal in practice with God's holiness, we must always remember that simultaneously there must be the reality of His love. And when we begin to deal in practice with God's love, we must remember that simultaneously there must be the reality of His holiness. It is not that we do one and then the other, like keeping a ball in the air with two Ping-Pong paddles. Both God's holiness and His love must be exhibited simultaneously, or we have fallen off one cliff or the other.

This doctrine is very practical. It relates not only to our intellectual and doctrinal thinking, but to our practice as individuals and groups. *True* love will always produce true holiness both in doctrine and in life. And, on the other hand, *true* holiness will always produce love both in doctrine and in life. All of this is true, I say again, because neither love nor holiness hangs in midair; they both rest upon the character of the God who is there, the God who is holy and the God who is love. And we are called upon to exhibit His existence and His character at every moment of our lives.

Objectivity and Subjectivity of History
We come now to the second major classification. All the absolute
limits I have discussed above (with the exception of the one corollary) have been intrinsic—that is, they are as true before the Fall as
after the Fall. I come now to those absolute limits which are true
only after the Fall, which are related to the abnormality of the
universe since the Fall. The first limit under this category is this:
the historic space-time nature of the Fall.

Words have become so devalued today that we often have to use
cumbersome terms to ensure that what we mean is understood.
The word *fact* does not necessarily mean anything anymore. *Fact*
can just mean upper-story religious truth, and therefore we have
to use an awkward term like *brute fact*. In this particular case, we
are fortunate because the liberal theologians themselves at one
time used the term *brute fact* for what they don't mean by facts. At
least for that time we had a term that we could agree on. Orthodox Christians, for example, believe in the *brute fact* of the historic,
space-time Fall. The historic Fall is not an interpretation; it is a
brute fact. There is no room for hermeneutics here, if by hermeneutics we mean explaining away the *brute factness* of the Fall. That
there was a Fall is not an upper-story statement—that is, it is not in
this sense a "theological" or "religious" statement. Rather, it is a
historic, space-time, *brute fact,* propositional statement.

Furthermore, as a result of this historic, space-time fall the
world is no longer the way it was when God made it, and the
change came as a result of the historic Fall. To say it another way,
there was a time before the Fall when the world was not abnormal
but normal. The denial of this concept is like a greased plank. The
grease on the plank which will cause our feet to slip out from
beneath us is the abnormality of the present universe.

Rationalistic philosophy and theology begin with the concept of
the normality of the world.[3] The rationalist begins with himself
and with the world around him and assumes that what he sees is
representative of the normal state of affairs. But this is not the
case. The Christian thinker begins with the infinite-personal God
who created the world (a normal world), and then he recognizes
the fact that after the historic, space-time Fall the world became
abnormal.

Likewise, Christ's death and resurrection are historic, space-
time *brute facts* that have already occurred, and the second coming
of Christ is a historic, space-time *brute fact* that will occur in the

future. What a contrast to neo-orthodox eschatology which does not refer to future space-time history, but to present, here-and-now purpose! There is no compromise at this point: either these things are space-time *brute facts* or they aren't.

One should wake up in the night saying to himself, "We live in an abnormal universe!" All of what we write, teach, preach and discuss should be grounded in the realization that creation, the Fall, Christ's death, His resurrection, and His second coming are propositional; they are *brute facts*.

We can carry this further. If we are children of God, there was a historic, space-time moment when we passed from death to life; there was a historic, space-time moment when God as Judge declared us individually justified, a moment when God declared that our true moral guilt was forgiven on the basis of the finished work of Jesus Christ in history. Furthermore, there will be a historic future complete salvation at the coming of the Lord Jesus, the resurrection of our bodies, and the restoration of all creation. When we do not affirm these things, then we fall off the cliff on one side.

But there is another cliff that we can fall off just as easily. We do so, if we fail to stress that these things are not *only* bare doctrines, not *only* bare propositions or *bare* facts. These *brute facts* have meaning in the present. All of the past, present and future historic events that we have insisted are *brute facts* have a present meaning in the history of our own lives. Christ's death has a present meaning in history, at this moment in my life; so does His resurrection. To put it another way, we must reject the concept of subjectivity with regard to these historical events; but we must also realize that these *brute facts* are not just theological abstractions or bare propositions. They are to have meaning in our present lives, and they are to be acted upon in our present lives. There is no Christian doctrine that does not have meaning in the existential, moment-by-moment life. For example, the doctrine of the Trinity is affirmed in our Christian lives as we practice the reality and the importance of personality at this present moment. This is true both in the practice of personal relationship toward God and toward people.

Jesus' first commandment is to "love the Lord your God with all your heart and soul and mind." And the second commandment is like it, "to love your neighbor as yourself." The emphasis in our generation is on subjective "religious truth," and this is our great enemy. But it is also true that in the midst of fighting this enemy it is possible to back off the other side of the cliff, to think of these things only as dogmas, only as creeds, only as bare propositions, and to forget that they have a personal aspect as well. The end of the matter is not the bare dogma—even proper theological dogma; it is the propositional, true knowledge that has the result of our loving the Lord with all our heart and our neighbors as ourselves in our present moment-by-moment lives.

Justification and Sanctification
Let us now look at a second absolute limit that falls under the category of those things which are true after the Fall. Mistakes at this point do not rule out a person's being a Christian, but such mistakes do conflict with biblical lines and open the door to serious confusion. Justification must not be confused with sanctification. Again there are two sides to the absolute limit. Justification is once-for-all, and this justification is not to be confused with the moment-by-moment Christian life. Justification is once-for-all, and yet if there are no signs of such a moment-by-moment Christian life, we must question whether or not there has ever been justification.

Similarly within the area of sanctification, sanctification is a process and not an act. Yet there is often a crisis, at least in the sense of new knowledge that we are then called to act upon. Many people who do not fall off the cliff on the side of making sanctification a once-for-all act do fall off the other cliff by thinking and acting as though one is justified and sanctified by an automatic, unconscious process. Sanctification is a process, but it is not a mechanical process in which the Christian takes no conscious part. Very often there is a crisis in a Christian's life when he is told or when he learns for himself from Scripture what the work and the death of Christ can mean to his moment-by-moment life, and when he begins to act on this.

Related to this is the fact that it is fruitless to argue whether a Christian can be free from all known sin at any one moment. This is so for the simple reason that since the Fall we are complex people—very complex people—and each man is divided from himself. The whole question of complete victory at any one moment is foolish in the light of the way we fool ourselves deep into our own subconscious being. Since the Fall we lie to ourselves, and none of us is capable of knowing fully what is known and what is not known to ourselves.

At the same time, we can fall off the opposite cliff by failing to put sufficient emphasis on the Bible's call for a sinless life. The command is clear as a bell: no second-rate standards. "Be perfect as your Father in heaven is perfect." In his stand against the concept of a static perfectionism, the careful theologian will say that we sin daily in thought, word and deed. But woe betide us if we count this our norm. That is totally destructive. There is a difference between the declarative statement that we sin daily and the normative statement that such sinning is acceptable. We can say that we sin daily in thought, word and deed without then resting upon our oars and excusing ourselves. Again, to go over either side of the cliff is equally destructive.

We can summarize these points this way: (1) Justification is once-for-all, and yet if there is no Christian life, one must ask whether a person has been justified. (2) Sanctification is a process, not an act, and yet there are often one or more crises along the way as a Christian gains new knowledge of the meaning and the work of Christ in his present life and as he begins to act on that knowledge. (3) It is fruitless to discuss the question of whether we can have victory over all known sin, and yet we cannot let this become normative in the sense of forgetting that the standard is perfection. Put it this way: can you imagine the God of perfection, light and beauty saying, "Just sin a little bit"? As soon as we say it, we know it is false.

Absolute Right and Wrong
Finally, we come to the last absolute limit that I wish to deal with: there is such a thing as absolute right and absolute wrong in systems. Of course, in our generation the whole direction is toward being unwilling to say that any system is right or wrong. Even many who consider themselves evangelicals today are embarrassed by the sixteenth-century Reformers' saying that the Roman Catholic system as a system was wrong. But we must affirm the possibility of right and wrong with regard to systems and categories. We fall off the cliff on one side if we do not do so.

But there is another side to the cliff: none of us is completely consistent in our Christian thinking. We must declare non-Christian systems false. And furthermore we must declare as true the Christian system which begins with the existence of the infinite-personal God on the high order of the Trinity—a God who created all that now exists (except Himself, who has always been), and who can and does act into the universe He has made and who gives propositional knowledge in verbalized form to man. And yet we must understand that none of us is totally consistent in presenting the Christian system.

The Reformers expressed an important concept here. They first made a distinction between true churches and false churches. Then in reference to true churches, they distinguished those that are more and those that are less pure. The same thing, I suggest, is true not only of churches, but of the expression of Christian teaching. We must be careful not to see everything as relative, some systems being 90 percent, some systems being 50 percent, etc. For this is not so. Lines are crossed when churches and systems pass from the things that are true to those that are false. Yet, we must not fall off the other cliff by thinking that any of us expresses the Christian teaching in a completely perfect fashion. Since the Fall we are not perfect in our bodies; our bodies are yet to be raised from the dead. We are not perfect in our sanctification; our sanctification is yet to be completed. And we are not totally consistent in our expression of the Christian teaching either. Yet we must not fall off the cliff in failing to stress that everything is not relative. There is such a thing as a right and wrong in systems.

This balance keeps us from a sectarian way of thinking; it keeps us from chewing up everyone who differs with us on any point of Christian doctrine. This is a very practical cliff indeed. For example, some of us have experienced sending our children to a university town away from home. What are we to say to them then? Certainly we must not say, "Well, after all, it doesn't matter where you go to church; it's just a matter of averages anyway, so it doesn't matter." But neither should we say, "You've got to find a perfect church before you can go to it." Putting it more personally, what do I say? Do I say, "You have to find a church that agrees down to every last detail with what I teach"? That's ridiculous. Nor do I say, "It doesn't matter where you go." What I say is, "Find a church which has, and lives, an orthodoxy of doctrine and an orthodoxy of community and go there." This is not to say that one is going to agree with every detail that is taught, nor that there is no time or place to discuss our Christian distinctives. Within the circle of truth there is that which is more or less pure, according to our own light as we study the Scripture. But if a church is a Bible-believing church, it falls inside the circle and you are not falling off the cliff.

Form and Freedom Inside the Circle

I wish to conclude by summarizing. Christianity is not to be considered as a single point or a narrow, repetitive line, but as a circle which provides form. Within this circle there is freedom to move in terms of understanding and expression. Christianity is a circle with definite limits, limits which tend to be like twin cliffs. We find ourselves in danger of falling off one side or the other; that is, we have to be careful not to avoid one sort of doctrinal error by backing off into the opposite one.

We must ask God to help us not to fall off the cliffs, and we must help each other. There is room for discussion within each circle, but we must not forget that there is a circle to be in and that there is a limit to the circle.

The Mark of the Christian

The Mark of the Christian

Through the centuries men have displayed many different symbols to show that they are Christians. They have worn marks in the lapels of their coats, hung chains about their necks, even had special haircuts.

Of course, there is nothing intrinsically wrong with any of this, if one feels it is his calling. But there is a much better sign—a mark that has not been thought up just as a matter of expediency for use on some special occasion or in some specific era. It is a universal mark that is to last through all the ages of the church until Jesus comes back.

What is this mark?

At the close of His ministry, Jesus looks forward to His death on the cross, the open tomb and the ascension. Knowing that He is about to leave, Jesus prepares His disciples for what is to come. It is here that He makes clear what will be the distinguishing mark of the Christian.

> Little children, yet a little while I am with you. Ye shall seek me; and as I said unto the Jews, Where I go, ye cannot come; so now I say to you. A new commandment I give unto you, that ye love one another; as I have loved you, that ye also love one another. By this shall all men know that ye are my disciples, if ye have love one to another. (John 13:33-35)

This passage reveals the mark that Jesus gives to label a Christian not just in one era or in one locality, but at all times and all places until Jesus returns.

Notice that what He says here is not a statement or a fact. It is a command which includes a condition: "A new commandment I give unto you, that ye love one another; as I have loved you, that ye also love one another. By this shall all men know that ye are my disciples, *if* you have love one to another." An *if* is involved. If you obey, you will wear the badge Christ gave. But since this is a command, it can be violated.

The point is that it is possible to be a Christian without showing the mark; but if we expect non-Christians to know that we are Christians, we *must* show the mark.

In 1 John 3:11 John says, "For this is the message that ye heard from the beginning, that we should love one another." Years after Christ's death, John, in writing the epistle, calls us back to Christ's original command in John 13. Speaking to the church, John in effect says, "Don't forget this . . . Don't forget this. This command was given to us by Christ while He was still on the earth. This is to be your mark."

Men and Brothers

The command in John 13 and 1 John 3 is to love our fellow-Christians, our brothers. But, of course, we must strike a balance and not forget the other side of Jesus' teaching: we are to love our fellow men, to love *all* men in fact, as neighbors.

All men bear the image of God. They have value, not because they are redeemed, but because they are God's creation in God's image. Modern man, who has rejected this, has no clue as to who he is, and because of this he can find no real value for himself or for other men. Hence, he downgrades the value of other men and produces the horrible thing we face today—a sick culture in which men treat men as less than human, as machines. As Christians, however, we know the value of men.

All men are our neighbors, and we are to love them as ourselves. We are to do this on the basis of creation, even if they are not redeemed, for all men have value because they are made in the image of God. Therefore, they are to be loved even at great cost.

This is, of course, the whole point of Jesus' story of the good Samaritan: because a man is a man, he is to be loved at all cost.

So when Jesus gives the special command to love our Christian brothers, it does not negate the other command. The two are not antithetical. We are not to choose between loving all men as ourselves and loving the Christian in a special way. The two commands reinforce each other.

If Jesus has commanded so strongly that we love all men as our neighbors, then how important it is especially to love our fellow-Christians. If we are told to love all men as our neighbors—as ourselves—then surely, when it comes to those with whom we have the special bonds as fellow-Christians—having one Father through one Jesus Christ and being indwelt by one Spirit—we can understand how overwhelmingly important it is that all men be able to see an observable love toward those with whom we have these special ties. Paul makes the double obligation clear in Galatians 6:10—"As we have, therefore, opportunity, let us do good unto all men, especially unto them who are of the household of faith." He does not negate the command to do good to all men. But it is still not meaningless to add, "especially unto them who are of the household of faith." This dual goal should be our Christian mentality, the set of our minds; we should be consciously thinking about it and what it means in our one-moment-at-a-time lives. It should be the attitude that governs our outward observable actions.

Very often the true Bible-believing Christian, in his emphasis on two humanities—one lost, one saved—one still standing in rebellion against God, the other having returned to God through Christ—has given a picture of exclusiveness which is ugly.

There are two humanities. That is true. Some men made in the image of God still stand in rebellion against Him; some, by the grace of God, have cast themselves upon God's solution.

Nonetheless, there is in another very important sense only one humanity. All men derive from one origin. By creation all men bear the image of God. In this sense all men are of one flesh, one blood.

Hence, the exclusiveness of the existence of the two humanities is undergirded by the unity of all men. And Christians are not to love their believing brothers to the exclusion of their nonbelieving fellow men. We are to have the example of the good Samaritan consciously in mind at all times.

A Delicate Balance
The first commandment is to love the Lord our God with all our heart, soul and mind. The second commandment bears the uni-

versal command to love men. Notice that the second command-ment is not just to love Christians. It is far wider than this. We are to love our neighbor as ourselves.

First Thessalonians 3:12 carries the same double emphasis: "And the Lord make you to increase and abound in love one toward another, and toward all men, even as we do toward you." Here the order is reversed. First of all, we are to have love one toward another and then toward all men, but that does not change the double emphasis. Rather, it points up the delicate balance—a balance that is not in practice automatically maintained.

For True Christians Only
If we look again at the command in John 13, we will notice some important things. First of all, this is a command to have a special love to all true Christians, all born-again Christians. From the scriptural viewpoint, not all who call themselves Christians are Christians, and that is especially true in our generation. The mean-ing of the word *Christian* has been reduced to practically nothing. Surely, there is no word that has been so devalued unless it is the word *God* itself. Central to semantics is the idea that a word as a symbol has no meaning until content is put into it. This is quite correct. Because the word *Christian* as a symbol has been made to mean so little, it has come to mean everything and nothing.

Jesus, however, is talking about loving all true Christians. And this is a command that has two cutting edges, for it means that we must both distinguish true Christians from all pretenders and be sure that we leave no true Christians outside of our consideration. In other words, humanists and liberal theologians who continue to use the Christian label, or church members whose Christian des-ignation is only a formality, are not to be accounted true Christi-anity.

But we must be careful of the opposite error. We must include *everyone* who stands in the historic, biblical faith whether or not he is a member of our own party or our own group.

But even if a man is not among the true Christians, we still have the responsibility to love him as our neighbor. So we cannot say, "Now here's somebody that, as far as I can tell, does not stand among the group of true Christians, and therefore I don't have to think of him any more; I can just slough him off." Not at all. He is covered by the second commandment.

The Standard of Quality

The second thing to notice in these verses in John 13 is the quality of the love that is to be our standard. We are to love all Christians "as I," Jesus says, "have loved you." Now think of both the quality and the quantity of Jesus' love toward us. Of course, He is infinite and we are finite; He is God, we are men. Since He is infinite, our love can never be like His; it can never be an infinite love.

Nevertheless, the love He exhibited then and exhibits now is to be our standard. We dare have no lesser standard. We are to love true Christians as Christ has loved us. When we say this, either of two things can happen. We can just say, "I see! I see!" and we can make a little flag and write on it, "We Love All Christians!" You can see us trudging along with our little flags—all rolled up—"We Love All Christians!"—and at the appropriate moment, we take off all the rubber bands, unzip the cover, and put it up. We wave it as we carry it along—"We Love All Christians!" How ugly!

It can be either this exceedingly ugly thing, as ugly as anything anyone could imagine, or it can be something as profound as anyone could imagine. And if it is to be the latter, it will take a great deal of time, a great deal of conscious talking and writing about it, a great deal of thinking and praying about it on the part of the Bible-believing Christians.

The church is to be a loving church in a dying culture. How, then, is the dying culture going to consider us? Jesus says, "By this shall all men know that ye are my disciples, if ye have love one to another." In the midst of the world, in the midst of our present culture, Jesus is giving a right to the world. Upon His authority He gives the world the right to judge whether you and I are born-again Christians on the basis of our observable love toward all Christians.

That's pretty frightening. Jesus turns to the world and says, "I've something to say to you. On the basis of My authority, I give you a right: you may judge whether or not an individual is a Christian on the basis of the love he shows to all Christians." In other words, if people come up to us and cast in our teeth the judgment that we are not Christians because we have not shown love toward other Christians, we must understand that they are only exercising a prerogative which Jesus gave them.

And we must not get angry. If people say, "You don't love other Christians," we must go home, get down on our knees, and ask God whether or not what they say is true. And if it is, then they have a right to have said what they said.

Failure in Love

We must be very careful at this point, however. We may be true Christians, really born-again Christians, and yet fail in our love toward other Christians. As a matter of fact, to be completely realistic, it is stronger than this. There will be times (let us say it with tears), there will be times when we will fail in our love toward each other as Christians. In a fallen world, where there is no such thing as perfection until Jesus comes, we know this will be the case. And, of course, when we fail we must ask God's forgiveness. But Jesus is not here saying that our failure to love all Christians proves that we are not Christians.

Let each of us see this individually for ourselves. If I fail in my love toward Christians, it does not prove I am not a Christian. What Jesus is saying, however, is that if I do not have the love I should have toward all other Christians, the world has the right to make the judgment that I am not a Christian.

This distinction is imperative. If we fail in our love toward all Christians, we must not tear our heart out as though it were proof that we are lost. No one except Christ Himself has ever lived and not failed. If success in love toward our brothers in Christ were to be the standard of whether or not a man is a Christian, then there would be no Christians, because all men have failed. But Jesus gives the world a piece of litmus paper, a reasonable thermometer. There is a mark which, if the world does not see, allows them to conclude, "This man is not a Christian." Of course, the world may be making a wrong judgment because if the man is truly a Christian, as far as the reality goes, they made a mistake.

It is true that a non-Christian often hides behind what he sees in Christians and then screams, "Hypocrites!" when in reality he is a sinner who will not face the claims of Christ. But that is not what Jesus is talking about here. Here Jesus is talking about our responsibility as individuals and as groups to so love all other true Christians that the world will have no valid reason for saying that we are not Christians.

The Final Apologetic

But there is something even more sober. And to understand it we must look at John 17:21, a verse out of the midst of Christ's high priestly prayer. Jesus prays, "That they all may be one, as thou, Father, art in me, and I in thee, that they also may be one in us; that the world may believe that thou hast sent me." In this, His high priestly prayer, Jesus is praying for the oneness of the church, the oneness that should be found specifically among true Christians. Jesus is not praying for a humanistic, romantic oneness among men in general. Verse 9 makes this clear: "I pray not for the world, but for them whom thou hast given me; for they are thine." Jesus here makes a very careful distinction between those who have cast themselves upon Him in faith and those who still stand in rebellion. Hence, in the 21st verse, when He prays for oneness, the "they" He is referring to are the true Christians.

Notice, however, that verse 21 says, "that they all may be one . . ." The emphasis, interestingly enough, is exactly the same as in John 13—not that those in certain parties in the church should be one, but that all born-again Christians should be one.

Now comes the sobering part. Jesus goes on in this 21st verse to say something that always causes me to cringe. If as Christians we do not cringe, it seems to me we are not very sensitive or very honest, because Jesus here gives us the final apologetic. What is the final apologetic? *"That they all may be one, as thou, Father, art in me, and I in thee, that they also may be one in us; that the world may believe that thou hast sent me."* This is the final apologetic.

In John 13 the point was that if an individual Christian does not show love toward other true Christians, the world has a right to judge that he is not a Christian. Here Jesus is stating something else which is much more cutting, much more profound: we cannot expect the world to believe that the Father sent the Son, that Jesus' claims are true, and that Christianity is true, unless the world sees some reality of the oneness of true Christians.

Now that is frightening. Should we not feel some emotion at this point?

Look at it again. Jesus is not saying that Christians should judge each other (as to their being Christian or not) on this basis. Please notice this with tremendous care. The church is to judge whether a man is a Christian on the basis of his doctrine, the propositional content of his faith, and then his credible profession of faith. When a man comes before a local church that is doing its job, he will be quizzed on the content of what he believes. If, for example, a church is conducting a heresy trial (the New Testament indicates there are to be trials in the church of Christ), the question of heresy will turn on the content of the man's doctrine. The church has a right to judge—in fact it is commanded to judge—a man on the content of what he believes and teaches.

But we cannot expect the world to judge that way, because the world cares nothing about doctrine. That is especially true in the second half of the twentieth century when, on the basis of their epistemology, men no longer believe even in the possibility of absolute truth. And if we are surrounded by a world which no longer believes in the concept of truth, certainly we cannot expect people to have any interest in whether a man's doctrine is correct or not.

But Jesus did give the mark that will arrest the attention of the world, even the attention of the modern man who says he is just a machine. Because every man is made in the image of God and has therefore aspirations for love, there is something that can be in every geographical climate—in every point of time—which cannot fail to arrest his attention.

What is it? The love that true Christians show for each other and not just for their own party.

Honest Answers, Observable Love
Of course, as Christians we must not minimize the need to give honest answers to honest questions. We should have an intellectual apologetic. The Bible commands it, and Christ and Paul exemplify it. In the synagogue, in the marketplace, in homes, and in almost every conceivable kind of situation, Jesus and Paul discussed Christianity. It is likewise the Christian's task to be able to give an honest answer to an honest question and then to give it.

Yet, unless true Christians show observable love to each other, Christ says the world cannot be expected to listen, even when we give proper answers. Let us be careful, indeed, to spend a lifetime studying to give honest answers. For years the orthodox, evangelical church has done this very poorly. So it is well to spend time learning to answer the questions of those who are about us. But after we have done our best to communicate to a lost world, still we must never forget that the final apologetic which Jesus gives is the observable love of true Christians for true Christians.

While it is not the central consideration that I am dealing with at this time, yet the observable love and oneness among true Christians exhibited before the world must certainly cross all the lines which divide men. The New Testament says, Neither Greek nor barbarian, neither Jew nor Gentile, neither male nor female (1 Cor. 12:13; Gal. 3:28; Col. 3:11).

In the church at Antioch, the Christians included Jews and Gentiles and reached all the way from Herod's foster brother to the slaves; and the naturally proud Greek Christian Gentiles of Macedonia showed a practical concern for the material needs of the Christian Jews in Jerusalem. The observable and practical love among true Christians that the world has a right to be able to observe in our day certainly should cut without reservation across such lines as language, nationalities, national frontiers, younger and older, colors of skin, levels of education and economics, accent, line of birth, the class system in any particular locality, dress, short or long hair among whites and African and non-African hairdos among blacks, cultural differentiations, and the more traditional and less traditional forms of worship.

If the world does not see this down-to-earth practical love, it will not believe that Christ was sent by the Father. People will not believe only on the basis of the proper answers. The two should not be placed in antithesis. The world must have the proper answers to their honest questions, but at the same time there must be a oneness in love between all true Christians. This is what is needed if men are to know that Jesus was sent by the Father and that Christianity is true.

False Notions of Unity
Let us be clear, however, about what this oneness is. We can start by eliminating some false notions.

First, the oneness that Jesus is talking about is not just organizational oneness. In our generation we have a tremendous push for ecclesiastical oneness. It is in the air—like German measles in a time of epidemic—and it is all about us. Human beings can have all sorts of organizational unity and yet exhibit to the world no unity at all.

The classic example is the Roman Catholic Church down through the ages. The Roman Catholic Church has had a great external unity—probably the greatest outward organizational unity that has ever been seen in this world—but there have been at the same time titanic and hateful power struggles between the different orders within the one church. Today there is a still greater difference between the classical Roman Catholicism and progressive Roman Catholicism. The so-called "progressive" Roman Catholic theologians are the same as the liberal theologians in the Protestant groups. The Roman Catholic Church still tries to stand in organizational oneness, but there is only organizational unity, for here are two completely different religions, two concepts of God, two different concepts of truth.

And exactly the same thing is true in the Protestant ecumenical movement. There is an attempt to bring people together organizationally on the basis of Jesus' statement, but there is no real unity, because two completely different religions—biblical Christianity and a "Christianity" which is no Christianity whatsoever—are involved. It is perfectly possible to have organizational unity, to spend a whole lifetime of energy on it, and yet to come nowhere near the realm that Jesus is talking about in John 17.

I do not wish to disparage proper organizational unity on a proper doctrinal basis. But Jesus is here talking about something very different, for there can be a great organizational unity without any oneness at all—even in churches that have fought for purity of doctrine.

I believe very strongly in the principle and practice of the purity of the visible church, but I have seen churches that have fought for purity and are merely hotbeds of ugliness. No longer is there any observable, loving, personal relationship even in their own midst, let alone with other true Christians.

There is a further reason why one cannot interpret this unity of which Christ speaks as organizational. *All* Christians—"that they all may be one"—are to be one. It is obvious that there can be no organizational unity which could include all born-again Christians everywhere in the world. It is just not possible. For example, there are true, born-again Christians who belong to no organization at all. And what one organization could include those true Christians standing isolated from the outside world by persecution? Obviously organizational unity, while it has its proper place, is not the fulfillment of Christ's commands.

There is a second false notion of what this unity involves. This is the view under which evangelical Christians have often tried to escape. Too often the evangelical has said, "Well, of course Jesus is talking here about the mystical union of the invisible church." And then he lets it go at that and does not think about it any more—ever.

In theological terms there are, to be sure, a visible church and an invisible church. The invisible Church is the real Church—in a way, the only church that has a right to be spelled with a capital. It is most important because it is made up of all those who have thrown themselves upon Christ as Savior. It is Christ's Church. As soon as I become a Christian, as soon as I throw myself upon Christ, I become a member of this Church, and there is a mystical unity binding me to all other members. True. But this is not what Jesus is talking about in John 13 and John 17, for we cannot break up this unity no matter what we do. Thus, to relate Christ's words to the mystical unity of the invisible Church is to reduce Christ's words to a meaningless phrase.

Third, he is not talking about our positional unity in Christ. It is true that there is a positional unity in Christ—that as soon as we accept Christ as Savior we have one Lord, one baptism, one birth (the second birth), and we are clothed with Christ's righteousness. But that's not the point here.

Fourth, we have legal unity in Christ, but he is not talking about that. There is a beautiful and wonderful legal unity among all Christians. The Father (the Judge of the universe) forensically declares, on the basis of the finished work of Christ in space, time and history, that the true moral guilt of those who cast themselves upon Christ is gone. In that fact we have a wonderful unity; but that is not what Jesus is talking about here.

It will not do for the evangelical to try to escape into the concept of the invisible Church and these other related unities. To relate these verses in John 13 and John 17 only to the existence of the invisible Church makes Jesus' statement a meaningless statement. We make a mockery of what Jesus is saying unless we understand that He is talking about something visible.

This is the whole point: the world is going to judge whether Jesus has been sent by the Father on the basis of something that is open to observation.

True Oneness

In John 13 and later 17, Jesus talks about a real visible oneness, a practicing oneness, a practical oneness across all lines, among all true Christians.

The Christian really has a double task. He has to practice both God's holiness and God's love. The Christian is to exhibit that God exists as the infinite-personal God; and then he is to exhibit simultaneously God's character of holiness and love. Not His love without His holiness—that is only compromise. Anything that an individual Christian or Christian group does that fails to show the simultaneous balance of the holiness of God and the love of God presents to a watching world not a demonstration of the God who exists, but a caricature of the God who exists.

According to the Scripture and the teaching of Christ, the love that is to be shown is to be exceedingly strong—as Christ loved us. It's not just something you mention in words once in a while.

Visible Love
What, then, does this love mean? How can it be made visible?

First, it means a very simple thing: it means that when I have made a mistake and when I have failed to love my Christian brother, I go to him and say, "I'm sorry." That is first.

It may seem a letdown—that the first thing we speak of should be so simple! But if you think it is easy, you have never tried to practice it.

In our own groups, in our own close Christian communities, even in our families, when we have shown lack of love toward another, we as Christians do not just automatically go and say we are sorry. On even the very simplest level it is never very easy.

It may sound simplistic to start with saying we are sorry and asking forgiveness, but it is not. This is the way of renewed fellowship, whether it is between a husband and wife, a parent and child, within a Christian community, or between groups. When we have shown a lack of love toward the other, we are called by God to go and say, "I'm sorry . . . I really am sorry."

If I am not willing to say, "I'm sorry" when I have wronged somebody—especially when I have not shown him love—I have not even started to think about the meaning of a Christian oneness which the world can see. The world has a right to question whether I am a Christian. And more than that, let me say it again, if I am not willing to do this very simple thing, the world has a right to question whether Jesus was sent from God and whether Christianity is true.

How well have we consciously practiced this? How often, in the power of the Holy Spirit, have we gone to Christians in our own group and said, "I'm sorry"? How much time have we spent reestablishing contact with those in other groups, saying to them, "I'm sorry for what I've done, what I've said, or what I've written"? How frequently has one *group* gone to another *group* with whom it differed and said, "We're sorry"? This is so important that it is, for all practical purposes, a part of the preaching of the gospel itself. The observable practice of truth and the observable practice of love go hand in hand with the proclamation of the good news of Jesus Christ.

I have observed one thing *among true Christians* in their differences in many countries: what divides and severs true Christian groups and Christians—what leaves a bitterness that can last for twenty, thirty or forty years (or for fifty or sixty years in a son's memory)—is not the issue of doctrine or belief which caused the differences in the first place. Invariably it is lack of love—and the bitter things that are said by true Christians in the midst of differences. These stick in the mind like glue. And after time passes and the differences between the Christians or the groups appear less than they did, there are still those bitter, bitter things we said in the midst of what we thought was a good and sufficient objective discussion. It is these things—these unloving attitudes and words—that cause the stench that the world can smell in the church of Jesus Christ among those who are really true Christians.

If, when we feel we must disagree as true Christians, we could simply guard our tongues and speak in love, then in five or ten years the bitterness could be gone. Instead of that, we leave scars—a curse for generations. Not just a curse in the church, but a curse in the world. Newspaper headlines bear it in our Christian press, and it boils over into the secular press at times—Christians saying such bitter things about other Christians.

The world looks, shrugs its shoulders, and turns away. It has not seen even the beginning of a living church in the midst of a dying culture. It has not seen the beginning of what Jesus indicates is the final apologetic—observable oneness among true Christians who are truly brothers in Christ. Our sharp tongues, the lack of love between us—not the necessary statement of differences that may exist between true Christians—these are what properly trouble the world.

How different this is from the straightforward and direct command of Jesus Christ to show an observable oneness which may be seen by a watching world!

Forgiveness
But there is more to observable love than saying we are sorry. There must also be open forgiveness. And though it's hard to say,

"I'm sorry," it's even harder to forgive. The Bible, however, makes plain that the world must observe a forgiving spirit in the midst of God's people.

In the Lord's prayer, Jesus Himself teaches us to pray, "Forgive us our trespasses, as we forgive those who trespass against us." Now we must say at once, this prayer is not for salvation. It has nothing to do with being born again, for we are born again on the basis of the finished work of Christ plus nothing. But it does have to do with a Christian's existential, moment-by-moment experiential relationship to God. We need a once-for-all forgiveness at justification, and we need a moment-by-moment forgiveness for our sins on the basis of Christ's work in order to be in open fellowship with God. What the Lord has taught us to pray in the Lord's prayer should make a Christian very sober every day of his life: we are asking the Lord to open to us the experiential realities of fellowship with Himself as we forgive others.

Some Christians say that the Lord's prayer is not for this present era; but most of us would say it is. And yet at the same time we hardly think once in a year about our lack of a forgiving heart in relationship to God's forgiving us. Many Christians rarely or never seem to connect their own lack of reality of fellowship with God with their lack of forgiveness to men, even though they may say the Lord's prayer in a formal way over and over in their weekly Sunday worship services.

We must all continually acknowledge that we do not practice the forgiving heart as we should. And yet the prayer is, "Forgive us our debts, our trespasses, as we forgive our debtors." We are to have a forgiving spirit even before the other person expresses regret for his wrong. The Lord's prayer does not suggest that when the other man is sorry, then we are to show a oneness by having a forgiving spirit. Rather, we are called upon to have a forgiving spirit without the other man having made the first step. We may still say that he is wrong, but in the midst of saying that he is wrong, we must be forgiving.

We are to have this forgiving spirit not only toward Christians, but toward all men. But surely if it is toward all men, it is important toward Christians.

Such a forgiving spirit registers an attitude of love toward others. But even though one can call this an attitude, true forgiveness is observable. Believe me, you can look on a man's face and know where he is as far as forgiveness is concerned. And the world is called on to look at us and see whether we have love across the groups, love across party lines. Do they observe that we say, "I'm sorry," and do they observe a forgiving heart? Let me repeat: our love will not be perfect, but it must be substantial enough for the world to be able to observe or it does not fit into the structure of the verses in John 13 and John 17. And if the world does not observe this among true Christians, the world has a right to make the two awful judgments which these verses indicate: that we are not Christians, and that Christ was not sent by the Father.

When Christians Disagree
What happens, then, when we must differ with our brothers in Christ because of the need also to show forth God's holiness either in doctrine or in life? In the matter of life, Paul clearly shows us the balance in 1 and 2 Corinthians. The same thing applies in doctrine as well.

First, in 1 Corinthains 5:1-5 he scolds the Corinthian church for allowing a man who is an active fornicator to stay in the church without discipline. Because of the holiness of God, because of the need to exhibit this holiness to a watching world, and because such judgment on the basis of God's revealed law is right in God's sight, Paul scolds the church for not disciplining the man.

After they have disciplined him, Paul writes again to them in 2 Corinthians 2:6-8 and scolds them because they are not showing love toward him. These two things must stand together.

I am thankful that we have the record of Paul writing this way, in his first letter and his second, for here you see a passage of time. The Corinthians have taken his advice, they have disciplined the Christian, and now Paul writes to them, "You're disciplining him, but why don't you show your love toward him?" He could have gone on and quoted Jesus in saying, "Don't you realize that the surrounding pagans of Corinth have a right to say that Jesus was not sent by the Father because you are not showing love to this man that you properly disciplined?"

A very important question arises at this point: how can we exhibit the oneness Christ commands without sharing in the other people's mistakes? I would suggest a few ways by which we can practice and show this oneness even across the lines where we must differ.

Regret

First, we should never come to such difference with true Christians without regret and without tears. Sounds simple, doesn't it? Believe me, evangelicals often have not shown it. We rush in, being very, very pleased, it would seem at times, to find other people's mistakes. We build ourselves up by tearing other people down. This can never show a real oneness among Christians.

There is only one kind of person who can fight the Lord's battles in anywhere near a proper way, and that is the person who by nature is unbelligerent. A belligerent man tends to do it because he is belligerent; at least it looks that way. The world must observe that when we must differ with each other as true Christians, we do it not because we love the smell of blood, the smell of the arena, the smell of the bullfight, but because we must for God's sake. If there are tears when we must speak, then something beautiful can be observed.

Second, in proportion to the gravity of what is wrong between true Christians, it is important consciously to exhibit an observable love to the world. Not all differences among Christians are equally serious. There are some that are very minor. Others are overwhelmingly important.

The more serious the wrongness is, the more important it is to exhibit the holiness of God, to speak out concerning what is wrong. At the same time, the more serious the differences become, the more important it becomes that we look to the Holy Spirit to enable us to show love to the true Christians with whom we must differ.

If it is only a minor difference, showing love does not take much conscious consideration. But where the difference becomes really important, it becomes proportionately more important to speak for God's holiness. And it becomes increasingly important in that place to show the world that we still love each other.

Humanly we function in exactly the opposite direction: in the less important differences we show more love toward true Christians; but as the difference gets into more important areas, we tend to show less love. The reverse must be the case: as the differences among true Christians get greater, we must *consciously* love and show a love which has some manifestation the world may see.

So let us consider this: is my difference with my brother in Christ crucially important? If so, it is doubly important that I spend time upon my knees asking the Holy Spirit, asking Christ, to do His work through me and my group, that I and we might show love even in this larger difference that we have come to with a brother in Christ or with another group of true Christians.

Costly Love

Third, we must show a *practical* demonstration of love in the midst of the dilemma, even when it is costly. The word *love* should not be just a banner. In other words, we must do whatever must be done, at whatever cost, to show this love. We must not say "I love you," and then—bang, bang, bang!

So often people think that Christianity is only something soft, only a kind of gooey love that loves evil equally with good. This is not the biblical position. The holiness of God is to be exhibited simultaneously with love. We must be careful, therefore, not to say that what is wrong is right, whether it is in the area of doctrine or of life, in our own group or another. What is wrong is wrong anywhere, and we have a responsibility in that situation to say that what is wrong is wrong. But the observable love must be there regardless of the cost.

The Bible does not make these things escapable. First Corinthians 6:1-7 reads:

> Dare any of you, having a matter against another, go to law before the unjust (that is, the unsaved people), and not before the saints? Do ye not know that the saints shall judge the world? And if the world shall be judged by you, are ye unworthy to judge the smallest matters? Know ye not that we shall judge angels? How much more things that pertain to this life? If, then, ye have judgments of things pertaining to this life, set them to judge who are least esteemed in the church. I speak to your shame. Is it so, that there is not a wise man among you? No, not one that shall be able to judge between his brethren? But brother goeth to law with brother, and that before the unbelievers. Now, therefore, there is utterly a fault among you, because ye go to law with another. Why do ye not rather take wrong? Why do ye not rather suffer yourselves to be defrauded?

What does this mean? The church is not to let pass what is wrong; but the Christian should suffer practical, monetary loss to show the oneness true Christians should have rather than to go to court against other true Christians; that would destroy such an observable oneness before the watching world. This is costly love, but it is just such practicing love that can be seen.

Paul is talking about something which is observable, something that is very real: the Christian is to show such love in the midst of an unavoidable difference with his brother that he is willing to suffer loss—not just monetary loss (though most Christians seem to forget all love and oneness when money gets involved), but whatever loss is involved.

Whatever the specifics are, there is to be a practical demonstration of love appropriate to a particular place. The Bible is a strong and down-to-earth book.

A fourth way we can show and exhibit love without sharing in our brother's mistake is to approach the problem with a desire to solve it, rather than with a desire to win.

We all love to win. In fact, there is nobody who loves to win more than the theologian. The history of theology is all too often a long exhibition of a desire to win.

But we should understand that what we are working for in the midst of our difference is a *solution*—a solution that will give God the glory, that will be true to the Bible, but will exhibit the love of God simultaneously with His holiness. What is our attitude as we sit down to talk to our brother or as group meets with group to discuss differences? A desire to come out on top? To play one-upmanship? If there is any desire for love whatsoever, every time we discuss a difference we will desire a solution and not just that we can be proven right.

The Difference of Differences

A fifth way in which we can show a practicing, observable love to the world without sharing in our brother's mistake is to realize, to keep *consciously* before us and to help each other to be aware, that it is easy to compromise and to call what is wrong right, but that it is equally easy to forget to exhibit our oneness in Christ. This attitude must be constantly and consciously developed—talked about and written about in and among our groups and among ourselves as individuals.

In fact, this must be talked about and written about *before* differences arise between true Christians. We have conferences about everything else. Who has ever heard of a conference to consider how true Christians can exhibit in practice a fidelity to the holiness of God and yet simultaneously exhibit in practice a fidelity to the love of God before the watching world? Have you heard of sermons or writings which carefully present the simultaneous practice of two principles which at first seem to work against each other: (1) the principle of the practice of the purity of the visible church in regard to doctrine and life; and (2) the principle of the practice of an observable love and oneness among *all* true Christians?

If there is no careful preaching and writing about these things, are we so foolish as to think that there will be anything beautiful in practice when differences between true Christians must honestly be faced?

Before a watching world, an observable love in the midst of difference will show a difference between Christians' differences and other men's differences. The world may not understand what the Christians are disagreeing about, but they will very quickly understand the difference of our differences from the world's differences if they see us having our differences in an open and observable love on a practical level.

That *is* different. Can you see why Jesus said this was the thing that would arrest the attention of the world? You cannot expect the world to understand doctrinal differences, especially in our day when the existence of truth and absolutes are considered unthinkable even as concepts.

We cannot expect the world to understand that on the basis of the holiness of God we are having a different kind of difference, because we are dealing with God's absolutes. But when they see differences among true Christians who also show an observable unity, this will open the way for them to consider the truth of Christianity and Christ's claim that the Father did send the Son.

As a matter of fact, we have a greater possibility of showing what Jesus is speaking about here, in the midst of our differences, than we do if we are not differing. Obviously we ought not to go out looking for differences among Christians; there are enough without looking for more. But even so, it is in the midst of a difference that we have our golden opportunity. When everything is going well and we are all standing around in a nice little circle, there is not much to be seen by the world. But when we come to the place where there is a real difference, and we exhibit uncompromised principles but at the same time observable love, then there is something that the world can see, something they can use to judge that these really are Christians, and that Jesus has indeed been sent by the Father.

Love in Practice

Let me give two beautiful examples of such observable love. One happened among the Brethren groups in Germany immediately after World War II.

In order to control the church, Hitler commanded the union of all religious groups in Germany, drawing them together by law. The Brethren divided over this issue. Half accepted Hitler's dictum and half refused. The ones who submitted, of course, had a much easier time, but gradually in this organizational oneness with the liberal groups their own doctrinal sharpness and spiritual life suffered. On the other hand, the group that stayed out remained spiritually virile, but there was hardly a family in which someone did not die in a German concentration camp.

Now can you imagine the emotional tension? The war is over, and these Christian brothers face each other again. They had the same doctrine, and they had previously worked together for more than a generation. Now what is going to happen? One man remembers that his father died in a concentration camp and knows that these people in the other group remained safe. But those on the other side have deep personal feelings as well.

Then gradually these brothers came to know that this situation just would not do. A time was appointed when the elders of the two groups could meet together in a certain quiet place. I asked the man who told me this, "What did you do?" He said, "Well, I'll tell you what we did. We came together, and we set aside several days in which each man would search his own heart." Here was a real difference; the emotions were deeply, deeply involved. "My father has gone to the concentration camp, my mother was dragged away." These things are not just little pebbles on the beach; they reach into the deep wellsprings of human emotions. But these people understood the command of Christ about this, and for several days every man did nothing except search his own heart concerning his own failures and the commands of Christ. Then they met together.

I asked the man, "What happened then?"

And he said, "We just were one."

To my mind, this is exactly what Jesus speaks about. The Father has sent the Son!

Divided But One

The principle we are talking about is universal, applicable in all times and places. Let me, then, give you a second illustration—a different practice of the same principle.

I have been waiting for years for a time when two groups of born-again Christians who for good reasons find it impossible to work together separate without saying bitter things against each other. I have longed for two groups who would continue to show a love to the watching world when they came to the place where organizational unity seems no longer possible between them.

Theoretically, of course, every local church ought to be able to minister to the whole spectrum of society. But in practice we must acknowledge that in certain places it becomes very difficult. The needs of different segments of society are different.

A problem of this nature arose in a church in a large city in the United States. A number of people attuned to the modern age were going to a certain church, but the pastor gradually concluded that he was not able to preach and minister to the two groups together. Some men can, but he personally did not find it possible to minister to the whole spectrum of his congregation—the counterculture people and the far-out ones they brought, and at the same time the people of the surrounding neighborhood.

The example of observable love I am going to present now must not be taken as an "of course" situation in our day. In our generation the lack of love can easily cut both ways. A middle-class people can all too easily be snobbish and unloving against the counterculture Christians, and the counterculture Christians can be equally snobbish and unloving against the middle-class Christians.

After trying for a long time to work together, the elders met and decided that they would make two churches. They made it very plain that they were not dividing because their doctrine was different; they were dividing as a matter of practicability. One member of the old session went to the new group. They worked under the whole session to make an orderly transition. Gradually they had two churches, and they were consciously practicing love toward each other.

Here is a lack of organizational unity that is a true love and unity which the world may observe. The Father has sent the Son!

I want to say with all my heart that as we struggle with the proper preaching of the gospel in the midst of the twentieth century, the importance of observable love must come into our message. We must not forget the final apologetic. The world has a right to look upon us as we, as true Christians, come to practical differences, and it should be able to observe that we *do* love each other. Our love must have a form that the world may observe; it must be visible.

The One True Mark

Let us look again at the biblical texts which so clearly indicate the mark of the Christian:

> A new commandment I give unto you, that ye love one another; as I have loved you, that ye also love one another. By this shall all men know that ye are my disciples, if ye have love one to another. (John 13:34, 35)

> That they all may be one as thou, Father, art in me, and I in thee, that they also may be one in us; that the world may believe that thou hast sent me. (John 17:21)

What then shall we conclude but that as the Samaritan loved the wounded man, we as Christians are called upon to love *all* men as neighbors, loving them as ourselves. Second, that we are to love all true Christian brothers in a way that the world may observe. This means showing love to our brothers in the midst of our differences—great or small—loving our brothers when it costs us something, loving them even under times of tremendous emotional tension, loving them in a way the world can see. In short, we are to practice and exhibit the holiness of God and the love of God, for without this we grieve the Holy Spirit.

Love—and the unity it attests to—is the mark Christ gave Christians to *wear* before the world. Only with this mark may the world know that Christians are indeed Christians and that Jesus was sent by the Father.

LAMENT

Weep, weep for those
Who do the work of the Lord
with a high look
And a proud heart.
Their voice is lifted up
In the streets, and their cry is heard.
The bruised reed they break
By their great strength, and the smoking flax
They trample.

Weep not for the quenched
(For their God will hear their cry
And the Lord will come to save them)
But weep, weep for the quenchers

For when the Day of the Lord
Is come, and the vales sing
And the hills clap their hands
And the light shines
Then their eyes shall be opened
On a waste place,
Smouldering,
The smoke of the flax bitter
In their nostrils,
Their feet pierced
By broken reed-stems . . .
Wood, hay, and stubble,
And no grass springing,
And all the birds flown.

Weep, weep for those
Who have made a desert
In the name of the Lord.

                                Evangeline Paterson

Death in the City

CHAPTER ONE

Death in the City

We live in a post-Christian world. What should be our perspective as individuals, as institutions, as orthodox Christians, as those who claim to be Bible-believing? How should we look at this post-Christian world and function as Christians in it?

This book will try to answer these questions. I will begin by asserting a proposition concerning the basic need of the orthodox church in our post-Christian world, and then I will consider that proposition in the biblical context of the books of Romans, Lamentations, and Jeremiah. Throughout we shall look at the situation we face in the modern world and the perspective we must have as Christians in that world.

First of all, I would like to set forth a proposition about reformation and revival. It will serve to focus our attention throughout the book. It is the basic need of the orthodox, evangelical church in our moment of history.

The church in our generation needs reformation, revival, and constructive revolution.

At times men think of the two words reformation *and* revival *as standing in contrast one to the other, but this is a mistake. Both words are related to the word* restore.

Reformation *refers to a restoration to pure doctrine;* revival *refers to a restoration in the Christian's life.* Reformation *speaks of a return to the teachings of Scripture;* revival *speaks of a life brought into its proper relationship to the Holy Spirit.*

The great moments of church history have come when these two restorations have simultaneously come into action so that the church has returned to pure doctrine and the lives of the Christians in the church have known the power of the Holy Spirit. There cannot be true revival unless there has been reformation; and reformation is not complete without revival.

Such a combination of reformation and revival would be revolutionary in our day—revolutionary in our individual lives as Christians, revolutionary not only in reference to the liberal church but constructively revolutionary in the evangelical, orthodox church as well.

May we be those who know the reality of both reformation and revival, so that this poor dark world may have an exhibition of a portion of the church returned to both pure doctrine and Spirit-filled life.

The latter portion of the first chapter of Romans speaks of man as he is, and two verses tell how he came to be in that position. Romans 1:21, 22 states, "Because, when they knew God, they glorified him not as God, neither were thankful, but became vain in their reasoning." It is important that we follow the Greek here with the word *reasoning* and not "imaginations" (as the King James Version renders it), because the emphasis is not on what our generation uses the word *imagination* to express, but on what it calls *reasoning.* What is involved here is men's thinking, that which is cognitive, thought processes, comprehension. Thus, they "became vain in their reasoning, and their foolish heart was darkened. Professing themselves to be wise, they became fools." When the Scripture speaks of man being thus foolish, it does not mean he is foolish only religiously. Rather, it means that he has accepted a position that is intellectually foolish not only with regard to what the Bible says, but also to what exists—the universe and its form, and the mannishness of man. In turning away from God and the truth which He has given, man has thus become *foolishly* foolish in regard to what man is and what the universe is. He is left with a position with which he cannot live, and he is caught in a multitude of intellectual and personal tensions.

Such is the biblical position regarding man. And if we are going to begin to think of reformation and revival, we must have the same mentality God has concerning the position of man.

The Scripture tells us how man came into that situation: "Be-

cause, when they knew God, they glorified him not as God, neither were thankful"; therefore, they became foolish in their
reasoning, in their comprehension, in their lives. This passage relates to the original fall, but it does not speak only about the
original fall. It speaks of any period when men knew the truth and
deliberately turned away from it.

Many periods of history could be described in this way. From
the biblical viewpoint there was a time when the ancestors of the
people of India knew the truth and turned away, a time when the
ancestors of the people of Africa knew the truth and turned away.
This is true of people anywhere who now do not know the truth.
But if we are looking across the history of the world to see those
times when men knew the truth and turned away, let us say
emphatically that there is no exhibition of this anywhere in history
so clearly—in such a short time—as in our own generation. We
who live in the northern European culture, including America and
Canada, have seen this verse carried out in our generation with
desperate force. Men of our time knew the truth and yet turned
away—turned away not only from the biblical truth, the religious
truth of the Reformation, but turned away from the total culture
built upon that truth, which included the balance of freedom and
form which the Reformation brought forth in northern Europe in
the state and in society, a balance which has never been known
anywhere in the world before.

Having turned away from the knowledge given by God, man
has now lost the whole Christian culture. In Europe, including
England, it took many years—in the United States only a few
decades. In the United States, in the short span from the twenties
to the sixties, we saw a complete shift. Of course, in the United
States in the twenties not everyone was a Christian, but in general
there was a Christian consensus. Now that consensus is gone.
Ours is a post-Christian world in which Christianity, not only in
the number of Christians but in cultural emphasis and cultural
result, is now in the minority. To ask young people to maintain
the status quo is folly. The status quo is no longer ours.

In four decades (from the twenties to the sixties) the change
came in *every portion* and in *every part* of life. If in the twenties you
had distributed a questionnaire in a place like Columbus Circle in
New York, you would have found that most of the people might
not personally have been Christians, but they would at least have
had an idea of what Christianity was. Trafalgar Square in London,

about 1890, would have been the same. But if today you distributed a questionnaire in these places, you would find that most of the people you asked would have little or no concept of true Christianity. They would know the word *Christianity*, but for most, in one way or another, the concepts they have about it would be erroneous. When we begin to think of them and preach the gospel to them, we must begin with the thought that they have no clear knowledge of biblical Christianity. But it is more than this; the whole culture has shifted from Christian to post-Christian.

Do not take this lightly! It is a horrible thing for a man like myself to look back and see my country and my culture go down the drain in my own lifetime. It is a horrible thing that sixty years ago you could move across this country and almost everyone, even non-Christians, would have known what the gospel was. A horrible thing that forty to fifty years ago our culture was built on the Christian consensus, and now we are in an absolute minority.

As Christians in this period of history we are faced with some crucial questions, the first one being this: what should our perspective be as we acknowledge the post-Christian character of our culture?

Let us refer to Romans 1:21, 22 again: "Because, when they knew God, they glorified him not as God, neither were thankful, but became vain in their reasoning, and their foolish heart was darkened. Professing themselves to be wise, they became fools." Verse 18 tells us the result of men turning away from and rebelling against the truth they know: "For the wrath of God is revealed from heaven against all ungodliness and unrighteousness of men, who hold the truth in unrighteousness." Man is justly under the wrath of the God who really exists and who deals with men on the basis of His character; and if the justice of that wrath is obvious concerning any generation, it is our own.

There is only one perspective we can have of the post-Christian world of our generation: an understanding that our culture and our country is under the wrath of God. *Our* country is under the wrath of God! Northern European culture is under the wrath of God. It will not do to say how great we are. It will not do to say the United States is God's country in some special way. It will not do to cover up the difference between the consensus today and the consensus of a Christian world. The last few generations have trampled upon the truth of the Reformation and all that those truths have brought forth. And we are under the wrath of God. This is the perspective we must have if we are going to understand what reformation, revival, and a true constructive revolution will mean.

What, then, should be our message in such a world—to the world, to the church, and to ourselves?

We do not have to guess what God would say about this because there was a period of history, biblical history, which greatly parallels our day. That is the day of Jeremiah. The book of Jeremiah and the book of Lamentations show how God looks at a culture which knew Him and deliberately turned away. But this is not just the character of Jeremiah's day of apostasy. It's my day. It's your day. And if we are going to help our own generation, our perspective must be that of Jeremiah, that weeping prophet whom Rembrandt so magnificently pictured weeping over Jerusalem, who in the midst of his tears spoke without mitigating his message of judgment to a people who had had so much and yet turned away.

In Jeremiah 1:2, 3, we are given the historic setting in which Jeremiah spoke.

> To whom the word of the Lord came in the days of Josiah, the son of Amon, king of Judah, in the thirteenth year of his reign. It came also in the days of Jehoiakim, the son of Josiah, king of Judah, unto the end of the eleventh year of Zedekiah, the son of Josiah, king of Judah, unto the carrying away of Jerusalem captive in the fifth month.

Here is Jeremiah rooted in history, during the reign of the last kings before the nation was carried into the Babylonian captivity.

The Bible puts its religious teaching in a historic setting. It is quite the opposite of the new theology and existential thought, quite the opposite of the twentieth century's reduction of religion to the "spiritual" and the subjective. Scripture relates true religion to space-time history which may be expressed in normal literary form. And that is important, because our generation takes the word *religion* and everything religious and turns it into something psychological or sociological.

The Bible also has another emphasis. Not all that occurs in space-time history is explainable on the basis of natural cause and effect—for example, economic, military, and psychological forces. Most modern men explain all of history this way, but the Bible does not. The Bible says that there is a true significant space-time history which God has made. Of course, history must be understood to be partially a product of the economic forces, of the flow of cultural thought, of military power, and so forth. If we had sufficient time to look at Jeremiah in detail, we would see various forces present: the great countries (Egypt on one side, Babylon on the other), tremendous external and internal forces. Still, history is not to be explained only on this basis. A holy and a loving God really exists, and He works into the significant history which exists. He works in history on the basis of His character; and when His people and their culture turn away from Him, He works in history in judgment.

We must understand that the "Christian culture" of Jeremiah's day was disintegrating into a "post-Christian culture." The holy God was dealing with that culture according to His character. Historic results were not just a product of chance, nor merely of mechanical, economic, and psychological forces. It was God working into that history as His people turned away from Him.

In Lamentations 1:1 Jeremiah speaks of the city of Jerusalem: "How doth the city sit solitary, that was full of people!" Jerusalem, a city which used to be close to God, has been changed by the choice of significant men. They have turned away from Him when they knew Him, and now their city is under siege. There is death in the city.

Furthermore, in Lamentations 1:9 Jeremiah says with brilliant realism: "Her filthiness is in her skirts." God's betrothed—this people and their total culture—has become filthy in her skirts. She is filled with spiritual adultery, and God says, "Her filthiness is in her skirts; she remembereth not her last end." This last phrase is tremendous: "She remembereth not her last [that is, her final] end."

Two factors are involved. She has forgotten what her end will be if she turns from God; but, even more fundamental, she has forgotten her purpose as a nation—she has forgotten her relationship to God. She has forgotten what was recorded in the Pentateuch, that the chief end is to love God. She has forgotten her purpose as the people of God. She has even forgotten the purpose of man. For man is not just a chance configuration of atoms in the slipstream of meaningless chance history. No. Man, made in the image of God, has a purpose—to be in relationship to the God who is there. And whether it is in Jeremiah's day, or in our own recent generations, the effect is the same. Man forgets his purpose, and thus he forgets who he is and what life means.

It was my generation and the generation that preceded me that forgot. The younger generation is not primarily to be blamed. Those who are struggling today, those who are far away and doing what is completely contrary to the Christian conscience, are not to be blamed first. It is my generation and the generation that preceded me who turned away. Today we are left largely not only with a religion and a church without meaning, but we are left with a culture without meaning. Man *himself* is dead.

Jeremiah says this of God's people who turned away in his day: "Her filthiness is in her skirts; she remembereth not her last end; therefore, she came down wonderfully, she had no comforter." Because the Jewish nation did not remember the purpose of its existence, it came down wonderfully. The people could not find a comforter.

What marks our own generation? It is the fact that modern man thinks there is nobody home in the universe. *Nobody* to love man, nobody to comfort him, even while he seeks desperately to find comfort in the limited, finite, horizontal relationships of life. But it doesn't go—in his art, in his music, or any other place. In his literature, in his drama, it doesn't go. In the sexual act, in human relationships, he finds only the devastatingly sterile and the ugly.

The Jews had tried Egypt, they had tried Babylon; but there was no comfort, for the true Comforter was gone. In hedonism, in pornography, and in much else our generation has tried a thousand Egypts and a thousand Babylons. But men have come down wonderfully because they have forgotten who man is and what his final purpose is. The true Comforter is gone.

But in Lamentations 1:11, Jeremiah continues: "All her people sigh, they seek bread; they have given their pleasant things for meat to relieve the soul." "To relieve the soul" may be translated, "to make the soul come again." In a city under siege, these Jews were physically starving; they were giving everything for bread.

Today most men in America are not physically starving. In fact, most Americans are suffocating in the stench of a completely affluent society. But no matter what their philosophic and intellectual system is, men, being made in the image of God, have human hungers that need to be satisfied. To some, the major need is intellectual; they must have answers. So they look into existential philosophy, linguistic analysis, and other non-Christian philosophies. But there is no final answer there. Other people have a deep longing for beauty. So they try to produce beauty out of their own fallenness and self-expression of fallenness. But the final answer and true comfort are not there.

Some hunger for beauty. Some hunger for answers. Still others are hungry for moral realities. Many modern sociologists, for example, are troubled by the lack of a firm basis for moral and social form. How is man to find firm categories to distinguish social good from social evil? They try relativism, the concept of social contract, and various types of totalitarianism, and comfort slips through their fingers.

And many men are hungry for love, for God has made man to love. So our generation has turned to sex as a fulfillment of the need for love in the human heart. But it doesn't work; sex, separated from humanness, is not love. So man cries out, "I am starving."

The hand of God is down into our culture in judgment, and men are hungry. Unlike Zeus, whom men imagined hurling down great thunderbolts, *God has turned away in judgment as our generation turned away from Him, and He is allowing cause and effect to take its course in history.*

God can bring His judgment in one of two ways: either by direct intervention in history or by the turning of the wheels of history. Often it is the peripheral blessings flowing from the gospel which when freed from the Christian base then become the things of judgment in the next generation. Consider freedom, for example. It is the results of the Reformation in the northern European world which have given us a balance of form and freedom in the area of the state and society, freedom for women, freedom for children, freedom in the area of the state under law. And yet, when once we are away from the Christian base, it is this very freedom, now as freedom without form, that brings a judgment upon us in the turning wheels of history.

As the wheels of history turn, our generation feels, as Proust said, the "dust of death" upon everything. And as man feels the transitoriness of the present life, he tries either to elongate it or, through all kinds of strange and devious devices, to give hope for life after death. Thus, for example, we find a strange thing: men who are naturalists and yet seek seances with those who have died. In men like Ingmar Bergman we find a denial of the existence of God but an interest in demonology.

As the Jews of Jeremiah's day were hungry for bread and had no comforter, our post-Christian world is hungry in state and society and in the individual longings of the heart, for it too has turned in our own day from the only sufficient Comforter.

Therefore, if we are going to understand anything about reformation, revival, and real constructive revolution in our own hearts and in the evangelical church, if we are going to start thinking about it and praying for it, we must be realistic. The place to begin is to understand that you and I live in a post-Christian world. Because man has turned from God, there are hungers on every side; there is death in the *polis,* there is death in the city!

CHAPTER TWO

The Loneliness of Man

Our generation is hungry—hungry for love, for beauty, for meaning, for stable morals and law. The "dust of death" covers all. And as in Jeremiah's day, there is with us the unsatisfied longing for a sufficient comforter.

Jeremiah said it well in Lamentations 1:16: "For these things I weep; mine eye, mine eye runneth down with water, because the comforter who should relieve [bring back] my soul is far from me." Why did the Jews in Jeremiah's day seek comfort and not find it, seek satisfaction and not find it? Because they had forgotten the end of man, the purpose of man. I want to commend something to you very strongly. Often when we in the evangelical and orthodox circles talk about the purpose of man, we quote from the first answer of the Westminster Catechism: "Man's chief end is to glorify God." And often the sentence is ended there. This completely changes our Reformation forefathers' understanding of the Scriptures. If you are going to give the complete biblical answer, you must finish their sentence: "Man's chief end is to glorify God, *and to enjoy Him forever.*" That changes the whole view of life.

Our calling is to enjoy God as well as glorify Him. Real fulfillment relates to the purpose for which we were made—to be in

219

reference to God, to be in personal relationship with Him, to be fulfilled by Him, and thus to have an affirmation of life. Christianity should never give any onlooker the right to conclude that Christianity believes in the negation of life. Christianity is able to make a real affirmation, because we affirm that it is possible to be in personal relationship to the personal God who is there and who is the final environment of all He created. All else but God is dependent; but being in the image of God, man can be in personal relationship to that which is ultimate and has always been. We can be fulfilled in the present and the future in the highest level of our personality and in all parts and portions of life.

There is nothing Platonic in Christianity. It is not the soul alone that is to be fulfilled and the body and the intellect to be minimized. There does exist an intellectualism which is destructive to Christianity, but that is not true Christian intellectual comprehension. The whole man is to be fulfilled; there is to be an affirmation of life that is filled with joy. I must say that when we look at many Christians, we do not find the excitement that Christianity should bring in their lives. We do not find them being fulfilled in *the whole man* in relationship to the God who is there.

And so too in the days of Jeremiah we find that the Jews had turned away from the true fulfillment. However, these ancient Jews were not nearly as bad off as the modern man of our own post-Christian world. They turned to false gods, but at least they still knew something was there. In a similar way the Greeks built their culture. Of course their gods were inadequate, so that, for example, Plato never found what to do with his absolutes because his gods weren't big enough, and the Greek writers didn't know what to do with the Fates because the gods were not great enough to always control them. But at least they knew something was there. It's only our foolish generation (and I am using "foolish" in the same sense it has in Romans 1) that lives in a universe which is purely material, everything being reduced to mass, energy, and motion. Thus we find that the Jews left the true God for false gods, just as the Greeks, the Romans, etc., had false gods, but they were not as far from the truth as our generation. Our generation has nobody home in the universe, nobody at all. Eventually, let us understand this: only a personal comforter can comfort man who is personal, and only one Comforter is great enough: the infinite-personal God who exists—that is, the God of Judeo-Christian Scripture. Only He is the sufficient Comforter.

The Song of Solomon beautifully depicts the need for a personal comforter. This magnificent love song in the midst of the Bible emphasizes the fact that God has made us man and woman. And because of this, there is a place for a love song in the Scriptures. In the Song of Solomon we find the girl has gone to her room for the night; she has anointed herself with perfumes and has retired. Then there's a knock at the door. Her lover has come, and he wants her to be with him. But she hesitates and remains inside. She has gone to bed and doesn't want to get up; after all, she has washed and her hands are anointed. Then suddenly he leaves, and as soon as she realizes this, she sees that all the perfume is absolutely worthless once the lover has gone. This is exactly the way it is with man. Struggling with the trappings of personality, man finds that if there is no one there to be a real and sufficient lover, if there is no infinite-personal God, then his wrestling with the trappings of personality is futile.

Jeremiah, here in Lamentations 1:16, turns and speaks this truth to the Jews with great force. He says, of course you are going to be without a Comforter. Of course, because you have turned away from Him. And the One who would be an adequate Comforter to you, to the Jews (and we can say it also to our twentieth century), is not there. So you are like the girl with the perfume on her hands; she's let the lover go, and there's no meaning to the perfume.

In Lamentations 1:18, we find that this chain of thought is taken a step further: "The Lord is righteous; for I have rebelled against his mouth." The Hebrew word is not "commandment" (KJV) but "mouth." The idea is not only that God has set up certain commandments which the Jews have broken. The Scripture here is more comprehensive than that; it says the Jews have rebelled against all that God has spoken—the propositional revelation of God in which God tells them the real answers to life, the way to please the God who is there, and the way to be in relationship with Him. The only reason men were in the place where they were in the days of Jeremiah, or are in our own post-Christian world, is that they have turned away from the propositional revelation of God, and as such they are under the moral judgment of God. You remember we saw in Romans 1 that Paul emphasized that because men knew the truth and turned from it, they were under the wrath of God. God is everywhere; but as the Jews of Jeremiah's day turned away from the revelation of God, they were morally separated from Him. And as the people of our generation turn away from the propositional revelation of God, they too are in the place where there is no sufficient Comforter—because they are morally separated from Him.

And then in Lamentations 1:19 we read this: "I called for my lovers, but they deceived me; my priests and mine elders gave up the ghost in the city, while they sought their meat to relieve their souls." And so we find this note of relieving the soul, bringing back the soul, is involved for the third time in the unity of this chain of references in Lamentations 1:11, 1:16, and 1:19.

What is the conclusion as man turns away from the revelation of God and from the true God who is there? From what perspective should we be looking at our post-Christian world? Certainly every Christian should have two reactions to our generation. The first is that we should cry because we watch our culture being destroyed—not only that individual men are lost, but that our whole culture is being destroyed as well. The second reaction is that we should be aware that insofar as the culture was built on biblical Reformation thought and that the generations immediately preceding us have turned from that truth, *there must be death in the city unless there is a turning to that truth.* We must know it will be!

When Jeremiah says, in Lamentations 1:19, that they gave up the ghost in the city, that there is death in the city, the specific city spoken of is Jerusalem. But the word *city* may be extended further. It can be related to the Greek word *polis*—that is, the sociological group or culture. Thus, because God is dealing with a culture that has turned away, Jeremiah has only one thing to say: "There's death in the city. There's death in the city!" That was true of Jeremiah's day, and it's true in our day.

I am amazed at the evangelical leaders who have been taken by surprise at the changes that have come in our culture. We should have predicted them. There's bound to be death in the city once people turn away from the base upon which our culture was built. The modern artists, the writers, understand that there is death in the city.

De Chirico, in his surrealistic paintings, saw the city, the modern culture, to be this way. In his paintings there are great cities, high towers, shadows, statues, puffing trains, but hardly a human being. The full force of what this meant dawned on me some years ago when I was riding in a train in Europe. In the first-class carriages there were nice colored pictures. In the second-class carriages there were uncolored pictures. I had an uncolored picture. In my carriage was a photograph of a city, the old city of Geneva. There were the streets that I knew very well. But suddenly I saw that in this photograph there were no people, there was nobody in the city, and I had a weird sensation of death. Then I understood what De Chirico was painting. In our generation there is death in the city.

What kind of death? Are people disappearing? No, rather it is the death of man. Personality is gone. We are reminded of American artists such as Edward Hopper who also painted that awful, terrible loneliness. Or we recall Nevil Shute's *On the Beach,* which pictured the world after the bombs have fallen and men have died. The scene is powerful: the lights are still burning, the generators are still running, but there's nobody there. It's an awful loneliness that Shute depicts. But what he is saying is something more profound than that we live in an age of potential nuclear destruction. He is saying, "Don't you understand? This is where man really is today, whether the bombs fall or not, because there's no final purpose to his existence." There is death in the city of man. And if we are really alive to the issues of our own day we should at least understand as well as the unbelieving poets, writers, painters, and the others, that this is the real dilemma: there's death in the city—death in the city of man.

What should we say about our country? Of course, we should be glad for the freedoms we do have. But having said that, should we not also understand that since our culture no longer has a Christian base, there's going to be death in the city? Death in the city will be increasingly all-consuming unless there is true reformation in the church and culture upon the foundation of God and His revelation. Do you think our country can remain as it has been, after it has thrown away the Christian base? Do not be foolish. Jeremiah would have looked at you and said, "You do not have the correct perspective. You should be crying, because it's going to be this way. Having turned from the One who can fulfill, the One who can give comfort, having turned away from His love, His propositional revelation, there will be death in *your* city, in *your* culture!" Modern man stands in that place. We see, therefore, that Jeremiah does give us the perspective we should have for our own day. This is his message. History, indeed, is not just mechanical. In Jeremiah's day God worked into history upon the basis of *His character,* and He continues to do so. Those people were going off to the Babylonian captivity not just for military reasons or economic reasons. God, as a holy God, judged them because they had turned away from Him. He will do the same in our generation.

This is the perspective that God's Word gives us. Being Christian means affirming certain doctrines, but it also means having a mentality attuned to what God has shown us in His book about the realities of history. And this must be our perspective, for only as men turn back to the One who can really fulfill, return to His revelation, and reaffirm the possibility of having a relationship with Him as He has provided the way through Jesus Christ, can they have the sufficient comfort which every man longs for. There *is* no other way. And if we aren't totally convinced that there is *no* other way, we are not ready for a reformation and revival. We are not ready for the revolution that will shake the evangelical church. If I think there are other final answers in the areas of art, history, psychology, sociology, philosophy, or whatever my subject and whatever my discipline; if I think there are other answers after man has turned away from God, I am not ready for the reformation, the revival, and the revolution—the constructive revolution—which the evangelical church so desperately needs. Our perspective must be the perspective of the Word of God. If it is, then we will offer no cheap solutions and we will not be surprised that there is judgment.

CHAPTER THREE

The Message of Judgment

Let us continue to look at Jeremiah and what he said to an age so much like our own. Jeremiah, you know, is called the "weeping prophet," for we find him crying over his people. And his attitude must be ours: we must weep over the church as it has turned away and weep over the culture that has followed it.

Jeremiah himself was born in Anathoth, as we are told in Jeremiah 1:1, and he died probably in his early sixties in Egypt. He did not have an easy life. In fact in Hebrews 11:36, 37, we read this: "And others had trial of cruel mockings and scourgings, yea, moreover, of bonds and imprisonment; they were stoned, they were sawn asunder." As you investigate, you can locate certain people in the Bible who went through all but one of the persecutions outlined in Hebrews 11. You don't find anybody who was sawn asunder. Tradition, however, tells us that after the Jewish nation was taken over by the Babylonians, some of the Jews carried Jeremiah down into Egypt, precisely where he did not want to go and where he told them not to go. The tradition (which may or may not be true) goes further and says that they put him in a hollow log and sawed through it. This might be what the writer

225

of Hebrews is referring to. In any case, Jeremiah's life, which we will look at in more detail, was not an easy one.

His message was not an easy one either. We learn what that basic message was in Jeremiah 1:10: "See, I have this day set thee over the nations and over the kingdoms, to root out, and to pull down, and to destroy, and to throw down, to build, and to plant." Notice the order. First, there was to be a strong negative message, and then the positive one. But the negative message was first. It was to be a message of judgment to the church which had turned away and to the culture which flowed from it. Judah had revolted against God and His revealed truth; and God says that Jeremiah's message was to be first a message of judgment. I believe the same message is to be ours today.

Christianity is not romantic, not soft. It is tough-fibered and realistic. And the Bible gives us the realistic message that Jeremiah preached into his own days, a message I am convinced the church today must preach if it is to be any help in the post-Christian world.

Let us not be surprised at the world's reaction. The Bible makes it plain that this message is going to be poorly received by a church in revolt and by a culture in revolt. We read in Jeremiah 1:18, 19, "For, behold, I have made thee this day a defenced city, and an iron pillar, and brasen walls against the whole land, against the kings of Judah, against its princes, against its priests, and against the people of the land. And they shall fight against thee, but they shall not prevail against thee; for I am with thee, saith the Lord, to deliver thee." In other words, God says, "This is the type of ministry you're going to have, Jeremiah." So if you are a Christian looking for an easy ministry in a post-Christian culture, you are unrealistic in your outlook. It was not to be so in Jeremiah's day, and it *cannot* be so in a day like our own.

Jeremiah in the book of Jeremiah then turns to analyze the various ways in which his culture was turning away from God. He focuses on a number of faults: the inadequacy of a merely external religion, the general apostasy of the church, a few specific sins, and the tendency to search for meaning and security apart from the God who is there.

Jeremiah points out that although there was plenty of external religion, that was not what God wanted. We read, for example, in Jeremiah 6:20, "To what purpose cometh there to me incense from Sheba, and the sweet cane from a far country? Your burnt offerings are not acceptable, nor your sacrifices sweet unto me." There was plenty of sacrifice, but it was no good. They were functioning in the wrong way, with the wrong motivation and the wrong propositions. So God said, "What good is your religion to Me?" The point is the same in Jeremiah 7:4: "Trust not in lying words, saying, The temple of the Lord, The temple of the Lord, The temple of the Lord." In other words the people said, "Is not the temple of the Lord with us? Then all will be well!" But God brought down His hands in anger and said, "I don't care anything about your temple once you have turned away from My revealed truth. Once you have done this, you can have the temple, but it doesn't mean a thing to Me."

So it is in our own generation. The fact that there is much religion means nothing to God and does nothing to remove His judgment. The new theology and the compromises, including compromises in regard to the Bible that one finds at times even in some so-called evangelicalism, remove the real thing that makes religion acceptable to God. As we saw in Lamentations, the Jews had turned away from the revelation of God; and when men turn away from the propositional revelation of God, it destroys the acceptability of our worship to God. We are not jousting over abstract theological terms. We are dealing with a question of believing God and believing His revealed truth.

Jeremiah, however, goes further in 7:10: ". . . and come and stand before me in this house, which is called by my name, and say, We are delivered to do all these abominations?" That is, "You come into the temple and then you go away and say, 'Now I can do anything I wish. I can live the hedonistic life.'" But God says through Jeremiah, "Not so. Mere external religion means nothing to Me." In 9:25 we find the same emphasis: "Behold, the days come, saith the Lord, that I will punish all them who are circumcised with the uncircumcised." They were circumcised, but what did it amount to? Nothing in the sight of God unless it was rooted in the truth of the revelation of God. The external forms alone mean *nothing* to God.

But through Jeremiah, God says more than this. Jeremiah speaks out expressly against apostasy. Here is a hallmark of our generation, one that shows the church today has been infiltrated by the relativism, the concept of synthesis: more and more since the thirties the church has ceased to use the word *apostasy*. It is easy to use the word in a hard and harsh way. That's wrong, of course.

Nevertheless, on the basis of the Word of God, there is such a thing as apostasy; and when we see a real turning away from God, we are not faithful to the Word of God unless we call it what it is.[1]

Through Jeremiah God speaks in strong, strict, even shocking terms about it: "They say, If a man put away his wife, and she go from him, and become another man's, shall he return unto her again? Shall not that land be greatly polluted? But thou hast played the harlot with many lovers" (Jeremiah 3:1). And then he gives the invitation, "Yet return again to me, saith the Lord." But the invitation is rooted in accepting the fact that what had been done before was real apostasy.

The picture in which the invitation is given is highly significant. Throughout Scripture God continually says, "You are My bride." For the church of God to turn away is spiritual adultery, *apostasy*. One must be careful not to use the word proudly, harshly, without love, without tears, or too easily, but there is a proper way. The picture is repeated in Jeremiah 3:6: "The Lord said also unto me in the days of Josiah, the king, Hast thou seen that which backsliding Israel hath done? She is gone up upon every high mountain and under every green tree, and there hath played the harlot." The Jews were turning away to false gods. But turning away to false theology is equal to turning away to false gods. Whenever the church of Jesus Christ turns away from the living God and His propositional truth, she is playing the harlot. In Jeremiah 3:9 we find the same: "And it came to pass through the lightness of her whoredom, that she hath defiled the land, and committed adultery with stones and with stocks."

Therefore, in a post-Christian world and in an often post-Christian church, it is imperative to point out with love where apostasy lies. We must openly discuss with all who will listen, treating all men as fellow men, but we must call apostasy, apostasy. If we do not do that, we are not ready for reformation, revival, and a revolutionary church in the power of the Holy Spirit.

We are all too easily infiltrated with relativism and synthesis in our own day. We tend to lack antithesis. There is that which is true God, and there is that which is no god. God is there as against His not being there. That's the big antithesis. And there are antitheses in relation to His revelation from Genesis 1 on. There is that which is given which is antithetical to its opposite. When we see men ignore or pervert the truth of God, we must say clearly—not in hate or anger—"You are wrong."

Jeremiah not only speaks against religious apostasy, but also against specific sins. This is likewise imperative in a generation such as our own. So God says, in Jeremiah 5:7, 8, "How shall I pardon thee for this? Thy children have forsaken me, and sworn by them that are no gods." That's the religious side again. But note the effect of the affluent society: "when I had fed them to the full, they then committed adultery, and assembled themselves by troops in the harlots' houses." They used their affluence for sin. Does that sound familiar?

Jeremiah continues in 5:8: "They were like fed horses in the morning." If a horse is well fed, says Jeremiah, it turns to sexual things. So, he says, that is the way you are in your affluent society, O Jews. And that is the way you are, O affluent United States and northern European Reformation countries, turning from the Reformation faith. "They are as fed horses in the morning; every one neighed after his neighbor's wife." Think of the novels today which express this escape into an adulterous community. In the 1960s many young people said to me, "Why shouldn't I take to drugs when the generation before me finds its escape in alcohol and adultery?" They were right: one is as bad as the other. Now in the 1980s drugs and alcohol are taken together for an attempted greater escape.

When the church does not speak against the prevailing sins in the post-Christian world, it does not follow God's example through Jeremiah as to what its message should include. External religion, apostasy, sexual sins, and lying—that too Jeremiah speaks about. In Jeremiah 9:2 we read, "Oh, that I had in the wilderness a lodging place of wayfaring men, that I might leave my people, and go from them! For they are all adulterers, an assembly of treacherous men." And in the fifth verse, "And they will deceive every one his neighbor, and will not speak the truth; they have taught their tongue to speak lies, and weary themselves to commit iniquity." God is also concerned about men speaking truth.

Men no longer believe that there are absolutes, and more and more it has become the accepted thing not to speak the truth. The business contract is not honored if, legally, a way can be found around it. The employer does not honor his promise. The employee responds in kind. As men have turned away from God, who alone gives a basis for absolutes in truth, men have become untruthful and hypocritical with each other. We accept hypocritical language in TV ads, and in medicine when the child, after it has been born, is called the "fetus-ex-utero" so that it can be gotten rid of more easily. We know we are surrounded by the untruthful and hypocritical, but our generation has come to accept it as normal and thus to be manipulated by it.

The younger generation had a phrase that relates to all this. They used the term, "a plastic culture." It fits. Ours is a plastic culture, and often ours is a plastic church. Men are simply carrying on by memory. They are living only by habit, not because they have a firm, rational, Christian base for their actions, and it is indeed ugly. It is so easy to see this hypocrisy and ugliness in both culture and church that we should not have had to wait to come to the present extremes. The church should have been saying these things for years. The beauty is gone if we continue outwardly to do even the right things once the base which produced these is gone.

We live in a day when truth is torn down in the philosophy of our generation. This is not so just in the chairs of philosophy, but in the places where living philosophy is being hammered out now; and we cannot expect truth to be torn down either in the university or in the arts without a result in the practice of society.

But Jeremiah speaks for God and says, "I'm not only speaking against sexual sin; I'm speaking about cutting down the force of truth." In 9:8 he says, "Their tongue is like an arrow shot out; it speaketh deceit. One speaketh peaceably to his neighbor with his mouth, but in heart he layeth his wait." It is easy for both the orthodox and the liberal church to talk of love and yet live without it. And it is easy for the modern generation outside the church to do the same. In the 1960s, drawn by the cry of "love," many a "flower child" was exploited and sucked empty of life by the time she was fourteen. And in the 1980s the word *love* continues to be used to mean hedonism, unlove and ugliness. Both inside the church and outside the church, to use the word *love* and other peaceable words in order to deceive is simply exploitation.

God spoke to Jeremiah against such falsehood and exploitation. And if the church is not speaking in strong terms against both the apostasy and the sins of our own day, we are not ready to see any sort of revolutionary movement into our generation. Our generation is properly sick of god words.

Jeremiah also speaks against looking to the world for help. In his day this was very specific. It was looking to Egypt and other great nations for protection against Babylon. In 2:18 we find Jeremiah saying, "And now what hast thou to do in the way of Egypt, to drink the waters of Shihor? Or what hast thou to do in the way of Assyria, to drink the waters of the river?" That is, "What are you doing looking to Egypt? What are you doing looking to Assyria? Why don't you look to God?" For Jeremiah it was a literal Assyria and Egypt. Our Egypt is the world and the world's cleverness. We cannot expect a cynical generation saturated by the glib and the plastic to take the church seriously if it uses the world's way. As Jeremiah says in 2:36, "Why gaddest thou about so much to change thy way? Thou also shalt be ashamed of Egypt, as thou wast ashamed of Assyria."

Or again in 37:7, 8, Jeremiah says, "Thus saith the Lord, the God of Israel, Thus shall ye say to the king of Judah, who sent you unto me to inquire of me, Behold, Pharaoh's army, which is come forth to help you, shall return to Egypt into their own land. And the Chaldeans shall come again, and fight against this city, and take it, and burn it with fire."

"Are you looking to the world for help?" God asks. "It is going to fail. You're going to be ashamed." The church that says there is truth in a generation of relativism, a church that says God is there, when the new theology turns religion into mere psychology—such a church must demonstrate that it really believes God is there. We must look directly to God for help. As Hudson Taylor used to say, it must be the Lord's work done in the Lord's way.

So what then is the message Jeremiah gave to the Jews? Was it a light message? What he said was, "You are going on to utter destruction because you have turned away from God and because you will not repent. The God who works in history is going to bring upon your culture utter destruction." And so he writes in 1:14, "Then the Lord said unto me, Out of the north an evil shall break forth upon all the inhabitants of the land." And in 5:15, "Lo, I will bring a nation upon you from far, O house of Israel, saith the Lord; it is a mighty nation, it is an ancient nation, a nation whose language thou knowest not, neither understandest what they say." The whole book is full of such prophecy. Utter destruction is coming upon your whole culture, utter destruction, unless there is reformation.

What we need are new John Bunyans to point out what occurs when men turn to Vanity Fair. When men turn away from God, the city becomes the city of destruction. "And I will make Jerusalem heaps, and a den of dragons; and I will make the cities of Judah desolate, without an inhabitant" (9:11). "Thus saith the Lord God of Israel, Behold, I will turn back the weapons of war that are in your hands" (21:4). To our generation God says, "O nation, O culture, do you think because of the knowledge you now have, a knowledge that's separated from what is really there (the universe in which there is a supernatural as well as a natural, in which everything is not merely economic cause and effect), do you think you can build weapons that will meet your need? No," says God, "these things are going to turn as a sword in a weak man's hand, and it's going to cut the man who holds it. You're trusting in increased technology. The technology will destroy you." Until we hear men preaching with this kind of contemporary courage, we cannot expect the church to be taken seriously.

> I will turn back the weapons of war that are in your hands, with which ye fight against the king of Babylon, and against the Chaldeans, who besiege you without the walls, and I will assemble them into the midst of this city. And I myself will fight against you with an outstretched hand and with a strong arm, even in anger, and in fury, and in great wrath. And I will smite the inhabitants of this city, both man and beast; they shall die of a great pestilence. And afterwards, saith the Lord, I will deliver Zedekiah, king of Judah, and his servants, and the people, and such as are left in this city from the pestilence, from the sword, and from the famine, into the hand of Nebuchadnezzar. (Jeremiah 21:4-7)

Our generation needs to be told that man cannot disregard God, that a culture like ours that has had such light and then has deliberately turned away stands under God's judgment. God is a God of grace, but the other side of the coin of grace is judgment. If God is there, if God is holy (and we need a holy God or we have no absolutes), there must be judgment.

I want to ask a question as I conclude this chapter. Do you really believe He is there? Why is there so much unreality among evangelicals, young and old? What is the final reality? The final reality is that God is really there. The Bible is what it is because the God who exists has spoken it in propositional, verbalized form. But does *your* Christianity end with something less than God who is there? In the teaching of your courses in Christian schools, do you believe He is there? In your learning, do you believe He is there? Do you *really* believe He is there, or are you only living in some sort of sociological belief? Are you only making the right theological statements, or do you believe God is there and you live before Him?

If He is really there and if He is a holy God, do you seriously think that God does not čare that a country like our own has turned from Him? There is only one kind of preaching that will do in a generation like ours—preaching which includes the preaching of the judgment of God.

CHAPTER FOUR

An Echo of the World

In the last chapter, we looked at the way Jeremiah spoke God's word into his own age. We saw how he preached judgment against a merely external religion, against the general apostasy, and against specific sins—adultery, lying, and hypocrisy. Jeremiah's voice was raised against the travesty his own people had made of God's revealed truth.

We turn now to examine not so much the sins of the people as the people themselves. Who was Jeremiah speaking to? Was it just the ordinary people in the next village? Whom did he accuse of turning away from God?

In Jeremiah 22:11, 12 we read, "For thus saith the Lord touching Shallum, the son of Josiah, king of Judah, who reigned instead of Josiah, his father, who went forth out of this place, He shall not return there any more, but he shall die in the place where they have led him captive, and shall see this land no more." Here we find immediately the preaching of an utter destruction which includes the king of the land. Jeremiah 22:18, 19 has the same emphasis: "Therefore, thus saith the Lord concerning Jehoiakim, the son of Josiah, king of Judah, They shall not lament for him, saying, Ah, my brother! or, Ah, sister! They shall not lament for him, saying, Ah, lord! or, Ah, his glory! He shall be buried with the burial of an ass, drawn and cast forth beyond the gates of Jerusalem."

Thus Jeremiah speaks soberly, using a very strong figure of speech. The judgment of God is coming upon this land because men have turned so far from Him that, rather than having the glorious funeral which the kings of Judah wanted to have, this king would be buried like an ass. How do you bury an ass? You drag him outside the city, abandon his carcass, and that's that. Such is the kind of judgment that is coming from God upon the generation and the leaders who have turned away. Again in 25:9-11 we feel the emphasis of utter destruction: "Behold, I will send and take all the families of the north, saith the Lord, and Nebuchadrezzar, the king of Babylon, my servant, and will bring them against this land, and against its inhabitants, and against all these nations round about, and will utterly destroy them, and make them an astonishment, and an hissing, and perpetual desolations. Moreover I will take from them the voice of mirth. . . ." Jeremiah's generation was seeking everywhere for the voice of mirth, even where there was no real mirth. And God says, "I'm going to take away from them the voice of mirth." "And what am I going to use as an instrument?" God asks. "I'm going to use a nation that is not My people, a military force that is not following the living God, and I'm going to use them against *you*."

I must say, when I pray for my country and our culture, I do not pray for God's justice. I can only plead for His mercy. If we had the justice of God, we would not have peace. We would have a situation like Jeremiah's. How dare we pray for justice upon our culture when we have so deliberately turned away from God and His revelation? Why should God bless us? Jeremiah was counted a traitor because he spoke like this, but it is what God put in his mouth: "Yes, you're the people of God; yes, externally you seem to have the real religion in the temple, but it's worth nothing to Me; and because you have turned from Me and from the propositional truth that I have given you, I am going to send an overwhelming judgment upon you." So I must say, for my generation and my country I pray for one thing—God's mercy.

But for Jeremiah's day the message of total destruction goes on: "And [I] will bring them against this land, and against its inhabitants, and against all these nations round about, and will utterly destroy them, and make them an astonishment, and an hissing, and perpetual desolations. Moreover, I will take from them the voice of mirth, and the voice of gladness, the voice of the bridegroom, and the voice of the bride. . . ." The central things of life are going to grind down to a close: "the sound of the millstones, and the light of the candle"—that is, the conduct of business as well as the joy of marriage. "And this whole land shall be a desolation, and an astonishment; and these nations shall serve the king of Babylon seventy years." Then, of course, comes that marvelous promise: after seventy years God will return them to the land. But Jeremiah's message to the generation to which he was preaching was destruction.

When Jeremiah preached destruction, he was not just talking in generalities. He preached against the dignitaries, the leaders of the land, who were drawing their people away from God. So we find in Jeremiah 8:1, "At that time, saith the Lord, they shall bring out the bones of the kings of Judah, and the bones of his princes, and the bones of the priests, and the bones of the prophets, and the bones of the inhabitants of Jerusalem, out of their graves." That is, Jeremiah says, "I'm talking against you, O kings. I'm talking against you, O priests. I'm talking against you, O prophets." Jeremiah preached against the dignitaries who might have been great in the hierarchy of that society and state, but who were leading the people astray. Today such dignitaries include not only church and governmental and judicial leaders, but those of education, the media and culture.

He continues this emphasis in 13:13, 14: "Then shalt thou say unto them, Thus saith the Lord, Behold, I will fill all the inhabitants of this land, even the kings who sit upon David's throne, and the priests, and the prophets, and all the inhabitants of Jerusalem, with drunkenness. And I will dash them one against another, even the fathers and the sons together, saith the Lord." He names those who are the leaders of the land, who stand in the social and state hierarchy—the kings, the prophets, and the priests. We also find a similar message toward the end of the book. (I am almost choosing at random, because the total message of Jeremiah is repeated over and over again throughout the many years he prophesied.) Thus in Jeremiah 34:19, 20: "The princes of Judah, and the princes of Jerusalem, the eunuchs, and the priests, and all the people of the land, who passed between the parts of the calf [that is, who made a covenant in God's name and then broke it], I will even give them into the hand of their enemies, and into the hand of those who seek their life; and their dead bodies shall be for meat unto the fowls of the heaven, and to the beasts of the earth." It is easy to preach like this to the common people, but what Jeremiah did under the moving of God was to have the courage to vocalize and to verbalize the preaching of God against the dignitaries who could do something about it. He even dared to name them. He dared to say, "*You* are leading us astray, and God's judgment is upon *you*." Naturally, as in our own day, such preaching brings a repercussion from those in power in either the church or state.

Jeremiah did not just preach against the political dignitaries, but, more than anyone else, against the religious leaders who were leading the people away from the propositional revelation of God. In Jeremiah 2:8 he says, "The priests said not, Where is the Lord? And they that handle the law knew me not. The pastors also transgressed against me, and the prophets prophesied by Baal, and walked after things that do not profit."

And so he turns here and asks, "The religious leaders—are they leading you aright?"

And he says, "No."

"Are they to be honored merely because they're religious leaders?"

"Not if they're not preaching the truth."

Surely this has something to do with the message we must speak to our post-Christian world. We must treat men with love, we must treat them and talk to them humanly. But we must not tone down our message; the religious leaders of our day too are often leading people astray. There is nothing in the Bible that removes a man from under the judgment of Scripture just because he is a religious leader. In fact, it is the other way around.

Further, we find in Jeremiah 5:13, "And the prophets shall become wind, and the word is not in them; thus shall it be done unto them." What's the matter with the prophets? The trouble is they are not speaking for God. They are merely taking the social consensus of their day and speaking as though that was the Word of God. In verse 31, "The prophets prophesy falsely, and the priests bear rule by their means, and my people love to have it so; and what will ye do in the end of it all?" What of these priests? What of these prophets? They merely echo what everyone around them is saying. Surely that sounds familiar. When we listen to the religion that is preached in our generation, it is largely the same thing the unbelieving philosophers and sociologists are saying. The only difference is that theological language is used. But God says, "It will not do. This brings you under my judgment."

In Jeremiah 12:10 God gives us a graphic picture of the destruction the religious leaders have brought on the people: "Many pastors have destroyed my vineyard, they have trodden my portion under foot, they have made my pleasant portion a desolate wilderness." The religious leaders have walked through God's garden and destroyed it. In Switzerland, every blade of grass is precious; you dare not walk through any field. It would be like walking through someone's rose garden. But here is God's field, and someone has trampled down the grass. Is it the common man? No, not primarily. Rather, it is the religious leaders who made the garden a desolate, desolate wilderness. Surely then, we cannot fail to speak against the religious leaders, when they are the ones who are bringing the desolation.

In Jeremiah 23:1, the figure of speech changes: "Woe be unto the pastors who destroy and scatter the sheep of my pasture! saith the Lord." Walking upon God's garden has now become scattering the sheep. Who scatters the sheep? Again it is the religious leaders. "Therefore," Jeremiah continues, "thus saith the Lord God of Israel against the pastors who feed my people, Ye have scattered my flock, and driven them away, and have not visited them; behold, I will visit upon you the evil of your doings, saith the Lord." Don't you care for the sheep? Well then I will visit upon you the natural results of what you have taught. Malcolm Muggeridge, when he wrote in *The New Statesman,* "The Death Wish of the Liberal," saw from his own liberal background exactly where liberalism has led. Removing the absolutes, liberalism has led into a wilderness. It has eliminated the categories that make the difference between love and nonlove. It led us all the way to Antonioni's movie, *Blow-up,* advertised as "Murder without guilt, love without meaning." The sheep are scattered.

The sheep of today are scattered even further than they were by the false prophets of Jeremiah's day. At least the Jews had still some kind of gods, false as they were. Our generation has become so ridden with folly that it lives in a materialistic world, shut up finally to the flow of atoms, to the flow of consciousness, contemplating itself without categories and without values. And by the 1980s it has added the folly of a multitude of countless mysticisms. No wonder God says, "I am going to judge you for what you have done." Who was responsible for this in Jeremiah's day? The religious leaders. Who has done it in our own? Surely the greatest judgment must be not upon those who have destroyed from the outside. Certainly the greatest guilt rests upon the church which knew the truth, deliberately turned away from it, and now only presents men with relativism, an echo of modern secular thought.

Jeremiah continues in 23:11: "For both prophet and priest are profane; yea, in my house have I found their wickedness, saith the Lord." It is a horrible thing to dwell in wickedness if you're one of God's people. But to bring the wickedness into the house of God is a double sin. And God says, "Where has this wickedness sprung from? It has sprung from My own house." Likewise, in our own culture what has cut the ground from under the base was on the inside. In the days of deism in our country, it was indeed true that in places there were few Christians, but rarely did the church itself become deistic. Rather, although the churches may have shrunk in size, when a man entered the church usually he could hear the truth. But in our generation, when men listen at the doors of many churches, what they hear is nontruth.

Furthermore, we find these words in 23:13-16: "And I have seen folly in the prophets of Samaria; they prophesied in Baal, and caused my people, Israel, to err." That was in the northern kingdom. But now Jeremiah swings around to the southern kingdom, and he says, Are you better? "I have seen also in the prophets of Jerusalem an horrible thing; they commit adultery, and walk in lies; they strengthen also the hands of evildoers. . . ." What is this? Is it not situational ethics? Jeremiah continues: ". . . that none doth return from his wickedness; they are all of them unto me like Sodom, and its inhabitants as Gomorrah. Therefore, thus saith the Lord of hosts concerning the prophets, Behold, I will feed them with wormwood, and make them drink the water of gall; for from the prophets of Jerusalem is profaneness gone forth into all the land." And the 21st verse, "I have not sent these prophets, yet they ran; I have not spoken to them, yet they prophesied." They have come and spoken in the name of God, and they have said, "God says," but they have not had the Word of God. It has merely been their own words welling up inside themselves and echoing the society which surrounds them. These men come and say, "Here is the message of God," but it's not. It's the message of man.

Do you think God is going to take this lightly? If you believe that a holy God is really there, do you think He can take it lightly when people move among the people of God, and say, "This is the Word of God," when they are speaking only from themselves and are directly contradicting what God has propositionally revealed? How do you expect God to take it lightly? What is He? Is He really an old man rocking in a chair, blind and hard of hearing?

Once more we read in this same chapter, verse 26: "How long shall this be in the heart of the prophets that prophesy lies? Yea, they are prophets of the deceit of their own heart." And finally, we read in the 30th verse, which is especially strong, "Therefore, behold, I am against the prophets, saith the Lord, that steal my words every one from his neighbor." What do the prophets say? This prophet hears that prophet, and then he repeats the message. And all you hear are echoes. It is like being in a hollow, boarded-up building; all you hear is echo, echo, echo, echo. Study the theology of our own day and all you hear is the echo, echo, echo, ECHO! Echoing what? Echoing what this man says, what that man says, what materialistic sociology teaches, what materialistic psychology teaches, what materialistic economics teaches, what materialistic philosophy teaches. Echoing, echoing, *echoing* as though the words were sprinkled with holy water because they now repeat these same things in theological terms.

And do you expect God to sit there and just rock in the heavens and say, "Isn't that nice; isn't that nice; isn't that nice"? What kind of a god do you have? And if such a god existed, what kind of a god would he be? What would be the use of having him? People have said that we who are evangelicals believe in a sort of old man with a beard. And we say it's not true. But I must say that in looking upon the evangelical church, it seems to me very often we give them the right to say it. And so I speak to you, O church; I speak to you, O generation, and even to that portion of the evangelical church that's getting wobbly—I speak to you and say *God will judge!* If we don't have the courage to say that, and mean it, we cannot expect our generation to do more than say, "god words, god words, god words."

But we come to the worst sin of all. In 6:14 we read, "They have healed also the hurt of the daughter of my people slightly, saying, Peace, peace; when there is no peace." The same language is used in Jeremiah 8:9-11. What does it mean? Imagine a bulging wall that is about ready to fall, and somebody comes and just whitewashes it. The prophets were giving just such cheap solutions, healing the hurt of my people, says God, slightly, slightly.

They were saying, "It's better than you think. Don't be despondent, don't get disturbed, take it easy, the day is not so bad, we can care for it rather lightly, don't worry too much, peace, peace." And God says, "I hate this above everything else; My people are under My judgment because they have revolted from Me, and the prophets who claim to speak for God say peace, peace, when there is no peace." Near the end of Jeremiah's prophecy, in 27:14, 15, we find him speaking in exactly the same way: "Therefore, hearken not unto the words of the prophets that speak unto you, saying, Ye shall not serve the king of Babylon; for they prophesy a lie unto you." They were saying, "Don't worry; Babylon isn't going to take this country. Really it's not going to be so bad; you're going to make it." And then God said this: "For I have not sent them, saith the Lord, yet they prophesy a lie in my name." And so here you have it again—speaking lightly of what is serious, giving all kinds of secondary solutions.

What caused such a breakdown in *our* culture? The two world wars? Don't believe it. If the house had been strong, it would not have come down with the earthquake. If the heart had not been eaten out of the culture, the world wars would not have broken it. "Don't worry," some say, "it's only a technological problem, and technology will be a solution." But that is not true. Man would not be in the position he is in simply because of technological problems if he had had a really Christian base. An energy crisis? Of course it is serious, but it is not the heart of the problem. The fact that the United States is now urban rather than agrarian? Is this the final problem? No. To solve only the urban problem would be to heal "slightly." You can hear it over and over again— all kinds of secondary solutions to secondary problems. Of course these are problems, but they are not the central problem. And men who use theological language to fasten our eyes upon them as the central problem stand under the judgment of God, because they have forgotten that the real reason we are in such a mess is that we have turned away from the God who is there and the truth which He has revealed. The problem is that the house is so rotten that even smaller earthquakes shake it to the core.

Jeremiah, in 28:1-15, gives us a specific example of a prophet, Hananiah, who said, "Don't worry, everything is going to go well." Hananiah prophesied that within two years God would bring back the hostages that had been taken to Babylon. But God, speaking through Jeremiah, said, "Hananiah, it's not so, and not only is it not so, but God is going to judge you, because you are telling the people a lie. You're saying it's not going to be so bad when, O people of God," says Jeremiah, "the trouble has hardly begun." It is a serious thing indeed to use the name of God to say that secondary solutions can cure our problems when the real problem is that people have turned away from God and the truth that He has revealed in verbalized, propositional form concerning Himself.

We must understand that Jeremiah did not only say these things to great men in general. He named them by name: Manasseh, the king (chapter 15); Pashur, the chief governor in the house of the Lord (chapter 20); Zedekiah, the king (chapter 21); Shallum, the king, Jehoiakim, the king, and Coniah, the king (chapter 22); Hananiah, the prophet (chapter 28); and Shemaiah, as he was in Babylon writing letters back to Palestine (chapter 29). Most of these names appear in the latter portions of his prophecy. As the situation became more serious, Jeremiah did not lessen his message; rather, he began to name the great people by name, saying to them, "Look at what you have done."

What then are the results of his message? We have one indication in Anathoth, Jeremiah's home town. "Therefore, thus saith the Lord of the men of Anathoth, who seek thy life, saying, Prophesy not in the name of the Lord, that thou die not by our hand" (11:21). That is, the people of his own town said, "Jeremiah, if you don't keep quiet, we're going to kill you. We don't want your prophecy of judgment." The priests, the prophets, and the people violently opposed him. So in Jeremiah 26:8, "Now it came to pass, when Jeremiah had made an end of speaking all that the Lord had commanded him to speak unto all the people, that the priests and the prophets and all the people took him, saying, Thou shalt surely die." And in verse 11, "Then spoke the priests and the prophets unto the princes and to all the people, saying, This man is worthy to die; for he hath prophesied against this city, as ye have heard with your ears." Those of you who mean to be tellers of the Word of God in a generation like our own must understand that men are going to say, "You're cutting out the optimism and, therefore, we're going to bring every pressure against you that we can bring." When a man stands up in the communist or other totalitarian countries today and really speaks of the judgment of God, he gets the same treatment as Jeremiah. Even in the West the results are similar. Men say, "You're against our culture, you're against the unity of our culture, you're against the progress of our culture, you're against the optimism of our culture and country, and we're going to do what we can against you." Our culture may do little if we preach only the positive message, but if we are faithful and also preach judgment in state or church, the result will be the same as with Jeremiah.

Men haven't changed, not one bit. For a man to think that he can preach the Word of God today and not experience the true price of the cross of Christ in the sense of not being accepted by the culture—for a man to think that he can be a teller, whether he be a teacher, a minister, a Christian artist, poet, musician, movie maker, or dramatist—any man who thinks he can speak truly of the things of God today into such a culture as our own and not have such words spoken against him is foolish. It is not possible. It is not possible whether one is the teller with his music or with his voice, whether one plays an instrument or speaks out behind a pulpit, whether one writes a book or paints a picture. To think that one can give the Christian message and not have the world with its monolithic, post-Christian culture bear down on us is not to understand the fierceness of the battle in such a day as Jeremiah's or such a day as our own.

In Jeremiah 36:22-24 we find the same thing: the priests, the prophets, the people rise up against the message. "Now the king sat in the winter house in the ninth month; and there was a fire on the hearth burning before him. And it came to pass that, when Jehudi had read three or four leaves, he cut it with the penknife, and cast it into the fire that was on the hearth, until all the roll was consumed in the fire that was on the hearth. Yet they were not afraid." And Jeremiah is astonished that they can take the Word of God, cut it up with a knife, cast it into the fire, and burn it until the message is totally consumed! And he says with wonder, "Yet they were not afraid, nor rent their garments, neither the king, nor any of his servants that heard all these words."

This is an exact picture of our own generation. Men today do not perhaps burn the Bible, nor does the Roman Catholic Church any longer put it on the index, as it once did. But men destroy it in the form of exegesis; they destroy it in the way they deal with it. They destroy it by not reading it as written in normal literary form, by ignoring historical-grammatical exegesis, by changing the Bible's own perspective of itself as propositional revelation in space and time, in history, by saying only the "spiritual" portions of the Bible have authority for us.

I would say to you who call yourselves Bible-believing Christians, if you see the Word of God diminished as it is in our day and are not moved to tears and indignation, I wonder if you have any comprehension of the day in which we live. If we as Bible-believing Christians can see God's Word, God's verbalized, propositional communication, treated as it is so often treated and are not filled with sorrow and do not cry out, "But don't you realize the end thereof?"—I wonder: do we love His Word? If we fight our philosophic battles, our artistic battles, our scientific battles, our battles in literature, our battles in drama, without emotional involvement, do we really love God? How can we do it without being moved as Jeremiah was moved? How can we speak of judgment and yet not stand like the weeping prophet with tears?

CHAPTER FIVE

The Persistence of Compassion

We have already had a glimpse of the personal results to Jeremiah that the preaching of judgment brings. In Anathoth, the people said, "Keep quiet or we're going to kill you." The threats to his liberty were not idle, for we read in Jeremiah 20:2, "Then Pashur smote Jeremiah, the prophet, and put him in the stocks that were in the high gate of Benjamin, which was by the house of the Lord." The first thing they did was to fasten him in the stocks. Poor Jeremiah, who has been preaching faithfully in the midst of this "post-Christian" culture, finds himself in the stocks. But his punishment didn't end there.

The stocks were not enough for him, so they put him in prison. "For then the king of Babylon's army besieged Jerusalem; and Jeremiah, the prophet, was shut up in the court of the prison, which was in the king of Judah's house" (Jeremiah 32:2). Just as his prophecy is coming true, just as the king of Babylon is at the doors, just as the false prophets are being proven wrong, Jeremiah is put into prison, the prison that is in the king's house. Those who know the Doge's palace in Venice can picture this, because that palace contained the most important prison. Apparently it was the same there.

Later on in 33:1 Jeremiah is still in prison: "Moreover, the word of the Lord came unto Jeremiah the second time, while he was yet shut up in the court of the prison." But even that was not the end. In Jeremiah 37:15, 16 we read, "Wherefore, the princes were wroth with Jeremiah, and smote him, and put him in prison in the house of Jonathan, the scribe; for they had made that the prison. When Jeremiah was entered into the dungeon, and into the cells, and Jeremiah had remained there many days . . ." So they gradually increased the punishment—from the stocks, to a prison, to a dungeon. Finally, as we read Jeremiah 38:4-6, every one of us must be moved. For here is a man of flesh and blood, like ourselves, in a historic space-time situation with his own aspirations, and he is carted off and put into a dungeon. And now his very life is threatened: "Therefore, the princes said unto the king, We beseech thee, let this man be put to death; for thus he weakeneth the hands of the men of war that remain in this city." That is, Jeremiah is not giving an optimistic answer; he isn't saying everything is going to turn out well. He isn't saying there is an easy solution; all we need is a little more technical advance to make the grade. He is cutting down their humanistic optimism, saying that they are under the judgment of God, and thereby weakening the people, undercutting their morale. "For this man seeketh not the welfare of this people, but the hurt." Of course it is not true. Jeremiah is wanting their real welfare. He is saying, "You must be healed of the real disease, which is your revolt against God, and not merely of some superficial, external wound." But that didn't please the dignitaries.

So we read, "Then Zedekiah, the king, said, Behold, he is in your hand; for the king is not he who can do any thing against you. Then took they Jeremiah, and cast him into the dungeon . . . that was in the court of the prison; and they let down Jeremiah with cords. And in the dungeon there was no water, but mire; so Jeremiah sunk in the mire." The story would make vivid drama, but it is not merely a piece of theater. Jeremiah, a man like yourself, was put into the innermost dungeon where they put a rope around his arms and lowered him down into the mire. As he went down, he must have wondered, "What are my feet going to touch?" He wasn't going to drown, but there was mud at the bottom, and as they let him down, he sunk, and he sunk, and he sunk—to his knees, to his waist, to his armpits? We do not know, but he was there as a result of his faithful preaching of God's judgment to a post-Christian world.

It's no small thing to stick with the message. It's easy to opt out. Evangelicals can easily opt out into their own little ghetto, saying nice things to themselves and closing their eyes to the real situation that surrounds them. One can opt out in many ways. But if one really preaches the Word of God to a post-Christian world, he must understand that he is likely to end up like Jeremiah.

We must not think that Jeremiah's trials were merely physical. They were psychological as well, for Jeremiah never saw any change in his own lifetime. He knew that seventy years later the people would return, but he didn't live to see it. Jeremiah, like every man, lived existentially on the knife-edge of time, moment by moment; like all of us, he lived day by day within the confines of his own lifetime.

Jeremiah was not just a piece of cardboard; he had a psychological life just as you and I have. How then was he affected? There were times when Jeremiah was discouraged and overwhelmed.

In Jeremiah 15:10 we read, "Woe is me, my mother, that thou hast borne me a man of strife and a man of contention to the whole earth! I have neither lent on usury, nor men have lent to me on usury, yet every one of them doth curse me." I am glad Jeremiah said that, because I have known discouragement too. And if you are being faithful in your preaching and not just opting out, in a culture like ours you too will experience times of discouragement.

And you say, how can a man of God be discouraged? Anybody who asks that has never been in the midst of the battle; he understands nothing about a real struggle for God. We are real men. We are on this side of the Fall. We are not perfect. We have our dreams, our psychological needs, and we want to be fulfilled. There are times of heroism as we stand firm and are faithful in preaching to men who will not listen. But there are also times when we feel overwhelmed.

In Jeremiah 20:14-18, we read one of the great cries of discouragement in the Bible, parallel to some of the cries of Job. But the intriguing thing is that neither Job, nor Jeremiah, nor David in the Psalms (where David often cried out to God, saying, "Have You turned away Your face forever, O God? Where are You?")—in none of these cases does God reprove His people as long as they do not turn from Him, nor blaspheme Him, nor give up their integrity in their attitude toward Him. There is no contradiction here. It is possible to be faithful to God, and yet to be overwhelmed with discouragement as we face the world. In fact, if we are never overwhelmed, I wonder if we are fighting the battle with compassion and reality, or whether we are jousting with paper swords against paper windmills.

So Jeremiah says in 20:14-18, "Cursed be the day on which I was born; let not the day on which my mother bore me be blessed. Cursed be the man who brought tidings to my father, saying, A man child is born unto thee; making him very glad. And let that man be like the cities which the Lord overthrew, and repented not; and let him hear the cry in the morning, and the shouting at noontide, because he slew me not from the womb; or that my mother might have been my grave, and her womb to be always great with me. Wherefore came I forth out of the womb to see labor and sorrow, that my days should be consumed with shame?" Jeremiah was discouraged because he was a man standing against a flood. And I want to say to you that nobody who is fighting the battle in our own generation can float on a Beautyrest mattress. If you love God and love men and have compassion for them, you will pay a real price psychologically.

So many people seem to think that if the Holy Spirit is working, then the work is easy. Don't believe it! As the Holy Spirit works, a man is consumed. This is the record of the revivals; it is the record of those places in which God has really done something. It is not easy!

As I stand and try to give a message out into the world—at the café tables and in the universities, to individuals and large seminars, publicly and privately—a price has to be paid. Often there is discouragement. Many times I say, "I can't go up the hill once more. I can't do it again." And what is God's answer? Well, first it is important to know that God doesn't scold a man when his tiredness comes from his battles and his tears from compassion. Second, it is learning to say, and mean, "Lord, please make your strength perfect in my weakness."

Jeremiah, we recall, was the weeping prophet. This has psychological depth as well as historic meaning. He is really *the man weeping*. But what does God expect of Jeremiah? What does God expect of every man who preaches into a lost age like ours? I'll tell you what God expects. He simply expects a man to go right on. He doesn't scold a man for being tired, but neither does He expect him to stop his message because people are against him. Jeremiah proclaimed the message to the very end. He was always against going down to Egypt for help. And, as the captivity came, he could have escaped to Babylon. Instead he stayed with the people of God to keep preaching the message even after the judgment had fallen. His people dragged him down to Egypt, and even there he continued to preach the same message, down in Egypt where he never, never wanted to go.

Jeremiah, then, provides us with an extended study of an era like our own, where men have turned away from God and society has become post-Christian. Now, before returning to the book of Romans with which this book began, we should tie together the exposition of Jeremiah.

First, we may say that there is a time, and ours is such a time, when a negative message is needed before anything positive can begin. There must first be the message of judgment, the tearing down. There are times—and Jeremiah's day and ours are such times—when we cannot expect a constructive revolution if we begin by overemphasizing the positive message. People often say to me, What would you do if you met a really modern man on a train and you had just an hour to talk to him about the gospel? And I've said over and over, I would spend forty-five or fifty minutes on the negative, to really show him his dilemma—to show him that he is more dead than even he thinks he is; that he is not just dead in the twentieth-century meaning of dead (not having significance in this life), but that he is morally dead because he is separated from the God who exists. Then I'd take ten or fifteen minutes to preach the gospel. And I believe this usually is the right way for the truly modern man, for often it takes a long time to bring a man to the place where he understands the negative. And unless he understands what's wrong, he will not be ready to listen to and understand the positive. I believe that much of our evangelistic and personal work today is not clear simply because we are too anxious to get to the answer without having a man realize the real cause of his sickness, which is true moral guilt (and not just psychological guilt-feelings) in the presence of God. But the same is true in a culture. If I am going to speak to a culture, such as my culture, the message must be the message of Jeremiah. It must be the same in both private and public discourse.

Secondly, with love we must face squarely the fact that our culture really is under the judgment of God. We must not heal the sickness slightly. We must emphasize the reality. We must proclaim the message with tears and give it with love. Through the work of the Holy Spirit there must be a simultaneous exhibition of

God's holiness and His love as we speak. We cannot shout at people or scream down upon them. They must feel that we are with them, that we are saying that both of us are sinners, and they must know these are not just words, but that we mean what we say. They must feel in our own attitudes that we know we too are sinners, that we are not innately good because we have been born into an evangelical home, attend an evangelical church or an evangelical school, or take some external sacraments.

There is in all of this a time for tears. It will not do to say these things coldly. Jeremiah cried, and we must cry for the poor lost world, for we are all of one kind. There is, of course, a sense in which there are two humanities—one saved, one lost. But the Bible also tells us that there is only one humanity; we all have a common ancestor, and all have been made in the image of God. So I *must* have tears for my kind. But with the tears the message must be clear: our culture, our country, our churches have walked upon what God has given us, and thus all these are under the judgment of God.

It is my experience that giving the realistic message does not turn people off—if they feel real compassion in you. As a matter of fact, it is the other way. The real thinkers and the serious artists understand the scream of modern man: "There's something wrong with my culture. It is a dead end."

Take, for example, the picture by Edvard Munch in which a man is screaming. Or listen to people crying, "It's plastic. Our culture is plastic." Modern man knows something is wrong, but no one tells him why. It is up to Christians to do so, to point out what is wrong and to show modern man why he is hung up and why his culture is plastic.

Often Christians, young and old alike, have not faced the facts about their own countries—that they are under the judgment of God. Perhaps that explains why they are often without enthusiasm in their proclamation of the gospel, why they just give the crumbling wall a coat of paint.

Third, we must say that if we believe in truth, we must practice truth. We live in an age of synthesis and relativism; men don't believe truth exists. How do we expect a world to take us seriously when we say we believe truth exists and then live in a relativistic way?

I would like to quote from the last appendix in my book, *The God Who Is There*. Its title is "The Practice of Truth." This gives in an abridged form the speech I gave in Berlin at The World Congress on Evangelism: "In regard to the first of the principles of which we spoke: *The full doctrinal position of historic Christianity must be clearly maintained,* it would seem to me that the central problem of evangelical orthodoxy in the second half of the twentieth century is the problem of the *practice* of this principle. This is especially so when we take into account the spiritual and intellectual mentality which is dominant in our century. . . . The unity of orthodox or evangelical Christianity should be centered around this emphasis on *truth*. It is always important, but doubly so when we are surrounded by so many for whom the concept of truth, in the sense of antithesis, is considered to be totally unthinkable. . . . Moreover, in our age of synthesis men will not take our protestations of truth seriously unless they see by our actions that we seriously *practice* truth and antithesis in the unity we try to establish and in our activities. . . . Both a clear comprehension of the importance of truth and a practice of it, even when it is costly to do so, are imperative if our witness and our evangelism are to be significant in our generation and in the flow of history. . . . In an age of relativity the *practice* of truth when it is costly is the only way to cause the world to take seriously our protestations concerning truth. Cooperation and unity that do not lead to purity of life and purity of doctrine are just as faulty and incomplete as an orthodoxy which does not lead to a concern for, and a reaching out towards, those who are lost. . . . All too often the only antithesis we have exhibited to the world and to our own children has been *talking* about holiness *or* our *talking* about love, rather than the consideration and practice of holiness and love together as truth— in antithesis to what is false in theology, in the church, and the surrounding culture."

I want to ask you something. Remember the false prophets in Jeremiah's day saying, "Peace, peace." Can you imagine Jeremiah saying to them, "We're all in one group because we all wear ecclesiastical colored ties"? I can't. He didn't do it. And I firmly believe that this is one of the things we must understand in our days of desperate need when men no longer believe in truth. We cannot expect them to take seriously our belief in objective truth, if in our practice we indicate only a quantitative difference between all men who are in ecclesiastical structures or who use certain forms of theological language. I do not mean that we should not have open dialogue with men; my words and practice emphasize that I believe love demands that. But I do mean that we should not give the impression in our practice that just because they are expressed in traditional Christian terminology all religious concepts are on a graduated, quantitative spectrum—that in regard to central doctrine no chasm exists between right and wrong.

Fourth, we must realize that to know the truth and to practice it will be costly. At times the price will be high in your individual family. Often there is a tremendous pressure upon young Christians as they face their non-Christian families. But the price is also high in society. You may not get the honor which you covet in the scholastic world, in the artistic world, in the medical world, or in the business world. The price may be high indeed.

Fifth, we must keep on speaking and acting even if the price is high. There is nothing in the Bible that says we are to stop. The Bible rather says, keep on, keep on. We may think of Paul as he writes in 2 Corinthians 11:24-28 (paraphrase): "I've been beaten by the Jews, I've been beaten by the Gentiles, I've battled the seas, I've known the wrath of men, and I've known the force of Satan." Did Paul stop? Paul said, "No, I want to come to Rome and preach the gospel there as well."

Perhaps you know this story of Martin Luther. When he had begun his preaching, he received word about the first Protestant martyrs. Some monks had read Martin Luther's work, turned to this way of thinking, and were burned alive in the Grand Place in Brussels. There is now a marker in the Grand Place where they were burned. And the story is that when Martin Luther heard that, he began to walk the floor and he said, "I can't go on. I can't do it any more. Because of me, other men are being killed. I can't go on!" Then as he wrestled with it, he understood that because it was truth, no matter what the cost to himself or anybody else, he must go on. Thank God, Martin Luther marched straight forward, and we had the Reformation.

Christianity is not a modern success story. It is to be preached with love and tears into the teeth of men, preached without compromise, without regard to the world's concept of success. If there seem to be no results, remember that Jeremiah did not see the results in his day. They came later. If there seem to be no results, it does not change God's imperative. It is simply up to you and to me to go on, go on, go on, whether we see the results or whether we don't. *Go on.*

We in L'Abri Fellowship have seen many results, and we have much to be thankful for. We have seen many things to encourage us, but there are also discouragements. And even if there were only discouragements, God's Word is still the message to Jeremiah: go on and teach and act, preach the truth of the revelation of God no matter what the cost; go on, go on, go on. If you are not willing to go on, you have to ask yourself the question, do I really believe Christianity is truth or is my Christianity only an upper-story religious concept? Do I really believe Christianity is truth, or does my Christianity rest only on an experience, an emotion—and when the experience, the emotion, cools, my Christianity collapses?

Our day is not totally unique. Time after time Christian cultures have thrown themselves away. Take, for example, the church of the Apostle Thomas in India. It began to whittle away at the truth. So the church largely died. There are two ways to bring about such death: one is to compromise the truth, and the other to have a dead orthodoxy. Both can equally grind down and destroy the message of a church in a generation, especially if the generation is hard. Do we realize that in China at about the year A.D. 800 there were Christian churches in almost every great city? Do we realize that there were hundreds of Christians in the Arabian peninsula just before Mohammed in A.D. 550? Why was it that Mohammedanism was able to rush over that country? Because of military force? Not only that. When Mohammed came forward and looked at the Christians he said, "There's nothing here." And he was largely right. Mohammedanism started, and it swept that portion of the world. The same thing was true with the church in North Africa, and the primitive church in Armenia, in Georgia, in Gaul. In each of these places there was a Christian church and a growing Christian culture, but the church collapsed. The pattern is clear: defection and then destruction.

And we as Christians today, what are we saying? We are saying that we want reformation and we want revival, but still we are not preaching into this generation, stating the negative things that are necessary. If there is to be a constructive revolution in the orthodox, evangelical church, then like Jeremiah we must speak of the judgment of individual men great and small, of the church, the state, and the culture, for many of them have known the truth of God and have turned away from Him and His propositional revelation. God exists, He is holy, and we must know that there will be judgment. And like Jeremiah, we must keep on so speaking regardless of the cost to ourselves.

My concluding sentence is simply this: The world is lost, the God of the Bible does exist; the world is *lost,* but truth is truth. Keep on! And for how long? I'll tell you. Keep on, keep on, keep on, keep on, and then KEEP ON!

CHAPTER SIX

The Significance of Man

This book began with an analysis of Romans 1:21, 22, verses which tell us why man is in the dilemma he is in. Man knew the truth and yet deliberately turned away. I spoke especially of how our generation has turned away in the last decades, and then I compared our age with Jeremiah's in order to show what sort of message we as Christians must speak into our twentieth-century post-Christian world.

In this chapter and in the two to follow I wish to return to the analysis of Romans. I will begin by looking again at the verses, Romans 1:21, 22, to see how the Bible considers man himself—his nature and his significance.

Increasingly, twentieth-century men tend to emphasize some sort of determinism. Usually it is one of three kinds: chemical determinism (such as the Marquis de Sade put forward and as Francis Crick maintains today), psychological determinism (as emphasized by Freud and those who follow him), or environmental determinism (as taught by B. F. Skinner and his followers). In the former, man is a pawn of chemical forces. In the second, every decision that a man makes is already determined on the basis of what has occurred to him psychologically in the past (especially when he was very young). In the third, we are only a product of our environment. In all three, man is no longer responsible for what he is or does. Man is no more than a part of a cosmic machine.

The Bible's view of man could not be more different. Romans 1:21, 22 says, "When they knew God, they glorified him not as God, neither were thankful, but became vain in their reasoning, and their foolish heart was darkened. Professing themselves to be wise, they became fools." The whole emphasis of these verses is that man has known the truth and deliberately turned away from it. But if that is so, then man is wonderful: he can really influence significant history. Since God has made man in His own image, man is not caught in the wheels of determinism. Rather, man is so great that he can influence history for himself and for others, for this life and the life to come.

I am convinced that one of the great weaknesses in evangelical preaching in the last years is that we have lost sight of the biblical fact that man is wonderful. We have seen the unbiblical humanism which surrounds us, and to resist this in our emphasis on man's lostness we have tended to reduce man to a zero. Man is indeed lost, but that does not mean he is nothing. We *must* resist humanism, but to make man a zero is not the right way to resist it. You can emphasize that man is totally lost and still have the biblical answer that man is really great. In fact, only the biblical position produces a real and proper "humanism." Naturalistic humanism leads to a diminishing of man and eventually to a zeroing of man. But the Christian position is that man is made in the image of God and even though he is now a sinner, he can do those things that are tremendous—he can influence history for this life and the life to come, for himself and for others.

Consequently, man's actions are not a piece of theater, not just a play. If you see a play one night and then you see it the next night, you know the ending is going to be the same because it is the same play. You see it the third night, and it is the same again. The actions of the characters are a piece of theater; they are not open to change. But the Bible's emphasis is that man is responsible; his choices influence history. Even sin is not nothingness. Romans 1:21, 22 implies the greatness of man.

Perhaps a figure of speech will help. Imagine history, space-time history, as feminine, and us (all men and women) as masculine. As masculine figures, we can impregnate history. We can plant into it seeds that come to fruition in the external world. Just as a man can so impregnate that what is brought forth are legitimate children or illegitimate children, so the Bible stresses that all people are able to impregnate history with what is either good or bad.

In short, therefore, man is not a cog in a machine; he is not a piece of theater; he really can influence history. From the biblical viewpoint, *man is lost, but great.*

We could spend a long time on this point because, I'm convinced, it is crucial to our discussion with twentieth-century people to make plain that Christianity does not destroy the meaningfulness of a man. In fact, it is the only system which gives a final and sufficient meaning to man. Man can influence history even if often, unhappily, that influence in history is not good.

Let us notice that Romans 1:21 says something else. It tells us how men begin to slide when they know the true God. Those of us who are Christians, true Bible-believing Christians, may take it as a warning to ourselves: "When they knew God, they glorified him not as God, neither were thankful." And I am convinced that the first step in God's people turning away from Him—even while they tenaciously and aggressively defend the orthodox position—is ceasing to be in relationship with Him with a thankful heart. Therefore, as we read this as Christians, though the central thrust is why lost man is in the position he is, it must also speak to us. Let us be careful—we who stand for the orthodox, historic Christian faith in the twentieth century—that we have a thankful heart. Otherwise it will not be many years until the orthodoxy is gone and we are faced with heterodoxy.

God through Paul puts Romans 1:21 into a very carefully reasoned setting. As a matter of fact, the first eight chapters of the book of Romans are the most systematic presentation of the Christian position in the New Testament. It is my theory that the reason the first eight chapters of Romans make a unity within the unity of the whole book of Romans is that they present Paul's basic message into the Greek and Roman world. Romans is the only book written by Paul to a church he had not visited. When he wrote to Ephesus or Corinth, Paul could assume they already had the basic message because he had preached it to them. But when he wrote to Rome, where he had not preached, he first carefully presented the total structure of the Christian position. Then, of course, he added to it the later chapters. The Greek and Roman world is not very distant from our own world in its intellectual setting. It was a world of thinkers, a highly developed world, such as our own. And we can see here both what Paul preached and what he thought men must know if they were to understand true Christianity.

The first eight chapters are divided into a very orderly sequence. Romans 1:1-15 is the introduction, and 1:16, 17 is the theme of all the rest: "For I am not ashamed of the gospel of Christ; for it is the power of God [the *dunamis* of God, the root of our word *dynamite*] unto salvation to everyone that believeth; to the Jew first, and also to the Greek. For in it is the righteousness of God revealed from faith to faith; as it is written, The just shall live by faith." Here Paul sets forth the theme of the Christian message. And Romans 1:18 through 8:39 is a running, full exegesis of these two verses.

This exegesis is divided into several sections. First is the need of salvation (1:18—3:20). And, as we have seen in the chapter prior to this, there is a necessary negative before men are ready to listen to a positive. Second is justification (3:21—4:25). So far Paul is talking about how to become a Christian. In the third section he assumes his readers are believers and talks about sanctification in the Christian life, and this is, of course, related to our theme of reformation and specifically to revival (5:1—8:17). Fourth is glorification, touching on the things in the future (8:18-25). Lastly, 8:26-39 tells us that eternal life is forever. Here, then, is a very closely argued structure.

Very often those who must travel and speak a great deal have a basic message which they adapt as they move. I think this was true of Jesus. I believe Jesus gave His teaching many times over. That is one possible explanation for the slight differences in the various Gospel accounts. He simply gave the same message in a slightly different way for each slightly different situation. If you had followed Paul, I think you would have heard him giving the same basic message over and over again in order that the gospel would have sufficient content. In fact, wherever there has been great preaching and great evangelizing, it has always stressed a sufficient content. People cannot be saved without it. Christianity must be communicated with sufficient content. Consequently, we find that Paul was careful to give sufficient information to those to whom he was preaching.

Now let us notice further the phrase from verse 16: "For I am not ashamed of the gospel." In Romans 1:16 and 5:5, I think Paul is playing upon the word *ashamed*. In chapter 5, Paul, talking to Christians, writes, "And hope maketh not ashamed, because the love of God is shed abroad in our hearts by the Holy Spirit which is given unto us." Paul says that in experience after you are a Christian, you will not be ashamed. But in 1:16 he is addressing those who are not yet Christians and is saying that he—Paul the preacher, Paul the educated man—was not ashamed of the *system* of the gospel, the *system* of Truth, the content of the gospel, as he presented it to the minds of men in the educated Greek and Roman world. He was *not ashamed,* because it gives the answers, the answers that nothing else gives.

I'm convinced that we today will not be able to speak out with confidence unless we understand that we need not be ashamed of the gospel and the *answers* it gives to men. If we do not have this confidence, men will feel our defensiveness, and it will not commend the gospel to them. It is just such intellectual defensiveness in preaching the gospel in the educated world that diminishes its effect. But Paul says, "I'm not ashamed when I stand on Mars Hill, because I have answers that the Greek philosopher does not have. I am not ashamed in the rough and tumble of the marketplace, because I know that the Bible is going to give me the true answers that men need and that nothing else gives."

Sadly enough, there is a kind of an anti-intellectualism among many Christians; spirituality is falsely pitted against intellectual comprehension as though they stood in a dichotomy. Such anti-intellectualism cuts away at the very heart of the Christian message. Of course, there is a false intellectualism which does destroy the work of the Holy Spirit. But it does not arise when men wrestle honestly with honest questions and then see that the Bible has the answers. This does not oppose true spirituality. So Paul writes, "I'm not ashamed. I'm not ashamed of the gospel because it will answer the questions of men; it is the *dunamis* of God unto salvation to everyone who believes, to the Jew first, and also to the Greek."

When Paul speaks here of *salvation,* he is not limiting the term to becoming a Christian. The concept of *salvation* in Scripture is much broader than the concept of justification. Salvation is the whole process that results from the finished work of Jesus Christ as He died in space and time upon the cross. In justification, our guilt is removed by God's forensic declaration that since a man has cast himself upon Jesus Christ and is relying on His finished work, his guilt is gone. But salvation is also sanctification (the Christian life) and glorification (that great day when the Lord Jesus Christ returns and the Christian's body is raised). And so what Paul is saying is, "I am not ashamed of the gospel which is the power of God for the salvation of the whole man, the whole of what was affected by the Fall, and the whole of our future into eternity."

Let us understand that true Christianity is not Platonic. Much, however, of what passes for Christianity does have the ring of Platonic thinking in it. Platonism says that the body is bad or is to be despised. The only thing that matters is the soul. But the Bible says God made the whole man, the whole man is to know salvation, and the whole man is to know the Lordship of Jesus Christ in the whole of life. The great teaching of the resurrection of the body is not just abstract doctrine; it stands as a pledge and reminder of a very important and a very hopeful fact. It says God made the whole man. God made man spirit and body, and He is interested in both. He made man with an intellect, and He is interested in the intellect. He made man with an artistic and creative sense of beauty, and He is interested in that. Body, mind, artistic sense: these things are not low; they are high. Of course, they can become wrong if they are put in the wrong perspective, but they are not wrong, nor unimportant, in themselves. Therefore, since God made the whole man and is interested in the whole man, the salvation which Paul preaches is a salvation which touches the whole man.

Salvation has something to say not only to the individual man, but also to the culture. Christianity is individual in the sense that each man must be converted, born again, one at a time. But it is not individualistic. The distinction is important. As God made man, He also made an Eve so that there could be finite, horizontal relationships between two people. And these human relationships are important to God, for "the power of God unto salvation" is also meant to give an answer to the sociological needs of man, the interplay between two people and all people. God is interested in the whole man and also in the culture which flows from people's relationship with each other.

So when Paul is saying here that he is not ashamed of the gospel which is the power of God unto salvation, do not think it covers just a small area. It has something to say about every division that has come because of the Fall. From the Christian viewpoint, all the alienations that we find in man have come because of man's historic, space-time fall. First of all, man is separated from God; second, he is separated from himself (thus the psychological problems of life); third, he is separated from other men (thus the sociological problems of life); fourth, he is separated from nature (thus the problems of living in the world—for example, the ecological problems). All these need healing.

No wonder Paul says, "I'm not ashamed of the gospel intellectually because it is going to have the answers that men need. I am not ashamed of the gospel because it is the power of God unto salvation in every single area; it has answers and meaning for both eternity and now." The gospel is great. If you are an evangelical Christian, you should be convinced that biblical Christianity is not tawdry; it is not a small thing dealing with a small area of life. If you are unsaved, you should realize that Christianity is titanic. It speaks to every need of man, not by a leap in the dark, but by good and sufficient reasons. In presenting the content of Christianity Paul says there is salvation—justification, sanctification, and glorification—for the whole man.

Notice too that Paul says, "to the Jew first and also to the Greek." One of the marks of the theology from Karl Barth onward is universalism, the notion that eventually all men are saved. In Barth this universalism was implicit; in those who follow him it was explicit. In Scripture there is no universalism of this type, but there is a universalism of another kind—the teaching that one message fulfills the need of all men. This is true biblical universalism: whether a man is a Jew or a Gentile, whether he lives in the West or the East, whether he lived in ages gone by or in the present, there is one message that will fulfill, or would have fulfilled, his needs: the message of the gospel of Jesus Christ. Paul speaks to both kinds of men—the Jew (the man with the Bible) and the Greek (the man without the Bible). That is, there is a universal message that is fitting for all men and for their total need.

In the 17th verse we read, "For in it is the righteousness of God revealed from faith to faith; as it is written, The just shall live by faith." He is quoting from Habakkuk 2:4. Paul is saying something more than that one becomes a Christian by faith. As a matter of fact, one must be careful to understand that phrase, for often it is presented so that it is no longer biblical. The *basis* of our salvation is not our faith. Faith is rather the instrument, the empty hands with which we accept the gift. We are not saved by faith in faith. The basis of our salvation is the finished work of Jesus

Christ in space and time. Paul emphasizes this in the third chapter where he says we are saved upon the basis of the work of Jesus Christ. Faith is raising empty hands in accepting the gift.

But if this is true for justification, it is also true for sanctification. And so we not only become Christians by faith, but we live existentially by faith. The word *existential* may be confusing, but the concept is important enough to warrant some explanation. There are two basic ways to use the term *existential*. It may refer to existentialism, a philosophy that says there is no real, or reasonable, meaning to man. This definition is perhaps too simple, but it will do. On the other hand *existential* refers to moment-by-moment reality. A Christian must reject the philosophy of existentialism, but he must emphasize what is truly existential, for the Bible does not teach a static situation in which one becomes a Christian and that's it. Rather, it teaches that time is moving, and a relationship to God is important at every given existential moment. Consequently, you do not begin the Christian life by faith and then remain static. You continue to live it by faith. Much of Paul's teaching from Romans 5 on deals with this. The Christian, then, should be the true existentialist, moving upon the knife-edge of time, in every given moment being in relationship with God. Moment-by-moment living by faith is what is taught here.

I have tried to set the stage for the carefully reasoned presentation which Paul makes in Romans 1:18 through 2:16 as he talks to *the man without the Bible*. All men—lost or saved—are great in their significance. Having been made in the image of God, man is magnificent even in ruin. God made man to be responsible for his thoughts and his actions, and man fashions a significant history. This is true of both Christians and non-Christians, both men with the Bible and men without the Bible.

CHAPTER SEVEN

The Man Without the Bible

In three different places Paul speaks solely to men without the Bible. The first is in Lystra (Acts 14:15-17), where the message is fragmentary because it was interrupted. The second is on Mars Hill (Acts 17:16-32), where he has a longer speech, but that also was broken off. Third is the Book of Romans, 1:18—2:16, where he can develop his argument at ease. We can see here what he was really saying in all these places, for the other two conform to this early section in Romans.

Here, I believe, is where God gives us the method of preaching to our generation, for our generation is largely made up of men without the Bible. How are you going to start talking to them? Are you only going to quote from the Bible if they don't know anything about it, or if they despise or ignore it or do not know its authority? Paul didn't. In this passage from Romans 1:18 to 2:16 he does not once quote from the Old Testament. When he begins to talk to the Jew, however, after 2:17, he does quote from the Scripture, because the Jews knew what the Bible was. But in the first part, where he talks to the Greek, the man without the Bible, he talks to him in a different way. And I repeat: I believe that we can learn from this the method of preaching to our generation.

How, then, does Paul begin to speak to the man without the

Bible? He says this in the 18th verse: "For the wrath of God is revealed from heaven against all ungodliness and unrighteousness of men, who hold the truth in unrighteousness." Many of the new translations read "hinder the truth," but I think "hold," from the King James Version, is the better translation. The first thing Paul says to the man without the Bible is this: "You're under the wrath of God because you hold the truth in unrighteousness." Notice that he immediately begins to preach the wrath of God. Think now of this man without the Bible (he is no different then than now). If you merely say what Paul said in verses 16 and 17, "Here's salvation," he will shrug his shoulders and say, "Why do I need salvation?" Or if modern man thinks he needs salvation, it will be some twentieth-century psychological salvation. But Paul says, "No. What you need is moral salvation. You are guilty. You have true guilt in the presence of God."

Terry Southern (who wrote *Candy* and *The Magic Christian*) had something important to say in the preface to *Writers in Revolt*. He made a distinction between the communist countries, in which the state has built arbitrary absolutes on the basis of arbitrary law, and the modern West, which has oriented everything psychologically. He had a clever sentence which said that we are the first generation in history to do away with crime. He did not mean there is no crime, but that we no longer call it crime; we explain everything as only psychological. When modern man (whether he is educated or not) thinks he needs salvation, usually he is not thinking of salvation from moral guilt, but rather relief from psychological guilt-feelings.

I am convinced that many men who preach the gospel and love the Lord are really misunderstood. People make a "profession of faith," but because they haven't understood the message, they are not really saved. They feel a psychological need and they want psychological relief, but they don't understand that the Christian message is not talking only about psychological relief (though it includes that), but is talking about true moral guilt in the presence of a holy God who exists. The real need is salvation from true moral guilt, not just relief from guilt-feelings. And I am certain many people who make a profession go away still unsaved, having not heard one word of the real gospel because they have filtered the message through their own thought-forms and their own intellectual framework in which the word *guilt* equals *guilt-feelings*.

But Paul will not allow this. He speaks immediately of the wrath of God, and anyone who is unwilling to speak of the wrath of God does not understand the Christian faith. We have a great verse telling us how to be saved: "He that believeth on the Son hath everlasting life" (John 3:36). But you must remember that the end of that verse is this: "and he that believeth not the Son shall not see life; but the wrath of God abideth on him." There is no real preaching of the Christian gospel except in light of the fact that man is under the wrath of God—the moral wrath of God. So Paul has a reply to the man who shrugs his shoulders and says, "Why do I need salvation?" His response is this: "You need salvation because you are under the wrath of God. You have broken God's law."

We must be careful here, for there is, of course, a very false Christian legalism. Paul preaches against it in Galatians. Nevertheless, there is no Christian message without a proper legalism. It is this that demarcates Christian from non-Christian thinking at this point. The non-Christian, in the twentieth century especially, has no legal and moral base. Everything floats in space: a 51 percent vote of some type of right-wing or left-wing authoritarianism must decide what is acceptable, or some form of hedonism must be adopted, because, as Plato understood so well, an absolute is necessary for real morality. Plato never found such an absolute, but he understood the problem and so did the Neoplatonic men of the Renaissance.

But the Bible is clear: there is a moral law of the universe. And that basic law is the character of God Himself. There is no law behind God that binds God. Rather, God Himself is the law because He is not a contentless God, but a God with a character. His character *is* the law of the universe. When He reveals this character to us in verbalized, propositional form, we have the commands of God for men. Thus there are absolutes and categories; the law which the God who exists has revealed and which is based upon His character is final. This is the biblical position.

Therefore, when men break these commands, they are guilty, guilty in the same way a man is guilty when he breaks the law of the state. When a man sins, he sins against the character of God, and he has moral guilt in the presence of the Great Judge. I know very well that people don't talk in these terms often any more. But it's to our loss. In contrast to left-wing or right-wing totalitarianism with its changing arbitrary absolutes and in contrast to modern man's relativistic, moral and legal chaos, the Bible's teaching alone gives moral answers to men.

We are told in this 18th verse that the man without the Bible *holds* the truth in unrighteousness. Or if you choose, you can say he *hinders* or *suppresses* the truth. I will deal later with the difference between *hold* and *hinder*. For the moment I will use the word *suppress,* which is used in many modern translations.

What truth then does *the man without the Bible* suppress? Formerly we talked about apostasy in a generation which knew the gospel and turned away from it. The Jews of Jeremiah's day suppressed the truth of the Bible which they had. But what truth does man suppress if he does not have the Bible? We read in verses 19 and 20, "Because that which may be known of God is manifest in them; for God hath shown it unto them. For the invisible things of him from the creation of the world are clearly seen, being understood by the things that are made."

Paul divides the truth which they suppress into two parts. It's interesting that they are the same two things that Carl Gustav Jung said cut across man's will: first of all, the external world; and secondly, those things that well up from inside the person. Jung, though he has no real solution, exactly identifies the two basic things that confront man—man himself, and the external universe. And Paul said long ago these are the two truths which man, even the man without the Bible, suppresses. As we have seen, Paul preached in other places to the Gentiles without Jews present, in Lystra and on Mars Hill. There too he used the same approach to the man without the Bible.

We should look in more detail at the truth about man which those without the Bible suppress. The list is rather long, for man is distinguished from both animals and machines on the basis of his creativity, his moral motions, his need for love, his fear of nonbeing, and his longings for beauty and for meaning. Only the biblical system has a way of explaining these factors which make man unique.

In Romans 2:15 Paul put special emphasis upon the moral motions of man: "Who show the work of the law written in their hearts, their conscience also bearing witness, and their thoughts the meanwhile accusing or else excusing one another."

God through Paul is saying here exactly what I feel we should say to modern man. And it is this: despite what a man may say in theory, he cannot escape having moral motions. The man who says morals do not exist is not amoral in the sense that he has no moral motions. Men may have different mores, but one never finds people without moral motions.

Talk to any man or woman, they may seem absolutely amoral. But if you can really talk to them, you find that they do have their own moral standards. They may be different; they may be very poor. But they are not just a machine. Modern people, as I have said, see themselves as in a deterministic situation where morals have no meaning; but they cannot, and do not, live this way.

We have a startling illustration of this in the Marquis de Sade, who was not only a pornographer, but a real philosopher. Those who are materialists have something to wrestle with in the Marquis de Sade's formulation, something that no determinist has ever been able to answer. The Marquis de Sade said that since everything is chemically determined, then whatever is, is right. Think about that for six months. The simple fact is that there is no way around that conclusion. De Sade is right. And sadism is the perfectly logical result. Obviously nature made man stronger than the woman; therefore, a man has the right to do anything he wants to a woman. That was de Sade's particular form of sadism. Nobody who holds any concept of determinism, either chemical or psychological, can explain why the Marquis de Sade is wrong. Determinism leads in the direction of cruelty and inhumanity, whether it takes the specific form of de Sade's sadism or not.

But even the Marquis de Sade, who indeed would have claimed that all men were merely determined, couldn't live this way. If you read carefully in what he wrote and examine his history, you find that at the end of his life, he was in an insane asylum in Charenton. What he was doing hardly seems possible. He was spending his time grumbling about the way he was being treated by the jailors, and he was reading the letters of his wife with meticulous care, having worked out some sort of system whereby he thought he could figure out from the number of letters in the lines the day he was going to get out. The simple fact is that men, even a Marquis de Sade, may say there is no such thing as morality and that all is a fixed situation, but in their own actions they demonstrate what they deny in their writings.

I have always enjoyed the thought of Khrushchev sitting at the United Nations, pounding on the table with his shoe and shouting, "It's wrong. It's wrong." Isn't that an interesting thing for a materialist to say? He didn't mean that something was merely counter to the best interests of the Soviet Union. He was saying something was wrong.

Moral motions distinguish man from non-man, but so does the need for love. Man feels the necessity of a love that means more than a sexual relationship. Many of the same people who say that love is only sexual go through marriage after marriage, hoping to find something more than physical satisfaction. Even when they say love is only sexual, they are looking for something to make *love* mean what the heart of man longs to have it mean. They simply cannot live consistently with their own view.

For a few men, the need for beauty is the point at which the mannishness of man most clearly shows through, even though on the basis of their own concept of man as a chance configuration of atoms in an impersonal universe, the very meaning of the word *beauty* is open to question.

All men, however, have a deep longing for significance, a longing for meaning. I was struck by the opening to Will and Ariel Durant's *The Lessons of History*. In the first paragraph they meditate on the cosmic dimensions of the universe, on the fact that the planets will remain not only when individual men are gone, but even after the whole race of man is gone. They were impressed with man's transience much as Proust was when he said that the dust of death is on everything human. But as to man's significance, all the Durants can point to is a kind of dignity that man has because he can observe the planets and they cannot observe him. It's quite clear: no man—no matter what his philosophy is, no matter what his era or his age—is able to escape the longing to be more than merely a stream of consciousness or a chance configuration of atoms now observing itself by chance.

In an extreme form, the longing for significance expresses itself most clearly in the fear of nonbeing. It has been obvious for centuries that men fear death, but depth-psychologists tell us that such a fear, while not found in animals, is for man a basic psychosis: no man, regardless of his theoretical system, is content to look at himself as a finally meaningless machine which can and will be discarded totally and forever. Even those who seek death and cry for the fulfillment of the death-wish still have a fear of nonbeing somewhere inside them. I am struck that when you talk to men contemplating suicide, somewhere inside they see themselves as a continuing spectator.

If you go back in art as far as you can go, you find that wherever man is, his essential mannishness is there too. Archaeologists unearthed a man that they say lived something like 40,000 years ago. They found him buried in a grave of flower petals. Now that's intriguing. You don't find animals burying their dead in flower petals. Or examine the Spanish and French cave paintings—the largest early work of art which gives us extended content. (I would accept the date of about 20,000 B.C. concerning these.) The paintings reveal that those cave-dwellers had the same human longings we have. Right there in the midst of the painting are indications that a man is crying out, "I know within myself that I am more than the dust that surrounds me." As a matter of fact, there is a theory that explains the cave paintings in southern France and northern Spain as a symbol system expressing the longings of man. Although it is open to discussion, I think it's probably right; and even if that theory proves not to be correct, still they do show man considering himself as uniquely distinguished from that which is non-man.

We may also mention the testimony of the scholar Levi-Strauss. Though his theories are highly controversial, Levi-Strauss has been a most important anthropologist. This French scientist put forth a concept that shook the world of anthropology. It is this: no matter where you go, into the past, into the present, to primitive peoples or cultured societies, you find that all men think in the same fashion. Man's thinking has not basically changed along the way. Thus, although primitive tribes may not make high-level, analyzed antitheses, still there is in tribal thinking a clear antithesis between *tribe* and *nontribe, hot* and *cold,* and so forth. The mannishness of man is evident as far back as anybody has been able to penetrate.

Michael Polanyi's arguments concerning the DNA template show much the same thing. Without going into details, let me say simply that Michael Polanyi specifically rejected the chemical determinism of Francis Crick. The chemical and physical properties of the DNA template do not give an explanation of what man is merely on the basis of those chemical and physical properties.

So Levi-Strauss said to look at the thinking of man; wherever you go into the past, into the present, man is man. Polanyi said the DNA template does not explain those peculiar things which man is. Mortimer Adler also testified to the problem of man's uniqueness in *The Difference of Man and the Difference It Makes.* He did not have an answer, but he said there is something different in man, and we had better identify it or we will start to treat people as nonhuman and even more tragedy will result. No matter what his theoretical system is, man knows within himself that he cannot be equated with non-man.

What Paul says in Romans is as up-to-date as the present ticking of the clock—men, even men without the Bible, suppress the truth of what they themselves are. Primitive man, cultured man, ancient man, modern man, Eastern man, Western man: all have a testimony that says man is more than their own theories explain.

Paul then turns to the second area in which men suppress the truth. In Romans 1:20 he says, "For the invisible things of him from the creation of the world are clearly seen, being understood by the things that are made." So the second testimony man suppresses is the truth of the external world. Jean-Paul Sartre has said that the basic philosophic question of all questions is this: why is it that *something* is there rather than *nothing*? He is correct. The great mystery to the materialist is that there is anything there at all.

However, it is not that something chaotic is there, but that something *orderly* is there. Einstein understood this very well at the end of his life. According to his friend Oppenheimer and what we know from his own writing, Einstein at the end of his life became a modern mystic. He didn't have the answer, he didn't turn to the Judeo-Christian position or the Bible, but he understood that there had to be a bigger answer because he saw in the universe an order that is indisputable. Einstein worded it beautifully when he said the world is like a well-constructed crossword puzzle; you can suggest any number of words, but only one will fit all the facts. And so Sartre says, "There's something there," and Einstein adds, "Yes. Look at the marvel of its form." Let's put it another way: there is a distinction between science and science fiction. In science fiction you may imagine any kind of universe, but in science you must deal with the universe that exists.

For several years Murray Eden at MIT used high-speed computers to calculate the possibility of whether on the basis of chance there could be so much complexity in the universe within any acceptable amount of time. His conclusion was that the possibility is zero.

We find the same thing in Charles Darwin himself in his autobiography and his letters. It's amazing that this old man toward the very end of his life said, "I cannot believe with my mind that all this was produced by chance." Not his emotions, but his mind.

And he has to excuse the testimony of his intelligence by saying that his mind has just come by evolution from a monkey mind, and who can trust that. But, of course, there's a trick in this. If he could not trust his mind on such a crucial point, how could he trust it to formulate the evolutionary hypothesis itself?

In short, the testimony of the existence and form of the external universe and of man himself, whether in the ancient world or the modern, constantly speaks to man and asks, "Do your presuppositions—your gods, your philosophy, or your naturalistic science—really explain what is?" Paul is saying that the truth that the man without the Bible suppresses is the truth of *what is,* a truth that surrounds him on every side. The Bible says, "They are without excuse." The man without the Bible is *without excuse* because he suppresses the truth of the nature of man and the nature of the external universe.

I would like to return now to a comment I made earlier in this chapter. You will recall that in the King James Version Romans 1:18 contains the phrase "hold the truth in unrighteousness," and that most modern translations render this verse as "hinder the truth in unrighteousness" or "suppress the truth." Some experts in Greek have told me that "hold" is better. Here, I believe, is the explanation. Paul is saying that men—because they refuse to bow to the God who is there and because they hold their presuppositions as an implicit faith—hold some of the truth about themselves and about the universe, but do not carry these things to their logical conclusions because they contradict their presuppositions. Therefore, they hold a portion of the truth, but they hold it in unrighteousness. They must hold some of the truth about themselves and the universe, for they must live in the universe as God made it; but they refuse to carry these truths to their reasonable conclusions. Whether they live in the ancient world or in the modern world, they adhere to their false presuppositions. Paul is saying, "Don't you understand? You really deserve the wrath of God because you, even you without the Bible, hold this testimony in unrighteousness."

So Paul continues in verses 21 and 22, on which we have already spent so much time. Men have become vain in their *reasoning,* their hearts have been darkened, and they have become foolishly foolish—holding positions in the very face of what exists. Men then are under God's judgment, not because God has scattered them like a handful of gravel, but because He has treated them as He created them—as significant. Man's own choices have led men where they are. In their own way all men are like the 1960 hippie who said, "Well, I don't care what happens to the next generation. I will take LSD even if it does split the chromosomes. I care only for the moment." In age after age men who had the truth have deliberately thrown it away. The world is what it is, not as a result of the cruelty of God to man, but of the cruelty of man to man.

In Romans 1:24 we read, "Wherefore, God gave them up to uncleanness through the lusts of their own hearts, to dishonor their bodies between themselves." Men in our own sociologically and psychologically oriented age have all kinds of explanations for the moral problems of man. But according to the Bible, it is not moral declension that causes doctrinal declension; it is just the opposite. Turning away from the truth—that which is cognitive, that which may be known about God—produces moral declension. The modern artists, the dramatists, and the novelists show how far modern man has turned away into moral byroads. The Bible tells us the cause: men who knew the truth turned away; they are followed by men who do not know the truth, and this results in all sorts of moral turning aside.

Paul repeats this concept three times, in 1:23-24, 25-27, and from 28 on. It seems to me he is saying, "Notice it, and notice it well. You haven't misread. Don't just read it lightly, because I'm going to say it three times so that you'll understand that you read it correctly in the first place. It's because men turn away from God that moral problems arise."

We must not accept minor secondary causes as to why man sins. Some psychological and sociological conditioning occurs in every man's life, and this affects the decisions he makes. But we must resist the modern concept that all sin can be explained merely on the basis of conditioning. In our generation there is a constant tendency to explain sin lightly and think that such an explanation is more humanitarian. But it isn't. It decreases the importance and the significance of man. Consequently, we can be glad for the sake of man that the Bible's explanation is so emphatic.

Paul repeats it in the 25th verse: "Who changed [the word *changed* is really *exchanged* in the Greek] the truth of God for a lie, and worshiped and served the creature [*creature* means that which has been created] rather than the Creator." This is the second of the three repetitions.

Paul was thinking of the gods of silver and stone and also the worship of the universe or any part of it. He says men have made such gods rather than worshiping the living God. Even on the basis of what they know themselves to be, they should have known better. Isaiah said 700 years before, "Aren't you silly to make gods that are less than yourself. You must carry them; they don't carry you. Now isn't it silly to make an integration point that is less than you yourself are." Paul used precisely the same argument on Mars Hill. Men who refuse to bow before God take the facts concerning the universe and man, push these facts through their own presuppositional grid, fail to carry their thinking to a reasonable conclusion, and so are faced with an overwhelming lie. Idols of stone are obvious lies because they are less than man, but so are non-Christian presuppositions such as the idea of the total uniformity of natural cause and effect in a closed system—the final explanation of the impersonal plus time plus chance—which ultimately makes man only a machine.

So Paul continues, "For this cause God gave them up unto vile affections; for their women did change the natural use for that which is against nature; and likewise also the men, leaving the natural use of the woman, burned in their lust one toward another, men with men working that which is unseemly, and receiving in themselves that recompense of their error which was meet."

Usually the first of these sins is taken to refer to lesbianism. But I am not sure that lesbianism is what is involved here. I think that this may be parallel to Isaiah 3:16: "Moreover, the Lord saith, Because the daughters of Zion are haughty, and walk with stretched forth necks and wanton eyes, walking and mincing as they go, and making a tinkling with their feet . . ." If this is so, Paul is first speaking of heterosexuality which has become twisted. Women turn away from the truth and misuse their natural femininity and all the strong sexuality connected with it. Sexuality here is a neutral word, for the rightness of sex depends on what you do with it. Paul would be saying, the women have used their bodies and their proper sexuality as a man-trap, twisting a good gift of God (which surely Eve had) into that which is wrong: "You have taken one of the most beautiful things that has ever existed, and ever will exist in the created world, and you have turned it into evil."

The 27th verse does, of course, refer to homosexuality and includes lesbianism. As people have turned from the truth, they have gotten their sexuality mixed up. A number of homosexuals and lesbians have come to L'Abri where they hoped they could get help. We must show compassion and not act as though this sin is greater than other sins, or as though we are superior since we are not caught in this. But at the same time we must point out that the practice (in contrast to the temptation) of homosexuality is wrong. It is not wrong in a way that makes them worse than other sins would do, but under the absolutes of God its practice is wrong.

The third of the three repetitions comes in verse 28: "And even as they did not like to retain God in their knowledge, God gave them over [or God gave them up] to a mind void of judgment." The King James translation ("a reprobate mind") misses the point. It's a mind void of judgment, a phrase referring back to verses 21 and 22, "they became vain in their reasoning," religiously but also intellectually foolish. These people do not understand what the universe is, and they do not understand who they themselves are. That sounds very modern indeed.

Gauguin, the French painter, brilliant as he was, provides an excellent example. Following Jean-Jacques Rousseau's idea that man is (or ought to be) autonomous, completely free, he said that what troubled him was that 2 and 2 always equaled 4. He wanted to be so free that on a Tuesday morning at eight o'clock he could say $2 + 2 = 4\frac{1}{2}$.

What Paul is stressing here is that when you turn away from God and follow other presuppositions, the more consistent you are to your presuppositions the further you get from reality itself. So you see Gauguin trying to paint an autonomous freedom, a primitive simplicity, and, as it were, stamping his feet and saying, "If my system is right, somehow or other $2 + 2$ should not always equal 4."

Let us summarize briefly the course of the argument in this chapter. We began by noticing that Paul speaks in a special way to the man without the Bible. The man without the Bible has not suppressed special revelation (that is, the revelation in the Bible), but the general revelation given by the mannishness of man and by the external world. It is then plain that the man without the Bible holds the truth in unrighteousness; he holds some of the truth about himself and the universe, but he does not follow it to its reasonable conclusions. Thereafter, a breakdown in morality occurs. God says to man in this position: You are under my judgment. And so these questions arise: "How are men without the Bible going to be judged?" and "Is this just?"

Those are the questions with which I close the present chapter.

CHAPTER EIGHT

The Justice of God

How is the man without the Bible to be judged by God? Is God just in this judgment? These are the questions with which we ended the last chapter.

If any of you have ever thought with honesty and not just sat under the evangelical umbrella, or if you have tried to talk to people on the outside, you immediately know that these questions deserve consideration. Is God really just in judging the man without the Bible?

We read in Romans 1:32—2:3, ". . . who, knowing the judgment of God, that they who commit such things are worthy of death [in other words, having moral motions regardless of their philosophic system], not only do the same, but consent with them that do them. Therefore, thou art inexcusable, O man [the man without the Bible], whosoever thou art that judgest; for wherein thou judgest another, thou condemnest thyself; for thou that judgest doest the same things. But we are sure that the judgment of God is according to truth against them who commit such things. And thinkest thou this, O man, that judgest them who do such things, and doest the same, that thou shalt escape the judgment of God?" Think about what is being said here.

Here are the people without the Bible scattered all over the world. Their ancestors (including the last two generations in our own culture), knowing the truth, have turned away from it, and this generation is unaware of it. Yet they have had the powerful testimony of the fact that their own system does not sufficiently explain what is—the mannishness of man and the existence and form of the universe. Further, all men have moral motions, even the modern man who by theory does not believe in morality. Although the standard of moral judgments may be much lower than those set forth in the Bible, moral judgments are still constantly being made.

Let us suppose for a moment that as each baby is born, a tape recorder is placed about its neck. Let us further suppose that this tape recorder works only when moral judgments are being made. Aesthetic judgments, etc., are not recorded, but every moral judgment is. Throughout one's whole life, every real moral motion is recorded upon the tape recorder. Finally, when each person dies and stands before God in judgment, God pushes a button and each person hears with his own ears his own moral judgments as they rolled out over the years: "You were wrong in doing this. You are wrong in doing that." Thousands of moral judgments pour forth, and God simply turns and says, "On the basis of your own words, have *you* kept these moral standards?" And each man is silent. No person in all the world has kept the moral standards with which he has tried to bind others. Consequently, God says, "I will judge you upon your own moral statements (those judgments upon which you have bound and condemned others), even if they are lower than moral statements should be. Are you guilty or not guilty?" No one will be able to raise his voice. The whole world will stand totally condemned before God in utter justice, because they will be judged not upon what they have not known, but upon what they have judged others and have not kept themselves. So all men must say, "Indeed I am justly condemned."

It is most significant that in Romans 2:15, 16, Paul concludes with this concept in the final two verses where he is addressing the man without the Bible, before he begins to speak to the man with the Bible: "who show the work of the law written in their hearts, their conscience also bearing witness, and their thoughts the meanwhile accusing or else excusing one another in the day when God shall judge the secrets of men by Jesus Christ according to my gospel."

The Bible emphasizes this in various places. Luke 12:2, 3 reads, "For there is nothing covered, that shall not be revealed; neither hidden, that shall not be known. Therefore, whatever ye have spoken in darkness shall be heard in the light; and that which ye have spoken in the ear in closets shall be proclaimed upon the housetops." I think that people may actually hear their own moral judgments, their own harsh words, being poured out against other men. And they will have to say, "You are just and I am condemned."

Revelation 20:12 speaks of the last great judgment: "And I saw the dead, small and great, stand before God, and the books were opened; and another book was opened, which is the book of life. And the dead were judged out of those things which were written in the books, according to their works." I have known evangelicals who have been somewhat embarrassed by this, and say that this passage really means that people will be judged on whether they have accepted Christ as Savior or not. That is not what God says. He says, "I'm going to judge you by your works, and your works will fail." They will fail on the basis of their moral judgments against others. There is no injustice in God's dealings with lost men, because they are judged on the standard by which they have bound others.

You will recall that up through Romans 4 Paul talks about how to become a Christian. From the fifth chapter on he talks to Christians. In Romans 5 there is a titanic statement about the historicity of the space-time fall of Adam. Paul is giving to Christians the explanation of the origin of evil. But I think it's highly significant that Paul did not mention this to the man without the Bible. When he talks to the man without the Bible he says to him, "I want to ask you a question: do you keep your own moral standards?" I have yet to find the man who, in an atmosphere of empathy, will not say, "No, sometimes I break them by mistake, but at times I deliberately break them." And this is what God's Word says will be the basis of the judgment of those who do not have the Bible. The judgment rests upon the individual's true moral choice.

I am convinced from my experience that without the biblical position concerning God's judgment of all men you cannot have really good answers for modern man when he asks his questions. Some of those questions, as I've been emphasizing, are: Who is man? What is man? Who am I? Does history have any significance? Do I have any significance? And if a Christian is to give answers that are tough-fibered enough to break into the thinking of honest people in the twentieth century, he must have an answer concerning significance that will bear full weight. Moral judgment is made on the basis of the standards a man holds and yet deliberately breaks. Such moral judgment has an effect, not only in this life, but in the life to come. The limitedness of this life never can give significance enough. But here when moral judgment is based on a man's choice which affects his present and future life far down into the reaches of foreverness, suddenly significance breaks like a great bursting bomb. This is the significance of finite man on the highest possible level. Here is the very opposite of Proust's concept of the dust of death on life now.

The only way that one can get rid of the lostness of men is to give up either one of two things. First is the emphasis upon God's true holiness. This, of course, removes this lostness of men. But the results are disastrous. What is lost is not just God, but man. If Nietzsche says God is dead, Sartre must say man is dead. For if you give up the true holiness of God, you give up any moral absolute in the universe, and you are back in a big circle where everything is adrift.

Second, one can give up the significance of history and the significance of man in that history. If neither has significance, then the concept of God's judgment of man can be ignored. But if you do that, man has no meaning. So if you give up the holiness of God, there are no absolutes and morality becomes a zero; if you give up the significance of man, man becomes a zero. If you want a significant man, with absolutes, morality, and meaning, then you must have what the Bible insists upon—that God will judge men justly, and they will not be able to raise their voices because of the base upon which He judges them.

This brings me to two conclusions. First of all, in Romans 2:1, Paul moves from abstract statements to personal application: "Therefore, thou art inexcusable, O man." The third verse repeats the personal emphasis: "And thinkest thou this, O man?" Paul is not just teaching abstract doctrine. It is my opinion, in fact, that every doctrine is meant to be practiced. Even the doctrine concerning the Trinity is meant to be practiced by the way our lives exhibit an understanding of the centrality of personality. And surely Paul's present message is to be practiced. All men are going to be judged, and all men are going to be found with a totally failing grade: "Therefore, O man"—you, individually.

Beginning at 2:17 Paul deals with the Jew, the man with the Bible. God says through Paul, "Just as I have explained that the man without the Bible is to be judged on the basis of the moral standards with which he binds others, I will explain to you, the man with the Bible, that I will judge you upon the higher standards of the Scripture." And as Paul continues on to 3:9, he concludes: the man with the Bible is no better than the man without the Bible, for both Jews and Gentiles have sinned.

You must understand that God's passing grade is 100 percent. If He is less than perfect or accepts less than perfection, the absolutes are gone! That's what an absolute means; it's a 100 percent affair. And so God says to the man without the Bible, "Have you kept 100 percent of the moral judgments with which you bound others?" And to the man with the Bible, "Have you kept 100 percent of the standards of Scripture?" The answer is no. In Galatians 3:21 Paul writes, "Is the law, then, against the promises of God? God forbid; for if there had been a law given which could have given life (or could make alive), verily righteousness should have been by the law." That is, if God could have given a law so that Jesus did not have to go to the cross, surely He would have done it! He didn't send Jesus to the cross as a piece of theater, as one arbitrary possibility in the midst of other arbitrary possibilities. Rather, since there is no law that man in his rebellion does not break, God had to provide a nonhumanist solution for the problem of man if there was to be a solution.

But in the book of Romans, as early as 1:16, 17, we are confronted with God's unexpected solution: "For I am not ashamed of the gospel of Christ; for it is the power of God unto salvation to everyone that believeth; to the Jew first, and also to the Greek." Paul says there is a solution for me personally and for you personally—a solution for the universal need of all men. God has provided a solution which fills the practical need *and* can be discussed on Mars Hill without shame. In that solution two great needs are fulfilled: the need for an absolute and the need for the significance of man.

What specifically is this solution? "For all have sinned, and come short of the glory of God" (3:23). The Greek is stronger: "For all *have* sinned [aorist tense] in the past, and all *are* coming short of the glory of God." In the past, we have sinned; in the present, we are sinning. But he continues, "being justified freely by his grace through the redemption that is in Christ Jesus." Many of you have been raised with these words from the Scripture until they have just become words. Some of you may say, "Oh, I've heard it ten million times, and it grinds through my mind like a phonograph."

Smash the record and *listen to the words!* "Whom God hath set forth [that is, Christ] to be propitiatory through faith in his blood [that is, Christ's finished work in space, time, and history, on the basis of the infinite value of His work because of His person as the eternal Son of God], to declare his righteousness for the remission of sins that are past, through the forbearance of God." God has provided a solution whereby His holiness and man's significance can stand, and yet not all men will be lost.

Then look at the great 26th verse. People pass by it much too easily, not understanding the wonder of what Paul is saying: "For the showing at this time his righteousness, that he himself might be just [that is, that He might keep His holiness—and thus there is an absolute], and yet [the word *yet* is not in the Greek, but the force of it is] the justifier of him who believeth in Jesus."

What is being said here? God has provided a way that no philosophy would have thought of. It is a way that would take us by surprise if we were not just thinking by evangelical habit. There should be everlasting surprise in it. I stand here. I am significant. God must be holy. Is all lost now that I have sinned? The answer is no! God has provided a propitiation, a substitute. The whole of God's answer rests upon the substitutionary death of Jesus Christ. Because of who He is, His death has infinite value; it can cover every spot; it can remove true moral guilt (and not just the guilt-feelings that exist) in the presence of God as the perfect Judge of the universe.

Thus three great things fall into place: God's holiness, man's significance, and the possibility of man's redemption. I don't know about you, but I believe it is time to stand up and sing the doxology. Here is an intellectual answer that nothing else has ever presented!

In 2:1-3, Paul brings the message down to the individual: "Therefore, thou art inexcusable, O man!" Paul's message is not just something for somebody else. It's for every one of us. God *is* holy. There *is* a moral absolute. I *am* significant. I *have* deliberately sinned. I *am* under that wrath of God. Note it well: unless by God's grace I have taken advantage of this unexpected and totally surprising answer to the dilemma, I am under the wrath of God.

Our second conclusion involves our attitude as Christians now that we know that the man without the Bible (not only the bushman but the educated modern man) is under the judgment of God. It's perfectly true that God in His mercy often brings men into contact with the gospel in very unexpected ways. L'Abri is a proof of this every day of the year. The amazing people that God brings in amazing ways from the ends of the earth to hear the content of the gospel in L'Abri! But we are not to wait like a piece of stone for God to bring men to us. Paul tells us very clearly what our attitude is to be. In 1:14, 15, he says, "I am debtor both to the Greeks and to the barbarians; both to the wise and to the unwise." I am a debtor, says Paul, to all classes of men. "So, as much as in me is, I am ready to preach the gospel to you that are at Rome also." And although that meant prison and finally death, he was willing to go. He went on in the same way as Jeremiah went on.

Later in 10:13-15, Paul writes, "For whosoever shall call upon the name of the Lord shall be saved. How, then, shall they call on him in whom they have not believed? And how shall they believe in him of whom they have not heard? And how shall they hear without a preacher? And how shall they preach, except they be sent? As it is written, How beautiful are the feet of them that preach the gospel of peace, and bring glad tidings of good things!" Paul's response is firm and strong. I am a debtor to be a teller of the content of the good news. The Christian is called to be the carrier of the content of the good news.

Milton understood properly: Satan was a horrible rebel, but what he did had a large meaning in history. And when men turn and revolt, it has meaning in history. When men who knew the truth turned and revolted against God, it meant that those who followed them in history did not have the content of the gospel. But there is a gospel. And God turns to those of mankind who know the content and He says: Take the gospel. And he continues to honor the way He made man as significant, for He now says, I have put the good news into your hands that you might have compassion upon your own kind!

Who are these, regardless of the color of their skin and the language they speak, scattered over the face of the world? Who are these that do not have the content of the gospel? Who are they? They are *my* kind; they are *my* people; they are not something else; they are that which I am. I can really understand them because I am who they are. It is the Christian who knows the real unity of the human race, for we have a common origin; we are of one flesh and blood.

I stand here now, a Christian who has the content of the gospel, and I say: Isn't it wonderful that we have an answer to modern man, who says man is a zero. I can say, You are not a zero. I can say: Proust is wrong; the dust of death is not on everything. There is real meaning that stretches out forever and ever into the future. Isn't that wonderful! And then if I'm listening and thinking at all, not only to the Word of God, but to the dictates of compassion in my heart, I realize that significance means something more. Significance should make me as the seraphim who cover their faces with their wings. I should put my hands over my face, because now *I am significant*. It's up to me in compassion to take the good news to *my kind*. This is who I now am.

It is Paul again who sounds the warning in 1 Corinthians 9:16: "For though I preach the gospel, I have nothing to glory of; for necessity is laid upon me; yea, woe is unto me, if I preach not the gospel!" Upon what basis should I preach and teach? Just some sociological group pressure from my church? The fact that the missionary candidate is a big wheel on some Christian college campuses and in some churches? Never! Ten thousand times no! The pressure upon me is this: *I am significant, and my kind needs the message that I know*.

Woe to us, woe to our evangelicalism with our lack of compassion. There is a decline in missionary interest across evangelical circles. What is lost? One of two things or both: a real sense of the lostness of the lost or compassion in our hearts. Many of us are intellectually embarrassed to speak of the lostness of the lost. We have been infiltrated by the naturalistic concepts of our own relativistic day. Across evangelicalism there is a great veil; regardless of what men affirm in their statements of faith, they no longer are facing the reality of the lostness of their own kind.

And as we have lost the sense of the lostness of the lost, we have also lost compassion. We are hard. What do you think when you see the newspaper pictures of those starving and displaced people? Do you have any compassion? What I find in much evangelicalism is not only weakness in sensing the lostness of the lost, but a tremendous weakness of compassion for the needs of my kind in the present life. What do you think of the overwhelming misery that almost every edition of the newspaper, almost every T.V. and radio news program brings us? Do you have any interest in helping them (or others in our own country) who need help in this life? And then as a Christian, does your world-view stand strong and consistent so that as you look at those starving people, you say: "Yes, they need help in this life. These are my kind; and there's an eternity out there, and these people *also* need the content of the gospel." Compassion for the needs of men, that's *our* need. In the midst of our affluence, we ought to have compassion for people in this life and in eternity as we understand the lostness of the lost. To separate these two things as though they can be divided, is not to understand the gospel.

All the church is to be made up of tellers. Not everyone is to be a missionary, not everyone is a minister, but there is no Christian who doesn't have laid upon him the admonition of Paul to be a debtor. Everyone is bound to be a teller in his own place, in his own calling, according to the individual vocation which God has given him.

What about missionary giving? Often we are proud to say we give more to missions than any other country in the world. But it seems to me that most Christians give their money out of sociological pressure in their group, and that group pressure is often generated by habit. It does not seem to me that most evangelicals give their money out of compassion and a sense of the lostness of the lost of their own kind.

People say to me at times, "But can you preach the gospel you have described in the midst of your intellectual presentation? Will twentieth-century man listen? Won't he say it's ugly?" I have never found a man who has thought orthodox Christianity as such is ugly once he understands the titanic answers it gives. I have never known a man who found that that was ugly! What men find ugly is what they see in Christians who hold to the orthodox doctrine that men are lost, but show no signs of compassion. This is what is ugly. This is what causes men in our generation to be turned off by evangelicalism.

At the conclusion of our study of Jeremiah and his message we said that if there is to be a constructive revolution in the orthodox, evangelical church, then like Jeremiah we must speak of judgment concerning individual men great and small and judgment of the church, the state, and the culture which have known the truth of God and have turned away from Him and His propositional revelation. God exists, He is a holy God, and we must know that there will be judgment. And like Jeremiah we must keep on—keep on so speaking regardless of the cost to ourselves. Now having completed our study in Romans we must add this: if there is to be a constructive revolution in the orthodox, evangelical church, we must comprehend and speak of the lostness of the lost, including the man without the Bible. And like Paul we must not be cold in our orthodoxy, but deeply compassionate for our own kind even when it is costly.

If we are Christians and do not have upon us the calling to respond to the lostness of the lost and a compassion for those of our kind for this life and eternity, our orthodoxy is ugly. And it is ugly in the presence of anybody who's an honest person. And more than that, orthodoxy without compassion is ugly to God.

CHAPTER NINE

The Universe and Two Chairs

In the course of these chapters we have focused attention on the way God looks at the culture of our day, and at both the men with the Bible and the men without the Bible who have turned away. In this final chapter, let us examine the way God looks at those who have the Bible and who have responded by believing in the God who is there and are relying on the finished work of Christ in space-time history for the removal of their guilt before a holy God.

You will recall that Paul says in Romans 1:17 that the just shall live by faith. That is, that they shall live existentially by reliance on God and faith in Him. We turn now in this final chapter to see what living by faith means in our twentieth-century world.

First let us note that we who live in the second half of the twentieth century live in an increasingly complicated universe— much more complicated for us than for men just a few years ago. Our telescopes see further, and we speak of light-years running up into great numbers; the very magnitude of these numbers tends to confuse us. On the other hand, our physicists deal with smaller and smaller particles, and as mass retreats into energy and energy into formulae, reality seems to slip through our fingers. As we look at those light-years, we shrink away. And as we look at the tiny particles, we grow like Alice in Wonderland. But our size here doesn't really help us because we tend to become uncomfortable as we see material reality reduced to sets of mathematic formulae and energy particles dashing about at furious speed. Yet we must understand, if we are going to live as Christians, that while these things indeed are complicated and confusing, nevertheless from the biblical viewpoint the universe is simple.

Let me illustrate this. Imagine the room where you are sitting with the curtains pulled and the doors locked. Let us suppose that room is the only universe that God has made. Now that would be possible. God could have made such a universe. So let us say that the only universe that exists is the room with the doors locked and the curtains pulled. There is nothing outside at all, absolutely nothing. We are in a universe that can be seen with one look around the room.

Now let us go further. Suppose we have two chairs in this room and that sitting on these two chairs are two men, the only two men in the universe. As we consider them, we find that they differ. One is a totally consistent materialist. As far as he is concerned, the universe is made up of nothing but mass, energy, and motion; that's all there is to it. On the other chair sits a Christian who lives in the light of the teaching of the Bible as the propositional revelation of God. And these two sit facing each other in a universe in which they sit alone.

After they have looked at each other awhile, the materialist says, "Now I'm going to explore our universe." And the Christian replies, "That's fine." So the materialist begins to analyze the universe, and it takes him a long time. He goes through all the scientific processes that we now use to examine our own universe. He uses the sciences of chemistry, biology, physics, etc. He goes back to the periodic table, and behind the periodic table into the atom and examines it. He examines everything from the paint on the wall to the more basic particles. All this takes him a long time.

Finally as an older man, he comes to the Bible-believing Christian and brings him a big set of books, and he says, "Now here's a set of books, they're nicely bound, and they give in great detail a description of our universe." So the Christian takes a number of months, even years, to study these books with care. Finally the Christian turns to the materialist and says, "Well, this is a tremendous work. You really told me a great deal about my universe that I wouldn't otherwise have known. However, my friend, though this is all very instructive, it's drastically incomplete." And you can imagine this man, who has spent his lifetime pouring out his heart to do his measuring and his weighing, suddenly taken aback. He turns and says to the Christian, "Well, now, I'm shocked that you tell me it's not all here. What have I missed?" And then the Christian responds something like this: "I have a book here, the Bible, and it tells me things that you do not know. It tells me the origin of the universe. Your scientific investigation by its very nature cannot do that. And your investigation also says nothing about where you and I as men came from. You have examined us because we, like the paint on the wall, are phenomena in the universe. You've studied something of our psychology and even given me several volumes on it, but you have not told me how we came to be here. In short, you don't know the origin of either the universe or us.

"Furthermore," the Christian continues, "I know from this book that there is more to the universe than you have described. There is an unseen portion as well as a seen portion. And there is a cause-and-effect relationship between them. They are not mutually exclusive, but are parts of one reality. It's as if you had taken an orange, sliced it in half, and only concerned yourself with one of the halves. To really understand reality in our universe, you have to consider both halves—both the seen and the unseen."

In this sense *supernatural* is not a good word to describe the unseen portion. We must understand that the unseen portion of the universe is just as natural and as real as is the seen portion. Furthermore, the seen and the unseen are not totally separated. When we do certain things, it makes a difference in the unseen world, and things in the unseen world make a difference in the seen world. The Christian would say to the materialist, "Your volume on the philosophy of history just does not hang together. The reason is that you are only looking at half of what's there; you are only looking at half of history; you do not take into account the unseen portion. Consequently, your philosophy of history will never be sound." He is right: nobody has ever produced a satisfactory philosophy of history beginning with the materialistic viewpoint. There is too much in the seen world that does not make sense when taken as if it were all there is. One cannot produce a philosophy of history based on only half of history.

Now what happens next? These two men look at each other

rather askance because their two primary views of the universe are set one against the other. The materialist replies, "You're crazy. You're talking about things you can't see." And the consistent Christian responds, "Well, you may say I am crazy because I'm talking about things I cannot see, but you are completely unbalanced. You only know half of your own universe."

Let us notice something extremely important: these two views can never be brought into synthesis. One man is not a little right and the other a little right and a synthesis better than both. These are two mutually exclusive views—one is right and one is wrong. If you say less than this, then you reduce Christianity to a psychological crutch, a glorified aspirin. That doesn't mean that the Christian can't glean much detail from the materialist's observation. But as far as the comprehensive view of the universe is concerned, there can be no synthesis. Either this man is right and that man is wrong, or that man is right and this man is wrong. It's a total antithesis.

I want to pursue their situation further. Suppose that on the wall of their room there's a large clock. All of a sudden it stops. And these two men turn around and say, "What a pity! The clock has stopped." The materialist says, "That will never do, and because there are only you and I in this universe, one of us must clamber up the wall and start the clock. There's nobody else to do it." The Christian replies, "Now wait a moment. Yes, it's possible for one of us to climb up and start the clock, but there is another possibility. I may talk to the One who made this universe (One who is not in the universe in the sense of it merely being an extension of His essence), and He can start the clock."

Here is a tremendous difference in attitude. You can imagine the materialist's reaction. "Now I know you're crazy. You're talking about someone we can't see starting a material clock." Anyone who has been doing modern twentieth-century thinking will realize the relevance of this. And I also think we may here see why so many Christians have no reality. They are not certain that it is possible for the God who made the universe "to start the clock" when a Christian talks to Him.

Let me give you an illustration from experience. Once I was flying at night over the North Atlantic. It was in 1947, and I was coming back from my first visit to Europe. Our plane, one of those old DC4's with two engines on each wing, was within two or three minutes of the middle of the Atlantic. Suddenly two engines on one wing stopped. I had already flown a lot, and so I could feel the engines going wrong. I remember thinking, If I'm going to go down into the ocean, I'd better get my coat. When I did, I said to the hostess, "There's something wrong with the engines." She was a bit snappy and said, "You people always think there's something wrong with the engines." So I shrugged my shoulder, but I took my coat. I had no sooner sat down than the lights came on and a very agitated copilot came out. "We're in trouble," he said. "Hurry and put on your life jackets."

So down we went, and we fell and fell, until in the middle of the night with no moon we could actually see the water breaking under us in the darkness. And as we were coming down, I prayed. Interestingly enough, a radio message had gone out, an SOS that was picked up and broadcast immediately all over the United States in a flash news announcement: "There is a plane falling in the middle of the Atlantic." My wife heard about this immediately, and she gathered our three little girls together and they knelt down and began to pray. They were praying in St. Louis, Missouri, and I was praying on the plane. And we were going down and down.

Then, while we could see the waves breaking beneath us and everybody was ready for the crash, suddenly the two motors started, and we went on into Gander. When we got down I found the pilot and asked what happened. "Well," he said, "it's a strange thing, something we can't explain. Only rarely do two motors stop on one wing, but you can make a rule that when they do, they don't start again. We don't understand it." So I turned to him and I said, "I can explain it." He looked at me. "How?" And I said, "My Father in Heaven started it because I was praying." That man got the strangest look on his face and he turned away. I'm sure he was the man sitting in the materialist's chair.

But here is the point: there is no distinction between the clock starting and those motors starting. Is it or isn't it possible for the God who made the mechanistic portion of the universe to start the clock or start the motors? Is it or isn't it? The materialist must say *no*; the Bible-believing Christian says *yes*.

Now then, let's get away from our small universe of a single room and suddenly throw wide the curtains, open the doors, push out the walls, the ceiling, and the floor, and have the universe as it is in its full size, as it has been created by God. Instead of two men, there are many men in the universe, but still represented by these two. What we must see is that no matter how deeply we get into the particles of matter and energy, or how much we learn by our telescopes and radiotelescopes about the vastness of the created universe, in reality the universe is no more complicated than the room we have been talking about. It is only larger; that's all. Looking at the bigger universe, we either see it as the materialist sees it or as the Christian sees it: we see it with the one set of presuppositions or the other.

However, what one must realize is that seeing the world as a Christian does not mean just saying, "I am a Christian. I believe in the supernatural world," and then stopping. It is possible to be saved through faith in Christ and then spend much of our lives in the materialist's chair. We can say we believe in a supernatural world, and yet live as though there were no supernatural in the universe at all. It is not enough merely to say, "I believe in a supernatural world." We must ask, "Which chair am I sitting in at this given existential moment?" We must live in the present: "Sufficient to the day is the evil thereof . . . Give us this day our *daily* bread." What counts is the chair I am sitting in *at any one existential moment.*

Christianity is not just a mental assent that certain doctrines are true—not even that the right doctrines are true. This is only the beginning. This would be rather like a starving man sitting in front of great heaps of food and saying, "I believe the food exists; I believe it is real," and yet never eating it. It is not enough merely to say, "I am a Christian," and then in practice to live as if present contact with the supernatural were something far-off and strange. Many Christians I know seem to act as though they come in contact with the supernatural just twice—once when they are justified and become a Christian, and once when they die. The rest of the time they act as though they were sitting in the materialist's chair.

The difference between a Christian who is being supernatural in practice and one who says he is a Christian but lives like a materialist can be illustrated by the difference between a storage battery and a light plug. Some Christians seem to think that when they are born again, they become a self-contained unit like a storage battery. From that time on they have to go on their own pep and their own power until they die. But this is wrong. After we are justified, once for all through faith in Christ, we are to live in supernatural communion with the Lord every moment; we are to be like lights plugged into an electric socket.

The Bible makes it plain that our joy and spiritual power depend on a continuing relation to God. If we do not love and draw on the Lord as we should, the plug gets pulled out and the spiritual power and the spiritual joy stop. Recall Paul's statement in the benediction, "The communion of the Holy Spirit be with you all." The reality of the communication of the Holy Spirit who lives within us and who is the agent of the whole Trinity is to be a continuing reality in the Christian's life.

Let's be more specific. The Bible says that Christ rose physically from the dead, that if you had been there that day you would have seen Christ stand up and walk away in a space-time, observable situation of true history. The materialist says, "No, I don't believe it. Christ was not raised from the dead." That is unbelief. Liberal theology is also unbelief because it says either that Jesus was not raised from the dead in history, or that maybe He was and maybe He wasn't because who knows what's going to happen in this world in which you can't be sure of anything. The historic resurrection of Christ doesn't really matter, says this theology; what matters is that the church got a big push from thinking He was raised in history. They see the importance of the resurrection as psychological, even though they may say they leave open the door to an actual resurrection since we live in a universe that we can not be sure of. Now I would say that the old liberalism, the new liberalism, and materialism are basically the same. To all of them finally the same word applies: *unbelief.*

But now, here we are, Bible-believing Christians. We stand and say, "No, I'm not going to accept that. I'm going to speak out against the materialist, and I'm going to speak out against the old and the new liberalism. Christ was raised from the dead, and He did ascend with the same body the disciples saw and touched. Between His resurrection and His ascension He appeared and disappeared many times. He often went back and forth between the seen and the unseen world in those forty days. And then finally, He took an official departure at the Mount of Olives." But the Bible says that if Christ is raised from the dead, we're supposed to act upon it in our moment-by-moment lives. Its importance is not just in past history.

So the Bible-believing Christian says, "Well, I believe it!" The materialist says, "I don't believe it!" and he sits in unbelief. But what shall we say about the man who says, "I believe it, I believe it," but then doesn't act upon this in faith in his daily life? I have made up a word for it. I call it *unfaith.*

The Bible tells us plainly that Christ promises to bear His fruit through us. In Romans 7:4 Paul says a very striking thing: "Wherefore, my brethren, ye also are become dead to the law by the body of Christ, in order that ye should be married to another, even to him who is raised from the dead, in order that we should bring forth fruit unto God." This verse says that each of us as a Christian is feminine. At conversion we are married to Christ, who is the Bridegroom, and as we put ourselves in His arms, moment by moment, He will produce His fruit through us into the external world. That's beautiful and overwhelming. Just as with the natural bride who gives herself to her husband and puts herself in his arms, there will be children born into a home. The bride can't just stand with the bridegroom at the wedding ceremony. She must give herself to him existentially, regularly, and then children will be born to him, through her body, into the external world.

As an example let us think of Mary and of Christ's birth. When Mary heard the annunciation, she did not say to the angel, "I won't give myself to God in order that the Messiah may be born. What would Joseph think?" It would have been reasonable to say that, because we know that later Joseph was indeed disturbed. On the other hand, she did not say, "Now that you've told me what is to happen, I can do it on my own." Mary herself could no more bring forth that baby than any other girl can will a virgin birth. She said the one thing she could say that could be right: "I am Your servant. I give my body into Your hands. Do with it as You will." This was an active passivity. She was passive in that God brought forth the baby. But she was not passive in her will. One can say it this way (and I say it with great care): God would not have raped Mary. She put herself into His hands, and He was the One who produced this marvel of the virgin birth. Of course the virgin birth of Christ to Mary is totally unique, but it can be a profound example to us.

In a very different way the same situation holds with each of us as Christians. If I will put myself in Christ's arms, moment by moment, He will bring forth *His* fruit through me into this poor, broken world. And if I'm not acting upon that, I am sitting in the chair of unfaith.

You will notice in Romans 6 (a very sober chapter to the Christian if he reads it with any delicacy of comprehension and feeling) in verses 13, 16 and 19 these words in the present tense: "Neither yield ye your members as instruments [it should be translated *arms* or *weapons* or *tools*] of unrighteousness unto sin, but yield yourselves unto God, as those that are alive from the dead, and your members as instruments [weapons or tools] of righteousness unto God." You continue to be significant after you become a Christian, and either you can yield yourself at any one moment into the hands of Christ for Him to use you as a tool or weapon in this world, or you can yield yourself in that moment as an instrument of unrighteousness even though you are a Christian.

Verse 16 says it again: "Know ye not that to whom ye yield yourselves servants to obey, his servants ye are whom ye obey, whether of sin unto death, or obedience unto righteousness?" Sitting in the believer's chair, am I yielding myself to Christ for Him to bear fruit through me, or am I yielding myself to be the servant of my old king Satan, in which case I am bringing forth death into the external world? The sober thing is that something important is at stake: the question of bearing the fruit of the Spirit into the external world, of being an exhibition of the existence of God and His character. The significance of man continues. You are not a programmed computer. Are you going to yield yourself to your Bridegroom or are you not? The 19th verse repeats the point: "I speak after the manner of men because of the infirmity of your flesh; for as ye have yielded your members servants to uncleanness and to iniquity, unto iniquity; even so now yield your members servants to righteousness, unto holiness."

The unbelieving man says, "Well, the resurrection—I really don't believe it." The Christian says, "I do believe it." But, surely, shouldn't we call it unfaith if I am not acting upon it and letting Christ, whom I say is raised from the dead, bring forth His fruit through me?

With this in mind, let's look at prayer. I feel that the determinism of our own generation has infiltrated us as evangelical Christians so that we tend not to be praying people. We must understand what prayer is. Prayer, according to the Bible, is speaking to God. The reason why we can speak to God is that He exists, He is personal, and we are made in His image. Since we are made in His image, it shouldn't be surprising that we can be in communication with Him, even though He is infinite and we are finite. When our guilt is removed through the finished work of Christ, communication with God is to be expected. You and I communicate in a horizontal direction with each other through verbalization. In

fact, many anthropologists say that verbalization more than anything else distinguishes man from non-man. God too communi-
cates to us in verbalization in Scripture, and we communicate to
God in verbalization by prayer. It's as simple and as profound as
that.

How then does prayer fit into the biblical view of the universe?
God made the universe. It is external to Himself, not spatially, but
in the sense that it is not an extension of His essence. There is, of
course, a machine portion of the universe, but neither God nor
man is caught in the machine. There is a uniformity of natural
causes, but not in a closed system. The course of nature can be
changed—can be reordered—just as I, through a choice of the will,
can interrupt something, for example by reaching over and turning off a light. This act of my will reorders the natural flow of
cause and effect. It is in this setting that the Bible sets forth its
teaching about prayer.

To return, therefore, to the airplane: I prayed, my family was
praying, and God started the airplane motors. That is not to say
that God always starts the motors. In this case He did. The distinction is that the Christian knows it is not absurd to think God can
"start the motors." To think, or act, otherwise is for the Christian
to be in the place of unfaith.

This is prayer, this is what it is supposed to be. God as well as
man can start the motors in the space-time world. Without the
true orthodox doctrine of God and man, prayer is just nonsense.
You have to understand that there is a personal God and that He
has created the universe, which is then not an extension of His
essence. If it were, we would have a pantheistic system in which
prayer is meaningless. At this point there is little difference between the pantheism of the East and many of the new theologians
of the West.

But let us notice that this emphasis must not be just a matter of
doctrine. We must really sit in the supernaturalist's chair and pray.
If a Christian does not pray, if he does not live in an attitude of
prayer, then no matter what he says about his doctrine, no matter
how many naughty names he calls the unbelieving materialist, the
Christian has moved over and is sitting in the materialist's chair.
He is living in unfaith if he is afraid to act upon the supernatural in
the present life.

Unfaith turns Christianity into only a philosophy. Of course,
Christianity is a philosophy—though not a rationalistic one be-

cause we have not worked it out beginning from ourselves. Rather, God has told us the answers. In this sense it is the true philosophy, for it gives the right answers to man's philosophic and intellectual questions. However, while it is the true philosophy, our Father in Heaven did not mean it to be only theoretical or abstract. He meant it to tell us about Himself—how we can get to Heaven, but equally how we can live right now in the universe as it is with both the seen and the unseen portions standing in equal reality. If Christians just use Christianity as a matter of mental assent between conversion and death, if they only use it to answer intellectual questions, it is like using a silver spoon for a screwdriver. I can believe that a silver spoon makes a good screwdriver at certain times. But it is made for something else. To take the silver spoon that's meant to feed you, moment by moment, and keep it in your tool box to use only as a screwdriver is silly.

But let's look further at the Christian living in unfaith. If the Bible-believing Christian has moved over and is in practice sitting in the materialist's chair, he is living as though the universe were something different than it is. He is out of step with the universe and is in practice living as though he is more ignorant than a pagan in a jungle.

Suppose three men were sitting together in a jet airliner, one against the window, one against the aisle, and one in the middle. The one at the window is a pagan who hasn't a clue as to how the airplane flies; he's terrified as the airplane goes up. The man on the aisle knows every nut and bolt in this airplane; he designed it. But he doesn't believe in any supernatural at all. Imagine that you as a Christian are sitting in the middle. Which of these two men would best understand the universe? The pagan doesn't have a clue about the airplane, but he knows that there is a seen and an unseen portion in the universe because he worships demons. The other man knows all about the airplane and he doesn't worship demons, but he also doesn't know that there is any unseen portion at all. The pagan is less ignorant of reality than the engineer, for the latter is living in only half of the universe. But what about you as the Christian? If you say that the universe has a spiritual dimension and yet do not live like it, you are acting as though you know less than the pagan.

Maybe now we will begin to see why in the evangelical church we often have a feeling of dustiness, unreality, and abstraction. I think the reason is that many are functioning as though they knew less about the universe than the pagan knows. They have moved over in unfaith and are living as though the universe is naturalistic. No wonder there is a dustiness! In such a case the evangelical church is a museum of dead artifacts representing what once was living practice of the doctrine we still say we believe.

If courses in a Christian college are being taught as though the professors are sitting in the materialist's chair, is it any wonder that there is an unreality? It's possible to teach our subjects that way. We can carry on our church life that way. We can carry on our evangelism that way. And our children then look at us, shake their heads and think, "Well, certainly there's something very unreal and musty in what I see in my teacher's, my pastor's, and my parents' Christian lives." If we sit in the chair of unfaith, that's the result we should expect.

But let's take note: there are only two chairs, not three. And at this present moment we are either sitting in one or the other. Unfaith is just the Christian sitting in the materialist's chair. At every moment, existentially, there are before us as Christians the two chairs. After I am a Christian, I do not lose my significance. I am either yielding my life to the living Christ at a given moment or I am not. I am either in one chair or the other.

Which chair are we in? How do we live our lives? What's the "set of the sail" in the way we live? None of us is perfect; this is true. All of us sometimes find ourselves in the materialist's chair. But is this where we habitually sit? Is this how we *usually* teach our subjects? Is this the way we *usually* study? Is it even the way we do what we call "the Lord's work"? Are we sitting in the chair of unfaith while we are trying to present the doctrines of belief?

Being a Bible-believing Christian, then, not only means believing with our heads, but in this present moment acting through faith on that belief. True spirituality is acting at the given moment upon the doctrines which one as a Christian says he believes.

We must fight the Lord's battles with the Lord's weapons in faith—sitting in the chair of belief. Only then can we have any part in the real battle. If we fight the Lord's battles merely by duplicating the way the world does its work, we are like little boys playing with wooden swords pretending they are in the battle while their big brothers are away at war in some distant and bloody land. The Lord will not honor with power the way of unfaith in His children because it does not give Him the honor. He is left out. That is true in Christian activities, in missionary work, in evangelism, in anything you name. Living supernaturally does not mean doing less work; nor does it mean less work getting done, but more. Who can do more? We with our own energy and wisdom, or the God who created Heaven and earth and who can work in space-time history with a power which none of us has? God exists. And if we through faith stay in the Bible-believing chair moment by moment in practice, and do not move into the chair of unfaith, Christ will bring forth His fruit through us. The fruit will differ with each of us, but it will be His fruit.

As I began this book I brought together the concepts of reformation and revival—the return to pure doctrine and the return of individuals and groups to a proper relationship to the Holy Spirit.

At the conclusion of our study of Jeremiah and his message, we said that if there is to be a constructive revolution in the orthodox, evangelical church, then like Jeremiah we must speak of God's judgment of individual men, great and small, and His judgment of the church, the state, and the culture, all of which have known the truth of God and have turned away from Him and His propositional revelation. God exists, He is a holy God, and we must know that there will be judgment. Like Jeremiah, we must keep on so speaking regardless of the cost to ourselves. At the conclusion of our study of Romans we added this: if there is to be a constructive revolution in the orthodox, evangelical church, we must comprehend and speak about the lostness of the lost, including the man without the Bible. As with Paul this must not be done with a cold orthodoxy, but with deep compassion for our own kind. Finally we must add that these things cannot be done once for all, nor by our own human effort alone; we must be in the believer's chair moment by moment.

Reformation and revival are related to God's people sitting moment by moment in the believer's chair. And with such reformation-revival will come constructive revolution in the evangelical, orthodox church. Even in the midst of death in the city, the evangelical church can have a really constructive revolution, a revolution that will shake it in all its parts and make it live before God, before the unseen world, and before the observing eyes of our post-Christian world.

The Great Evangelical Disaster

Preface

As you begin reading this book, I would like to mention that I have something of a dilemma, and I have had this now for a number of years. Let me try to explain what this is: During the last two decades I have written twenty-three books. My early books dealt especially with the intellectual questions of philosophy and matters in the area of culture. Then there were the books dealing with the Christian life and the church. More recently my books have dealt especially with the area of civil needs and the needs of law and government.

Throughout all of my work there is a common unifying theme, which I would define as "the Lordship of Christ in the totality of life." If Christ is indeed Lord, he must be Lord of all of life—in spiritual matters, of course, but just as much across the whole spectrum of life, including intellectual matters and the areas of culture, law, and government. I would want to emphasize from beginning to end throughout my work the importance of evangelism (helping men and women come to know Christ as Savior), the need to walk daily with the Lord, to study God's Word, to live a life of prayer, and to show forth the love, compassion, and holiness of our Lord. But we must emphasize equally and at the same time the need to live this out in every area of culture and society.

This book which you are reading now needs to be seen, then, within the context of my work as a whole. My dilemma is that many will not have had the opportunity to be familiar with the full range of my work, and it would be impossible to review or cover all of this within the pages of this book.

At the same time, however, this book stands on its own, in speaking to the critical issues of the day. Thus, for the person reading my work for the first time this book really does provide a good place to begin. On the other hand, those who are already familiar with my work should see that this new book grows out of the critical situation in which we live today, but also that it is a direct extension and application of what I have written over the years.

And if you find what I say in these pages interesting and helpful, I would encourage you to go back and study through my earlier work. This is now available in a five-volume set of my *Complete Works,* published by Crossway Books. The set is arranged so as to best follow the flow of my thought, and it includes twenty-two of my books, revised throughout for this new edition, with a comprehensive index.

One of the purposes of this present book was to reaffirm and restate some of the ideas and themes from my earlier work, as well as to make extensions and application of these to the situation in which we live today. The notes at the end of the book should be consulted to see where in my other works many of these themes and ideas are developed in greater detail.

Finally I would say that the statement which I am making in the pages of this book is perhaps the most important statement I have ever written. It concerns what I call "The Great Evangelical Disaster" and the greatest problem we who are Christians face in our generation.

FRANCIS A. SCHAEFFER
February 1984

PART I

Introduction

CHAPTER ONE

What Really Matters?

Time magazine recently published a special sixtieth anniversary edition with the title "The Most Amazing 60 Years." In recalling the world into which *Time* was born, this special issue began with the words: "The atom was unsplit. So were most marriages."[1] Here two things occurring in our era are properly brought together—one, the scientific technological explosion; and two, a moral breakdown. It is not just by accident that these two things have happened simultaneously. There is something which lies behind both phenomena, and in recognizing this *Time* really has shown amazing comprehension.

The Quest for Autonomy

Something happened during the last sixty years—something which cut the moral foundation out from under our culture. Devastating things have come in every area of culture, whether it be law or government, whether it is in the schools, our local communities or in the family. And these have happened within the lifetime of many who are reading this book. Our culture has been squandered and lost, and largely thrown away. Indeed, to call it a moral breakdown puts it mildly. Morality itself has been turned on its head with every form of moral perversion being praised and glorified in the media and the world of entertainment.

How can we make sense of what has happened? In the main essay of this special edition *Time* offers an explanation. The essay, entitled "What really mattered?" suggests: "To determine what really mattered in this jumble [of events] seems to require a sense of something beyond the particulars." We will need, *Time* says, to discover the "idea characterizing [our] age."[2]

Time is quite right in this. In order to make sense of these last sixty years, and equally in order to understand the present and how we as Christians are to live today, we will need to understand the idea of our age—or what we might call the spirit of the times which has transformed our culture so radically since the 1920s. This idea, this spirit, *Time* says, has been the idea of "freedom"—not just freedom as an abstract ideal, or in the sense of being free from injustice, but *freedom in an absolute sense:*

> The fundamental idea that America represented corresponded to the values of the times. America was not merely free; it was freed, unshackled. The image was of something previously held in check, an explosive force of a country that moved about in random particles of energy yet at the same time gained power and prospered. To be free was to be modern; to be modern was to take chances. The American century was to be the century of unleashing, of breaking away, at first from the 19th century (as Freud, Proust, Einstein and others had done), *and eventually from any constraints at all.*[3]

Further along in the same essay *Time* comments: "Behind most of these events lay the assumption, almost a moral *imperative,* that what was not free ought to be free, *that limits were intrinsically evil,*" and that science should go wherever it pleases in a spirit of "self-confident autonomy."[4] But, as *Time* concludes, "when people or ideas are unfettered, they are freed but not yet free."[5]

Form and Freedom
Here the problem of the 1920s to the 1980s is properly spelled out. It is the attempt to have absolute freedom—to be totally autonomous from any intrinsic limits. It is the attempt to throw off anything that would restrain one's own personal autonomy. But it is especially a direct and deliberate rebellion against God and his law.

In this essay *Time* has given that which indeed is central, namely the problem of form and freedom. It is a problem which every culture from the beginning of history has had to confront. The problem is this: If there is not a proper balance between form and freedom, then the society will move into either of two extremes. Freedom, without a proper balance of form, will lead to chaos and to the total breakdown of society. Form, without a proper balance of freedom, will lead to authoritarianism, and to the destruction of individual and social freedom. But note further: no society can exist in a state of chaos. And whenever chaos has reigned for even a short time, it has given birth to the imposition of arbitrary control.

In our own country we have enjoyed enormous human freedom. But at the same time this freedom has been founded upon forms of government, law, culture, and social morality which have given stability to individual and social life, and have kept our freedoms from leading to chaos. There is a balance here between form and freedom which we have come to take as natural in the world. But it is not natural. And we are utterly foolish if we do not recognize that this unique balance which we have inherited from the Reformation thought-forms is not automatic in a fallen world. This is clear when we look at the long span of history. But it is equally clear when we read the daily newspaper and see half the world locked in totalitarian oppression.

The Reformation not only brought forth a clear preaching of the gospel, it also gave shape to society as a whole—including government, how people viewed the world, and the full spectrum of culture. In Northern Europe, and in the countries such as the United States that are extensions of Northern Europe, the Reformation brought with it an enormous increase in knowledge of the Bible which spread through every level of society. This is not to say that the Reformation was ever a "golden age" or that everyone in the Reformation countries was a true Christian. But it is clear that through the Reformation many were brought to Christ and that the absolutes of the Bible became widely disseminated in the culture as a whole. The freedoms which grew out of this were tremendous; and yet, with the forms grounded in a biblical consensus or ethos,[6] the freedoms did not lead to chaos.

But something has happened in the last sixty years. The freedom that once was founded on a biblical consensus and a Christian ethos has now become autonomous freedom, cut loose from all constraints. Here we have the world spirit of our age—autonomous Man setting himself up as God, in defiance of the knowledge and the moral and spiritual truth which God has given. Here is the reason why we have a moral breakdown in every area of life. The titanic freedoms which we once enjoyed have been cut loose from their Christian restraints and are becoming a force of destruction leading to chaos. And when this happens, there really are very few alternatives. All morality becomes relative, law becomes arbitrary, and society moves toward disintegration. In personal and social life, compassion is swallowed up by self-interest. As I have pointed out in my earlier books, when the memory of the Christian consensus which gave us freedom within the biblical form is increasingly forgotten, a manipulating authoritarianism will tend to fill the vacuum. At this point the words "right" and "left" will make little difference. They are only two roads to the same end; the results are the same. An elite, an authoritarianism as such, will gradually force form on society so that it will not go into chaos—and most people would accept it.[7]

The Battle We Are In

As evangelical, Bible-believing Christians we have not done well in understanding this. The world spirit of our age rolls on and on claiming to be autonomous and crushing all that we cherish in its path. Sixty years ago could we have imagined that unborn children would be killed by the millions here in our own country? Or that we would have *no freedom of speech* when it comes to speaking of God and biblical truth in our public schools? Or that every form of sexual perversion would be promoted by the entertainment media? Or that marriage, raising children, and family life would be objects of attack? Sadly we must say that very few Christians have understood the battle that we are in. Very few have taken a strong and courageous stand against the world spirit of this age as it destroys our culture and the Christian ethos that once shaped our country.

But the Scriptures make clear that we as Bible-believing Christians are locked in a battle of cosmic proportions. It is a life and death struggle over the minds and souls of men for all eternity, but it is equally a life and death struggle over life on this earth. On one level this is a spiritual battle which is being fought in the heavenlies. Paul's letter to the Ephesians presents the classic expression:

> For our struggle is not against flesh and blood, but against the rulers, against the authorities, against the powers of this dark world and

against the spiritual forces of evil in the heavenly realms. (Ephesians 6:12)

Do we really believe that we are engaged in this cosmic battle? Do we really believe that there are "powers of this dark world" which rule our age? Or as the Apostle John says, do we really believe that "the whole world is under the control of the evil one" (1 John 5:19)? If we do not believe these things (and we must say that much of the evangelical world acts as if it does not believe these things), we certainly cannot expect to have much success in fighting the battle. Why has the Christian ethos in our culture been squandered? Why do we have so little impact upon the world today? Is it not because we have failed to take the primary battle seriously?

And if we have failed to take the battle seriously, we have certainly failed to use the weapons our Lord has provided. As the Apostle Paul writes:

> Finally, be strong in the Lord and in his mighty power. Put on the full armor of God so that you can take your stand against the devil's schemes . . . Therefore put on the full armor of God, so that when the day of evil comes, you may be able to stand your ground, and after you have done everything, to stand. Stand firm then, with the belt of truth buckled around your waist, with the breastplate of righteousness in place, and with your feet fitted with the readiness that comes from the gospel of peace. In addition to all this, take up the shield of faith, with which you can extinguish all the flaming arrows of the evil one. Take the helmet of salvation and the sword of the Spirit, which is the word of God. And pray in the Spirit on all occasions with all kinds of prayers and requests. With this in mind, be alert and always keep on praying for all the saints. (Ephesians 6:10, 11, 13-18)

Note that there is nothing in this list that the world accepts as a way of working, but there is no other way to fight the spiritual battle in the heavenlies. And if we do not use these weapons we have no hope of winning.

The primary battle is a spiritual battle in the heavenlies. But this does not mean, therefore, that the battle we are in is other-worldly or outside of human history. It is a real spiritual battle, but it is equally a battle here on earth in our own country, our own communities, our places of work and our schools, and even our own homes. The spiritual battle has its counterpart in the visible world, in the minds of men and women, and in every area of human culture. In the realm of space and time the heavenly battle is fought on the stage of human history.

But if we are to win the battle on the stage of human history, it will take a prior commitment to fighting the spiritual battle with the only weapons that will be effective. It will take a life committed to Christ, founded on truth, lived in righteousness and grounded in the gospel. It is interesting to note that all of the weapons which Paul lists up to this point are defensive. The only offensive weapon mentioned is "the sword of the Spirit, which is the word of God." While the others help to defend us against the attacks of Satan, the Bible is the weapon which enables us to join with our Lord on the offensive in defeating the spiritual hosts of wickedness. But it must be the Bible as the Word of God in *everything it teaches*— in matters of salvation, but just as much where it speaks of history and science and morality. If it is compromised in any of these areas, as is unhappily happening today among many who call themselves evangelicals, we destroy the power of the Word and put ourselves in the hands of the enemy. Finally, it will take a life of prayer: "pray in the spirit on all occasions."

On the level of human history, however, the battle is equally important. Here too there is a fundamental conflict going on which is the earthly counterpart to the heavenly battle. This conflict takes two forms. The first of these has to do with the way we think— the ideas we have and the way we view the world. The second has to do with the way we live and act. Both of these conflicts— in the area of ideas and in the area of actions—are important; and in both areas Bible-believing Christians find themselves locked in battle with the surrounding culture of our day.

The Wisdom of the World
The battle in the area of ideas is pointed out most clearly in the letters of the Apostle Paul.[8] Here we see that there is a fundamental conflict between "the wisdom of this world" and "the wisdom of God." Thus Paul writes:

> Where is the wise man? Where is the scholar? Where is the philosopher of this age? Has not God made foolish the wisdom of the world? For since in the wisdom of God the world through its wisdom did not know him, God was pleased through the foolishness of what was preached to save those who believe. (1 Corinthians 1:20, 21)

And again:

> Do not deceive yourselves. If any one of you thinks he is wise by the standards of this age, he should become a "fool" so that he may become wise. For the wisdom of this world is foolishness in God's sight. (1 Corinthians 3:18, 19)

Now we should say immediately that Paul is not saying that knowledge and education have no value. Paul himself was among the most highly educated of his time. Paul is speaking instead of a worldly wisdom which claims to be self-sufficient in itself, quite apart from God and his revelation. It is a kind of worldly wisdom which leaves God and his revelation out of the picture and thereby ends up with a completely distorted conception of reality. This can be seen most clearly in the first chapter of Romans where Paul writes:

> For although they knew God, they neither glorified him as God nor gave thanks to him, but their thinking became futile and their foolish hearts were darkened. Although they claimed to be wise, they became fools. . . .
> Therefore God gave them over in the sinful desires of their hearts to sexual impurity for the degrading of their bodies with one another. They exchanged the truth of God for a lie, and worshiped and served created things rather than the Creator. . . . (Romans 1:21-25)

What is involved here is the way men think, the process of reasoning, thought, and comprehension. Thus "their thinking became futile and their foolish hearts were darkened. Although they claimed to be wise, they became fools." When the Scripture speaks of man being foolish in this way, it does not mean he is only foolish religiously. Rather, it means that he has accepted a position that is intellectually foolish not only with regard to what the Bible says, but also to what exists concerning the universe and its form and what it means to be human. In turning away from God and the truth which he has given, man has thus become *foolishly* foolish in regard to what man is and what the universe is. Man is left with a position with which he cannot live, and he is caught in a multitude of intellectual and personal tensions.

The Scripture tells us how man came into this situation: Because "although they knew God, they neither glorified him as God nor gave thanks to him"; therefore, they became foolish in their rea-

soning, in their comprehension, in their lives. This passage relates
to the original fall, but it does not speak only about the original
fall. It speaks of any period when men knew the truth and deliberately turned away from it.

Many periods of history could be described in this way. From
the biblical viewpoint there was a time when the ancestors of the
people of India knew the truth and turned away, a time when the
ancestors of the people of Africa knew the truth and turned away.
This is true of people anywhere who now do not know the truth.
But if we are looking across the history of the world to see those
times when men knew the truth and turned away, let us say
emphatically that there is not an exhibition of this anywhere in
history so clearly—and in such a short time—as in our own generation. We who live in North America have seen this verse carried
out in our generation with desperate force. Men of our time knew
the truth and yet turned away—turned away not only from the
biblical truth but also turned away from the many blessings this
brought in every area of culture, including the balance of form
and freedom we once had.

A Post-Christian Culture
Having turned away from the knowledge given by God, the Christian influence on the whole of culture has been lost. In Europe,
including England, it took many years—in the United States only
a few decades. In the United States, in the short span from the
twenties to the sixties, we have seen a complete shift. Ours is a
post-Christian world in which Christianity, not only in the number of Christians but in cultural emphasis and cultural result, is
no longer the consensus or ethos of our society.

Do not take this lightly! It is a horrible thing for a man like
myself to look back and see my country and my culture go down
the drain in my own lifetime. It is a horrible thing that sixty years
ago you could move across this country and almost everyone,
even non-Christians, would have known what the gospel was. A
horrible thing that fifty to sixty years ago our culture was built
on the Christian consensus, and now this is no longer the case.

Once again I would refer to Romans 1:21, 22: "although they
knew God, they neither glorified him as God nor gave thanks to
him, but their thinking became futile and their foolish hearts were
darkened. Although they claimed to be wise, they became fools."
Verse 18 tells us of the result of turning away from and rebelling
against the truth they know: "The wrath of God is being revealed

from heaven against all the godlessness and wickedness of men who suppress the truth by their wickedness." Man is justly under the wrath of the God who really exists and who deals with men on the basis of his character; and if the justice of that wrath is obvious concerning any generation it is our own. Wrath may come either in the cause and effect of the turning wheels of history, or in the direct action of God.

There is only one perspective we can have of the post-Christian world of our generation: an understanding that our culture and our country deserves to be under the wrath of God. It will not do to say the United States is God's country in some special way. It will not do to cover up the difference between the consensus today and the Christian consensus that prevailed sixty years ago. The last few generations have trampled upon the truth of the Bible and all that those truths have brought forth.[9]

Ideas and Actions

We have seen then that as Bible-believing Christians we are locked in a battle in the area of ideas. But in the area of actions there is a direct parallel. Ideas are never neutral and abstract. Ideas have consequences in the way we live and act, both in our personal lives and in the culture as a whole. We can look again to the first chapter of Romans to see what the consequences of these ideas are in the form of actions:

> Therefore God gave them over in the sinful desires of their hearts to sexual impurity for the degrading of their bodies with one another. . . .
>
> Furthermore, since they did not think it worthwhile to retain the knowledge of God, he gave them over to a depraved mind, to do what ought not to be done. They have become filled with every kind of wickedness, evil, greed and depravity. They are full of envy, murder, strife, deceit and malice. They are gossips, slanderers, God-haters, insolent, arrogant and boastful; they invent ways of doing evil; they disobey their parents; they are senseless, faithless, heartless, ruthless. Although they know God's righteous decree that those who do such things deserve death, they not only continue to do these very things but also approve of those who practice them. (Romans 1:24, 28-32)

There hardly could be a more fitting description of our own culture today. Bent on the pursuit of autonomous freedom—freedom from any restraint, and especially from God's truth and moral absolutes—our culture has set itself on the course of self-destruction. Autonomous freedom! How the voices of our day cry out! I must be free to kill the child in my womb. I must be free even to kill the newborn child if I don't think he or she measures up to my standards of "quality life." I must be free to desert my husband or wife, and abandon my children. I must be free to commit shameless acts with those of my own sex. The last verse really is frightening when we think of it in relationship to our culture today: "Although they know God's righteous decree that those who do such things deserve death, they not only continue to do these very things but also approve of those who practice them."

And if this is not enough, I would urge you to read the second chapter of 2 Peter. The whole chapter is as accurate a picture of our culture as can be found anywhere—of the knowledge we once had, of the rejection of the truth, of the moral degeneration, and of the judgment that awaits those who have known the truth and turned from it. Thus Peter concludes the chapter:

> For they mouth empty, boastful words and, by appealing to the lustful desires of sinful human nature, they entice people who are just escaping from those who live in error. They promise them freedom, while they themselves are slaves of depravity—for a man is a slave to whatever has mastered him. If they have escaped the corruption of the world by knowing our Lord and Savior Jesus Christ and are again entangled in it and overcome, they are worse off at the end than they were at the beginning. It would have been better for them not to have known the way of righteousness, than to have known it and then to turn their backs on the sacred commandment that was passed on to them. (2 Peter 2:18-21)

Make no mistake. We as Bible-believing evangelical Christians are locked in a battle. This is not a friendly gentleman's discussion. It is a life and death conflict between the spiritual hosts of wickedness and those who claim the name of Christ. It is a conflict on the level of ideas between two fundamentally opposed views of truth and reality. It is a conflict on the level of actions between a complete moral perversion and chaos and God's absolutes. But do we really believe that we are in a life and death battle? Do we really believe that the part we play in the battle has consequences for whether or not men and women will spend eternity in hell? Or whether or not in this life people will live with meaning or meaninglessness? Or whether or not those who do live will live in a climate of moral perversion and degradation? Sadly, we must say that very few in the evangelical world have acted as if these things are true. Rather than trumpet our accomplishments and revel in our growing numbers, it would be closer to the truth to admit that our response has been a disaster.

The Antithesis of Christian Truth
In thinking back over what I have said to this point, we have seen that the spirit of the age is autonomous freedom—that is, freedom from all restraints and especially rebellion against God's truth and moral absolutes. And we have seen that over the last sixty years the pursuit of autonomous freedom has undercut the Christian ethos that once had a profound influence in shaping our culture. How did this come about? In one sense we may say that it is due to willful rebellion against God's truth and the revelation of his Word. And we would be right in this. But in another sense the changes which have come flow out of the intellectual and religious history of our culture and the Western world. In a number of my books I have dealt at length with the rise of humanism in the Western world and the devastating effect this has had, and I would encourage you to review this.[10] Here, however, I would refer to just one aspect of this—that is, the influence of the Enlightenment, and how this relates specifically to the shift that has taken place in our country over the last sixty years.

At the end of the nineteenth century the ideas of the Enlightenment began to have a significant influence upon Christianity in America. Now it is important to understand what the views of the Enlightenment were, for they have left a radical mark upon religion in America up to this day. The Enlightenment was a movement of thought which began to appear in the mid-seventeenth century and reached its most clear-cut form in eighteenth-century Germany. In general, it was an intellectual movement which emphasized the sufficiency of human reason and skepticism concerning the validity of the traditional authority of the past. It is instructive to note exactly how the Enlightenment is defined in *The Oxford Dictionary of the Christian Church:*

> The Enlightenment combines opposition to all supernatural religion and belief in the all-sufficiency of human reason with an ardent desire to promote the happiness of men in this life. . . . Most of its representatives . . . rejected the Christian dogma and were hostile to Catholicism as well as Protestant orthodoxy, which they regarded as powers of spiritual darkness depriving humanity of the use of its

rational faculties. . . . Their fundamental belief in the goodness of human nature, which blinded them to the fact of sin, produced an easy optimism and absolute faith of human society once the principles of enlightened reason had been recognized. The spirit of the Enlightenment penetrated deeply into German Protestantism [in the 19th century], where it disintegrated faith in the authority of the Bible and encouraged Biblical criticism on the one hand and an emotional "Pietism" on the other.[11]

This could be summarized in a few words: The central ideas of the Enlightenment stand in complete antithesis to Christian truth. More than this, they are an attack on God himself and his character.

In the late nineteenth century it was these ideas which began to radically transform Christianity in America. This started especially with the acceptance of the 'higher critical" methods that had been developed in Germany. Using these methods, the new liberal theologians completely undercut the authority of Scripture. We can be thankful for those who argued strenuously against the new methods and in defense of the full inspiration and inerrancy of Scripture. One would remember especially the great Princeton theologians A. A. Hodge and B. B. Warfield, and later J. Gresham Machen. But in spite of the efforts of these men and scores of other Bible-believing Christian leaders, and in spite of the fact that the vast majority of lay Christians were truly Bible-believing, those holding the liberal ideas of the Enlightenment and the destructive methods of biblical criticism came into power and control in the denominations. By the 1930s liberalism had swept through most of the denominations and the battle was all but lost.

The Turning-Point
Then in the mid 1930s, there occurred an event which I would say marks the turning-point of the century concerning the breakdown of our culture. By 1936 the liberals were so in control of the Northern Presbyterian Church that they were able to defrock Dr. J. Gresham Machen. Machen, as I mentioned, had been a brilliant defender of Bible-believing Christianity, as can be seen, for example, in his book entitled *Christianity and Liberalism*[12] published in 1924. Machen's defrocking and the resulting division of the Northern Presbyterian Church was front-page news in the secular news media in much of the country. (I would just comment that this is something we know nothing about today. In the 1930s religious events were still considered important enough to be

front-page news.) However much conscious forethought this showed on the editors' and broadcasters' part, this was rightfully page-one news, for it marked the culmination of the drift of the Protestant churches from 1900-1936. It was this drift which laid the base for the cultural, social, moral, legal, and governmental changes from that time to the present. Without this drift in the denominations, I am convinced that the changes in our society over the last fifty years would have produced very different results from what we have now. When the Reformation churches shifted, the Reformation consensus was undercut. A good case could be made that the news about Machen was the most significant U.S. news in the first half of the twentieth century. It was the culmination of a long trend toward liberalism within the Presbyterian Church and represented the same trend in most other denominations. Even if we were only interested in sociology, this change in the churches and the resulting shift of our culture to a post-Christian consensus is important to understand if we are to grasp what is happening in the United States today.[13] It is interesting to note that there was a span of approximately eighty years from the time when the higher critical methods originated and became widely accepted in Germany to the disintegration of German culture and the rise of totalitarianism under Hitler.

The New Consensus

Do you understand now what the battle is about in the area of culture and ideas? In the last sixty years the consensus upon which our culture was built has shifted from one that was largely Christian (though we must say immediately it was far from perfect) to a consensus growing out of the Enlightenment: that is, to a consensus that stands in total antithesis to Christian truth at every point—including the denial of the supernatural; belief in the all-sufficiency of human reason; the rejection of the fall; denial of the deity of Christ and his resurrection; belief in the perfectibility of Man; and the destruction of the Bible. And with this has come a nearly total moral breakdown. There is no way to make a synthesis of these ideas and Christian truth. They stand in total antithesis.

In a number of my other books I have described this new consensus as secular humanism. The Enlightenment world view and the world view of secular humanism really are essentially the same, with the same intellectual heritage. What we have here is a total world view. As I said in *A Christian Manifesto,* the problems we face today have:

come about due to a shift in world view—that is, through a fundamental change in the overall way people think and view the world
and life as a whole. This shift has been *away from* a world view that
was at least vaguely Christian in people's memory (even if they were
not individually Christian) *toward* something completely different—
toward a world view based upon the idea that the final reality is
impersonal matter or energy shaped into its present form by impersonal chance.[14]

And if we hold this world view we live in a universe that is
ultimately silent, with no meaning and purpose, with no basis for
law and morality, with no concept of what it means to be human
and of the value of human life. All is relative and arbitrary. And
so modern man is left with nothing to fill the void but hedonism
or materialism or whatever other "ism" may be blowing in the
wind.

Accommodation
And now we must ask where we as evangelicals have been in the
battle for truth and morality in our culture. Have we as evangelicals
been on the front lines contending for the faith and confronting
the moral breakdown over the last forty to sixty years? Have we
even been aware that there is a battle going on—not just a heavenly
battle, but a life-and-death struggle over what will happen to men
and women and children in both this life and the next? If the truth
of the Christian faith is in fact *truth,* then it stands in antithesis to
the ideas and the immorality of our age, and it must be *practiced*
both in teaching and practical action. Truth demands confrontation. It must be loving confrontation, but there must be confrontation nonetheless.

Sadly we must say that this has seldom happened. Most of the
evangelical world has not been active in the battle, or even been
able to see that we are in a battle. And when it comes to the issues
of the day the evangelical world most often has said nothing; or
worse has said nothing different from what the world would say.

Here is the great evangelical disaster—the failure of the evangelical world to stand for truth as truth. There is only one word
for this—namely *accommodation:* the evangelical church has accommodated to the world spirit of the age. First, there has been accommodation on Scripture, so that many who call themselves
evangelicals hold a weakened view of the Bible and no longer
affirm the truth of all the Bible teaches—truth not only in religious

matters but in the areas of science and history and morality. As part of this, many evangelicals are now accepting the higher critical methods in the study of the Bible. Remember, it was these same methods which destroyed the authority of the Bible for the Protestant church in Germany in the last century, and which have destroyed the Bible for the liberal in our own country from the beginning of this century. And second, there has been accommodation on the issues, with no clear stand being taken even on matters of life and death.

This accommodation has been costly, first in destroying the power of the Scriptures to confront the spirit of our age; second, in allowing the further slide of our culture. Thus we must say with tears that it is the evangelical accommodation to the world spirit around us, to the wisdom of this age, which removes the evangelical church from standing against the further breakdown of our culture. It is my firm belief that when we stand before Jesus Christ, we will find that it has been the weakness and accommodation of the evangelical group on the issues of the day that has been largely responsible for the loss of the Christian ethos which has taken place in the area of culture in our own country over the last forty to sixty years.

And let us understand that to accommodate to the world spirit about us in our age is nothing less than the most gross form of worldliness in the proper definition of that word. And with this proper definition of worldliness, we must say with tears that, with exceptions, the evangelical church is worldly and not faithful to the living Christ.

What Really Matters?
In concluding this chapter I would ask one final question: What really matters? What is it that matters so much in my life and in your life that it sets the priorities for everything we do? Our Lord Jesus was asked essentially this same question and his reply was:

> " 'Love the Lord your God with all your heart and with all your soul and with all your mind.' This is the first and greatest commandment. And the second is like it: 'Love your neighbor as yourself.' All the Law and the Prophets hang on these two commandments." (Matthew 22:37-40)

Here is what really matters—to love the Lord our God, to love his Son, and to know him personally as our Savior. And if we love him, to do the things that please him; simultaneously to show forth his character of holiness and love in our lives; to be faithful to his truth; to walk day by day with the living Christ; to live a life of prayer.

And the other half of what really matters is to love our neighbor as ourselves. The two go together; they cannot be separated. "On these two commandments hang all the Law and the Prophets." *Because* we love the Lord Jesus Christ and know him personally as our Savior *we must,* through God's grace, love our neighbor as ourselves. And if we love our neighbor as Christ would have us love our neighbor, we will certainly want to share the gospel with our neighbor; and beyond this we will want to show forth the law of God in all our relationships with our neighbor.

But it does not stop here. Evangelism is primary, but it is not the end of our work and indeed cannot be separated from the rest of the Christian life.[15] We must acknowledge and then act upon the fact that if Christ is our Savior, he is also our Lord in *all* of life. He is our Lord not just in religious things and not just in cultural things such as the arts and music, but in our intellectual lives, and in business, and in our relation to society, and in our attitude toward the moral breakdown of our culture. Acknowledging Christ's Lordship and placing ourselves under what is taught in the whole Bible includes thinking and acting as citizens in relation to our government and its laws.[16] Making Christ Lord in our lives means taking a stand in very direct and practical ways against the world spirit of our age as it rolls along claiming to be autonomous, crushing all that we cherish in its path.

If we truly love our Lord and if we truly love our neighbor, we will ache with compassion for humanity today in our own country and across the world. We must do all we can to help people see the truth of Christianity and accept Christ as Savior. And we must not allow the Bible to be weakened by any compromise in its authority, no matter how subtle the means. This is especially so when those doing this call themselves "evangelical." But we must stand equally against the spirit of our age in the breakdown of morality and the terrible loss of humanness that it has brought. It will mean especially standing for human life and showing by our actions that every life is sacred and worthwhile in itself—not only to us as human beings, but precious also to God. Every person is worth fighting for, regardless of whether he is young or old, sick or well, child or adult, born or unborn, or brown, red, yellow, black, or white.

It is God's life-changing power that is able to touch every individual, who then has the responsibility to touch the world around him with the absolutes found in the Bible. In the end we must realize that the spirit of the age—with all the loss of truth and beauty, and the loss of compassion and humanness that it has brought—is not merely a cultural ill. It is a spiritual ill that the truth given us in the Bible and Christ alone can cure.

PART II

The Watershed of the Evangelical World

CHAPTER TWO

Marking the Watershed

A Watershed

Not far from where we live in Switzerland is a high ridge of rock with a valley on both sides. One time I was there when there was snow on the ground along that ridge. The snow was lying there unbroken, a seeming unity. However, that unity was an illusion, for it lay along a great divide; it lay along a watershed. One portion of the snow when it melted would flow into one valley. The snow which lay close beside would flow into another valley when it melted.

Now it just so happens on that particular ridge that the melting snow which flows down one side of that ridge goes down into a valley, into a small river, and then down into the Rhine River. The Rhine then flows on through Germany and the water ends up in the cold waters of the North Sea. The water from the snow that started out so close along that watershed on the other side of the ridge, when this snow melts, drops off sharply down the ridge into the Rhone Valley. This water flows into Lac Leman—or as it is known in the English-speaking world, Lake Geneva—and then goes down below that into the Rhone River which flows through France and into the warm waters of the Mediterranean.

The snow lies along that watershed, unbroken, as a seeming unity. But when it melts, where it ends in its destinations is literally a thousand miles apart. That is a watershed. That is what a watershed is. A watershed divides. A clear line can be drawn between what seems at first to be the same or at least very close, but in reality ends in very different situations. In a watershed there is a line.

A House Divided
What does this illustration have to do with the evangelical world today? I would suggest that it is a very accurate description of what is happening. Evangelicals today are facing a watershed concerning the nature of biblical inspiration and authority. It is a watershed issue in very much the same sense as described in the illustration. Within evangelicalism there are a growing number who are modifying their views on the inerrancy of the Bible so that the full authority of Scripture is completely undercut. But it is happening in very subtle ways. Like the snow lying side-by-side on the ridge, the new views on biblical authority often seem at first glance not to be so very far from what evangelicals, until just recently, have always believed. But also, like the snow lying side-by-side on the ridge, the new views when followed consistently end up a thousand miles apart.

What may seem like a minor difference at first, in the end makes all the difference in the world. It makes all the difference, as we might expect, in things pertaining to theology, doctrine and spiritual matters, but it also makes all the difference in things pertaining to the daily Christian life and how we as Christians are to relate to the world around us. In other words, *compromising the full authority of Scripture eventually affects what it means to be a Christian theologically and how we live in the full spectrum of human life.*

There is a sense in which the problem of full biblical authority is fairly recent. Up until the last two hundred years or so virtually every Christian believed in the complete inerrancy of the Bible, or in the equivalent of this expressed in similar terms. This was true both before the Reformation and after. The problem with the pre-Reformation medieval church was not so much that it did not hold to belief in an inerrant Bible as that it allowed the whole range of nonbiblical theological ideas and superstitions to grow up within the church. These ideas were then placed alongside of the Bible and even over the Bible, so that the Bible's authority and teaching were subordinated to nonbiblical teachings. This resulted in the abuses which led to the Reformation. But note that the problem was not that the pre-Reformation church did not *believe* in the inerrancy of Scripture; the problem was that it did not *practice* the inerrancy of Scripture, because it subordinated the Bible to its fallible teachings.

Thus it is important to note that, up until recent times, 1) belief in the inerrancy of Scripture (even when it was not practiced fully) and 2) claiming to be a Christian were seen as two things which necessarily went together. If you were a Christian, you also trusted in the complete reliability of God's written Word, the Bible. If you did not believe the Bible, you did not claim to be a Christian. But no one, until the past two hundred years or so, tried to say, "I am a Christian, but at the same time I believe the Bible to be full of errors." As incredible as this would have seemed to Christians in the past, and as incredible as this may seem to Bible-believing Christians today, this is what is now happening within the evangelical world.

This problem which started some two hundred years ago has within the past two decades come to the forefront among evangelicals. It is a problem which I (and others) began to address publicly in the mid-sixties, again in the seventies and repeatedly in the eighties. We can be thankful for the many who have taken a strong stand on this; but we must also say, sadly, that the problem continues and is growing. Evangelicalism is divided, deeply divided. And it will not be helpful or truthful for anyone to deny this. It is something that will not simply go away, and it cannot be swept under the rug. What follows in this chapter grows out of the study, thinking, and prayer, often with tears, which I have done concerning this watershed issue during my whole life as a Christian, but especially as I have dealt with this in my speaking and writing during the past two decades. The following, then, is a restatement on further development as a unified whole of my work in this area.

The Ground Cut out from Under
There are two reasons in our day for holding to a strong uncompromising view of Scripture. First and foremost, this is the only way to be faithful to what the Bible teaches about itself, to what Christ teaches about Scripture, and to what the church has consistently held through the ages. This should be reason enough in itself. But today there is a second reason why we should hold to a strong, uncompromising view of Scripture. There are hard days

ahead of us—for ourselves and for our spiritual and physical children. And without a strong view of Scripture as a foundation, we
will not be ready for the hard days to come. Unless the Bible is
without error, not only when it speaks of salvation matters, but
also when it speaks of history and the cosmos, we have no foundation for answering questions concerning the existence of the
universe and its form and the uniqueness of man. Nor do we have
any moral absolutes, or certainty of salvation, and the next generation of Christians will have nothing on which to stand. Our
spiritual and physical children will be left with the ground cut out
from under them, with no foundation upon which to build their
faith or their lives.

Christianity is no longer providing the consensus for our society. And Christianity is no longer providing the consensus upon
which our law is based. That is not to say that the United States
ever was a "Christian nation" in the sense that all or most of our
citizens were Christians, nor in the sense that the nation, its laws,
and social life were ever a full and complete expression of Christian
truth. There is no golden age in the past which we can idealize—
whether it is early America, the Reformation, or the early church.
But until recent decades something did exist which can rightly be
called a Christian consensus or ethos which gave a distinctive shape
to Western society and to the United States in a definite way. Now
that consensus is all but gone, and the freedoms that it brought
are being destroyed before our eyes. We are at a time when humanism is coming to its natural conclusion in morals, in values,
and in law. All that society has today are relativistic values based
upon statistical averages, or the arbitrary decisions of those who
hold legal and political power.

Freedom with Form or Chaos
The Reformation with its emphasis upon the Bible, in all that it
teaches, as being the revelation of God, provided a freedom in
society and yet a form in society as well. Thus, there were freedoms in the Reformation countries (such as the world had never
known before) without those freedoms leading to chaos—because
both laws and morals were surrounded by a consensus resting
upon what the Bible taught. That situation is now finished, and
we cannot understand society today for ourselves or our spiritual
and physical children unless we understand in reality what has
happened. In retrospect we can see that ever since the 1930s in the
United States, the Christian consensus has been an increasingly

minority view and no longer provides a consensus for society in morals or law. We who are Bible-believing Christians no longer represent the prevailing legal and moral outlook of our society, and no longer have the major influence in shaping this.

The primary emphasis of biblical Christianity is the teaching that the infinite-personal God is the final reality, the Creator of all else, and that an individual can come openly to the holy God upon the basis of the finished work of Christ and that alone. Nothing needs to be added to Christ's finished work, and nothing *can* be added to Christ's finished work. But at the same time where Christianity provides the consensus, as it did in the Reformation countries (and did in the United States up to a relatively few years ago), Christianity also brings with it many secondary blessings. One of these has been titanic freedoms, yet without those freedoms leading to chaos, because the Bible's *absolutes* provide a consensus within which freedom can operate. But once the Christian consensus has been removed, as it has been today, then the very freedoms which have come out of the Reformation become a destructive force leading to chaos in society. This is why we see the breakdown of morality everywhere in our society today—the complete devaluation of human life, a total moral relativism, and a thoroughgoing hedonism.

Relativism or God's Absolutes
In such a setting, we who are Bible-believing Christians, or our children, face days of decision ahead. Soft days for evangelical Christians are past, and only a strong view of Scripture is sufficient to withstand the pressure of an all-pervasive culture built upon relativism and relativistic thinking. We must remember that it was a strong view of the absolutes which the infinite-personal God gave to the early church in the Old Testament, in the revelation of Christ through the Incarnation, and in the then growing New Testament—absolutes which enabled the early church to withstand the pressure of the Roman Empire. Without a strong commitment to God's absolutes, the early church could never have remained faithful in the face of the constant Roman harassment and persecution. And our situation today is remarkably similar as our own legal, moral, and social structure is based on an increasingly anti-Christian, secularist consensus.

But what is happening in evangelicalism today? Is there the same commitment to God's absolutes which the early church had? Sadly we must say that this commitment is not there. Although growing in numbers as far as name is concerned, throughout the world and the United States, evangelicalism is not unitedly standing for a strong view of Scripture. But we must say if evangelicals are to be evangelicals, we must not compromise our view of Scripture. There is no use of evangelicalism seeming to get larger and larger, if at the same time appreciable parts of evangelicalism are getting soft concerning the Scriptures.

We must say with sadness that in some places seminaries, institutions, and individuals who are known as evangelicals no longer hold to a full view of Scripture. The issue is clear. Is the Bible true truth and infallible wherever it speaks, including where it touches history and the cosmos, or is it only in some sense revelational where it touches religious subjects? That is the issue.

The New Neo-Orthodoxy
There is only one way to describe those who no longer hold to a full view of Scripture. Although many of these would like to retain the evangelical name for themselves, the only accurate way to describe this view is that it is a form of neo-orthodox existential theology. The heart of neo-orthodox existential theology is that the Bible gives us a quarry out of which to have religious experience, but that the Bible contains mistakes where it touches that which is verifiable—namely history and science. But unhappily we must say that in some circles this concept now has come into some of that which is called evangelicalism. In short, in these circles the neo-orthodox existential theology is being taught under the name of evangelicalism.

The issue is whether the Bible gives propositional truth (that is, truth which may be stated in propositions) where it touches history and the cosmos, and this all the way back to pre-Abrahamic history, all the way back to the first eleven chapters of Genesis; or whether instead of that, it is only meaningful where it touches that which is considered religious. T. H. Huxley, the biologist friend of Darwin, the grandfather of Aldous and Julian Huxley, wrote in 1890 that he visualized the day not far hence in which faith would be separated from all fact, and especially all pre-Abrahamic history, and that faith would then go on triumphant forever. This is an amazing statement for 1890, before the birth of existential philosophy or existential theology. Huxley indeed foresaw something clearly. I am sure that he and his friends considered this some kind of a joke, because they would have understood well that if faith is separated from fact and specifically pre-Abrahamic space-time history, it is only another form of what we today call a trip.

But unhappily, it is not only the avowedly neo-orthodox existential theologians who now hold that which T. H. Huxley foresaw, but some who call themselves evangelicals as well. This may come from the theological side in saying that not all the Bible is revelational. Or it may come from the scientific side in saying that the Bible teaches little or nothing when it speaks of the cosmos. Or it may come from the cultural side in saying that the moral teachings of the Bible were merely expressions of the culturally determined and relative situation in which the Bible was written and therefore not authoritative today.

Martin Luther said, "If I profess with the loudest voice and clearest exposition every portion of the truth of God except precisely that little point which the world and the devil are at the moment attacking, I am not confessing Christ, however boldly I may be professing Christ. Where the battle rages, there the loyalty of the soldier is proved and to be steady on all the battle front besides, is mere flight and disgrace if he flinches at that point."

Marking a Line

In our day that point is the question of Scripture. Holding to a strong view of Scripture or not holding to it is the watershed of the evangelical world.

The first direction in which we must face is to say most lovingly but clearly: evangelicalism is not consistently evangelical *unless there is a line drawn* between those who take a full view of Scripture and those who do not.

What is often forgotten is that where there is a watershed there is a line which can be observed and marked. If one had the responsibility in Switzerland, for example, for the development of hydroelectric power from the flow of water, one would have a great responsibility to determine the topography of the country and then mark where the line would fall, and where the water would divide and flow. In the watershed of the evangelical world, what does marking such a line mean? It means lovingly marking visibly where that line falls, lovingly showing that some are on the other side of the line, and making clear to everyone on both sides of the line what the consequences of this are.

In making visible where the line falls, we must understand what is really happening. With the denial of the full authority of Scripture, a significant section of what is called evangelicalism has allowed itself to be infiltrated by the general world view or view-point of our day. This infiltration *is really a variant of what had dominated liberal theological circles under the name of neo-orthodoxy.*

An Inner Feeling or Objective Truth

It is surprising to see how clearly the liberal, neo-orthodox way of thinking is reflected in the new weakened evangelical view. For example, some time ago I was on Milt Rosenberg's radio show "Extension 720" in Chicago (WGN) along with a young liberal pastor who graduated from a very well-known liberal theological seminary. The program was set up as a three-way discussion between myself, the liberal pastor, and Rosenberg, who does not consider himself to be a religious person. Rosenberg is a clever master of discussion. And with *A Christian Manifesto* and the question of abortion as the discussion points, he kept digging deeper and deeper into the difference between the young liberal pastor and myself. The young liberal pastor brought up Karl Barth, Niebuhr, and Tillich, and we discussed them. But it became very clear in that three-way discussion that the young liberal pastor never could appeal to the Bible without qualifications. And then the young liberal pastor said, "But I appeal to Jesus." My reply on the radio was that in view of his view of the Bible, he could not really be sure that Jesus lived. His answer was that he had an inner feeling, an inner response, that told him that Jesus had existed.

The intriguing thing to me was that one of the leading men of the weakened view of the Bible who is called an evangelical, and who certainly does love the Lord, in a long and strenuous but pleasant discussion in my home a few years ago, when pressed backwards as to how he was certain concerning the resurrection of Jesus Christ, used almost the same words. He said he was sure of the resurrection of Jesus Christ because of the inward witness. They both answered finally in the same way.

My point is that a significant and influential section of what is called evangelicalism has become infiltrated by a point of view which is directly related to the view that had dominated liberal theological circles under the name of neo-orthodoxy. To me, this was curious at the time when I saw it happening a certain number of years ago because where this ends had already been demonstrated by the Niebuhr-Tillich-"God-is-dead" syndrome. Neo-orthodoxy leads to a dead end with a dead God, as has already been demonstrated by the theology of the sixties. And is it not curious that some evangelicals are just now picking this up as if it were the thing we should hold if we are to be "with it" today? But equally significant, note that the liberal pastor and the leader with the weakened view of Scripture who calls himself an evangelical both end up in the same place—with no other final plea than "an inner witness." They have no final, objective authority.

This points up just how encompassing the infiltration is. Namely, just as the neo-orthodox roots are only a theological expression of the surrounding world view and methodology of existentialism, so what is being put forth as a new view of Scripture in evangelicalism is also an infiltration of the general world view and methodology of existentialism. By placing a radical emphasis on subjective human experience, existentialism undercuts the objective side of existence. For the existentialist it is an illusion to think that we can know anything truly, that there is such a thing as certain objective truth or moral absolutes. All we have is subjective experience, with no final basis for right or wrong or truth or beauty. This existential world view dominates philosophy, and much of art and the general culture such as the novel, poetry, and the cinema. And although this is apparent in the thinking in academic and philosophical circles, it is equally pervasive in popular culture. It is impossible to turn on the TV, or read the newspaper, or leaf through a popular magazine without being bombarded with the philosophy of moral relativism, subjective experience, and the denial of objective truth. In the new view of Scripture among evangelicals we find the same thing—namely, that the Bible is not objective truth; that in the area of what is verifiable it has many mistakes in it; that where it touches on history and the cosmos it cannot be trusted; and that even what it teaches concerning morality is culturally conditioned and cannot be accepted in an absolute sense. But nevertheless this new weakened view stresses that "a religious word" somehow breaks through from the Bible—which finally ends in some expression such as "an inner feeling," "an inner response," or "an inner witness."

A Divided Bible
The following two quotations are clear examples of this. They come from men widely separated geographically across the world, both of whom are in evangelical circles, but who advocate the idea that in the area where reason operates the Bible contains mistakes. The first writes:

But there are some today who regard the Bible's plenary and verbal
inspiration as insuring its inerrancy not only in its declared intention
to recount and interpret God's mighty redemptive acts, but also in
any and in all of its incidental statements or aspects of statements that
have to do with such nonrevelational matters as geology, meteorol-
ogy, cosmology, botany, astronomy, geography, etc.

In other words, the Bible is divided into halves. To someone like
myself this is all very familiar—in the writings of Jean-Paul Sartre,
of Albert Camus, of Martin Heidegger, of Karl Jaspers, and in
the case of thousands of modern people who have accepted the
existential methodology. This quotation is saying the same thing
they would say, but specifically relating this existential methodology to the Bible.

In a similar quote another evangelical leader in a country far
from the United States writes:

More problematic in my estimation is the fundamentalist extension
of the principle of noncontradictory Scriptures to include the historic,
geographic, statistical and other biblical statements, which do not
touch in every case on the question of salvation and which do belong
to the human element of Scripture.

Both of these statements do the same thing. They make a dichotomy; they make a division. They say that there are mistakes in
the Bible but nevertheless we are to keep hold of the meaning
system, the value system, and the religious things. This then is
the form in which the existential methodology has come into
evangelical circles. In the end it cuts the truth of the Scriptures off
from the objective world and replaces it with the subjective experience of an "inner witness." It reminds us in particular of the
secular existential philosopher Karl Jaspers' term "the final experience," and any number of other terms which are some form of
the concept of final authority being an inner witness. In the neo-
orthodox form, the secular existential form, and this new evangelical form, truth is left finally as only subjective.

All this stands in sharp contrast to the historic view presented
by Christ himself and the historic view of the Scripture in the
Christian church, which is the Bible being objective, absolute
truth. Of course we all know that there are subjective elements
involved in our personal reading of the Bible and in the church's
reading of the Bible. But nevertheless, the Bible *is* objective, absolute truth in all the areas it touches upon. And therefore we

know that Christ lived, and that Christ was raised from the dead, and all the rest, not because of some subjective inner experience, but because the Bible stands as an objective, absolute authority. This is the way we know. I do not downplay the experience that rests upon this objective reality, but this is the way we know— upon the basis that the Bible is objective, absolute truth.

Or to say it another way: the culture is to be constantly judged by the Bible, rather than the Bible being bent to conform to the surrounding culture. The early church did this in regard to the Roman-Greek culture of its day. The Reformation did this in its day in relation to the culture coming at the end of the Middle Ages. And we must never forget that all the great revivalists did this concerning the surrounding culture of their day. And the Christian church did this at every one of its great points of history.

The New Loophole

But to complicate things further, there are those within evangelicalism who are quite happy to use the words "infallibility," "inerrancy," and "without error," but upon careful analysis they really mean something quite different from what these words have meant to the church historically. This problem can be seen in what has happened to the statement on Scripture in the Lausanne Covenant of 1974. The statement reads:

> We affirm the divine inspiration, truthfulness and authority of both Old and New Testament Scriptures in their entirety as the only written Word of God, without error in all that it affirms, and the only infallible rule of faith and practice.

Upon first reading, this seems to make a strong statement in support of the full authority of the Bible. But a problem has come up concerning the phrase "in all that it affirms." For many this is being used as a loophole. I ought to say that this little phrase was not a part of my own contribution to the Lausanne Congress. I did not know that this phrase was going to be included in the Covenant until I saw it in printed form, and I was not completely happy with it. Nevertheless, it is a proper statement if the words are dealt with fairly. We do not, of course, want to say that the Bible is without error in things it does *not* affirm. One of the clearest examples is where the Bible says, "The fool has said in his heart, 'There is no God.' " The Bible does not teach that "there is no God." This is not something that the Bible affirms, even though it makes this statement. Furthermore, we are not saying the Bible is without error in all *the projections* which people have made on the basis of the Bible. So that statement, as it appeared in the Lausanne Covenant, is a perfectly proper statement in itself.

However, as soon as I saw it in printed form I knew it was going to be abused. Unhappily, this statement, "in all that it affirms," has indeed been made a loophole by many. How has it been made a loophole? It has been made a loophole through the existential methodology which would say that the Bible affirms the value system and certain religious things set forth in the Bible. But on the basis of the existential methodology, these men and women say in the back of their minds, even as they sign the Covenant, "But the Bible does not affirm without error that which it teaches in the area of history and the cosmos."

Because of the widely accepted existential methodology in certain parts of the evangelical community, the old words *infallibility, inerrancy* and *without error* are meaningless today unless some phrase is added such as: the Bible is without error not only when it speaks of values, the meaning system, and religious things, but it is also without error when it speaks of history and the cosmos. If some such phrase is not added, these words today are meaningless. It should be especially noted that the word *infallibility* is used today by men who do not apply it to the whole of Scripture, but only to the meaning system, to the value system, and certain religious things, leaving out any place where the Bible speaks of history and the things which would interest science.

In Spite of All the Mistakes
Just a few months ago a very clear example of this was brought to my attention. Today we find that the same view of Scripture which is held by the modern liberal theologian is being taught in seminaries which call themselves evangelical. This view follows the existential methodology of secular thinkers which says that the Bible has mistakes but that it is to be believed somehow or other anyway. For example I recently received a letter from a very able thinker in Great Britain, in which he wrote:

> There are many problems facing evangelicals today not the least of which is the neo-orthodoxy in relation to Scripture. I am studying at Tyndale House [a study center in Cambridge, England] for a few days. And down the corridor from me is a very amiable professor, from a prominent seminary in California which calls itself evangelical,

who calls himself an "open evangelical." He has stated publicly in theological debate that he believes the Bible "despite all the mistakes in it."

This Christian leader in England who wrote this letter to me is quite right in calling this neo-orthodoxy under the name of evangelical. Isn't it curious that evangelicals have picked this up now as that which is progressive, just at a time when the liberals have found that neo-orthodoxy led to the "God is dead" theology? And when it was clear a few years ago that this seminary and others were simply presenting a form of neo-orthodoxy in regard to Scripture under the evangelical name, did the evangelical leadership quickly draw a line? Was there a rush of the evangelical leadership to the cause of defending the Scriptures and the faith? Sadly we must say no. Except for a few lone voices there was a great, vast silence.[1]

Cultural Infiltration

Those weakening the Bible in the area of history and where it touches the cosmos do so by saying these things in the Bible are *culturally oriented*. That is, in places where the Bible speaks of history and the cosmos, it only shows forth views held by the culture in the day in which that portion of the Bible was written. For example, when Genesis and Paul affirm, as they clearly do, that Eve came from Adam, this is said to be only borrowed from the general cultural views of the day in which these books were written. Thus not just the first eleven chapters of Genesis, but the New Testament is seen to be relative instead of absolute.

But let us realize that one cannot begin such a process without going still further. These things have gone further among some who still call themselves evangelicals. They have been still trying to hold on to the value system, the meaning system, and the religious things given in the Bible; but for them the Bible is only culturally oriented when it speaks of history and the cosmos. In more recent years an extension has come to this. Now certain moral absolutes in the area of personal relationships given in the Bible are also said to be culturally oriented. I would mention two examples, although many others could be given. First, there is easy divorce and remarriage. What the Bible clearly teaches about the limitations placed upon divorce and remarriage is now put by some evangelicals in the area of cultural orientation. They say these were just the ideas of that moment when the New Testament was written. What the Bible teaches on these matters is to them only one more culturally oriented thing, and that is all. There are members, elders, and ministers in churches known as evangelical who no longer feel bound by what the Scripture affirms concerning this matter. They say that what the Bible teaches in this area is culturally oriented and is not to be taken as an absolute.

As a second example, we find the same thing happening in the area of the clear biblical teaching regarding order in the home and the church. The commands in regard to this order are now also considered culturally oriented by some speakers and writers under the name of evangelical.

In other words, in the last few years the situation has moved from hanging on to the value system, the meaning system, and the religious things while saying that what the Bible affirms in regard to history and the cosmos is culturally oriented to the further step of still trying to hold on to the value system, the meaning system, and religious things, but now lumping these moral commands along with the things of history and the cosmos as culturally oriented. There is no end to this. The Bible is made to say only that which echoes the surrounding culture at *our* moment of history. *The Bible is bent to the culture instead of the Bible judging our society and culture.*

Once men and women begin to go down the path of the existential methodology under the name of evangelicalism, the Bible is no longer the Word of God without error—each part may be eaten away step by step. When men and women come to this place, what then has the Bible become? It has become what the liberal theologians said it was back in the days of the twenties and thirties. We are back in the days of a scholar like J. Gresham Machen, who pointed out that the foundation upon which Christianity rests was being destroyed. What is that foundation? It is that the infinite-personal God who exists has not been silent, but has spoken propositional truth in *all* that the Bible teaches—including what it teaches concerning history, concerning the cosmos, and in moral absolutes as well as what it teaches concerning religious subjects.

Notice though what the primary problem was, and is: infiltration by a form of the world view which surrounds us, rather than the Bible being the unmovable base for judging the ever-shifting fallen culture. As evangelicals, we need to stand at the point of the call *not* to be infiltrated by this ever-shifting fallen culture which surrounds us, but rather judging that culture upon the basis of the Bible.

What Difference Does It Make?

Does inerrancy make a difference? Overwhelmingly; the difference is that with the Bible being what it is, God's Word and so absolute, God's objective truth, we do not need to be, *and we should not be,* caught in the ever-changing fallen cultures which surround us. Those who do not hold the inerrancy of Scripture do not have this high privilege. To some extent, they are at the mercy of the fallen, changing culture. And Scripture is thus bent to conform to the changing world spirit of the day, and they therefore have no solid authority upon which to judge and to resist the views and values of that changing, shifting world spirit.

We, however, must be careful before the Lord. If we say we believe the Bible to be the inerrant and authoritative "Thus saith the Lord," we do not face the howling winds of change which surround us with confusion and terror. And yet, the other side of the coin is that if this *is* the "Thus saith the Lord," we must live under it. And without that, we don't understand what we have said when we say we stand for an inerrant Scripture.

I would ask again, Does inerrancy really make a difference—in the way we live our lives across the whole spectrum of human existence? Sadly we must say that we evangelicals who truly hold to the full authority of Scripture have not always done well in this respect. I have said that inerrancy is the watershed of the evangelical world. But it is not just a theological debating point. *It is the obeying of the Scripture which is the watershed! It is believing and applying it to our lives* which demonstrate whether we in fact believe it.

Hedonism

We live in a society today where all things are relative and the final value is whatever makes the individual or society "happy" or feel good at the moment. This is not just the hedonistic young person doing what feels good; it is society as a whole. This has many facets, but one is the breakdown of all stability in society. Nothing is fixed, there are no final standards; only what makes one "happy" is dominant. This is even true with regard to human life. The January 11, 1982, issue of *Newsweek* had a cover story of about five or six pages which showed conclusively that human life begins at conception. All students of biology should have known this all along. Then one turns the page, and the next article is entitled "But Is It a Person?" The conclusion of that page is, "The problem is not determining when actual human life begins, but when the value of that life begins to outweigh other considerations, such as the health or even the happiness of the mother." The terrifying phrase is, "or even the happiness." Thus, even acknowledged human life can be and is ended for the sake of someone else's happiness.

With no set values, all that matters is my or society's happiness at the moment. I must say I cannot understand why even the liberal lawyers of the American Civil Liberties Union are not terrified at that point.

And, of course, it is increasingly accepted that if a newborn baby is going to make the family or society unhappy, it too should be allowed to die. All you have to do is look at your television programs and this comes across increasingly like a flood. It is upon such a view that Stalin and Mao allowed (and I'm using a very gentle word when I say "allowed") millions to die for what they considered the happiness of society. This then is the terror that surrounds the church today. The individual's or society's happiness takes supreme preference even over human life.

Now let us realize that we are in as much danger of being infiltrated by the surrounding amoral thought-forms of our culture as we are in danger of being infiltrated by the existential thought-forms. Why? Because we are surrounded by a society with no fixed standards and "no-fault" everything. Each thing is psychologically pushed away or explained away so that there is no right or wrong. And, as with the "happiness" of the mother taking precedence over human life, so anything which interferes with the "happiness" of the individual or society is dispensed with.

Bending the Bible
It is obeying the Scriptures which really is the watershed. We can say the Bible is without mistake and still destroy it if we bend the Scriptures by our lives to fit this culture instead of judging the culture by Scripture. And today we see this happening more and more as in the case of easy divorce and remarriage. The no-fault divorce laws in many of our states are not really based upon humanitarianism or kindness. They are based on the view that there is no right and wrong. And thus all is relative, which means that society and the individual act on what seems to give them happiness for the moment.

Do we not have to agree that even much of the evangelical church, which claims to believe that the Bible is without error, has bent Scripture at the point of divorce to conform to the culture rather than the Scripture judging the present viewpoints of the fallen culture? Do we not have to agree that in the area of divorce and remarriage there has been a lack of biblical teaching and discipline even among evangelicals? When I, contrary to Scripture, claim the right to attack the family—not the family in general, but to attack and break up my own family—is it not the same as a mother claiming the right to kill her own baby for her "happiness"? I find it hard to say, but here is an infiltration of the surrounding society that is as destructive to Scripture as is a theological attack upon Scripture. Both are a tragedy. Both bend the Scripture to conform to the surrounding culture.

The Mark of Our Age
What is the use of evangelicalism seeming to get larger and larger if sufficient numbers of those under the name evangelical no longer hold to that which makes evangelicalism evangelical? If this continues, we are not faithful to what the Bible claims for itself, and we are not faithful to what Jesus Christ claims for the Scriptures. But also—let us not ever forget—if this continues, we and our children will not be ready for difficult days ahead.

Furthermore, if we acquiesce, we will no longer be the redeeming salt for our culture—a culture which is committed to the concept that both morals and laws are only a matter of cultural orientation, of statistical averages. That is the hallmark—the mark of our age. And if we are marked with the same mark, how can we be the redeeming salt to this broken, fragmented generation in which we live?

Here then is the watershed of the evangelical world. We must say most lovingly but clearly: evangelicalism is not consistently evangelical unless there is a line drawn between those who take a full view of Scripture and those who do not. But remember that we are not just talking about an abstract theological doctrine. It makes little difference in the end if Scripture is compromised by theological infiltration or by infiltration from the surrounding culture. It is the obeying of Scripture which is the watershed— obeying the Bible equally in doctrine and in the way we live in the full spectrum of life.

Confrontation
But if we truly believe this, then something must be considered. *Truth carries with it confrontation.* Truth *demands* confrontation; loving confrontation, but confrontation nevertheless. If our reflex

action is always accommodation regardless of the centrality of the truth involved, there is something wrong. Just as what we may call holiness without love is not God's kind of holiness, so also what we may call love without holiness, including when necessary confrontation, is not God's kind of love. God is holy, and God is love.

We must, with prayer, say no to the theological attack upon Scripture. We must say no to this, clearly and lovingly, with strength. And we must say no to the attack upon Scripture which comes from our being infiltrated in our lives by the current world view of no-fault in moral issues. We must say no to these things equally.

The world of our day has no fixed values and standards, and therefore what people conceive as their personal or society's happiness covers everything. We are not in that position. We have the inerrant Scripture. Looking to Christ for strength against tremendous pressure because our whole culture is against us at this point, we must reject the infiltration in theology and in life equally. We both must affirm the inerrancy of Scripture and then live under it in our personal lives and in society.

God's Word will never pass away, but looking back to the Old Testament and since the time of Christ, with tears we must say that because of lack of fortitude and faithfulness on the part of God's people, God's Word has many times been allowed to be bent, to conform to the surrounding, passing, changing culture of that moment rather than to stand as the inerrant Word of God judging the form of the world spirit and the surrounding culture of that moment. In the name of the Lord Jesus Christ, may our children and grandchildren not say that such can be said about us.

CHAPTER THREE

The Practice of Truth

When the Scriptures are being destroyed by theological infiltration and compromise, and equally by cultural infiltration and compromise, will we have the courage as Bible-believing Christians to mark the watershed? Will we have the courage to draw a line, and to do it publicly, between those who take a full view of Scripture and those who have been infiltrated theologically and culturally? If we do not have the courage, we will cut the ground out from under the feet of our children, and we will destroy any hope of being the redeeming salt and light of our dying culture.

We cannot wait for others to draw the line. *We* must draw the line. It will not be easy, and for many it may be costly. It certainly will not be popular. But if we truly believe in the infinite-personal God—the God of holiness and love—if we truly love the Lord and his Word and his church, we have no other choice.

A New "Fundamentalist Legalism"
When Dr. C. Everett Koop, my son Franky, and I were in the midst of seminars for the film *Whatever Happened to the Human Race?* an interesting thing happened. One of us received a letter from a prominent evangelical leader. He holds a good view the-

ologically concerning Scripture, and I would also say that I like him. In his letter, however, he said, "I see the emergence of a new sort of fundamentalist legalism." He went on to explain what he meant like this: "That was the case in the thrust concerning false evangelicals in the inerrancy issue, and is also the case on the part of some who are now saying that the evangelical cause is betrayed by any who allow any exceptions of any sort in government funding to abortion." This needs some clarification. Basically he is saying that those who believe that we must hold to the inerrancy of Scripture in order to be truly evangelical, and those who also take a strong stand against abortion, are expressing a "new sort of fundamentalist legalism."

In one sense this evangelical leader is quite right. A high view of Scripture and a high view of life go hand-in-hand. You cannot be faithful to what the Bible teaches about the value of human life and be in favor of abortion. But the opposite is also true. Theological infiltration in the form of a low view of Scripture and cultural infiltration in the form of the devaluation of human life likewise go hand-in-hand. He correctly linked the two issues together.

But the term "fundamentalist legalism" presents a problem. Is this what we mean when we speak of drawing the line? Is that what we mean by being faithful to the love and holiness of God?

If what is involved is the heartless, loveless, "fundamentalist legalism" some of us have known so well in the past, of course we do not want it, and we reject it in the name of Christ. The love of God and the holiness of God must always be evident simultaneously. And if anyone has wandered off and returns, the attitude should not be one of pride that we have been right, but rather joy and the playing of songs, happy music, joyous music, singing of joyous songs, and I would add, even dancing in the streets because, and if, there has been a true return.

Again, if the term "fundamentalist legalism" means the downplaying of the humanities, as unhappily has so often been the case, the failure to know that the intellect is important, that human creativity by Christians and non-Christians is worth study; if it means the down-playing of the scholarly; if it means the downplaying of the Lordship of Christ in all of life—then my work of some forty years and all my books and films speak of my total rejection of this.

Again, if the term "fundamentalist legalism" means a confusion of primary and secondary points of doctrine and life, that too should be rejected.

Love and Holiness

But when we have said all of this, when we come to the central things of doctrine and to the central things of life itself, then something must be profoundly considered. As I mentioned at the close of the last chapter, truth carries with it confrontation—loving confrontation, but confrontation nonetheless. And if our reflex action is always accommodation regardless of the centrality of the truth involved, then something is profoundly wrong. If we use the word *love* as our excuse for avoiding confrontation when it is necessary, then we have denied the holiness of God and failed to be faithful to him and his true character. In reality we have denied God himself.

It is hard to imagine how far things have gone in just a few years. Something is profoundly wrong when a Bible teacher at a prominent evangelical college teaches that one of the Gospel writers made up some of the stories about the birth of Jesus, and that some of the things which Jesus said as recorded in the Gospels really were not said by Jesus at all, but were made up by other people later. Something is profoundly wrong when many evangelical college and seminary professors now use higher-critical methods to study the Scripture, when it was these same methods which began eighty to one hundred years ago to destroy the Scriptures for the liberal church in the United States. Something is profoundly wrong when the chairman of the philosophy and ethics department at a prominent Christian college holds a proabortion position. Something is profoundly wrong when a leading evangelical changes his position on the full authority of Scripture, endorses the neo-orthodox existential method, and ridicules those who uphold the full authority of Scripture by calling them "Fundamentalist obscurantists."[1]

How must we respond to this—when it is really the gospel itself that is at stake? And more than this, when the future of our culture and the lives of millions are being destroyed?

To be really Bible-believing Christians we need to practice, *simultaneously*, at each step of the way, two biblical principles. One principle is that of the purity of the visible church. Scripture commands that we must do more than just talk about the purity of the visible church; we must actually practice it, even when it is costly.

The second principle is that of an observable love among all true Christians. In the flesh we can stress purity without love, or we can stress love without purity; we cannot stress both simultaneously. To do so we must look moment by moment to the work of Christ and of the Holy Spirit. Without that, a stress on purity becomes hard, proud, and legalistic; likewise, without it a stress on love becomes sheer compromise. Spirituality begins to have real meaning in our lives as we begin to exhibit simultaneously the holiness of God and the love of God. We never do this perfectly, but we must look to the living Christ to help us do it truly. Without this simultaneous exhibition our marvelous God and Lord is not set forth. It is rather a caricature of him that is shown, and he is dishonored.

What Was at Stake?
This is the basis for how we need to respond today. But if we really want to know how these principles apply in the present religious situation, we need to understand what happened in the early decades of this century. We touched on this briefly in Chapter 1, but now we need to look at this much more carefully. During this time a whole course of events took place which left their mark on the church right up to our present day, and they surely will for generations to come. This was the time when the denominations in the United States were in the midst of what often is called the modernist/fundamentalist conflict. But I hesitate to even use this term because most people have a very mistaken understanding of this, especially with the total and deliberate distortion of the word *fundamentalist*.

At the end of the nineteenth and the beginning of the twentieth century, the ideas of liberal German theology came sweeping into this country. These ideas grew out of the German and Western European philosophy current at the time, which basically was an attempt to synthesize the idea of the Enlightenment with theology and thereby to arrive at a "modern" approach to religion in contrast to the "unscientific superstitions" of the past. But there is a problem here: the primary themes of the Enlightenment, as we have seen in Chapter 1, are the complete antithesis to Christian truth. The Enlightenment was founded on the opposition to the supernatural and upon belief in the all-sufficiency in human reason. It held to the fundamental goodness of human nature and believed in the perfectibility of human society. By the time these ideas reached the United States in the late 1800s, they had already penetrated deeply into German Protestantism, disintegrating faith in the Bible through the methods of "higher criticism."[2] Later these ideas entered into portions of the Roman Catholic Church as well.

In the early years of this century, this new liberal theology was coming into the United States like a flood. Most of the large Protestant denominations were being knocked down like a row of tenpins, one after the other, being taken over by liberal theology. But what was really at stake? It was the gospel itself. We are not talking about minor variations in the interpretation of secondary doctrines. We are not talking about denominational differences. The things being denied by the liberals were at the heart of the Christian faith—the authority of the Bible, the deity of Christ, the meaning of salvation. Harry Emerson Fosdick, pastor of the First Presbyterian Church of New York and one of the most influential spokesmen of modernism, was a clear example. In his famous sermon, "Shall the Fundamentalists Win?" given in 1922, he explained what the liberal means by the return of Christ. The liberals, Fosdick preached,

> say "Christ is coming!" They say it with all their hearts; but they are *not thinking of an external arrival on the clouds.* They have *assimilated as part of divine revelation* the exhilarating insight which these recent generations have given to us, that *development* [i.e., modern progress] is *God's way of working out His will. . . .* When they say that Christ is coming, they mean that, slowly it may be, but surely, *His will and principles will be worked out . . . in human institutions.*[3]

Here we have what is at stake—the denial of the work of Christ and the actual return of Christ; the "new revelation" of modern thought replacing the Bible; salvation as the modern progress of human institutions. This is heretical denial of the gospel, and is directly related to the Enlightenment view of the perfectibility of Man.

Defending the Faith
In response to the wave of liberalism sweeping the denominations in the first three decades of this century, Bible-believing Christians tried to mount a spiritual defense of Christian truth. Here again the common understanding today is terribly distorted. The defense was led by some of the greatest minds and scholars of the day— men such as Benjamin B. Warfield, James Orr, W. H. Griffith Thomas, and G. Campbell Morgan. A key strategy in the defense was the publication of twelve paperback volumes from 1910 through 1915 called *The Fundamentals* and the later reissue of these in an edited four-volume set at the end of the decade. As one Christian historian pointed out recently, this was published as "a

great 'Testimony to the Truth' and [was] even something of a scholarly *tour de force* . . . [which] assembled a rather formidable array of conservative American and British scholars. . . ."[4] Likewise, there was Dr. J. Gresham Machen, the distinguished professor of New Testament at Princeton Theological Seminary. In 1923 Machen published *Christianity and Liberalism*. In this brilliant defense of Christian truth Machen argued that liberalism was really a new religion and not Christianity at all. Since liberalism did not believe in the fact that Christ died in history to atone for the sins of men and women, and that this was the only basis for salvation, liberalism was really religious faith in man dressed up in Christian language and symbols. Thus, Machen explained, the only honest thing for the liberal to do would be to leave the churches which were founded on biblical truth.[5]

At the heart of the defense was the affirmation of the "essential fundamentals of the faith" by a broad base of Christian laymen and the defense of these by leading Christian scholars. The fundamentals themselves are usually identified in terms of five essential truths: 1) the inspiration and inerrancy of the Bible; 2) the deity of Christ and his virgin birth; 3) the substitutionary atonement of Christ's death; 4) the literal resurrection of Christ from the dead; and 5) the literal return of Christ.

Two Groups

As Bible-believing Christians today we have nothing to be ashamed of concerning the early "fundamentalists' " attempts to defend the truth of the gospel. Indeed, the specific doctrines which were defended as *The Fundamentals* are what have always been affirmed through the ages. And those defending them were Christian scholars of the highest order. But then in the 1930s something began to change. Prior to the 1930s the Bible-believing Christians had stood together as liberalism came in to steal the churches. Then at different speeds the liberals achieved their theft of the various denominations by gaining control of the power centers of the seminaries and the bureaucracies. At this point onward, Bible-believing Christians, instead of standing together, divided into two groups; those who held to the principle of the purity of the visible church, and those who accepted and acted upon the concept of a pluralistic church. There was a line just like that. It is a line that began back there in the 1930s, that has continued, and that marks the religious life of the United States excruciatingly to this day. On one hand there are those who hold to the principle of the purity of the visible church, and on the other hand those who accept the concept of the pluralistic church. Looking back over the years, we can see that there have been problems on both sides.

Looking first at those who affirmed the purity of the visible church and left the liberal denominations, we must admit there was often a hardness, a lack of love. It didn't have to be that way, but it was a mistake that marked the "separatist movement" for years to come. What happened in the Presbyterian Church in the United States (the Northern branch of the Presbyterian Church) was typical of what happened in most of the denominations. There were many who said before the division that they would not allow a liberal takeover. But when the time came, many of these remained in the denomination. It is true to say of those who came out, without judging their motives, that they felt deserted and betrayed. Some of those who stayed in the Northern Presbyterian Church urged that the Constitutional Convention Union—the vehicle for all of their working together previously—should not be dissolved, so as to enable those who stayed in and those who came out to continue to work together. But in exasperation and perhaps some anger, those who left dissolved it at once. All the lines of a practical example of observable love among the brethren were destroyed.

The periodicals of those who left tended to devote more space to attacking people who differed with them on the issue of leaving than to dealing with the liberals. Things were said that are difficult to forget even now. Those who came out refused at times to pray with those who had not come out. Many who left broke off all forms of fellowship with true brothers in Christ who had not left. Christ's command to love one another was destroyed. What was left was frequently a turning inward, a self-righteousness, a hardness. The impression often was left that coming out had made those who departed so right that anything could then be excused. Having learned such bad habits, they later treated each other badly when the resulting new groups had minor differences among themselves.

The Christian's Calling

In the midst of anger, frustration, and even self-righteousness, those who came out forgot what our calling as Christians always must be. Our calling is to exhibit the existence of God and to exhibit his character, individually and collectively. God is holy and God is love, and our calling is simultaneously to show forth holiness and love in every aspect of life—as parent and child, as husband and wife, in business, in our Christian organizations, in the church, in government, in everything—an exhibition of the character of God showing forth his holiness and love simultaneously. If we depend on the flesh rather than the work of the Spirit, it is easy to say we are showing holiness and yet it is only egotistic pride and hardness. Equally, in the flesh rather than the work of the Spirit, it is easy to say we are showing forth love and it is only egotistic compromise, latitudinarianism, and accommodation. Both are equally easy in the flesh. Both are equally egotistic. To show forth both simultaneously, in personal matters or in church and public life, can only be done in any real degree by our consciously bowing, denying our egotistic selves, and letting Christ bring forth his fruit through us—not merely as a "religious" statement, but with some ongoing reality.

Thus whenever it becomes necessary to draw a line in the defense of a central Christian truth it is so easy to be proud, to be hard. It is easy to be self-righteous and to self-righteously think that we are so right on this one point that anything else may be excused—this is very easy, a very easy thing to fall into. These mistakes were indeed made, and we have suffered from this and the cause of Christ has suffered from this through some fifty years. By God's grace, let us consciously look to our Lord for his help not to give Satan the victory by making this tragic error again.

The Real Chasm

A second problem of those who left the Presbyterian Church was a confusion over where to place the chasm that marks off our identity. Is the chasm placed between Bible-believing churches and those that are not? Or is it between those who are part of our own denomination and those who are not? When we go into a town to start a church, do we go there primarily motivated to build a church that is loyal to Presbyterianism and the Reformed faith, or to the Baptistic position on baptism, or to the Lutheran view of the sacraments, etc., etc.? Or do we go to build a church that will preach the gospel that historic, Bible-believing churches of all denominations hold, and then, on this side of that chasm, teach what we believe is true to the Bible with respect to our own denominational distinctives? The answers to these questions make a great deal of difference. There is a difference of motivation, of breadth and outreach. One view is catholic and biblical and gives promise of success—on two levels: first, in church growth and then a healthy outlook among those we reach; second, in providing leadership to the whole church of Christ. The other view is inverted and self-limiting—and sectarian.

As Bible-believing Christians we come from a variety of backgrounds. But in our moment of history we need each other. Let us keep our doctrinal distinctives. Let us talk to each other about them. But let us recognize the proper hierarchy of things. The real chasm is not between Presbyterians and everyone else, or Lutherans and everyone else, or Anglicans and everyone else, or Baptists and everyone else. The real chasm is between those who have bowed to the living God and thus also to the verbal, propositional communication of God's inerrant Word, the Scriptures, and those who have not.

Latitudinarianism

Now for those who did not leave the liberally controlled denominations fifty years ago, there were also two problems. First there was the birth of a general latitudinarianism—a kind of acceptance of theological pluralism which easily slips into compromise and accommodation. If those who came out were inclined to become hard, some of those who stayed in tended to become soft. Some said: This is not the moment to come out, but we will do so if such-and-such occurs. These in principle did not accept the concept of a pluralistic church. Some developed their own kind of hardness—a decision to stay in, no matter what happened.

If one accepts an ecclesiastical latitudinarianism, it is easy to step into a cooperative latitudinarianism that easily encompasses doctrine, including one's view of Scripture. This is what happened historically. Out of the ecclesiastical latitudinarianism of the thirties and the forties has come the letdown with regard to Scripture in certain areas of evangelicalism in the eighties. Large sections of evangelicalism act as though it makes no real difference whether one holds the historic view of Scripture, or whether one holds the existential methodology that says the Bible is authoritative when it teaches religious things but not when it touches on what is historic or scientific, or on such things as the male/female relationship.

Not all who stayed in the liberal-dominated denominations have done this, by any means. I do not believe, however, that those who made the choice to stay in "no matter what happens" can escape a latitudinarian mentality. They will struggle to paper over the difference regarding Scripture so as to keep an external veneer of evangelical unity—when indeed today there is no unity at that crucial point of Scripture. When doctrinal latitudinarianism sets in, we can be sure both from church history and from personal observation that in one or two generations those who are taught by the churches and schools that hold this mentality will lose still more, and the line between evangelical and liberal will be lost.

Moving Back the Line
The second problem for those who did not leave the liberally controlled denominations is the natural tendency to continually move back the line at which the final stand must be taken. For example, could such well-known evangelical Presbyterians in the 1930s as Clarence McCartney, Donald Grey Barnhouse, and T. Roland Phillips have stayed in a denomination where there is no possibility of disciplining those who hold patently heretical views? Take for instance the case of Professor John Hick, the author of *The Myth of God Incarnate*. How can a man who holds that the Incarnation is a myth call himself a Christian? Yet he was recently received into the Presbytery of Claremont, California as a minister in good standing. How could these men have stayed in a denomination which takes a militantly proabortion stand? Or where it is considered a "victory" to have stalled the ordination of practicing homosexuals and lesbians? What do you think McCartney, Barnhouse, and Phillips would have said? Such a situation in their denomination would have been inconceivable to them.

False Victories
Evangelicals must be aware of false victories. The liberal denominational power structure knows how to keep Bible-believing Christians off balance. There are many possible false victories they can throw to evangelicals to prevent them from making a clear stand. There are still those who say, "Don't break up our ranks. Wait a while longer. Wait for this, wait for that." Always wait, never act. But fifty years is a long time to wait while things are getting worse. Because of my failing health, I am in a good position to say that we do not have forever to take that courageous and costly stand for Christ we sometimes talk about.

Even what seems to be a major victory may end up having no practical effect. Again, a clear example of this happened in the Northern Presbyterian Church. In 1924 the conservatives decided the best way to meet the liberal challenge was to elect a moderator of the General Assembly who would clearly be Bible-believing.

As a result, 1924 saw elected as the moderator of the Northern Presbyterian Church an orthodox, Bible-believing man, Dr. Clarence Edward McCartney. The conservatives were jubilant. The secular newspapers carried the story of the conservative victory, and the conservatives rejoiced. But while all the rejoicing was going on, the liberals consolidated their power in the church bureaucracy. And because they were allowed to do so, the election of the conservative moderator proved to mean nothing. By 1936 the liberals were so in control that they were able to defrock Dr. J. Gresham Machen, putting him out of the ministry.

It seems to me that by the end of the 1930s almost all the major Protestant denominations in the United States came under the control of those holding liberal theological views, and that now in the 1980s those denominations not dominated by liberal theology in the 1930s are in the same place of decision as the others were in the 1930s. It should be noted that the Roman Catholic Church now also has many in the hierarchy, many theologians and teachers, called progressives, who are existential theologians who believe and teach the same things as the existential theologians in the Protestant churches do, but using traditional Roman Catholic, rather than Protestant, terms.

Two of the Protestant denominations in the United States now in the place of decision, interestingly enough, have recently tried to protect themselves, as did the Northern Presbyterian Church, by electing a conservative executive officer. But I would urge the true Christian today in these denominations to learn from the mistakes of the Presbyterian Church. Do not think that merely because a Bible-believing man is elected as an executive officer or is appointed to an important position, this will give safety to a denomination. If the two power centers in modern denominations—the bureaucracy and the seminaries—remain in the control of the liberals, nothing will be permanently changed. There must be a loving but definite *practice* of the purity of the visible church in any denomination if it is really to dwell in safety. The holiness of God must be exhibited in ecclesiastical affairs. We must practice truth, not just speak about it.

Flaming Truth
It must be understood that the new humanism and the new theology have no concept of true truth—absolute truth. Relativism has triumphed in the church as well as in the university and in society. The true Christian, however, is called upon not only to

teach truth, but to practice truth in the midst of such relativism. And if we are ever to practice truth, it certainly must be in a day such as ours.

This means, among other things, that after we have done all we can on a personal level, if the liberals in the church persist in their liberalism, they should come under discipline. As I have shown at length in *The Church Before the Watching World,* the church must remain the faithful bride of Christ.[6] And, as I explained there in detail, the liberals are not faithful to the God of the Bible, the God who is there.[7] Historic Christianity, biblical Christianity, believes that Christianity is not just doctrinal truth, but flaming truth—true to what is there, true to the great final environment, the infinite-personal God. Liberalism, on the other hand, is unfaithfulness; *it is spiritual adultery toward the divine Bridegroom.* We are involved, therefore, in a matter of loyalty—loyalty not only to the creeds, but to the Scripture, and beyond that to the divine Bridegroom—the infinite-personal divine Bridegroom who is there in an absolute antithesis to his not being there.

We not only believe in the existence of truth, but we believe we have the truth—a truth that has content and can be verbalized (and *then* can be lived)—a truth we can share with the twentieth-century world. Christ and the Bible have given us this truth. Do you think our contemporaries will take us seriously if we do not practice truth? Do you think for a moment that the really serious-minded twentieth-century young people—our own youth as they go off to universities, who are taught in the fields of sociology, psychology, philosophy, etc., that all is relative—will they take us seriously if we do not *practice* truth in very practical ways? In an age that does not believe that truth exists, do you really believe they will take seriously that their parents are speaking truth and believe in truth? Will their parents have credibility if they do not practice antithesis in religious matters?

It is therefore necessary for the true Christians in the church to oppose McLuhanesque "cool" communication employed by the liberal theologians with the "hot" communication of theological and biblical content. It is only thus that we can practice the exhibition of the holiness of God.

We believe in the hot communication of content, and as our age cools off more and more in its communication, as content is played down and reason is plowed under, I believe the historic Christian faith must more and more consciously emphasize content, content, and then more content. In this we are brought face-to-face in a complete antithesis with the existential theologian. If we are to talk truth at all, we must have content on the basis of antithesis; and to do this, we must have discipline with regard to those who depart from the historic Christian faith. It is thus that we can practice the exhibition of the holiness of God.

At the same time, however, we must show forth the love of God to those with whom we differ. Fifty years ago in the Presbyterian crisis in the United States, we forgot that. We did not speak with love about those with whom we differed, and we have been paying a price for it ever since. We must love men, including the existential theologians, even if they have given up content entirely. We must deal with them as our neighbors, for Christ gave us the second commandment telling us that we are to love all men as our neighbors.

We must stand clearly for the principle of the purity of the visible church, and we must call for the appropriate discipline of those who take a position which is not according to Scripture. But at the same time we must visibly love them as people as we speak and write about them. We must show it before both the church and the world. We must say that the liberals are desperately wrong and that they require discipline in and by the church, but we must do so in terms that show it is not merely the flesh speaking. This is beyond us, but not beyond the work of the Holy Spirit. I regret that years ago we did not do this in the Presbyterian Church; we did not talk of the need to show love as we stood against liberalism. And as the Presbyterian Church was lost, that lack has cost us dearly.

The Tragedy of Bishop Pike

But with prayer, both love and concern for truth can be shown. Several years ago at the Roosevelt University auditorium in Chicago, I had a dialogue with Bishop James Pike. (Bishop Pike was a leading liberal in the Episcopal Church.) Some years before our dialogue, he had been brought to trial in the Episcopal Church on heresy charges. However, the charges were eventually dropped— not because his views were in fact orthodox, but because the Episcopal denomination had accepted theological pluralism and relativism and therefore had no real basis upon which to practice discipline.

Before the dialogue, I asked those in L'Abri to pray for one thing—that I would be able to present a clear Christian position to him and to the audience, and at the same time end with a good human relationship between the two of us. It was something I could not do in myself, but God answered that prayer. A clear statement was raised, with a clear statement of differences, without destroying him as a human being. At the close he said, "If you ever come to California, please visit me in Santa Barbara." Later, when Edith and I were out in Santa Barbara, we went to his place and were able to carry on further a discussion with him without one iota of compromise, and yet again not destroying him, but letting him know that we respected him as a human being.

We also talked about the possibility that his belief that he was talking to his son "on the other side" was really a matter of demonology. This was some time after Bishop Pike's son had committed suicide, and he had tried to communicate with his son through a medium. And he did not get angry, though he was close to crying. It is possible to make clear statements, even the necessary negative ones, if simultaneously we treat people as people.

I will never forget the last time I saw him as Edith and I were leaving the Center for the Study of Democratic Institutions. He said one of the saddest things I have ever heard: "When I turned from being agnostic, I went to Union Theological Seminary, eager for and expecting bread; but when I graduated, all that it left me was a handful of pebbles."

Who is responsible for the tragedy of Bishop James Pike? His liberal theological professors who robbed him of everything real and human. We cannot take lightly the fact that liberal theological professors in any theological school are leaving young men and women with a handful of pebbles and nothing more.

Yet, even in the midst of this situation, by God's grace we must do two things simultaneously. We must do all that is necessary for the purity of the visible church to exhibit the holiness of God; and yet, no matter how bitter the liberals become or what nasty things they say or what they release to the press, we must show forth the love of God in the midst of the strongest speaking we can do. If we let down one side or the other, we will not bear our testimony to God who is holy and who is love.

Discipline
Let us again go back to the Presbyterian struggles of the thirties when true Christians did not remember to keep this balance. On the one hand, they waited far too long to exert discipline, and so they lost the denomination, as did the Christians in almost every

other denomination. On the other hand, some of them treated the liberals as less than human, and therefore they learned such bad habits that later, when those who formed new groups developed minor differences among themselves, they continued to treat each other badly. Beware of the habits we learn in controversy. Both must appear together: the holiness of God and the love of God exhibited simultaneously by the grace of God. It will not come automatically. It takes prayer. We must write about it in our denominational papers. We must talk about it to our congregations; we must preach sermons pointing out the necessity of standing for the holiness of God and the love of God *simultaneously,* and by our attitudes we must *exhibit* it to our congregations and to our own children.

It is important to notice the principle we are speaking about here and the language we use to express that principle. It is not the principle of *separation.* It is the *practice of the principle of the purity of the visible church.* Words are important at this point, because we make attitudes with the words we choose and use year after year. So I repeat: the principle is the practice of the purity of the visible church. That principle may have to be exhibited in various ways, but that is the principle. The church belongs to those who by the grace of God are faithful to the Scriptures. Almost every church has in its history a process for exercising discipline, and when needed this should be used in the practice of the positive principle.

Between the 1890s and the 1930s we can see how the practice of discipline was turned on its head. In the early 1890s, disciplinary action was taken against Dr. Charles A. Briggs. Dr. Briggs was a vigorous advocate of higher criticism and a leader in the introduction of liberalism to Union Theological Seminary in New York. In 1881 he was tried for heresy and was eventually suspended from the ministry in 1883 by the General Assembly of the Northern Presbyterian Church. But by the 1930s the older type of liberals had taken over the denomination, and the situation was completely reversed. In 1936 the *liberals* were able to put Dr. Machen out of the denomination for his firm and practical stand for orthodoxy in belief and practice.

Dr. Machen was disciplined and put out of the ministry. What had happened in the intervening years? Discipline had not been consistently applied by the faithful men of the church. The church was able to discipline Dr. Briggs in the 1880s, but after that faithful men waited too long. Though they had achieved one outstanding victory, after that first burst of discipline they did nothing, until it was far too late. Discipline in the church and in our Christian organizations—as in the family—is not something that can be done in one great burst of enthusiasm, one great conference, one great anything. Men must be treated in love as human beings, but it is a case of continual, moment-by-moment care, for we are not dealing with a merely human organization but with the church of Christ. Hence, the practice of the purity of the visible church first means discipline of those who do not take a proper position in regard to the teaching of Scripture.

Why is it so unthinkable today to have discipline? Why is it that at least two denominations in the United States are now so much in the hands of liberals that it is officially and formally no longer possible to have a discipline trial, ever—even in theory? It is because both the world and the liberal church are totally caught up in the grasp of synthesis and relativism. It was not unthinkable to our forefathers to conduct discipline hearings, because they believed that truth existed. But because the world and the liberal church no longer believe in truth as truth, any concept of discipline in regard to doctrine has become unthinkable.

A Second Step

Let us now shift our focus. What does the future hold? What can we expect for ourselves, our congregations, our physical and spiritual children in the days ahead? America is moving at great speed toward a totally humanistic society and state. Do we suppose this trend will leave our own little projects, lives, and churches untouched? When a San Francisco Orthodox Presbyterian congregation can be dragged into court for breaking the law against discrimination because it dismissed an avowed, practicing homosexual as an organist, can we be so deaf as not to hear all the warning bells?

In what presbytery in the Presbyterian Church U.S.A. can you bring an ordained man under biblical discipline for holding false views of doctrine and expect him to be disciplined? The same is true in many other denominations. We should first of all, of course, do all we can on a personal, loving level to help the liberal; but if he persists in his liberalism he should be brought under discipline, because the visible church should remain the faithful bride of Christ.

The church is not the world. When a denomination comes to a place where such discipline cannot operate, then before the Lord her members must consider a second step: that step, with regard to the practice of the principle of the purity of the visible church, is with tears to step out. Not with flags flying, not with shouts of hurrah or thoughts that in this fallen world we can build a perfect church, but that step is taken with tears.

Evangelicals who come to this point must still keep on loving the liberals, and must do so because it is right. If we do not know how to take a firm stand against organized liberalism and still love the liberals, we have failed in half of the call to exhibit simultaneously the love and the holiness of God—before a watching world, before a watching church, before our children, before the watching angels, and before the face of the Lord himself.

Learning from the Past

As we face the watershed issue concerning the full authority and inerrancy of the Scriptures, what can we learn from the past? First, we must recognize that there is a direct parallel between what happened in the early decades of this century and what we are facing today. Will we repeat the mistakes we made in the past, or will we learn from these and remain faithful to God by simultaneously expressing his love and holiness?

Within the evangelical circles things are moving rapidly in the direction of what happened fifty years ago in the denominations. But there still is time to head off a complete takeover of the leadership and key organizations within evangelicalism by those who hold a weakened view of Scripture and have been infiltrated theologically and culturally by the surrounding world view—if we have the courage to clearly but lovingly draw a line. Sadly though, we must say that things *are* moving rapidly and in precisely the same way that the denominations went some fifty years ago. There is the growing acceptance of higher critical methods in our colleges and seminaries. There is a growing acceptance of the neo-orthodox existential methodology. There is a growing infiltration of humanistic ideas into both *theology and practice.* There is a growing acceptance of pluralism and accommodation. And what has been the response of the evangelical leadership? Overwhelmingly it has been to keep silent, to let the slide go further and further, to paper over the differences. Here again we see the great evangelical disaster—the failure of the evangelical leadership to take a stand really on anything that would stand decisively over against the relativistic moral slide of our culture—the failure to take a stand on anything that would "rock the boat" concerning our personal projects and acceptance. And now when our culture is all but lost, can we expect anything but further disaster in the form of a complete moral breakdown and the rise of a new humanistic authoritarianism if we do not take a stand?

Practical Steps
On a very practical level, in our evangelical organizations and institutions, as well as our churches and denominations, we will need to take some very specific steps. Where there is a departure from the historic view of Scripture and from obedience to God's Word, then those who take this weakened view need to be brought under discipline. It must be done according to all that has been said so far in this chapter—with genuine love, without self-righteousness, and everything else that I have said. But a clear line must be drawn—by those who sit on the boards of evangelical organizations and colleges and seminaries; when we recommend schools for students to attend or avoid; when we are asked to work together for the sake of the gospel with others who hold a weakened view of the Bible; when we decide who and what we will publish in our magazines and publishing houses. In organizations such as these, and especially in the colleges and seminaries, the issues are crucial. For it was the failure of evangelicals fifty years ago to practice discipline and maintain control of the denominational centers of influence—in colleges and seminaries, in publishing, and in the organizational structures—which allowed the liberals to take control.

And if the moment should come for you when loyalty to Christ brings you to the place of bringing discipline to bear, or even to leaving your local church or denomination or Christian organization, I plead with you to find some way to show observable love among *true* Christians before the world. The practice of truth requires that a line be drawn between those who hold the historic view of Scripture and the new weaker one. But this is not to say that those who hold this view are not often brothers and sisters in Christ, nor that we should not have loving personal relationships with them. Don't just divide into ugly parties. If you do, the world will see an ugliness which will turn it off. Your children will see the ugliness, and you will lose some of your sons and daughters. They will hear such harsh things from your lips against men who they know have been your friends that they will turn away from you. Don't throw your children away; don't throw other people away by forgetting to observe, by God's grace, the two principles simultaneously—to show love and holiness.

When the World Is on Fire

Finally, we must not forget that the world is on fire. We are not only losing the church, but our entire culture as well. We live in the post-Christian world which is under the judgment of God. I believe today that we must speak as Jeremiah did. Some people think that just because the United States of America is the United States of America, because Britain is Britain, they will not come under the judgment of God. This is not so. I believe that we of Northern Europe since the Reformation have had such light as few others have ever possessed. We have stamped upon that light in our culture. Our cinemas, our novels, our art museums, our schools scream out as they stamp upon that light. And worst of all, modern theology screams out as it stamps upon that light. Do you think God will not judge our countries simply because they are our countries? Do you think that the holy God will not judge?

And if this is true in our moment of history, we need each other. Let us keep our denominational distinctives. And let us talk to each other about our distinctives as we keep them.

But in a day like ours, let us recognize a proper hierarchy of things. Our distinctives are not to be the chasm. We hold our distinctives because we are convinced that they are biblical. But God's call is to love and be one with all those who are in Christ Jesus, and then to let God's truth speak into the whole spectrum of life and the whole spectrum of society. That is our calling. The limiting circle is not to be the distinctives of our own particular denomination. We hold these things because we believe indeed they are taught in Scripture. But beyond that there is the responsibility, there is the call, to be something to the whole church of the Lord Jesus Christ, and beyond the church of the Lord Jesus Christ to the whole society and to the whole culture. If we don't understand this, we understand neither how rich Christianity is and God's truth is, nor do we understand how wide is the call placed upon the Christian into the totality of life. Jesus cannot be said to be Savior unless we also say he is Lord. And we cannot honestly and rightly say he is our Lord if he is only a Lord of part of life and not of the totality of life, including all the social and political and cultural life.

In a day like ours, when the world is on fire, let us be careful to keep things in proper order. We must have the courage to draw the line between those who have compromised the full authority of the Scriptures, either by *theological infiltration* or *cultural infiltration,* and those who have not. But we must at the same time practice an observable oneness among all who have bowed to the living God and thus to the verbal propositional communication of God's Word, the Scriptures. Learning from the mistakes of the past, let us raise a testimony that may still turn both the churches and society around—for the salvation of souls, the building of God's people, and at least the slowing down of the slide toward a totally humanistic society and an authoritarian suppressive state.

PART III

Names and Issues

CHAPTER FOUR

Connotations and Compromise

Names are funny things, and especially in the connotations they are given. Names can be used either to enhance or to destroy.

As we have seen in the preceding chapter, the name "fundamentalism" first came into use in the mid-1920s. During this time and before, liberalism was sweeping through the major denominations and the liberals were taking over the positions of leadership and control in the seminaries, in many Christian publications, and in the denominational structures.

Fundamental Truths
In response, the Bible-believing Christians, under the leadership of such scholars as J. Gresham Machen and Robert Dick Wilson, issued what they called *The Fundamentals of the Faith*. Dr. Machen and the other men never thought of making this an "ism." They considered these things to be a true expression of the historic Christian faith and doctrine. They were the *fundamental truths of the Christian faith*—doctrine which was true to the Bible; *truth* which they were interested in and committed to. And as we have seen in the preceding chapter, this truth was presented and published in a series of books written by the outstanding Christian

thinkers of–the day. Dr. Machen, whom I knew as a student, simply called himself a "Bible-believing Christian." The same thing was true of the many publications which were also committed in that day to doctrine and teaching which is true to the Bible.

Soon, however, the word *fundamentalist* came into use. As used at first, it had nothing problematic in its use either in definition or in connotation. I personally, however, preferred Machen's term "Bible-believing Christian" because that was what the discussion was all about.

As time passed, however, the term *fundamentalist* took on a connotation for many people which had no necessary relationship to its original meaning. It came to connote a form of pietism which shut Christian interest up to only a very limited view of spirituality. In this new connotation, many things having to do with the arts, culture, education, and social involvement were considered to be "unspiritual" and not a proper area of concern for the Christian. Spirituality had to do with a very narrow sphere of the Christian's life, and all other things were considered to be suspect. Fundamentalism also, at times, became overly harsh and lacking in love, while properly saying that the liberal doctrine that was false to the Bible had to be met with confrontation.

The Full Spectrum of Life
Therefore, at a certain point in this country a new name was entered—*evangelical*. This was picked up largely from the British scene. In Britain during the twenties and thirties, *evangelical* largely meant what Machen and the others had stood for in this country—namely, Bible-believing Christianity as opposed to the inroads of various forms and degrees of liberal theology. By the mid-1940s the name *evangelical* had come into common use in the United States. It was especially used here with the connotation of being Bible-believing without shutting one's self off from the full spectrum of life, and in trying to bring Christianity into effective contact with the current needs of society, government, and culture. It had a connotation of leading people to Christ as Savior, but then trying to be salt and light in the culture.

It was in this general period that my lectures and books began to be of some influence—from the 1950s onward. My lectures and early books stressed the Lordship of Christ over all of life in the areas of culture, art, philosophy, and so on while also strongly stressing the need to be Bible-believing with loving but true confrontation against not only false theology, but also against the destructive results of the false world view about us.

While not overemphasizing their importance, for many of that period and especially in the radical sixties, these books did help open a new door. Many discovered a Christianity which is viable in this age of collapsing values when the older cultural norms are being turned on their heads by the ethos dominating our age. And many came to understand that this new ethos—namely, the concept that the final reality is energy which has existed forever in some form and takes its present form by chance—has totally destructive consequences for life. The young people of the sixties sensed that this position left all standards in a relativistic flux and life as meaningless, and they began to think and live in these terms. In this setting, happily a certain number did find that L'Abri's presentation of Christianity—as touching all of thought and life, along with a life of prayer—did demonstrate Christianity's viability, and they became Bible-believing, consecrated Christians.

But note: this rested upon two things: 1) being truly Bible-believing; and 2) facing the results of the surrounding wrong world view that was current with loving but definite confrontation. By the grace of God this emphasis had some influence in many countries and in many disciplines.

Now, however, we find this matter of names with their connotations entering again. Gradually, though there was no need for it from the original use of the word, an appreciable section of those known as evangelical began a drift toward *accommodation*. Note, there was no need for this from the original use of the word, nor largely from the stance of the men and women who originally had begun to use the word. Those who originally called themselves evangelicals were both Bible-believing and did not take a compromising position in relation to the world.

The "Blue Jean" Mentality

It is important to see what the effect of this has been. This drift toward accommodation is a kind of mirror situation of what occurred previously with fundamentalism. After the denominational turmoil of the thirties, fundamentalism fell increasingly into a mistaken pietism which saw any challenge to the surrounding culture as unspiritual—that the Christian's job was only to lead people to Christ and then to know something of a personalized Christianity. Thus, the changing, destructive surrounding culture tended to stand increasingly unchallenged. In the case of an accommodating evangelicalism, there has been a tendency to talk about a wider, richer Christianity and to become more deeply involved in culture, but at the same time to accommodate to the world spirit about us at each crucial point. Note that the result is then the same. Despite claims of cultural relevance, an accommodating evangelicalism also leaves the destructive surrounding culture increasingly unchallenged. Thus the two positions end up with similar results.

This rather reminds me of young people whom we worked with at Berkeley and other universities, including certain Christian colleges, and those who came to us in large numbers with packs on their backs to L'Abri in the 1960s. They were rebels. They knew they were, for they wore the rebel's mark—the worn-out blue jeans. But they did not seem to notice that the blue jeans had become the mark of accommodation—that indeed, everyone was in blue jeans. This does seem to me to be a close parallel to what we see in much of the connotation which grew out of the new uses of the word *evangelical*. What they are saying is this: "We are the 'new evangelicals,' the 'open evangelicals'; we have thrown off the cultural isolation and anti-intellectualism of the old fundamentalists." But what they have not noticed is that they have nothing to say which stands in clear confrontation and antithesis to the surrounding culture. It is so easy to be a radical in the wearing of blue jeans when it fits in with the general climate of wearing blue jeans.

This is really nothing new. Christianity has been plagued by accommodation time and again through the centuries, and in particular in this century. It is interesting to note what Dr. Harold J. Ockenga wrote about the liberalism at the turn of this century:

> Destructive higher criticism of the Bible became the dominant approach among the theologians at the close of the nineteenth century and during the early twentieth century. When joined with naturalistic evolution, it produced liberalism. . . . It [liberalism] *accommodated Christianity to modern scientific naturalism* . . . whenever objections arose on the details of the Christian religion.[1]

It is interesting to note further that even some liberals have begun to recognize the devastating effect of theological accommodation and are beginning to grow weary of it and are wondering what to do. One such liberal recently wrote:

The central theme of contemporary theology is *accommodation to modernity*. It is the underlying motif that unites the seemingly vast differences between existential theology, process theology, liberation theology, demythologization, and many varieties of liberal theology—all are searching for some more compatible adjustment to modernity.

The spirit of accommodation has . . . [led to] the steady deterioration of a hundred years and the disaster of the last two decades. . . .[2]

Yet accommodation has become fashionable among many evangelicals—in spite of the devastating effect this has had theologically and culturally.

Holiness and Love

Complicating the matter is our own tendency to lack a proper balance. As we confront the issues, there must be a proper balance under the leadership of the Holy Spirit while carefully living within the circle of that which is taught in Scripture. Each issue must be met with holiness and love simultaneously. To be really Bible-believing and true to our living Christ, each issue demands a balance which says "no" to two opposite errors: we can neither compromise love in the name of holiness; nor can we compromise holiness in the name of love. Or to say it another way: the devil never gives us the luxury of fighting the battle on just one front.

In every generation God calls his people to show forth his love and holiness, to be faithful to him, and to stand against accommodation with the world's values of the day. In order to show forth God's love and holiness and to present the Good News to our generation in such a way that the message has viability, we must try in a balanced way not to fall into the "blue-jean" mistake of thinking that we are courageous and "being with it" when we are really only fitting into what is the accepted thought-form of the age around us.

We must admit we have not done well here. And I do not think that the evangelical leaders in positions of influence—in schools, in publishing, in other spheres of influence—have been helpful in these things. All too often, it seems to me that "being with it" simply has meant dealing with the current popular topics, but really not being in balanced but clear confrontation with them. This, of course, is in line with the spirit of relativism that dominates in our age. Since the prevailing world view teaches that the final reality is a silent universe which can give no value judgments, truth as final truth therefore does not exist. Thus, there can be various differences of personal opinions, but not the confrontation of truth versus error, as not only the Christians but also the classical philosophers and thinkers of the past believed to be the case. We are left with no basis for saying something is right or wrong. Thus when confronting the crucial issues of the day, the prevailing world view teaches that there is neither right nor wrong, only personal opinion. Relativism rules, and we are surrounded by a spirit of accommodation.

"Don't Rock the Boat"

The matter of human life is a good case in point. "I am personally against abortion, but. . . ." with any number of qualifications added—this became the mediating phrase not only of Christians in government, but also of many in the pulpit and in publications as well. The end result is the same as moral relativism; the issue of abortion is reduced to a personal opinion which has no relationship to the way one lives one's life in the world. In the mid-1970s when Dr. C. Everett Koop, Franky Schaeffer, and I began to work on the project *Whatever Happened to the Human Race?* there were in fact so few Protestants involved that the battle was being lost simply by its being called a Roman Catholic issue. Why were there so few Protestants involved? The mistaken pietists thought battles in the area of government were "unspiritual"; the other stream had acquired the habit of accommodation and it would have meant "rocking the boat" badly to take a clear stand. Happily more are committed now, but still the damage has been done. If voices had been clearly raised in confrontation when abortion and the general lowering of the view of human life began to be openly advocated, the original flood of these concepts in all probability could not have prevailed and the *Roe* v. *Wade* ruling by the Supreme Court might never have been made. And if the heat had been kept on by Christian leaders and publications, the Christians who are in Congress would not have found it so convenient to say they were personally against abortion, but then, for example, vote against limitations on government funding of abortions.

It is ironic that so many who were opposed to Christianity's being shut up to a removed and isolated spirituality by a poor pietism now have by a process of accommodation ended up just as silently on all those issues which go against the current commonly accepted thought-forms. It is so easy to be radical in wearing blue jeans when it fits into a general wearing of blue jeans.

Truth really does bring forth confrontation—loving confrontation, but confrontation—whether it is in regard to those who take a lower view of the Scriptures than both the original users of the terms 'fundamentalist" and "evangelical" took, or in regard to holding a lower view of human life. This lowering of the view of human life may begin with talking about extreme cases in regard to abortion, but it flows on to infanticide and on to all of human life being open to arbitrary, pragmatic judgments of what human life is worthy to be lived—including your human life when you become a burden to society.

In the preceding chapter I quoted from a letter from a Christian leader which tied the issue of Scripture and abortion. I would stress again what I said there—that on the basis of what the word *evangelical* originally meant in regard to Scripture, we must be willing in love to draw a line in regard to those who take a lowered view of Scripture. On the basis of the original term *evangelical,* they are false evangelicals. Not to do so is accommodation to the world's spirit about us at a crucial point which will eventually carry everything else down with it.

But the same principle applies equally in the crucial issues of human life. A lowered view of life and a lowered view of Scripture go hand-in-hand. The watershed issue is *obedience to the Bible* just as much as it is belief in the doctrine of inerrancy. Since the Bible teaches that life in the womb is human life, one cannot accept abortion without denying the authority and truth of Scripture in practice. In drawing or not drawing a line on the issue of Scripture, and indeed in regard to human life, the evangelical establishment has also produced little or no leadership. Most of the time they seem to understand nothing in regard to the real issue involved. Either from a false practice of pietism or a fear of rocking their own boat, they have not been evident in the fray at this crucial point of the question of human life. Or if at all, they have come very late into the battle.

The Real Issue
It is curious how the world often seems to understand these issues better than most Christians and Christian leaders. For example, a recent essay in *Time* magazine entitled "Thinking Animal Thoughts" spells out the real issue. In discussing "animal rights,"

Time tries to discover whether or not there is really any difference between animal life and human life:

> If human beings assume that they were created in the image of God, it is not difficult for them to see the vast and qualitative distance between themselves and the lesser orders of creation. The Bible teaches that man has dominion over the fish of the sea, the fowl of the air, the cattle and every creeping thing. Perhaps the rise of the animal rights movement is a symptom of a more secular and self-doubting spirit. . . .
>
> The human difference is known, to some, as the immortal soul, an absolute distinction belonging to man and woman alone, not to the animal. The soul is the human pedigree—and presumably the dispensation to slay and eat any inferior life that crosses the path. *But in a secular sense how is human life different from animal life?* Intelligence? Some pygmy chimps and even lesser creatures are as intelligent as, say, a severely retarded child; if it is not permissible to kill a retarded child, why kill the animals?[3]

Thus *Time* points out that when we take away the biblical teaching that God is the final reality and that God created man uniquely in his own image, then man as man has no intrinsic value. In a secular sense, human life is no different from animal life. Or in other words, when one accepts the secular world view that the final reality is only material or energy shaped by chance, then human life is lowered to the level of animal existence. There are only two classifications—nonlife and life. And if one thinks of human life as basically no different from animal life, why not treat people the same way? It would only be religious nostalgia to do otherwise. And so it first becomes easy to kill children in the womb, and then if one does not like the way they turn out, to kill children after they are born. And then it goes on to the euthanasia of anyone who becomes a burden or inconvenience. After all, according to the secular world view, human life is not intrinsically different from animal life—so why should it be treated differently?

One would have wished the Christian press and Christian leaders would have had the same comprehension as *Time* and seen these implications. But on the few occasions when secularism and secular humanism have been dealt with, has the Christian press exposed the real implications of this world view? One Christian magazine came out with the conclusion that the concern over secular humanism and its resulting impact on society was only a bogeyman.[4] Rightly defined, secular humanism—or humanism, or secularism, or whatever name you may wish to use—is no bogeyman; it is a vicious enemy. Here again balance is important by means of careful definition. The word *humanism* is not to be confused with humanitarianism, nor with the word humanities.[5] But humanism is the defiant denial of the God who is there, with Man defiantly set up in the place of God as the measure of all things. For if the final reality is only material or energy which has existed forever and has its present form only by chance, then there is no one but finite man to set purely relative values and a purely relativistic base for law and government. This is no bogeyman! It stands totally against all that the original fundamentalists stood for, and totally against what the original meaning of evangelical stood for, and totally against all that the Bible stands for. How could any Christian be so foolish as not to see that this "bogeyman" *guarantees destruction to the individual in the life to come, and in the present life as well?*

Religious Mumbo Jumbo

Do you realize what the implications of this are? Do you really understand that the biblical view of man and the secularist view are a total antithesis—and as such, they result in a totally conflicting view of human life, with totally different consequences? The secular world understands this, as can be seen clearly in the comments of Dr. Peter Singer. Writing in the prestigious medical journal *Pediatrics,* Dr. Singer explains:

> The ethical outlook that holds human life to be sacrosanct—I shall call it the "sanctity-of-life view"—is under attack. The first major blow to the sanctity-of-life view was the spreading acceptance of abortion throughout the Western world. Supporters of the sanctity-of-life view have pointed out that some premature babies are less developed than some of the fetuses that are killed in late abortions. They add, very plausibly, that the location of the fetus/infant—inside or outside the womb—cannot make a crucial difference to its moral status. Allowing abortions, especially these late abortions, therefore does seem to breach our defense of the allegedly universal sanctity of innocent human life.
>
> A second blow to the sanctity-of-life view has been the revelation that it is standard practice in many major public hospitals to refrain from providing necessary life-saving treatment to certain patients. . . .
>
> Is the erosion of the sanctity-of-life view really so alarming? Change is often, in itself, alarming, especially change in something that for centuries has been spoken of in such hushed tones that to question it is automatically to commit sacrilege. . . .
>
> Whatever the future holds, it is likely to prove impossible to restore

in full the sanctity-of-life view. The philosophical foundations of this view have been knocked asunder. We can no longer base our ethics on the idea that human beings are a special form of creation, made in the image of God, singled out from all other animals, and alone possessing an immortal soul. Our better understanding of our own nature has bridged the gulf that was once thought to lie between ourselves and other species, so why should we believe that the mere fact that a being is a member of the species *Homo sapiens* endows its life with some unique, almost infinite, value?

Once the religious mumbo jumbo surrounding the term "human" has been stripped away, we may continue to see normal members of our species as possessing greater capacities of rationality, self-consciousness, communication, and so on, than members of any other species, but we will not regard as sacrosanct the life of each and every member of our species, no matter how limited its capacity for intelligent or even conscious life may be. If we compare a severely defective human infant with a nonhuman animal, a dog or a pig, for example, we will often find the nonhuman to have superior capacities, both actual and potential, for rationality, self-consciousness, communication, and anything else that can plausibly be considered morally significant. Only the fact that the defective infant is a member of the species *Homo sapiens* leads it to be treated differently from the dog or pig. Species membership alone, however, is not morally relevant. . . .

If we can put aside the obsolete and erroneous notion of the sanctity of all human life, we may start to look at human life as it really is: at the quality of life that each human being has or can achieve. Then it will be possible to approach these difficult questions of life and death with the ethical sensitivity that each case demands, rather than with the blindness to individual differences that is embodied in the Department of Health and Human Services' rigid instruction to disregard all handicaps when deciding whether to keep a child alive.[6]

Do you understand what you have just read? If you take away the biblical teaching of the sanctity of human life and of man created in the image of God (as Dr. Singer has shown so clearly), there is no final basis for placing value on human life. And this applies whether we are talking about the unborn or those who are already born. If human life can be taken before birth, there is no logical reason why it cannot be taken after birth. Thus the quality of life, arbitrarily judged by fallible and sinful people, becomes the standard for killing or not killing human life—whether unborn, newly born, the rich, or the aged. But what then does this say about the handicapped now alive? Isn't their life wrongly and tragically devalued? There are people who will read this book who would be allowed to die under these criteria if they were born today.[7]

The question of human life truly is a watershed issue. Those who accept abortion try to conceal the horrible reality behind respectable language such as the "quality of life," or "the happiness and well-being of the mother," or "the need for every child to be wanted." Although such language may sound close to what the Bible teaches—that all human life is created in the image of God and as such has unique, intrinsic value—it results in the total devaluation of life. The unborn child is a human being created in the image of God, and to deny this is to deny the authority of the Bible. It is impossible to read Psalm 139 and truly believe what it says without realizing that life in the womb is human life. It is impossible to truly believe in the Incarnation and not realize that the child conceived in Mary by the power of the Holy Spirit was indeed the Son of God from the time of conception. If we truly believe the Bible, there is no question when human life begins.[8] And to deny this is to deny the authority of the Bible.

But the question is not just abortion, as important as that is. Are we so blind not to see what is involved? It is human life as human life that is involved. Yet much of the evangelical world carries on business as usual, saying they are not for abortion except for this or that; or saying that we should not make an issue of this because it might be divisive; or saying we should not draw a line— even when millions of human lives are at stake. *But if we are not willing to take a stand even for human life, is there anything for which we will stand?*

CHAPTER FIVE

Forms of the World Spirit

It is comfortable to accommodate to that which is in vogue about us, to the forms of the world spirit in our age. This accommodation has been deadly—in the loss of twelve million human lives over the last ten years by abortion. But it does not stop with questions of human life; it is just as evident on virtually every other issue which has been made fashionable by the secularist mentality of the day.

The Socialistic Mentality

Thus in another area we find that a large section of evangelicalism is confusing the kingdom of God with a socialistic program. This too is sheer accommodation to the world spirit around us. A clear example can be found in a newsletter published by a leading evangelical magazine. In a recent issue the newsletter featured the work of Evangelicals for Social Action (ESA), their social strategy, and their critique of society. As ESA explains:

> Summarized briefly, the critique claims that the social problems Christians in this nation are most concerned about (i.e., crime, abortion, lack of prayer, secular humanism, etc.) are important, but are actually

379

symptoms of much larger problems—*unjust social structures in the United States*—which underlie these legitimate Christian concerns.

The obvious answer, then, is to attack the causes of the disease so the symptoms will go away. ESA spends much of its educational effort trying to acquaint biblical Christians with crucial areas of basic injustices in society and the need to change these for the better.

What are these basic "unjust structures"? ESA believes that most of them (but certainly not all) stem from poverty and the maldistribution of wealth, both on the national and international levels.[1]

Do you understand what is being said here? Remarkably, ESA is saying that "unjust social structures" and in particular "the maldistribution of wealth" are the real causes of evil in the world. According to ESA it is these things (e.g., unjust social structures/maldistribution of wealth) which cause "crime, abortion, lack of prayer, secular humanism, etc." Just on a factual level this is foolish. There is crime at all levels of society irrespective of wealth; abortion is supported most strongly by the wealthy. And does ESA really believe that changing economic structures would solve the problem of "lack of prayer"? Here the gospel has been reduced to a program for transforming social structures. This is the Marxist line. It does not mean that those who take this position are Communists. But it does mean they have made a complete confusion of the kingdom of God with the basic socialistic concepts. In back of this stands the Enlightenment idea of the perfectibility of man if only the cultural and economic chains are removed.[2]

But think further what this means theologically. What has happened to the fall and sin? ESA seems to be saying that changing economic structures is the means of salvation for modern man since only this deals with the basic "causes of the disease." Ironically their program is not radical enough! The basic problem is that of the fall and sin and the heart of man. The basic problem is much deeper than social structures, and by not recognizing this ESA ends up with an understanding of salvation which is very different from what the Scriptures teach. Sin is the problem, and there is no greater sin than modern man's willful defiance of God and his laws both in the area of ideas and actions.

The socialist mentality as promoted by Evangelicals for Social Action and others, and endorsed by much of the evangelical world, is based upon a double error. First and foremost it is wrong theologically, fundamentally distorting the meaning of the gospel. But it is equally wrong in its naive assessment of the redistribution of wealth and its consequences. The answer is not some kind of socialistic or egalitarian redistribution. This would be much more unjust and oppressive than our own system, imperfect though it is. To understand this all we need to do is look at the repressive societies which have resulted from attempts to radically redistribute wealth along socialistic or egalitarian lines. Every attempt at radical redistribution has wrecked the economy and the culture of the country where it was tried, and every Marxist revolution has ended in a blood bath. It has left the people with less, not more, as well as putting them under a totalitarian government. In this respect the comments of economist and historian Herbert Schlossberg are very helpful. Schlossberg points out the "hatred in principle" in the statements of the opinion-makers of the day who call for socialistic redistribution:

> The hatred revealed in such statements is all that can be expected in a society that has institutionalized envy and uses the term social justice to describe a system of legalized theft. That should alert us to the cant in the old fraud that property rights can somehow be separated from human rights and are inferior to them. There are no societies that are cavalier toward property rights but which safeguard human rights. The state that lays its hand on your purse will lay it on your person. Both are the acts of a government that despises transcendent law.
>
> Those who think they will replace the competition of capitalism with the cooperation of socialism know nothing of either. . . . Soviet "cooperation" cost by 1959 some 110 million lives. The alternative to free economic activity is not cooperation but coercion.[3]

I would ask you to think back once again to the illustration of the watershed at the beginning of the second chapter. There I mentioned how the snow lying side by side when it melted would end up a thousand miles apart. And we saw how, in the case of Scripture, two views which seemed at first to be fairly close end up in completely different places, with disastrous consequences both for theology and the culture in which we live. Now when we consider evangelical accommodation to the socialistic mentality, we really find the same thing happening. With its call for justice and compassion it sounds at first like it is the same as, or very close to, what Scripture teaches on justice and compassion. Those advocating the socialist mentality try to use all the right evangelical words and avoid any red-flag socialistic rhetoric. But what they are in fact talking about is "another gospel." And when we look more carefully at what is involved, we find that the socialist mentality ends up in a completely different place, with disastrous consequences theologically and in terms of human rights and human life. A socialistic program is not the answer.[4] And when a large section of evangelicalism begins confusing the kingdom of God with a socialistic program,[5] this is sheer accommodation to the world spirit of this age. Our response must be confrontation—loving confrontation but nonetheless confrontation. A line must be drawn.

Three Great Weaknesses
But here again we must be careful and have a proper balance. In taking a stand against the socialistic mentality, we need to be careful not to baptize everything in America's past. This is something which I have stressed over the years beginning with my earliest books and lectures, but it needs to be repeated again. There never has been a golden age in the past. There is no age we can look back to, including the Reformation, or the early church, or early America, that was perfect or fully Christian. There were great weaknesses which as Christians we must reject and then work to redress, and I would mention three of these here.

First there is the matter of race, where there were two kinds of abuse. There was slavery based on race, and also racial prejudice as such. Both practices are wrong, and often both were present when Christians had a stronger influence on the consensus than they now have. And yet the church, as the church, did not speak out sufficiently against them. Sadly, Americans indulged in the lie that the black man was not a person and could therefore be treated as a thing. It is remarkable that exactly the same argument was used in the *Roe* v. *Wade* decision of 1973 to legalize abortion. One hundred and fifty years ago the black man could be enslaved because he was not legally a person; in the last ten years twelve million unborn children have been killed because the Supreme Court decided that they are not persons. As Christians, by identification with our forebears, we must acknowledge this wrong and twisted view of race and beyond this make every effort to eliminate racial prejudice today. We can be grateful for Christian men like Shaftesbury, Wilberforce, and Wesley who, on the basis of the biblical view that there are absolutes, could say that these evils and injustices are absolutely wrong. But we can hardly sit in judgment of past generations if the same lie is used in the wanton destruction of human life today.[6]

Second, there is the question of the compassionate use of wealth.

As I have stressed in the past, this means two things: first, making it with justice; and then using it with real compassion. As a matter of fact, I have said a number of times and places where I hope it counted that I think when Christians get to heaven and they speak of how much they gave to missions, to build schools, and so on, that the Lord is going to tell them it would have been better if they had had less money to give and had made their money with justice.

Third, there is the danger of confusing Christianity with the country. In this area I have stressed first that we must not wrap Christianity in our country's flag,[7] and second that we must protest the notion of "manifest destiny" that would permit our nation to do anything it chooses. We are responsible for all that we do and all that God has given to us, and if we trample on his great gifts we will one day know his judgment.[8]

The Devaluation of History
After acknowledging these grave weaknesses, we must nonetheless recognize that Christianity did in fact have a profoundly positive influence in shaping this country. When historians devaluate too far the Christian influence in founding the country it is neither good history nor honoring to God for the good things which came out of this influence and especially out of Reformation Christianity. There was a massive amount of biblical knowledge in the country in that day which existed in general and especially out of the Great Awakening. This did have a profound influence, and many secular historians agree that there was a general Christian consensus or ethos.

But this is not to be so foolish as to think that all the founders of the United States were Christians. They were not. Everyone knows, for example, that Jefferson was a deist. But even as a deist he knew that a God existed, and this made a drastic difference in how he understood the world. In particular it meant that Jefferson grounded the concept of inalienable rights in the Creator. Even if the concept was defective in Jefferson's case, for example, there is a drastic difference between this and the ideas of the Enlightenment, which produced the wholesale slaughter of the French and Russian Revolutions. Or there is the example of John Witherspoon, the Presbyterian minister and president of what is now Princeton University and the only pastor to sign the Declaration of Independence. He was not always consistent in his thinking, as none of us are. But it is most striking to note what the issue was when, in a sermon, Witherspoon openly named and attacked Thomas Paine, the "Enlightenment man." Witherspoon directly challenged Paine's Enlightenment views concerning the perfectibility of man, contrasting this with the biblical view of the fall and the lostness of man and therefore the lack of perfection in all realms of government.[9] Witherspoon was not always correct in his political views. But his Christianity did make a difference in his understanding of the political realities of the day.

But there are those within evangelical circles today who would, under the guise of scholarship, belittle all of this and act as though the Christian consensus was always in a total muddle. Just how far this can be taken may be shown by the example of one Christian historian who carries the muddle all the way back to the Reformation itself. Thus he writes:

> [Schaeffer's] confusion rests on his inability to see Protestantism as the religious form of Renaissance humanism. To be sure, Protestants *said* that their consciences were informed by the Bible, on which authority alone rested (*"sola scriptura"*). Yet we all know of Protestant inability to agree on what the Bible said, or even on what kind of a book it is.
>
> In his triumphalism, Schaeffer cannot see the ironic and tragic in the Protestant movement, because he refuses to see it as an aspect of the humanist movement itself. In his various works Schaeffer repeatedly invokes the Reformation as the answer to the problem of humanism, when in reality it is part of the problem.[10]

Do you understand what is being said here? The significance of the Reformation is completely devalued and subordinated to humanism. The Reformation and the Reformers' view of *sola scriptura*—the Bible as the sole basis for Christian truth—is thrown out completely. Everything the Reformation stood for is swallowed up in a morass of synthesis and relativity. Exactly the same line is taken by the relativistic, non-Christian, secularized historians of our day. This is not a dispute over the facts of history; in fact, many non-Christian historians would disagree with this radically disparaging view of Reformation ideas. What we have here is the infiltration of thoroughly secularized thinking presented as if it were evangelical scholarship. Yes, we must stand against those who would naively baptize all in the past and that would wrap Christianity in the country's flag. But we must equally stand against those who would accommodate to the world spirit of this age under the guise of scholarship, and in the process not only distort the facts of history but Christian truth as well.[11]

Academic Infiltration

Sadly we must say that in the area of scholarship the evangelical world has not done well. In every academic discipline the temptation and pressure to accommodate is overwhelming. Evangelicals were right in their rejection of a poor pietism which shut Christianity up into a very narrow area of spiritual life. Evangelicals were right in emphasizing the Lordship of Christ over all areas of culture—art, philosophy, society, government, academics, and so on. But then what happened? Many young evangelicals heard this message, went out into the academic world, and earned their undergraduate and graduate degrees from the finest secular schools. But something happened in the process. In the midst of totally humanistic colleges and universities, and a totally humanistic orientation in the academic disciplines, many of these young evangelicals began to be infiltrated by the anti-Christian world view which dominated the thinking of their colleges and professors. In the process, any distinctively evangelical Christian point of view was accommodated to the secularistic thinking in their discipline and to the surrounding world spirit of our age.[12] To make the cycle complete, many of these have now returned to teach at evangelical colleges where what they present in their classes has very little that is distinctively Christian.

Note that this criticism is not a call for intellectual retreat and a new anti-intellectualism. Evangelical Christians should be better scholars than non-Christians because they know that there is truth in contrast to the relativism and narrow reductionism of every discipline. But too often Christians have naively entered the academic world with a glassy-eyed fascination and left their critical judgment and Christian truth behind.

The battle we are in rages most intensely in the academic world. Every academic discipline has dominated secularist thinking—especially in the behavioral sciences, the humanities, and the arts. Part of our task as Christians is to carefully understand and study these areas—but then to respond critically from a distinctively Christian point of view. But note, as I pointed out in the preceding chapter, this involves two things: 1) being truly Bible-believing; and 2) facing the results of the surrounding wrong world view with loving, but definite confrontation. Please do not take this lightly. We cannot retreat and shut Christianity up to a narrow view of spirituality; but in the totally secularistic academic world the dangers and the temptations are profound. It is very difficult to live in this world as a college or university student for four years or longer and not become infiltrated by the surrounding world view. And if one is a teacher, the dangers go far beyond this with the overwhelming pressure to compromise one's thinking in order to gain scholarly respectability within disciplines dominated by secularist thinking.

And for those who are professors at evangelical Christian colleges, the responsibility is awesome. Yes, you must clearly and carefully present the full range of learning in your discipline. But this is barely the beginning of your responsibility. Will you then go on to explain the points at which there are fundamental conflicts between the ideas in your discipline and biblical truth? Or will you—in the name of academic freedom, or tolerance, or neutrality—let it all slip by without confrontation? This is not the way the world works. The Marxist sociology professor at the secular university is not interested in neutrality, but will make sure that his ideological position gets across in the classroom. Again I would say, in the area of academic scholarship the evangelical world has often failed to take a clear stand. This of course has not been true of everyone, and we can be thankful for those who have taken a stand. But there has been and is a growing accommodation to the spirit of the age as it finds expression in the various disciplines. And because of this, how many will have come to our schools looking for the bread of life, and leave with only a handful of pebbles? This danger is present in the colleges which are thought of as the best Christian colleges. The problem is not future but present.

False Prophecy
Accommodation, accommodation. How the mindset of accommodation grows and expands. It can be seen once again in the new evangelical call for participation in the World Council of Churches (WCC). It is ironic that just when the secular press was exposing the hypocrisy of the WCC and severely criticizing it, evangelical leaders and influential evangelical publications were praising it. Because it shows such remarkable perception, I will quote at length from *Time's* article entitled "The Curious Politics of Ecumenism":

> To many conservative Christians in Western Europe and the U.S., the World Council of Churches, an umbrella organization for 301 Protestant and Orthodox denominations with more than 400 million members, appears to be an ecclesiastical clone of the United Nations. Responsive to the growing influence of churches in the Third World,

the council has seemingly evolved into a forum for relentless denunciations of the sins of American policy and capitalism. Meanwhile, the WCC has what some critics call a see-no-evil policy toward Communist regimes. . . .

The WCC's sixth assembly at the University of British Columbia in Vancouver, which was attended by 838 delegates from 100 countries as well as thousands of visitors, did nothing to dispel the suspicions of anti-Western bias. For example, a committee headed by William P. Thompson, one of the two top leaders of the Presbyterian Church (U.S.), was responsible for drafting last week's formal statement on Afghanistan. Working closely with delegates from Soviet churches, the committee produced a muted document that asked for withdrawal of Soviet troops as part of an overall political settlement; that was one of the few times the U.S.S.R. has been named specifically in a political declaration by the WCC. But the statement also said in effect that Soviet troops should be allowed to stay in Afghanistan until such a settlement is reached, and recommended that aid to the anti-Communist Afghan rebels be cut off. Thompson's committee also produced a harshly worded attack on U.S. Central American policy. The document praised "the life-affirming achievements" of the Nicaraguan government; Cuba was mentioned not at all.

Bishop Alexander Malik of the Church of Pakistan, a union of Anglican and Protestant bodies, demanded that the Afghanistan statement be sent back to committee for a suitable injection of candor: "If any Western nation were involved, I am sure we would have jumped on it with the strongest language available in the dictionary. The U.S.S.R. has committed a great aggression upon a neighbor, and it must be condemned." Malik's recommendation was rejected after Russian Orthodox Archbishop Kirill warned that any stronger statement would present "terrible difficulties" for his church and would be a "challenge to our loyalty to the ecumenical movement."

This was vintage WCC politics. The council is willing to risk further damage to its image, not only because many Western church leaders agree with the attacks on the policies of the U.S. and its allies, but also because silence is supposedly the price that must be paid to keep Soviet bloc churches in the council. This pragmatic—some would say shortsighted—approach also prevents the WCC from addressing the plight of religious believers in the Soviet Union. The most dramatic event of the last assembly, in Nairobi eight years ago, was the publication of an open letter from two Soviet dissidents, Father Gleb Yakunin and Lev Regelson, claiming that the council had been silent when "the Russian Orthodox Church was half destroyed" in the early 1960's, and pleading for action against Soviet persecution.[13]

Later the same article turns to the topic of witnessing and evangelism. Here *Time* notes that

There was a flurry of excitement at the assembly involving a non-political document titled "Witnessing in a Divided World." Bishop Per Lonning of the Church of Norway (Lutheran) called it a "dangerous setback," because it showed a "lack of missionary urgency" and did not emphasize the uniqueness of Christianity. Agreeing, the delegates voted nearly unanimously for a revision, but in dealing with a bushel of political statements on everything from nuclear arms (yes to a freeze) to Palestinian rights (an emphatic endorsement), they never had a chance to act on the rewritten statement.[14]

Now contrast this with what our own evangelical leaders and press reported. An article in *Christianity Today* stated:

Evangelicals have been delighted with the new WCC statement on Mission and Evangelism, which shows influence of evangelical theology in its strong call for proclaiming the gospel and personal conversion to Christ. . . .

Subjectively, this was one of the great spiritual experiences of my life. We are dealing with intangibles, but I must report that I have never been among so many supernaturally courteous, gracious Christian people [i.e., the WCC delegates]. . . . Everything seemed dignified by the presence of the Spirit. The only arguments I had in Vancouver were with my fellow evangelicals. . . .

The majority of evangelicals who caucused at the assembly were also enthusiastic, so much so that they produced a statement commending the World Council and inviting evangelicals to add their gifts to the process.[15]

This report went on to discount any Marxist influence, to minimize the Council's being "fuzzy about the uniqueness of salvation in Christ," to defend the Council's call for unilateral disarmament, and in general tried to find some way to make everything that happened at the Vancouver Assembly sound palatable.

Is it possible that the writer of the *Christianity Today* report was at the same WCC Sixth Assembly meeting that *Time* was at? One would think that he would have had at least as much insight into the Assembly as a secular magazine such as *Time*. Again we see that the world often does understand better than an accommodating evangelicalism. It is hard to imagine how this observer could come away with such a naively favorable report—especially if we consider some of the other things that happened at the Vancouver Assembly.

As an example of how far the accommodation has gone, 200 evangelicals, many of whom are prominent leaders in the evangelical world, signed the statement commending the WCC and calling for more evangelical participation. One of the few evangelical leaders at the Assembly who did not sign the statement endorsing the WCC was Dr. Peter Beyerhaus, a professor at the University of Tübingen in Germany. In an alternative statement, Dr. Beyerhaus, who has been a long-time observer of the WCC, reported on the Assembly as follows:

> To see history in a materialistic context is the chief characteristic of Marxist ideology which in the form of the "Theology of the Poor" has found entrance even into the mission documents of Vancouver. . . .
>
> Speakers who represented traditional Christian doctrines [were featured] side by side with others who expounded radical beliefs incompatible with orthodox biblical convictions. One outstanding example was Dr. Dorothee Sölle. She denounced the biblical concept of God and His Lordship, speaking of a "god-movement," and even encouraged her listeners to write "new bibles."
>
> Other speakers encouraged women to make their female experience the starting point of developing a profoundly new theology in which the reverence for the biblically revealed God as our Father is changed into the cult of god-mother.
>
> Non-Christian religions are presented as ways through which Christ Himself gives life to their followers and also speaks to us as Christians. The fear of many that the WCC could move into an increasing syncretism is confirmed by the inclusion of Indian mythology in the worship program . . . and by the explicit statement by a leading WCC official . . . that an evangelistic revival endangers our dialogue with other religions.
>
> The credibility of the WCC's claim to be a prophetic voice decrying the oppression of human rights is damaged once again by the political one-sidedness in which such violations are pointed out only in the non-Marxist world, while serious offenses by socialist states, whose ecumenical representatives are applauded by the Assembly as passionate advocates for peace and justice, are dealt with mildly or passed over in silence. This applies particularly to the harassment of the churches and the persecution of confessing Christians in these areas.
>
> The decisive shortcoming of the Assembly is the lack of a truly biblical diagnosis of mankind's basic predicament: our separation from God through our sin, and of the biblical remedy, our regeneration by the Holy Spirit through repentance and personal faith in Jesus Christ, resulting in the transformation of our present life and in our everlasting fellowship with God. A rather optimistic view of the human nature and our capability to help ourselves is once again leading to a universalistic view of redemption.[16]

Dr. Beyerhaus' statement includes much more than this, all giving evidence of the fundamental incompatibility of the WCC program and philosophy with historic, Christian orthodoxy. But note carefully. The issue here is not even whether or not we should be in a denomination which is a member of the World Council. This is a matter of individual conscience (though I could not be in such a denomination). Rather, the real issue concerns discipline as one of the true marks of a true church. And here we now have evangelical leaders abandoning the principle of discipline concerning even the central doctrines of the faith, and calling for evangelicals to be content to remain in denominations which are permanently pluralistic—with a mixture of Bible-believing Christians and those holding even the most extreme views of liberal theology. Having given up any idea or any hope of ever using discipline to purify the church, any amount of heresy and untruth is accepted as normal in the church of Christ. Dr. Beyerhaus' conclusion is very much to the point: "All these observations contribute to our apprehension that the WCC is in danger of becoming a mouthpiece of false prophecy to Christianity."[17]

The New Utopianism
It is interesting to note that within the WCC agenda there is a whole catalog of issues on which the World Council has "come down on the wrong side,"and with which the evangelical world has increasingly accommodated. One that I would mention in particular is related to the proper need for Christians to stand against tyranny—from whatever side it might come, right or left. This includes the tyranny that exists in the Soviet bloc, and the extended tyranny that exists around the globe because of the natural expansionist philosophy of Marxism and the Soviet Union. And note that the Soviet system is *totally* based on the same view of final reality which under the name "humanism" is producing the destruction of our own country and our own culture.

This of course also needs balance: I would say again that our country was never perfect—our country was never perfect, and now it is certainly less perfect. It has been years since I have prayed for justice on our country; I pray only for mercy. With all the light we have had and the results of the biblical influence, and then to have trampled on what we have had—we deserve God's judgment. However,this cannot cause us to forget that the Soviet position is even further down the road. Loving our neighbor as we should means, first, doing all we can to help those persecuted by that system now (and especially never minimizing the persecution of our Christian brothers and sisters in the Soviet bloc); and second, not assisting the spread of this oppression to other countries when failing to remember that we live in a fallen world, we then support the contemporary vogue of utopian views on disarmament.

The Bible is clear here: I am to love my neighbor as myself, in the manner needed, in a practical way, in the midst of the fallen world, at my particular point of history. This is why I am not a pacifist. Pacifism in this poor world in which we live—this lost world—means that we desert the people who need our greatest help.

Let me illustrate. I am walking down the street and I come upon a big, burly man beating a tiny tot to death—beating this little girl—beating her—beating her. I plead with him to stop. Suppose he refuses? What does love mean now? Love means that I stop him in any way I can, including hitting him. To me this is not only necessary for humanitarian reasons: it is loyalty to Christ's commands concerning Christian love in a fallen world. What about that little girl? If I desert her to the bully, I have deserted the true meaning of Christian love—responsibility to my neighbor. She, as well as he, is my neighbor.

We have, in the Second World War, the clearest illustration anyone could ask for on this point. What about Hitler's terrorism? There was no possible way to stop the awful terror in Hitler's Germany without the use of force. There was no way. As far as I am concerned, this was the necessary outworking of Christian love in the fallen world as it is. The world is an abnormal world. Because of the fall, it is not what God meant it to be. There are many things in this world which grieve us, but we must face them. We never have the luxury of acting in a merely utopian way. Utopian schemes in this fallen world have always brought tragedy. The Bible is never utopian.

We all grieve at any war, and especially at the prospect of nuclear war. But in a fallen world there are many things we grieve over but must nevertheless face. Since World War II, Europeans more than Americans have wanted the protection of nuclear weapons and have demanded this protection. We have arrived at a crazy place, with a wild proliferation of nuclear weapons on both sides. Clearly there must be discussion here, and reduction of this capability if possible. But the fundamental factor has not changed: Europe, even more today than in Winston Churchill's day, would be under the threat of Soviet military and political domination if it were not for the existence of NATO's nuclear weaponry.

In connection with this, it is interesting to note the recent comments of Yves Montand, the French left-wing movie actor. Montand, incidentally, is the husband of Simon Signoret who has been known as the voice of the left for thirty-five years in France, and who has been deep in leftist political activity in Europe. In light of this, Montand's recent statement is remarkable: that the present peace movement and peace demonstrations are more dangerous than Stalin himself.

Unilateral disarmament in this fallen world, especially in the face of aggressive Soviet materialism with its anti-God basis, would be altogether utopian and romantic. It would lead, as utopianism always has in this fallen world, to disaster. It may sound reasonable to talk of a freeze at the present level, or to say, "We won't ever use atomic weapons first." But if we think it through, either of these equals practical unilateral disarmament. It must not be forgotten, in this connection, that a freeze does not impose constraints on existing weapons; no present guarantee of safety would be achieved by such a measure.

One can understand the romanticism of liberal theologians in these matters, since liberalism does not agree with the biblical stress on the fallen nature of this world. One can also understand the pacifism of the "peace churches": they have always taken Christ's command to individuals to turn the other cheek and misguidedly extended it to the state. They ignore the God-given responsibility of the state to protect its people and to stand for justice in a fallen world. Both of these points of view are understandable; but both are mistaken. If they carry the day and determine government policy, then the mistake will become a tragedy.

But when those who call themselves evangelical begin to troop along in the popular, unthinking parade of our day, and begin to be romantic and utopian, it is time to speak openly in opposition. If we accept accommodation at this point, how can we say we love our neighbor?[18]

The Feminist Subversion
There is one final area that I would mention where evangelicals have, with tragic results, accommodated to the world spirit of this age. This has to do with the whole area of marriage, family, sexual morality, feminism, homosexuality, and divorce. I bring these together as one topic because they are all directly related and indeed

all are part of one of the most significant aspects of human existence.

The Biblical Pattern.   Why are marriage and these related aspects of human sexuality so important? The Bible teaches that the marriage relationship is not just a human institution, but rather it is in fact a sacred mystery which, when honored, reveals something about the character of God himself. Thus we find the man-woman relationship of marriage is stressed throughout the Scriptures as a picture, an illustration, a type of the wonderful relationship between the individual and Christ, and between the church and Christ. Thus, Ephesians 5:25-32 reads:

> Christ loved the church and gave himself up for her to make her holy, cleansing her by the washing with water through the word, and to present her to himself as a radiant church, without stain or wrinkle or any other blemish, but holy and blameless. In this same way, husbands ought to love their wives as their own bodies. He who loves his wife loves himself. After all, no one ever hated his own body, but he feeds and cares for it, just as Christ does the church—for we are members of his body. "For this reason a man will leave his father and mother and be united to his wife, and the two will become one flesh." This is a profound mystery—but I am talking about Christ and the church.

Notice how the Word of God very carefully intertwines this description of the normative marriage relationship with the description of the church's relationship to Christ. The two ideas are so fused that it is almost impossible to separate them even with, as it were, an instrument as sharp as a surgeon's scalpel. Thus we read in Ephesians 5:21-25 and 33:

> Submit to one another out of reverence for Christ. Wives, submit to your husbands as to the Lord. For the husband is the head of the wife as Christ is the head of the church, his body, of which he is the Savior. Now as the church submits to Christ, so also wives should submit to their husbands in everything. Husbands, love your wives, just as Christ loved the church and gave himself up for her. . . . However, each one of you also must love his wife as he loves himself, and the wife must respect her husband.

Nor is this an isolated passage, for we find the same image of bride and bridegroom repeatedly in the Old and New Testaments.

(See, for example, John 3:28, 29; Romans 7:1-4; Jeremiah 3:14; 2 Corinthians 11:1, 2 and Revelation 19:6-9.)

Thus the husband-wife relationship in marriage, and the relationship of the individual and the church to Christ are intimately related. Just as there is a real oneness between the human bride and bridegroom who really love each other, and yet the two personalities are not confused, so in our oneness with Christ, Christ remains Christ and the bride remains the bride. This great understanding of the way Scripture parallels the human man-woman relationship and our union with Christ guides our thinking in two directions. First, it makes us understand the greatness and the wonder and the beauty of marriage; and second, it helps us to understand profoundly something of the relationship between God and his people and between Christ and his church.

Shattered Lives.   Now what has happened to this beautiful picture of marriage in our generation? It has been destroyed. And we must say with tears that the destruction has been nearly as complete in our own evangelical circles. If we look at many of our evangelical leaders and at much of our evangelical literature we find the same destructive views on divorce, extreme feminism, and even homosexuality as we find in the world. Just how far the situation has gone among evangelicals in the area of divorce is illustrated clearly by the following observations and quotes provided by Os Guinness:

> For instance, a Christian conservative writes that the break-up of his marriage was a sad but "healthy new beginning for each of us in our own way." And he continues that he was called by faith like Abraham to leave the security of marriage to embark on a spiritual pilgrimage toward emotional authenticity.
>
> Another writes, "I hope my wife will never divorce me, because I love her with all my heart. But if one day she feels I am minimizing her or making her feel inferior or in any way standing in the light that she needs to become a person God meant her to be, I hope she'll be free to throw me out even if she's one hundred. There is something more important than our staying married, and it has to do with integrity, personhood, and purpose."
>
> The ultimate in refinement are the disingenuous ones who claim to be *separating out of faithfulness to Christ!* Once this would have meant a Christian husband or wife left by the non-Christian partner because of the faith itself. Now it often means a Christian divorcing another Christian over a Christian issue.

Would you have thought, for example, that a commitment to a simple lifestyle could ever lead to divorce? Yes, one writer urges today, "The split finally comes when one recognizes that this kind of conscience can't be compromised. There are levels of importance and urgency in biblical morality. And Jesus' driving concern for the coming of the Kingdom, as a counter to the culture, far outweighed his concern for the maintenance of family structures. There can be as much sin involved in trying to perpetuate a dead or meaningless relationship as in accepting the brokenness, offering it to God, and going on from there." Disobeying Christ out of faithfulness to Christ! The irony is exquisite.[19]

Yes, there must be balance here too. We must have compassion for the divorced person—and for all of those in the whole range of relationships that are shattered by divorce. But under the guise of love, much of the evangelical world has abandoned any concept of right or wrong in divorce and any pretext of dealing with divorce according to the boundaries established in the Scriptures.

Subversive Influence. And we cannot talk about divorce without speaking immediately about extreme feminism, for this certainly is one of the largest influences contributing to divorce today. It is interesting to note what the editor of one magazine which calls itself evangelical says about feminism:

For years, the right has argued that feminism threatens to corrupt Western values and to undermine American institutions. I have never understood their concern; I thought they were just afraid of change.

But increasingly I suspect they are correct. Feminism, at least in some forms, is profoundly subversive.

That's why I like it.[20]

This evangelical editor is right at least in one sense. The world spirit of our age espouses an extremely strong and subversive feminist view which teaches that the home and family are ways of oppressing women; that personal fulfillment and career must come before one's marriage and the needs of children; that housework and child care are demeaning; that it is a waste of one's talents to be a full-time homemaker. All of this, of course, has had a devastating effect upon the family, but just as much upon the whole of society as those who have grown up with deprived family relationships live their shattered lives in the world.[21]

The key to understanding extreme feminism centers around the idea of total equality, or more properly the idea of *equality without distinction*. Here again we must have balance. The Bible does not teach the inequality of men and women. Each person, man or woman, stands equally before God as a person created in his image, and at the same time as a sinner in need of salvation. And because of this, each person, whether male or female, has at the same time both an *infinite equality of worth* before God and one another, and a *total equality of need* for Christ as Savior. But at the same time, this equality is not an equality of monolithic uniformity or "sameness" between men and women. It is an equality which preserves the fundamental differences between the sexes and which allows for the realization and fulfillment of these differences; but at the same time, it affirms everything that men and women have in common—as both being created in the image of God, and as *complementary expressions of his image*. Thus we must affirm two things simultaneously: because men and women are both created in the image of God there is a common equality which has enormous implications for all of life; and because men and women are both created with distinctions as *complementary expressions of the image of God,* this has enormous implications for all of life—in the family, in the church, and in the society as a whole. And in this wonderful complementarity there is an enormous range of diversity. But at the same time, this is not freedom without form. The Bible gives enormous freedom to men and women, but it is freedom within the bounds of biblical truth and within the bounds of what it means to be complementary expressions of the image of God.

In balance, it must also be emphasized that because we are all fallen, men have often corrupted their place by turning it into tyranny. It is part of the husband's responsibility to see that, as far as possible, the wife is fulfilled. This too is part of the biblical form.

In contrast to this marvelous balance, the world spirit in our day would have us aspire to autonomous absolute freedom in the area of male and female relationships—to throw off all form and boundaries in these relationships and especially those boundaries taught in the Scriptures. Thus our age aspires not to biblical equality and complementarity in expressing the image of God, but a monolithic equality which can best be described as *equality without distinction*—that is, without taking into account any differences between men and women and how these affect every area of life. In the end equality without distinction is destructive to both men and women because it does not take into account their true identity and the distinctives as well as the commonalities that are bound up in what it means to be man and woman.

Tragic Consequences. I have dwelt at length on this because it is an absolutely crucial point. To deny the truth of what it means to be male and female as taught in the Scriptures is to deny something essential about the nature of man and about the character of God and his relationship to man. But this denial has equally tragic consequences for society and human life. If we accept the idea of equality without distinction, we logically must accept the ideas of abortion and homosexuality. For if there are no significant distinctions between men and women, then certainly we cannot condemn homosexual relationships. And if there are no significant distinctions, this fiction can be maintained only by the use of abortion-on-demand as a means of coping with the most profound evidence that distinctions really do exist.

Again we see that an idea which sounds at first so close to a genuinely biblical idea ends up in a completely different place. The idea of absolute, autonomous freedom from God's boundaries flows into the idea of equality without distinction, which flows into the denial of what it truly means to be male and female, which flows into abortion and homosexuality, and the destruction of the home and the family, and ultimately to the destruction of our culture. Once more we must say sadly that the evangelical world has not done well here. There are those who call themselves evangelicals and who are among the evangelical leadership who completely deny the biblical pattern for male and female relationships in the home and church. There are many who accept the idea of equality without distinction and deliberately set aside what the Scriptures teach at this point.[22] And there are others who call themselves evangelical and then affirm the acceptability of homosexuality and even the idea of homosexual "marriage."[23]

Bending the Bible. But note: this cannot be done without directly denying the authority of Scripture in the area of sexual morality. This is not a dispute over a matter of interpretation; it is a direct and deliberate denial of what the Bible teaches in this area. Some evangelical leaders, in fact, have changed their views about inerrancy as a direct consequence of trying to come to terms with feminism. There is no other word for this than accommodation. It is a direct and deliberate bending of the Bible to conform to the world spirit of our age at the point where the modern spirit conflicts with what the Bible teaches. Another example of this in the area of homosexuality, by an author who calls herself an evangelical, is the following:

> It's true that some Christians insist that homosexuals *can* change how they feel—indeed that they should change. But other Christians have begun questioning that notion—and not just capriciously but after careful Scriptural, theological, historical, and scientific study.[24]

Perhaps unwittingly this author has given a concise description of how accommodation works. First one starts questioning, based upon what the world about us is saying, then one looks at Scripture, then theology, then scientific study—until finally what the Scriptures teach is completely subjected to whatever view is currently accepted by the world. The above author's conclusions reflect this in a remarkably creative way: homosexuality is similar to "handedness." That is, some people are right-handed and some people are left-handed; some people are heterosexual and some people are homosexual. And one is just as good as the other.

It is hard to imagine how far these things have gone. Evangelicalism is deeply infiltrated with the world spirit of our age when it comes to marriage and sexual morality. Few would go so far as the extremes mentioned above. But there are many who quietly tolerate these views and in practice, if not in principle, view the biblical teaching on marriage and order in the home and church as quaint anachronisms which are culturally irrelevant in the modern world. For some the accommodation is conscious and intentional; for many more it involves our unreflective acquiescence to the prevailing spirit of the age. But in either case the results are essentially the same.

Believing God's Word. Why is this whole area of marriage and sexuality so important? First, because the Bible says that it is and speaks in the strongest terms about those who violate what God has established in this area:

> Do you not know that the wicked will not inherit the kingdom of God? Do not be deceived: neither the sexually immoral nor idolaters nor adulterers nor male prostitutes nor homosexual offenders nor thieves nor the greedy nor drunkards nor slanderers nor swindlers will inherit the kingdom of God. (1 Corinthians 6:9, 10)

And again speaking specifically about homosexuality:

> . . . God gave them over to shameful lusts. Even their women exchanged natural relations for unnatural ones. In the same way the men abandoned natural relations with women and were inflamed with lust for one another. Men committed indecent acts with other men, and received in themselves the due penalty for their perversion. (Romans 1:26, 27)[25]

God condemns sexual sin in the strongest language. This is not to say that sexual sin is worse than any other sin. And to be consistent with what the Bible teaches, we must take a strong stand against every kind of sin. At the same time, we can never forget that God very strongly condemns sexual sin and he never allows us to tone down on the condemnation of that sin.

Why is this point so important? The first reason, of course, is simply because God says so. God is the Creator and the Judge of the universe; his character is the law of the universe, and when he tells us a thing is wrong, it *is* wrong.

Second, we must never forget that God has made us in our relationships to really fulfill that which he made us to be, and therefore a right sexual relationship is for our good as we are made. If we do not follow God's pattern for marriage and sexual morality, it will be destructive to us personally and for our society as a whole.

Third, the denial of God's pattern for marriage and sexual morality shatters the meaning of God's relationship with his people as illustrated in the Scriptures' teaching on marriage and sexual morality. It is not just a matter of what is right and wrong on a human level; it is a denial of the truth of God and his relationship to his people. If we do not follow God's pattern, we destroy the true picture of what a Christian individually and as part of the church is.

Finally, we must say that this applies in particular to the order within the family. As we have seen already, the Bible paints a beautiful picture of the relationship of husband and wife in marriage, likening this to the relationship between Christ and the church:

> Submit to one another out of reverence for Christ. Wives, submit to your husbands as to the Lord. For the husband is the head of the wife as Christ is the head of the church, his body, of which he is the Savior.

Now as the church submits to Christ, so also wives should submit to their husbands in everything. Husbands, love your wives, just as Christ loved the church and gave himself up for her to make her holy, cleansing her by the washing with water through the word, and to present her to himself as a radiant church, without stain or wrinkle or any other blemish, but holy and blameless. In this same way, husbands ought to love their wives as their own bodies. He who loves his wife loves himself. After all, no one ever hated his own body, but he feeds and cares for it, just as Christ does the church—for we are members of his body. "For this reason a man will leave his father and mother and be united to his wife, and the two will become one flesh." This is a profound mystery—but I am talking about Christ and the church. However, each one of you also must love his wife as he loves himself, and the wife must respect her husband. (Ephesians 5:21-33)

This is not oppression, as so many today even in the evangelical world would have us believe. It is a beautiful picture of what marriage should be, but equally of the love of Christ for the church. To reject this not only destroys the marriage relationship, but it equally destroys the truth of Christ's unchanging love for the church and the authority of the Bible in the area of sexual morality.

CHAPTER SIX

The Great Evangelical Disaster

Accommodation, accommodation. How the mindset of accommodation grows and expands. The last sixty years have given birth to a moral disaster, and what have we done? Sadly we must say that the evangelical world has been part of the disaster. More than this, the evangelical response itself has been a disaster. Where is the clear voice speaking to the crucial issues of the day with distinctively biblical, Christian answers? With tears we must say it is not there and that a large segment of the evangelical world has become seduced by the world spirit of this present age. And more than this, we can expect the future to be a further disaster if the evangelical world does not take a stand for biblical truth and morality in the full spectrum of life. *For the evangelical accommodation to the world of our age represents the removal of the last barrier against the breakdown of our culture.* And with the final removal of this barrier will come social chaos and the rise of authoritarianism in some form to restore social order.

Worldliness
Whether we see this as the judgment of God (which surely it is) or the inevitable results of social chaos makes little difference.

Unless the mentality of accommodation within the evangelical world changes, this is surely what we can expect. This will certainly mean that the fiction of a united evangelicalism will have to be faced with honesty, and some will have the courage to draw a line—drawing a line lovingly, and drawing a line publicly. There must be loving confrontation, but confrontation. This also means not accommodating to the form that the world spirit takes today as it rolls on with no limits, claiming to be autonomous. In contrast to this, the Bible offers true freedom with form and a way of life which meets the deepest human needs. The Bible gives not just moral limits but absolutes and truth in regard to the whole spectrum of life.

The next sentence is crucial. *To accommodate to the world spirit about us in our age is the most gross form of worldliness in the proper definition of the word.* And unhappily, today we must say that in general the evangelical establishment has been accommodating to the forms of the world spirit as it finds expression in our day. I would say this with tears—and we must not in any way give up hoping and praying. We must with regret remember that many of those with whom we have a basic disagreement over these issues of accommodation are brothers and sisters in Christ. But in the most basic sense, the evangelical establishment has become deeply worldly.[1]

Confrontation

All that I have said in my book *The Mark of the Christian* and in the preceding chapters of this book must stand.[2] We must indeed give a practical demonstration of love in the midst of the differences. But at the same time God's truth and the work of Christ's church both insist that *truth demands loving confrontation, but confrontation.* And know that it is not as if we are talking about minor differences. The differences are already there in the evangelical world, and trying to cover them over is neither faithfulness to truth nor faithfulness to love.

There are three possible positions: 1) unloving confrontation; 2) no confrontation; and 3) loving confrontation. Only the third is biblical. And there must be hierarchy of priorities. All things may be important, but all are not on the same level of needing confrontation at a given time and place. The chasm is: not conforming to the world spirit of autonomous freedom in our age and obedience to God's Word. And this means living in obedience to the full inerrant authority of the Bible in the crucial moral and social issues of the day just as much as in the area of doctrine. Obedience to God's Word is the watershed. And the failure of the evangelical world to take a clear and distinctively biblical stand on the crucial issues of the day can only be seen as a failure to live under the full authority of God's Word in the full spectrum of life.

Yes, there must be balance and holiness standing together with love. But that does not mean constant and growing accommodation and compromise—moving along step by step, fitting into the world's position in our day. It does not mean pretending that there is such a thing as a unified evangelicalism. Evangelicalism is already divided at the point of the watershed. And the two halves will end up miles apart. If truth is indeed truth, it stands in antithesis to nontruth. This must be practiced in both teaching and practical action. A line must be drawn.

The Weapon of Connotations

Now we come back to where we started this part of the book, with names and issues: I used to shift away uncomfortably when I was called a "fundamentalist," because of the negative connotation which had become attached to it. But now it seems that as soon as one stands in confrontation against that which is unbiblical (instead of accommodation), as soon as one takes such a stand, one is automatically labeled "fundamentalist." That is the way Kenneth Woodward used it in *Newsweek*—as a putdown. And when Bible-believing Christians who are brothers and sisters in Christ get taken in this way by the connotation of words, it is much sadder.[3]

Let us also think of the term "The New Right." There is an extreme right to be leaned against. But this term "The New Right" too has become a term with a negative connotation and is used as a putdown. When one examines this, it too is usually not defined and often seems to refer to anyone who is ready to stand against the slide in our day rather than going along with accommodation. But note. If it is fair to talk of "The New Right" and the religious "Right Wing," then it must be equally fair to speak of the religious "Left Wing"—concerning those within evangelicalism who have accommodated to the dominant form of the world spirit of our day. I have not done so, for I dislike the name-calling attacks which some have used, instead of dealing with facts and content as I have tried to do. But if I had used "Left Wing" to discredit what I have been describing, it would not have been unfair.

I would say again there must be balance. Our country never was fully Christian, but it was different from that which grew out of the world view of the French Revolution and the Russian Revolution. And up until the lifetime of many who will read this book, it was vastly different than it is today—because there was the clear influence of a Christian consensus or ethos. Certainly what I have stressed many times is correct: merely being conservative is no better than being nonconservative *per se*. Conservative humanism is no better than liberal humanism; authoritarianism from the left is no better than authoritarianism from the right. What is wrong is wrong, no matter what tag is placed on it.

But with the term "The New Right," as it is often used today— and too often by Christians—it seems to mean that on all the issues we have spoken of in this chapter, there is a willingness to take a stand (even to have balanced and loving confrontation) rather than the automatic mentality of accommodation. And if this is so, we must not shy away from the issues merely because some would use the weapon of connotations against us, especially when these terms can have the possibility of meaning something quite different when analyzed. A sensible person must conclude that all such terms can mean different things as used in different ways. And then we should go on hoping that our brothers and sisters in Christ who should know better will not use the wrong connotations, without proper definition and analysis. *This is the case whether we do or do not care to use any of these terms in regard to ourselves.* We are to reject what is wrong regardless of tags, not fearing proper confrontation regardless of the tags then applied.

May Day
In closing this chapter, I would ask each one reading this book one final question. If the Christians in this country, and the evangelical leaders in particular, had been in Poland over the last few years instead of in the United States, would they have been on the side of confrontation or on the side of accommodation? Would they have marched in great personal danger in the Constitution Day protests and in the May Day demonstrations? Or would they have been in the ranks of acceptable accommodation? The Polish government is great in using terms with adverse connotations as weapons: "hooligans"; "extremists"! They know how to use names to shut up the people.

I cannot be sure where many Christians in this country would have marched in light of the extent of the accommodation in our country—where there are no bullets, no water cannons, no tear gas, and most rarely any prison sentences.

It does seem to me that evangelical leaders, and every evangelical Christian, have a very special responsibility not to just go along with the "blue-jean syndrome" of not noticing that their attempts to be "with it" so often take the same forms as those who deny the existence or holiness of the living God.

Accommodation leads to accommodation—which leads to accommodation . . .

PART FOUR

Conclusion

CHAPTER SEVEN

Radicals For Truth

In September of 1965, when I spoke at Wheaton College for the Spiritual Emphasis Week, my message was "Speaking the Historic Christian Position into the Twentieth Century." At that time the youth rebellion, which began at Berkeley in the early 1960s, was underway. There were those at Wheaton, including the student body president, who were called "rebels," and the administration was having problems with them. However, it was this radical group who understood my message that if Christianity is true, it touches all life, and that it is a radical voice in the modern world. The rebels listened. And there were some of them who turned around in their thinking.

We need a revolutionary message in the midst of today's relativistic thinking. By revolutionary, or radical, I mean standing against the all-pervasive form which the world spirit has taken in our day. This is the real meaning of radical.

God has given his answers in the Bible—the Bible that is true when it speaks of history and of the cosmos, as well as when it speaks of religious things. And it therefore gives truth concerning all reality. It thus sustains radical rebellion against the relativism and the syncretism which are the hallmark of our own day—

whether that syncretism is expressed in secular or religious terminology, including evangelical terminology.

As we have now come to the famed year 1984, what we need in light of the accommodation about us is a generation of radicals for truth and for Christ. We need a young generation and others who will be willing to stand in loving confrontation, but real confrontation, in contrast to the mentality of constant accommodation with the current forms of the world spirit as they surround us today, and in contrast to the way in which so much of *evangelicalism* has developed the automatic mentality of accommodation at each successive point.

Evangelicalism has done many things for which we can be greatly thankful. But the mentality of accommodation is indeed a disaster. We should note, however, that in holding to the same Bible principles, there could come a time when we will have to lean against an opposite swing of the pendulum. In this fallen world, things constantly swing like a pendulum, from being wrong in one extreme way to being wrong in another extreme. The devil never gives us the luxury of fighting on only one front, and this will always be the case.

However, the problem of evangelical accommodation, in the years we have been considering, and especially at this crucial moment in history, is that the evangelical accommodation has constantly been in one direction—that is, to accommodate with whatever is in vogue with the form of the world spirit which is dominant today. It is this same world spirit which is destroying both church and society. Balance must be considered constantly. But the accommodation we have been speaking of has constantly taken the form of giving in to the humanistic, secular consensus which is the dominant destructive force of our day. And if no change in this comes, our opportunity will be past. Not only will the compromising portion of evangelicalism go down in collapse, all of us will be carried down with it.

We cannot think that all of this is unrelated to us. It will all come crashing down unless you and I and each one of us who loves the Lord and his church are willing to act. And so I challenge you. I call for Christian radicals, and especially young Christian radicals, to stand up in loving confrontation, but confrontation—looking to the living Christ moment by moment for strength—in loving confrontation with all that is wrong and destructive in the church, our culture, and the state.

If there is not loving confrontation, but courageous confrontation, and if we do not have the courage to draw lines even when we wish we did not have to, then history will look back at this time as the time when certain "evangelical colleges" went the way of Harvard and Yale, when certain "evangelical seminaries" went the way of Union Seminary in New York, and the time when other "evangelical organizations" were lost to Christ's cause—forever.

Notes to Volume IV

THE CHURCH AT THE END OF THE TWENTIETH CENTURY

Chapter 1: The Roots of the Student Revolution
[1]The problem of epistemology is central to the problem of modern man, and I have discussed it in much more detail in *He Is There and He Is Not Silent*.

[2]See Giovanni Gentile, *Leonardo da Vinci* (New York: Raynal and Company, 1956), p. 174.

[3]"Upstairs"—an "upper-story experience"—is a term used to denote that which, in modern thinking, deals with values, significance and meaning, but is not open to contact with the world of facts or reason.

[4]There are four ways that evangelicals have tended to drift unknowingly in this same direction: (1) by saying, "Don't ask questions; just believe"; (2) by decreasing the content of their preaching and teaching until at times the modern man hears their message as, "Drop out and take a trip with Jesus"; (3) by praising Karl Barth without realizing that he opened the door to the whole of the theology of the leap; and (4) by applying to the early chapters of Genesis the same approach that Barth did to the whole Bible; that is, by separating the Bible's statements about space-time history from "religious truth."

Chapter 2: The International Student Revolution
[1]See *The Mark of the Christian*.

Chapter 4: Form and Freedom in the Church
[1]It seems clear to me that the opposite cannot be held—namely, that only that which is commanded is allowed. If this were the case, then, for example, to have a church building would be wrong and so would having church bells or a pulpit, using books for singing, following any specific order of service, standing to sing, and many other like things. If consistently held in practice, I doubt if any church could function or worship.

Chapter 7: Modern Man the Manipulator
[1]For a book-length treatment of this, see *Pollution and the Death of Man: The Christian View of Ecology*.

THE CHURCH BEFORE THE WATCHING WORLD

Introduction
[1]See *The Mark of the Christian,* and "The Practice of Truth" in *The God Who Is There.* Much in *Death in the City* is also related to these two principles.

Chapter 1: A Historical Critique of Theological Liberalism
[1]See *Escape from Reason* and *The God Who Is There.*
[2]For a consideration of this at much greater length from a philosophical perspective, considering metaphysics, morals and epistemology, see *He Is There and He Is Not Silent.*
[3]Those who wish to pursue the subject of the biblical perspective in somewhat more detail may wish to refer at this point to the appendix, "Some Absolute Limits."
[4]This problem in epistemology is developed in detail in *He Is There and He Is Not Silent.*
[5]J. S. Bezzant, *Objections to Christian Belief* (London: Constable and Co. Ltd., 1963), pp. 90, 91. See also *The God Who Is There.*
[6]As an example, see Raymond Panikkar, *The Unknown Christ of Hinduism* (London: Darton, Longman and Todd, 1964).
[7]See Chapter 3 of *He Is There and He Is Not Silent* for a more complete consideration of Wittgenstein's importance at this point.
[8]See *The God Who Is There,* page 64.

Chapter 2: Adultery and Apostasy—the Bride and Bridegroom Theme
[1]*The Mark of the Christian* and *The Church at the End of the Twentieth Century* should be read together with this book.

Chapter 3: Practicing Purity in the Visible Church
[1]See also *True Spirituality.*
[2]Machen's defrocking and the resulting division of the Northern Presbyterian Church was front-page news in the secular news media in much of the country. However much conscious foresight this showed on the editors' and broadcasters' part, this was rightfully page-one news, for it marked the culmination of the drift of the Protestant churches from 1900 to 1936. It was this drift that contributed greatly to the cultural, sociological, moral, legal and governmental changes from that time to the present. Without this drift in the churches, I am convinced that the changes from a rural to urban society, etc., would not have produced the same results they now have. When the Reformation churches shifted, the Reformation consensus was undercut. A good case could be made that the news about Machen was the most significant U.S. news in the first half of the twentieth century. It was the culmination of a long trend toward liberalism within the Presbyterian Church and represented the same trend in most other denominations. Even if we were interested only in sociology, this change in the churches and the resulting shift to a post-Christian sociological base is important to understand if we are to grasp what is happening in the United States and other Northern European Reformation countries today.
[3]According to Marshall McLuhan's theories of communication, *hot* communication is communication that has content, that appeals to men and moves men

through the mind on the basis of that content. *Cool* communication is a kind of personal first-order experience wherein one is moved but without any content passing through his mind, his reason. It is a manipulation based on electronics. Father John Culkin, who was director of communications at Fordham University, a follower of McLuhan, said this: "Gutenberg came and the Reformation came. Electronics comes and the ecumenical movement comes." He means that the ecumenical movement is rooted for its unity in the midst of a contentless situation, a situation that is completely cool and has nothing to do with objective doctrinal truth. I feel he is right. I do not believe that the modern ecumenical movement could have been built even in the day of the old liberals. The ecumenical movement is built, I believe, in organizational oneness on the basis of a lack of content.

Equally, the new existential theologians in our churches live only in the area of cool communication. They have denied content—content is of no, or limited, importance to them. An existential, upper-story experience is separated from all reason and from all that is open either to verification or falsification. T. H. Huxley in 1890 saw that the day would come when theology would be separated from everything that has anything to do with the fact, especially pre-Abrahamic historical fact, and as such would never be open to challenge (*Science and Hebrew Tradition,* Vol. 4 of *Collected Essays,* London: Macmillan, 1902). But of course that kind of theology has no real meaning either. If a thing has no point for possible verification or falsification, it is only a "religious truth" in an upper-story situation.

[4]Unhappily in the 1980s this tendency has become evident among a considerable number of those who wish to keep the name *evangelical,* but who have taken the view of Scripture that follows the influence of Karl Barth. The modern form of this is that the Bible has authority when it speaks of "religious" or "spiritual" matters, but not when it touches upon history and the cosmos. For them to take this position is curious because the end results of this "methodology" have been demonstrated by what happened in the optimistic beginning and the dead end of neo-orthodoxy.

Appendix

[1]With either of these two methods, a careful study of the Bible must be the basis for the limits. The bounds are set not by *any* "method" but by the truth God has given us in propositional form in the whole Bible. Notice I say the whole Bible. It will not do to make a part of the Bible, or certain proof-texts, into an iron grid through which the rest of the Bible is forced. The context of each verse is, first, the immediate context, then the context of the entirety of that specific book, and then the whole Bible.

There is one absolute limit that is crucial, but which I am not dealing with in this appendix because it is dealt with in book length in *He Is There and He Is Not Silent.* In that book I deal with God's "being there" *and His not being silent* in regard to propositional, verbalized communication from God to man in the areas of metaphysics (being), morals and epistemology (knowing).

[2]The nonhumanistic *basis* for a man's salvation is the infinite value of the death of Christ (as the second person of the Trinity) in space-time history on the cross. The nonhumanistic *instrument* is the empty hands of faith.

[3]The later Heidegger showed that he at least felt a problem here in that he brought in the concept of epistemological abnormality with Aristotle. See *The God Who Is There*.

DEATH IN THE CITY

Chapter 3: The Message of Judgment
[1]See "Adultery and Apostasy," Chapter 2 in *The Church Before the Watching World*.

BOOK FIVE: THE GREAT EVANGELICAL DISASTER

Chapter 1: What Really Matters?
[1]Henry Grunwald, "*Time* at 60," *Time*. October [60th Anniversary Issue] 1983, p. 5.
[2]Roger Rosenblatt, "What Really Mattered?" *Time*. October [60th Anniversary Issue] 1983, pp. 24, 25.
[3]Rosenblatt, p. 25. Emphasis added.
[4]Rosenblatt, p. 26. Emphasis added.
[5]Rosenblatt, p. 27.
[6]The terms "biblical consensus" and "Christian consensus," as used throughout this chapter and the book, need some clarification. In using these terms I do not mean to say that everyone at the time of the Reformation in Northern Europe was truly a Christian; nor, when these terms are used in reference to our own country, that everyone in our country was a genuine Christian. Rather this refers to the fact that the Christian world view, and biblical knowledge in particular, were widely disseminated throughout the culture and were a decisive influence in giving shape to the culture. In other words, at the time of the Reformation and in our country up until the last forty to sixty years, the large majority of people believed in basic Christian truths such as: the existence of God; that Jesus was God's Son; that there is an afterlife; that morality is concerned with what truly is right and wrong (as opposed to relative morality); that God is righteous and will punish those who do wrong; that there truly is evil in the world as a result of the fall; and that the Bible truly is God's Word. In the Reformation countries and in our own country up until the last forty to sixty years, most people believed these things—albeit sometimes only in a vague way and often not in the sense that they personally trusted in Christ as their Savior.

Going back to the founding of the United States, this consensus was crucial. This does not mean that it was a golden age, nor that the Founders were personally Christian, nor that those who were Christians were always consistent in their political thinking. But the concept of a Creator and a Christian consensus or ethos was crucial in their work, and the difference between the American Revolution, as compared to the French and Russian Revolutions, cannot be understood without recognizing the significance of the Christian consensus or ethos.

This vast dissemination of biblical knowledge can properly be called a "biblical consensus," a "Christian consensus" or a "Christian ethos." And it may correctly be stated that this "consensus" had a decisive influence in shaping the culture of the Reformation and the extensions of these cultures in North America, Australia, and New Zealand. We must be careful, however, not to overstate the case and imply that the United States ever was a "Christian nation" in a truly biblical sense of what it means to be a Christian, or that the United States could ever properly be called God's "chosen nation."

Moreover, we must acknowledge that there is no "golden age" in the past to which we can return, and that as a nation we have always been far from perfect. As I have mentioned in the past we have had blind spots and serious shortcomings, particularly in three areas: 1) in the area of race; 2) in the area of the compassionate use of wealth—both in how money is made and how money is used; and 3) in wrongly subscribing to the idea of "manifest destiny" as some have done. But having made all of these qualifications, we must nevertheless acknowledge that insofar as the Northern European countries of the Reformation and the extensions of these countries such as the United States do in fact represent a Christian consensus, this consensus has profoundly shaped these cultures, bringing forth many wonderful blessings across the whole spectrum of life. Moreover, the opposite is also true: insofar as our culture has departed from a Christian consensus, as it has so rapidly over the last forty to sixty years, this has had a devastating effect upon human life and culture, bringing with it a sweeping breakdown in morality and in many other ways as well.

[7]See further, *How Should We Then Live?* in *The Complete Works of Francis Schaeffer,* Vol. V (Westchester, Ill.: Crossway Books, 1982), pp. 243, 244.

[8]See further the way I have developed the material in the next two sections in a slightly different form, for example, in *Death in the City* in *The Complete Works,* Vol. IV, pp. 210-212.

[9]See further, *Death in the City* in *The Complete Works,* Vol. IV, pp. 207-299, especially 209-213.

[10]See the treatment of this in *A Christian Manifesto* in *The Complete Works,* Vol. V, pp. 423-430; in Francis A. Schaeffer, Vladimir Bukovsky, and James Hitchcock, *Who Is For Peace?* (Nashville: Thomas Nelson, 1983), pp. 13-19; and my critique of secular humanism found especially in *The God Who Is There (The Complete Works,* Vol. I, pp. 5-202) and in my later work, especially *How Should We Then Live?* and *Whatever Happened to the Human Race?* in *The Complete Works,* Vol. V, pp. 83-227 and pp. 281-419 respectively. See also the excellent discussions of secular humanism by James Hitchcock, *What Is Secular Humanism? Why Humanism Became Secular and How It Is Changing the World* (Ann Arbor, Mich.: Servant Books, 1982); Herbert Schlossberg, *Idols for Destruction: Christian Faith and Its Confrontation with American Society* (Nashville: Thomas Nelson), esp. chap. 2; and Os Guinness, *The Gravedigger File: Papers on the Subversion of the Modern Church* (Downers Grove, Ill.: InterVarsity Press, 1983).

[11]F. L. Cross, ed., *The Oxford Dictionary of the Christian Church* (London: Oxford University Press, 1958), pp. 104, 105. Note that the quote as it appears in the original text of the *Dictionary* uses the German form of the word *Aufklärung* instead of the English "Enlightenment," and that the English form has been substituted in the quote as it appears here.

[12]J. Gresham Machen, *Christianity and Liberalism* (Grand Rapids, Mich.: Eerdmans, 1924).

418 A CHRISTIAN VIEW OF THE CHURCH

¹³See further *The Church Before the Watching World* in *The Complete Works,* Vol. IV, pp. 153-162, and esp. note 2, p. 302.

¹⁴See further *A Christian Manifesto* in *The Complete Works,* Vol. V, p. 423; and Chapter 1, Note 9 of this book.

¹⁵See further the way I have developed this in an expanded form in *Whatever Happened . . .* in *The Complete Works,* Vol. V, pp. 407-410.

¹⁶In recent years I have been criticized for allegedly having left my earlier concerns as reflected in my earlier books and work, and for allegedly having moved in a new direction. This criticism, however, really is not accurate. A more correct way to look at my work would be to see a continuity from beginning to the end. My earlier books dealt especially with intellectual matters and the area of culture. Then there were the books dealing with the Christian life and the church. My later books have made specific application of my earlier work to the area of law and the society as a whole, especially in relation to the crucial issues of human life and freedom of religious expression. Through all of this there has been my continued interest in evangelism (helping men and women come to know Christ as Savior) and an emphasis upon the Lordship of Christ in the totality of life. Finally I would want to emphasize, from beginning to end, the need to walk daily with the Lord, to study the Word of God, to live a life of prayer, and to show forth the love, compassion, and holiness of our Lord in daily life.

The proper way to view my work is to see my later work as a direct extension and application of my earlier work, and to see that I have not in any way abandoned my earlier concerns. I must admit that since my writing has filled so many pages and covered such a wide range, I do face a problem concerning those who are familiar with only some of my work, or those who would like to give priority of one part over another. I would stress simply that my work needs to be taken as a whole, with continuity from beginning to end. Probably the best way to see this would be to consult my *Complete Works* and read it through from beginning to end.

Chapter 2: Marking the Watershed

¹There was indeed at least one person who raised a lonely and courageous voice when this seminary began to accept a neo-orthodox view of the Scripture. This was Jay Grimstead, a graduate of the seminary, and I would mention him and honor him for his efforts. Jay Grimstead played a decisive role in founding the International Council on Biblical Inerrancy. The Council was formally organized on May 16, 1977 in Chicago with ten of us present. It still did not have the backing of most of the evangelical leadership, and there was no rush of the evangelical leadership to this cause.

The council was formed specifically for the purpose of defending the historic orthodox position concerning Scripture. Of particular note are the two statements issued by the Council. The first statement, issued in October 1978, is entitled "The Chicago Statement on Biblical Inerrancy." The second statement, issued in November 1982, deals with "Hermeneutics." Both statements are extremely valuable in setting forth first what it means to say that the Bible is without error, and second how this applies to the understanding and interpretation of the Bible. The second statement on hermeneutics presents a remarkably balanced and helpful series of twenty-five "affirmations and denials" concerning how the Scriptures are properly to be studied and interpreted. Together these statements set forth the total integrity of biblical inerrancy.

Chapter 3: The Practice of Truth

¹See further Bernard Ramm, *Beyond Fundamentalism: The Future of Evangelical Theology* (San Francisco: Harper and Row, 1983), especially pp. 19-22 and 43, 44.

²The issue here is not really a question of scholarship. Bible-believing Christians should never be opposed to genuine scholarship in any field. Constantly through the years great Bible-believing scholars have engaged in what is usually called "lower criticism"—the question of what the best Bible text really is. It is natural that biblical Christians should find textual study important, because, since Scripture is propositional communication from God to mankind, obviously we are interested in the very best texts possible. Consequently, Christian scholars have labored through the years in the area of "lower criticism."

"Higher criticism" is quite a different matter. Picking up where lower criticism leaves off, it attempts to determine upon its own subjective basis what is to be accepted and what is to be rejected after the best text has been established. The real difference between liberalism and biblical Christianity is not a matter of scholarship but a matter of presuppositions. Both the old liberalism and the new liberalism operate on a set of presuppositions common to both of them, but different from those of historic, orthodox Christianity.

See further chapter 1 of my book *The Church Before the Watching World* (Downers Grove, Ill.: InterVarsity, 1971), p. 9-34, also my *The Complete Works,* Vol. IV (Westchester, Ill.: Crossway Books, 1982), p. 117-132.

³Quoted in George C. Bedell, Leo Sandon, Jr., and Charles T. Welborn, *Religion in America* (New York: Macmillan, 1975), p. 237, emphasis added.

⁴George M. Marsden, *Fundamentalism and American Culture: The Shaping of Twentieth Century Evangelicalism: 1870-1925* (New York: Oxford University Press, 1980), pp. 118, 119.

⁵See further *Eerdmans' Handbook to Christianity in America,* Mark A. Noll et al, eds. (Grand Rapids, Mich.: Eerdmans, 1983), p. 379.

⁶See further *The Church Before . . . ,* Chapter 2, p. 35-60; also in *The Complete Works,* Vol. IV, pp. 133-149.

⁷See further *The Church Before . . . ,* Chapter 1, pp. 9-34; also in *The Complete Works,* Vol. IV, pp. 117-132.

Chapter 4: Connotations and Compromise

¹Harold J. Ockenga, "From Fundamentalism, Through New Evangelicalism, to Evangelicalism," in Kenneth S. Kantzer, ed., *Evangelical Roots: A Tribute to Wilbur Smith* (Nashville: Thomas Nelson, 1978), p. 36, emphasis added.

²Thomas C. Oden, *Agenda for Theology: Recovering Christian Roots* (San Francisco: Harper and Row, 1979), pp. 29-31, emphasis added. Oden is a very interesting example. He was a thoroughgoing liberal who recognized that liberalism had completely failed, and we can commend him in his courage to say this publicly and decisively. This has led him toward what is essentially a neo-orthodox position, but one that tries at the same time to take the full range of historic Christianity seriously. Since, however, he does not accept the full authority and inerrancy of the Bible he is still left with a serious problem—namely, upon what will he finally base his faith? Without the objective truth of the Bible as his foundation, Oden is still left without any way to appropriate with confidence the truth of the Scriptures, nor really to sort through the mixture of truth and error in the life and theology of the church through the centuries. Thus we can commend Oden for rediscovering the stream of historic orthodoxy, but we

must say that his theology is still seriously deficient with regard to his under-standing of the authority of the Bible. Without the full authority and inerrancy of the Bible, he is left without any final authority and caught in the same basic problem that he started with. It is interesting to note that the issue which started Oden to reconsider his liberalism was the liberal stance on abortion. Thus Oden comments:

> So when I am speaking of a diarrhea of religious accommodation, I am not thinking of "the other guys" or speaking in the abstract, but out of my own personal history. . . .
> The shocker is not merely that I rode every bandwagon in sight, but that I thought I was doing Christian teaching a marvelous favor by it, and at times considered it the very substance of the Christian teaching office. . . .
> It was the abortion movement, more than anything else, that brought me to movement revulsiveness. The climbing abortion statistics made me move-ment weary, movement demoralized. I now suspect that a fair amount of my own idealistic history of political action was ill conceived by self-deception romanticisms, in search of power in the form of prestige, that were from the beginning willing to destroy human traditions in the name of humanity, and at the end willing to extinguish the futures of countless unborn children in the name of individual autonomy. (pp. 24, 25)

³Lance Morrow, "Thinking Animal Thoughts," *Time.* October 3, 1983, p. 86, emphasis added.
⁴David Neff, "Who's Afraid of the Secular Humanists?" *His.* March 1983, pp. 4-7, 31.
⁵See further how I have carefully defined "humanism" in Francis A. Schaeffer, *A Christian Manifesto* (Westchester, Ill.: Crossway Books, 1981), pp. 22-24, in *The Complete Works,* Vol. V (Westchester, Ill.: Crossway Books, 1982), pp. 425-527. On the question of what humanism is, see further James Hitchcock, *What Is Secular Humanism?* (Ann Arbor, Mich.: Servant Books, 1982).
⁶Peter Singer, "Sanctity of Life or Quality of Life?" *Pediatrics.* July 1983, pp. 128, 129.
⁷Once abortion is accepted there is no logical boundary as to how far the de-valuation of human life can be taken. Think how quickly there is discussion concerning the use of fetuses for experimentation. It is a horror even to think about. But once the unborn human life is not legally accepted and protected as a person, this is a most logical extension. Concerning the implications of fetal experimentation and documented cases of this see "On Human Experimenta-tion," Donald DeMarco, *The Human Life Review,* Fall 1983, pp. 48-60.

Chapter 5: Forms of the World Spirit
¹Russ Williams, "Spotlight: Evangelicals for Social Action," *Evangelical News-letter.* October 15, 1982, p. 4, emphasis added.
²For an expanded treatment and an incisive critique of the "socialist mentality" see further Franky Schaeffer, *Bad News for Modern Man* (Westchester, Ill.: Cross-way Books, 1984).
³Herbert Schlossberg, *Idols for Destruction: Christian Faith and Its Confrontation with American Society* (Nashville: Thomas Nelson, 1983), pp. 133, 134.

Alexander Solzhenitsyn's comments are also instructive here. In an article entitled "Three Key Moments in Japanese History," *National Review,* December 9, 1983, Solzhenitsyn writes:

> This is an appropriate place to touch briefly upon a fashionable and widespread myth about socialism. Although this term lacks any precise, unambiguous meaning, it has come to stand, the world over, for some vague dream of a "just society." At the heart of socialism lies the fallacy that all human problems can be solved by social reorganization. But even when socialism promises to take the very mildest of forms, it always attempts to implement by force the contrived and unattainable notion that all people must be equal. One of the most brilliant thinkers in Russia today, physicist Yuri Orlov (now ill and close to death after more than five years' confinement in a Communist labor camp), has demonstrated that *pure* socialism is always and inevitably totalitarian. Orlov shows that it is immaterial how mild and gradual the measures of advancing socialism may be: if they are consistent, then the conveyor-belt-like sequence of socialist reforms will hurl that country (or the entire world) into the abyss of Communist totalitarianism. And totalitarianism is what the physicist calls an "energy well." It is easy to tumble in, but it takes extraordinary effort and exceptional circumstances to effect an escape.

[4]See further the work of John Perkins for an outstanding example of an alternative to the "socialist mentality"—an alternative which is at once biblical, compassionate, and practical. Perkins, who is a black himself, emphasizes the need for blacks to be active in the economic system, to be given opportunity, and to be treated justly, and to build equity within the economic system. See especially John Perkins, *Let Justice Roll Down* (Ventura, Calif.: Regal Books, 1976), *A Quiet Revolution: The Christian Response to Human Need, A Strategy for Today* (Waco, Texas: Word, 1976), and *With Justice For All* (Ventura, Calif.: Regal Books, 1982).

[5]It is interesting to note that while many evangelicals are beginning to sing the praises of socialism, a growing number of secular socialists are growing weary of socialism. Of particular interest is the *"Nouveaux Philsophes,"* Bernard-Henri Levy, whom *The Christian Science Monitor* calls "one of France's greatest contemporary philosophers." Levy is not a Christian by any means, but his insight into the problem of morality, social ethics, and law is remarkable. Levy comments:

> I am not a man of faith but I think if we are looking for a new foundation of ethics, the best ground is the old biblical tradition. These old manuscripts contain the principles of human rights, the idea of individuality, the idea of exile and cosmopolitanism. Marxism maintains there is no absolute ethics, truth, evil, and good; it all depends on the circumstance and the class which is expressing it. If you want, however, to escape this relativity of ethics you'll find the tools and inspiration in the Bible.

Remarkably, Levy sees the total incompatibility of Marxism with Christianity better than many evangelical Christians. See further the complete article by Stewart McBride, " 'New Philosopher' Bernard-Henri Levy: A French Leftist Takes Out After Socialism," *The Christian Science Monitor* (Pullout Section). January 20, 1983, pp. B1-B3.

⁶See further how I have developed this in *How Should We Then Live?* (Westchester, Ill.: Crossway Books, 1976), pp. 113, 114 and 127, 128; in *The Complete Works,* Vol. V, p. 141, 142 and pp. 152, 153. I would mention further that in the matter of race, all the way back to the time that I was a pastor in St. Louis in the 1940s and the black neighborhood was getting closer to our church building, I was stressing to my elders that color must *never* be a factor in determining who was to be accepted as a member of the church, and that I would resign as the pastor if it were. And through the years, a number of blacks have found L'Abri to be the first place where race made no difference at all. In the 1940s, many of our leading evangelical schools—and I'm not thinking of schools such as Bob Jones here at all—still held strict racial dating laws and all the rest. I will never forget one black who attended such a school who said at L'Abri, "This is the first place I was treated as a man." When he said it, I wept. I'm glad he could say that.

⁷See further *A Christian Manifesto,* p. 121; and in *The Complete Works,* Vol. V, p. 486.

⁸See further, Francis A. Schaeffer, Vladimir Bukovsky, and James Hitchcock, *Who Is For Peace?* (Nashville: Thomas Nelson, 1983), p. 19.

⁹*Witherspoon's Works,* Vol. 5, p. 184.

¹⁰Ronald A. Wells, "Francis Schaeffer's Jeremiad," *Reformed Journal.* May 1982, p. 18.

¹¹This is not just abstract academic discussion. For if Christian truth makes no or little difference in society (without it ever being a golden age) and if all is only a mixture, including the Reformation concept of *sola scriptura*—if this is only an illusion, then indeed Christianity is only one more piece of data in a world of probability, uncertainty, and constant flux. We should not be surprised that the historian I quoted above (see Note 10) who so devaluated the Reformation and its claim of *sola scriptura* in another article urges evangelicals to look at Walter Rauschenbusch and Reinhold Niebuhr and to their social gospel as our basis of having something to say to modern culture. For those of you who know these two men, you know what this means. The earlier evangelicals saw themselves in complete conflict with Niebuhr's social gospel.

¹²For a personal account of how this can happen, for example in psychology, see the remarkable chapter entitled "Wolf in the Fold" in William Kirk Kilpatrick's book *Psychological Seduction* (Nashville: Thomas Nelson, 1983), pp. 13-27.

¹³Richard N. Ostling, "The Curious Politics of Ecumenism," *Time.* August 22, 1983, p. 46. On the Marxist influence in the WCC contributions to guerilla warfare causes see further: Richard N. Ostling, "Warring Over Where Donations Go," *Time.* March 28, 1983, pp. 58, 59; Kenneth L. Woodward and David Gates, "Ideology Under the Alms," *Newsweek.* February 7, 1983, pp. 61, 62; and Raël Jean Isaac, "Do You Know Where Your Church Offerings Go?" *Readers Digest.* January 1983, pp. 120-125.

¹⁴Ostling, "The Curious Politics," p. 46.

¹⁵Richard Lovelace, "Are There Winds of Change at the World Council?" *Christianity Today.* September 16, 1983, pp. 33, 34.

¹⁶Peter Beyerhaus, Arthur Johnston, and Myung Yuk Kim, "An Evangelical Evaluation of the WCC's Sixth Assembly in Vancouver," as reprinted in *Theological Student Fellowship Bulletin.* September-October, 1983, pp. 19, 20.

[17]Beyerhaus, p. 20.

[18]For an expanded treatment concerning the related questions of nuclear defense and pacifism see Schaeffer, *Who Is For Peace?*, esp. pp. 19-30. For an excellent treatment in a longer format see Jerram Barrs, *Who Are the Peacemakers? The Christian Case for Nuclear Deterrence* (Westchester, Ill.: Crossway Books, 1983).

[19]Os Guinness, *The Gravedigger File: Papers on the Subversion of the Modern Church* (Downers Grove, Ill.: InterVarsity Press, 1983), pp. 99, 100, emphasis in the original.

[20]John F. Alexander, "Feminism as a Subversive Activity," *The Other Side.* July 1982, p. 8.

[21]It is interesting to note how sociologists Brigitte Berger and Peter L. Berger link the breakdown of the family and the prevailing antifamily attitude in our culture with a whole range of other issues. The Bergers write:

Those who would do away with the bourgeois family would like, if at all possible, to do away with *all* risks. This fantasy of a risk-free existence expresses itself in some of its central causes; the ideal of the "swinging single," with no ties on his or her project of endless self-realization; the idealization of abortion, once and for all eliminating the vestigial risk of pregnancy in sexual relations; the insistence that a "gay life-style" is as socially legitimate as heterosexual marriage, thereby putting on the same level a relatively risk-free (since childless) relationship with the most risky relationship at all. All these themes can be subsumed under the category of "antinatalism." They can then be seen in a perfectly logical configuration with other ideological themes prevalent in the same strata: *political leftism, zero-growth and zero-population theories, anti-nuclear and more generally anti-technological sentiments, pacifism and a benignly nonaggressive posture in international relations, a deep suspicion of patriotism* (which always has an at least potentially military dimension), *and a generally negative attitude to the values of discipline, achievement, and competitiveness.* In the aggregate, this is indeed a constellation of decadence. A society dominated by these themes has rather poor prospects in the real world, which is mostly inhabited by people with very contrary norms and habits.

We recognize the likelihood that some readers will be offended by the above paragraphs; we certainly do not expect to persuade anyone by such a sketchy argument. We only make it here to indicate that the fate of the bourgeois family *is linked, in our opinion, with much broader questions of the survival chances of contemporary Western societies.* In any case, our defense of the bourgeois family does not necessarily depend on agreement concerning these wider issues. But there is one more point that should be stressed if one places this topic in the framework of decadence: That is the point that the decadent syndrome is not distributed uniformly throughout our societies. Both in North America and in Western Europe it is concentrated in those strata that we have described as the new "knowledge class" (in the case of evangelicalism this corresponds to the evangelical leadership, especially as found in evangelical "knowledge industries" such as education and print media) though it radiates into other strata from this epicenter. There are other classes (notably the lower-middle and working classes) and large, relatively unassimilated ethnic groups that are much less marked by this syndrome and, in some instances, not touched at all by it. The fate of the bourgeois family (*and, we believe, the future survivability of these societies*) thus hinges on the future development of these groups. (pp. 135-146, emphasis added)

Or in other words, as this applied to evangelical leadership, the Bergers are pointing out that the leadership within evangelicalism has accommodated to the ideas which happen to be in vogue among the secular "knowledge class." See further the Bergers' very insightful book entitled *The War Over the Family: Capturing the Middle Ground* (New York: Doubleday, 1983).

[22]See for example, Paul K. Jewett, *Man as Male and Female* (Grand Rapids, Mich.: Eerdmans, 1975); and Virginia R. Mollenkott, *Women, Men and the Bible* (Nashville: Abingdon, 1977).

[23]See for example, Letha Dawson Scanzoni and Virginia R. Mollenkott, *Is the Homosexual My Neighbor?* (San Francisco: Harper and Row, 1980).

[24]Letha Dawson Scanzoni, "Can Homosexuals Change?" *The Other Side.* January 1984, p. 14.

[25]See further: 1 Corinthians 6:9, 10; 1 Timothy 1:9, 10; Jude 6, 7; 2 Peter 2:4, 6-8; Leviticus 18:22 and 20:13.

Chapter 6: The Great Evangelical Disaster

[1]Although I would not agree with Richard Quebedeaux in his theology, the main sociological conclusion he reaches in his influential book *The Worldly Evangelicals* (San Francisco: Harper and Row, 1978) is very much to the point— namely, that the leadership of evangelicalism has become worldly in the proper sense of the word.

[2]See Francis A. Schaeffer, *The Mark of the Christian* (Downers Grove, Ill.: InterVarsity, 1970); in *The Complete Works,* Vol. IV, pp. 183-205.

[3]Note, for example, the comments of Gill Davis, in "Christians for Socialism," which appeared in *The Other Side:* "I am concerned with those mealy-mouthed preachers . . . In this counry, the mythological support for fascism is often right-wing fundamentalism." As reported in Lloyd Billingsley, "First Church of Christ Socialist," *National Review.* October 28, 1983, p. 1339.

List of Translated Editions and Publishers of the Books in Volume Four

THE CHURCH AT THE END OF THE TWENTIETH CENTURY

First United States edition, InterVarsity Press, 1970.
First British edition, Norfolk Press, 1970.
La Chiesa alla Fine del XX Secolo (Italian), Ugo Guanda Editore, Parma, 1970.
Korean edition, Word of Life Press, Seoul, 1970.
Kirche am Ende des 20 Jahrhunderts (German), Haus der Bibel, Geneva, R. Brockhaus Verlag, Wuppertal, 1970.
La Iglesia al Final del Siglo XX (Spanish), Ediciones Evangélicas Europeas, Barcelona, 1973.
A Igreja No Ano 2001 (Portuguese), Casa Editora APLIC, Goiânia, Goias, Brasil, 1975.
De Kerk Tegen Het Eind van de 20e Eeuw (Dutch), Buijten & Schipperheijn Publishing Co., 1978.

THE CHURCH BEFORE THE WATCHING WORLD

First United States edition, InterVarsity Press, 1971.
First British edition, Inter-Varsity Press, 1972.
Chinese edition, Christian Chinese Translation Center, New York, 1974.
Korean edition, Word of Life Press, Seoul, 1975.
Die Kirche Jesu Christi—Auftrag und Irrweg (German), Hanssler-Verlag, Neuhausen-Stuttgart, 1981.

THE MARK OF THE CHRISTIAN

First United States edition, InterVarsity Press, 1970.
First British edition, Inter-Varsity Press, 1971.
Den Kristnes Kännetecken (Swedish), Gospel Publications AB, Her-
rljunga, 1973.
Chinese edition, Christian Witness Press, Hong Kong, 1972.
Das Kennzeichen des Christen (German), Haus der Bibel, Geneva R.
Brockhaus Verlag, Wuppertal, 1971.
La Marque du Chrétien (French), Telos, Fontenay-sous-Bois, 1973.
Urdu edition, Masihi Ishaat Khana, Inc., Lahore.
Kaerlighed der kan Ses (Danish), Lohses Forlag, Fredericia, 1974.
Het Kenmerk van de Christen (Dutch), Buijten & Schipperheijn
Publishing Co., Amsterdam, 1973.
Sérkenni Kristins Manns (Icelandish), Kristilegt Studenta félag,
Reykjavik, 1974.
Korean edition, Word of Life Press, Seoul, 1973.
O Sinal do Cristao (Portuguese), Alianca Biblica Universitaria do
Brasil and Casa Editora APLIC, Joiãnia, Goias, 1975.
Russian edition published in *Christianin* Toronto Christian Mis-
sion, Toronto, January, February, and March, 1977.
Japanese edition, Japan Alliance Mission, 1979.
Kristityn Tuntomerkki (Finnish), Uusi Tie, Helsinki, 1978.
Ciri Khas Kristen (Indonesian), BBK Gunung Mulia, Jakarta Pasat,
Untuk OMF, 1980.

DEATH IN THE CITY

First United States edition, InterVarsity Press, 1969.
First British edition, Inter-Varsity Press, 1969.
Kuolema Kaupungissa (Finnish), Suomennetter Inter-Varsity Press-
in, Poukkusilta, 1970.
De good over de stad (Dutch), Buijten & Schipperheijn, Amsterdam,
1971.
Muerte en la Ciudad (Spanish), Ediciones Evangélicas; Europeas,
Barcelona, 1973.
Tod in der Stadt (German), Haus der Bible, Geneva, R. Brockhaus
Verlag, Wuppertal, 1973.

Zycia Chrzescijanskiego; Czyli Prawdziwego Uduchowienie (Polish) (2 volumes—*Death in the City, Escape From Reason, True Spirituality*), Powielono Staraniem Prezydium Rady Zjednoczonego Kosciola Ewangelicznego, Warsaw, 1971.

Morte Nella Cittá (Italian), Edizioni Gruppi Biblici Universitari, Rome, 1971.

Jeg Skammer Meg Ikke ved Evangelict (Norwegian), Credo/Lutherstiftelsen, Oslo, 1973.

Dokad? (Polish), (*Escape From Reason; Death in the City*), Powielono Staraniem Prezydium Rady Zjednoczonego Kosciola Ewangelicznego, Warsaw, 1973.

La Mort dans la Cité (French), La Maison de la Bible, Geneva, 1974.

Halal a Varosban (Hungarian), Evangéliumi Kiado, 1979.

Acknowledgments

THE CHURCH AT THE END OF THE TWENTIETH CENTURY

Material from the *International Herald Tribune* is reprinted by permission of The Associated Press.

Appendix A, "Learning From the Past to Do Better in the Future," is an address delivered at the Consultation on Presbyterian Alternatives in May of 1980. It was first published in the April 10, 1981, issue of *Christianity Today*.

Appendix B, "What Difference Does Inerrancy Make?" is an address delivered in March of 1982 at the plenary sessions of the Congress on the Bible. It is here published for the first time.

THE MARK OF THE CHRISTIAN

The poem "Lament," copyright 1966 by *Christianity Today,* is used by permission of *Christianity Today*.

THE GREAT EVANGELICAL DISASTER

As some of you will know, for seven weeks following Thanksgiving Day, 1983, I was critically ill. I was taken first to the hospital in Aigle, Switzerland, and then, after a literally life and death dash across the Atlantic as a stretcher case, I spent the major part of the next six weeks in St. Mary's Hospital, connected with Mayo Clinic. While in St. Mary's, Edith and our children were told three times that I was expected to die. Happily the time has passed. And as I write this now I am convalescing in one of the houses of the Rochester, Minnesota branch of L'Abri.

Thus, that seven weeks was totally snatched from my life along with most of the work I had hoped to do. In that situation this book never would have made the deadline for the seminars bearing the same name, if it had not been for the long hours and devotion of Lane Dennis, vice-president and general manager of Crossway Books.

Lane is a friend, and one who knows my work "forward and backwards." He is the publisher of my *Complete Works* and *A Christian Manifesto*. He brought his whole family to spend three months at L'Abri in the summer of 1978. He has listened to many hours of my tapes, and he wrote his Ph.D. dissertation as a sociological study of L'Abri.

When I got out of the hospital I found that the seven weeks when I was in the hospital had not been lost. During this time Lane had been working long hours doing research and preparing my materials for the final manuscript. Thus, when a little time had passed and I felt a bit better, the manuscript was in a form ready for me to work. As I write this, we are still spending long hours on the phone and exchanging the last phases of the manuscript by Federal Express. There is every reason to believe now that the book will soon be on the Crossway presses and ready for the seminars as they begin early in March.

But the point is, if it had not been for Lane Dennis none of this would have been possible.

Nothing like this has ever occurred with my previous books and I, and everyone helped by the book, owe a debt of gratitude to Lane Dennis.

FRANCIS A. SCHAEFFER
February 7, 1984

The publisher would like to express special appreciation to those who assisted in doing research for this volume, especially to Melinda Delahoyde, Director of Education for the Americans United for Life, and to Jonathan D. Lauer, Head of Public Services for the Wheaton College Library.

The publisher also would express special thanks to Denise Gill for her excellent work in typing the manuscript for the book— sometimes on a few minutes notice, often late at night, but always with a very professional and willing spirit.

Finally, the publisher would like to express appreciation for permission to quote from the following:

The *Holy Bible: New International Version,* copyright © 1978 by the New York International Bible Society. Used by permission of Zondervan Bible Publishers. All Scripture quotations are taken from this translation of the Bible.

Who Is for Peace? by Francis A. Schaeffer, copyright © 1983 by Francis A. Schaeffer, used by permission of Thomas Nelson Publishers, Nashville, Tennessee.

Some of the material in Chapter Two previously appeared in print in a different form in *Action* magazine, Fall 1976, a publication of the National Association of Evangelicals.